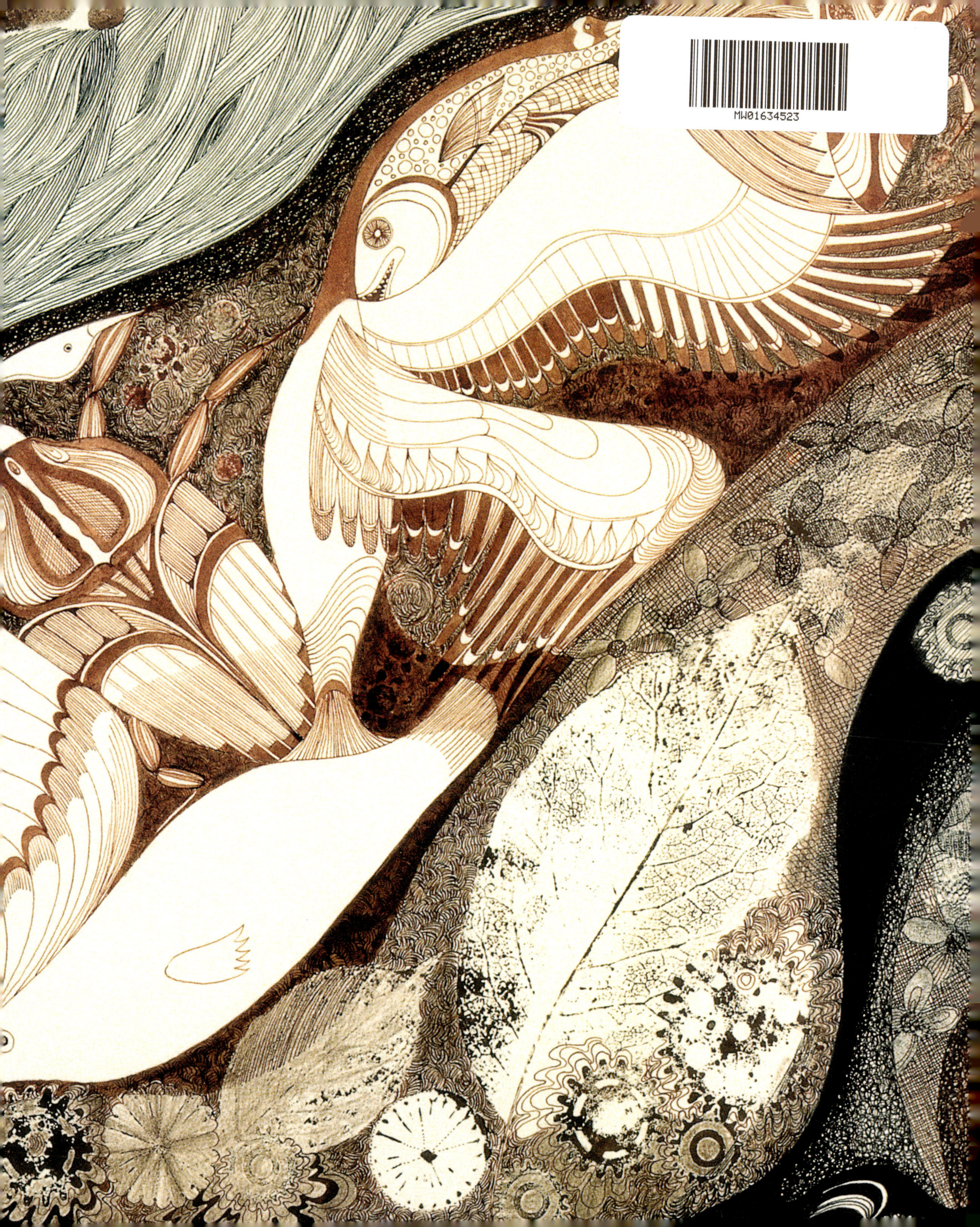

PNINA GRANIRER

PORTRAIT OF AN

ARTIST

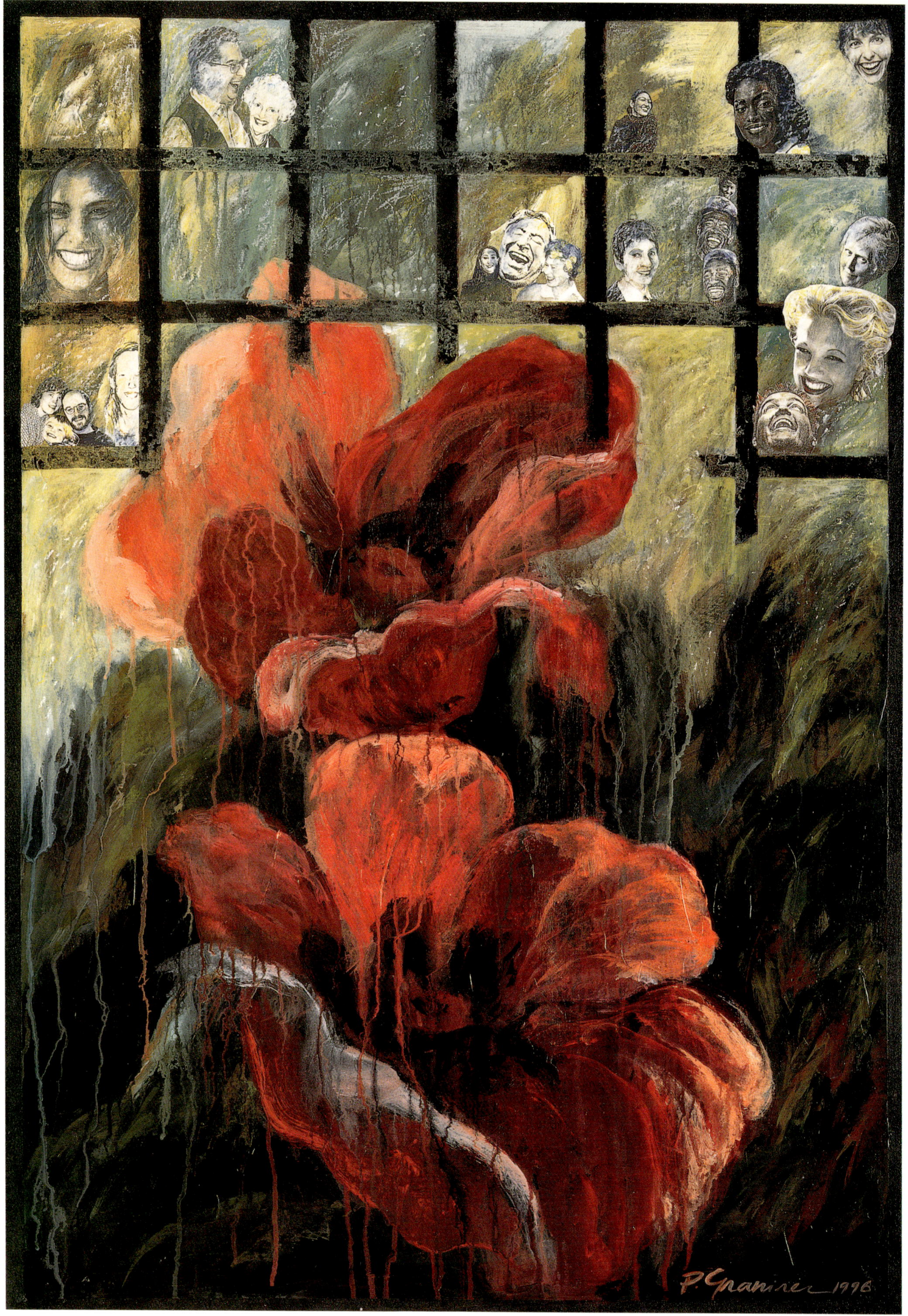
P. Granirer 1996

PNINA GRANIRER

PORTRAIT OF AN ARTIST

To Joyce and Louis – affectionately and with very best wishes Pnina March 24, 1998

by

TED LINDBERG

RONSDALE
1998

RONSDALE PRESS
3350 West 21st Avenue
Vancouver, B.C., Canada
V6S 1G7

Set in Garamond, 12 pt on 16
Typesetting: Julie Cochrane
Printing: Kings Time Industries Ltd.
Cover Design: Julie Cochrane
Cover: *Sculptor Unknown,* 1988, 56.5 x 76 cm (22 1/4 x 29 7/8)
Frontispiece: *A Gift of Laughter,* 1996, 104 x 74 cm (41 x 29 in)
Detail on endpapers: *Child's Magic,* 1974 (ill. 45)

Ronsdale Press wishes to thank the Canada Council for the Arts, the Department of Heritage, and the British Columbia Cultural Services Branch for their support of its publishing program.

CANADIAN CATALOGUING IN PUBLICATION DATA
Lindberg, E. Theodore.
Pnina Granirer

Includes bibliographical references and index.
ISBN 0-921870-54-X

1. Granirer, Pnina, 1935 — Criticism and interpretation.
2. Painters — Canada — Biography. 3. Granirer, Pnina, 1935–
I. Title.
ND249.G713L56 1998 759.11 C97-910839-X

She was feeling toward the discovery that there is no sum total of being; it flows from what has been, through what is, and so on to what is becoming.

— NADINE GORDIMER

Contents

Foreword by William Gough

Being a great believer in synchronicity it was no accident that, when I began to write about the amazing art of Pnina Granirer, I found myself in a coffee house underneath a typed quotation from Joseph Campbell. Pen touching paper, I looked up to read this quote: "The demon you can swallow gives you the power and, the greater life's pain, the greater life's reply."

As I'd been thinking about the birth of an artist, the trails that follow all her life from her birthplace, the circumstances that surround the family — the way mothers and fathers look at the world — wondering where a street may lead, what shadows a deep night may hold, the quote on the wall matched what I'd come to believe.

I don't, for a moment, think it's necessary to suffer in order to create art but, when an artist has suffered — has seen, as a child, how fragile the world is, how it may shape-shift in a second; knows what a delicate balance keeps the world in tenuous kindness, and accepts this instead of avoiding it — her art becomes empowered. What helps a family, a child, survive disaster and find meaning in a world of flux, is the same power that gives an artist the ability to allow her talent to grow with each passing year. Pnina did not ignore the demons of life, she faced them and consumed them in the fire of her creation.

Born Jewish into a Jew-hating part of the world, protected by the kindness of neighbours, seeing war sweep through Romania when she was only five years old, knowing that many of the Jews in her country were slaughtered, she was in a family that had to grasp life, hold it close and cherish every small detail, savour each safe second as if it might last forever. There are two ways to stretch time using the power of our being

— either by escaping extreme danger or being enfolded by extreme danger. In Pnina's escape, in knowing the horror she had missed, time shifted and so did the nature of her world and, through her eyes, so did our world.

As her family lost house and possessions, as the war ended and Communism decreed that Art must be utilitarian, her family's escape to Israel and her wanderings carried the concept of home as a portable, nurturing center not dependent on geographic location. She carried with her, like a wanderer in a fairy tale, two pieces of knowledge. The first was a way of looking at the world that remained always connected to the five year old who, seeing a world fragment and vanish, understood that it is *detail* that saves. The second gift was the expanding, visceral knowledge that, when the world disintegrates, a family may hold, through the power of love and care, a safe place that moves with them — the true home that we all seek.

Holding in one hand a golden imp — the playful eyes of childhood, shaped by an adult craft — and, in the other hand, a lace angel from her early years, she moved into becoming an adult artist. And that is where the personal revolution for Pnina Granirer occurred. I don't believe she consciously chose at the beginning this path — but, she made certain choices that turned her into the kind of revolutionary that she has become, and the one that we will learn from as she moves gradually towards her future paintings.

Obviously the century she was born into was a century of war and revolution: two World Wars, countless insurrections, as well as the spread and melt and reformation of Communism. But these events were not events of the real revolution, for they all ended up fitting into the constricting mantle of Patriarchy, a world where humans are divided from nature, where nature is seen as something to be controlled, and where family and career are to be divided. Pnina's art has always been so unique a vision that it was, by nature, as I see it, although she may deny it, revolutionary. Under the fine hand of a major creator another gift was needed to make the shifts which would carry her art into that final form, shedding light over all the mutating creations she has done before. It needed the world of raising her own family, of understanding fully, in gut and heart, hand and spine, the oppression of an Art world where men are placed in the forefront and where a division of artist from family is as expected as the separation of science and technology from the natural expression of Nature. Pnina speaks movingly in the pages of this book of her choice to be both mother and artist, and the results of these choices show in dazzling form in her art.

The more I read of her life, the more I opened myself to her eye-heart-view of our return to a universe that is more organic; the more I saw linkages throughout her startling variety of art. It is startling because of the specialization expected in an age characterized by buying, selling and then endless talk about buying and selling. Specialization, the narrowing of art, makes a market easier to describe. Narrowing in the life-veins of an artist kills every artist and finally Art itself. Because Pnina has allowed a childlike, child-conscious, curiosity to lead her inside the world of her eyes, she explores many forms — but her explorations are organic, and natural; the same power that allows a mother to know how different each of her children may be and still be loved the same. The more we come to understand that it is not the achievements of our children, but the *being* of our children that is the true measure of how we helped them grow, the more that understanding of the world may be applied to art. In art there is no "has to" there is always "What if?"

As a creator myself, and one who prays for re-generation every day of my life, one who understands this is a time to reconnect with the Mother, I believe that Pnina has created a remarkable body of work, diverse and yet with connecting threads that weave through every disparate piece. Even in her early work we can see the combination of the particular with the emphasized essence of form. The power of *Alley in Jerusalem,* 1959, comes from the combination of the dark sweep of adult and child, hand-in-hand, moving into the pulsing, angled, narrow alley we must all travel in life's journey. By the time of *Child's Magic,* 1974, the child now travels through the Shamanic form of life enfolding life. The coloured India ink, combined with the actual footprints of Dan, her youngest son, traces the journey with the detail of Dan's own footprints standing in for all children — for all of us. The forms flow and unfold, revealing a curved universe, one that enters the eye to participate, to sweep and glide and seek the center. The flowing lines of the work of art duplicate the ocean-ebb-and-flow lines of the whorls in her child's feet. The particular and the form. There is room in this painting; lots of room for any viewer.

By the time we reach Pnina's exploration of the extraordinary power of the Gabriola Millstone creations, her rendering of the details of life in a world carved and distorted by technology has made the wounds and scars on the body of the Earth part of Nature's skin. Nature enfolds and holds and makes ponds of civilization's carvings.

In her shifting, glowing work, there's also great tactility. Feathers and other found objects become embedded in paintings. Our eyes not only see, they feel the surface, they become hands reaching out to connect with the creation. When Michelangelo has God reach out to touch Adam the point is not above and below, the point is finger to finger — the transmission of touch from the invisible to the visible. Tactility is the mantle of life on earth, that which makes us human.

I also believe that Pnina is now ready to create the new works of art that will synthesize everything she has already done, bringing her works of art into a *unified individuality* — and that will happen, because she stands facing her future, where those canvases, those blends of texture and word and fold and undulation and colour-spring and cloud-drift will create new works from this revolutionary artist which will help us all find our way into the new world that awaits those with open eyes and hearts.

William Gough
Toronto, 1997

Preface

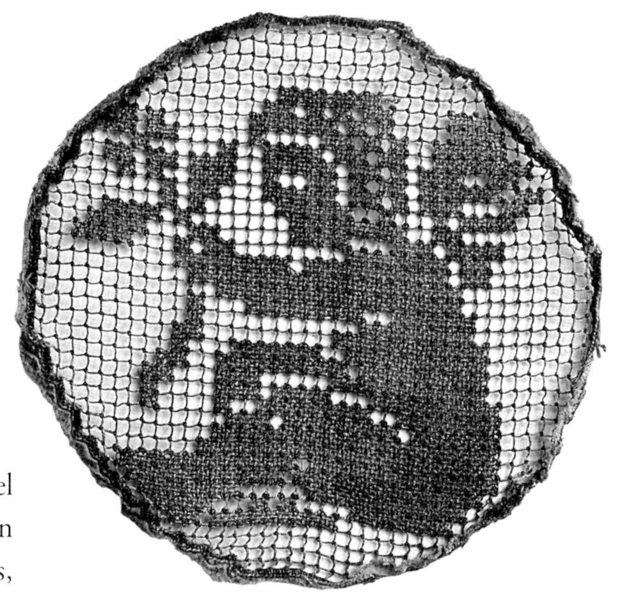

1. Lace cherub from embroidered sheet, brought out of Romania. This image has been a constant presence in Granirer's *Childhood Magic Series.*

At the periphery of Pnina Granirer's consciousness, a cherubic angel and an impish devil hover — twin imagistic "muses" implanted in childhood memory. These seemingly fanciful metaphysical symbols, when interplayed in their various guises, suggest an eternal dichotomy or polarity: the tension between light and dark, truth and beauty, heaven and hell — the universal yin and yang evinced in this artist's perception and expression.

Strictly speaking, women have historically been deprived of muses. The original muses were Greek goddesses, enlisted to tantalize and inspire male artists, particularly poets and musicians. Throughout most of the two-thousand-year period of the Judeo-Greco-Christian cultural configuration we have been pleased to call Western Civilization, women as artists have not been thought of as practitioners in the art mythos. Rather, they have been objectified and fictionalized, beginning perhaps with the Myth of Eve.

The art establishment has been notably unreceptive to women in general and to women who enjoy conventional marital and maternal status in particular, relegating them to the ranks of dilettantism, to the status of less-than-fully committed. Pnina Granirer is one of the few women artists who have reconciled the personal and the professional aspects of her vocation as a painter. As an artist of more than thirty years' standing, she has learned to explore metaphors which develop from her personal life in order to give artistic expression to her deepest observations and convictions.

The concept of "muse" is itself a metaphor: it is a word/picture for that which drives us, urges us forward. What has impelled Granirer from the beginning is the conviction that the content of her art must have some literal meaning. In her early work, content was easy, because

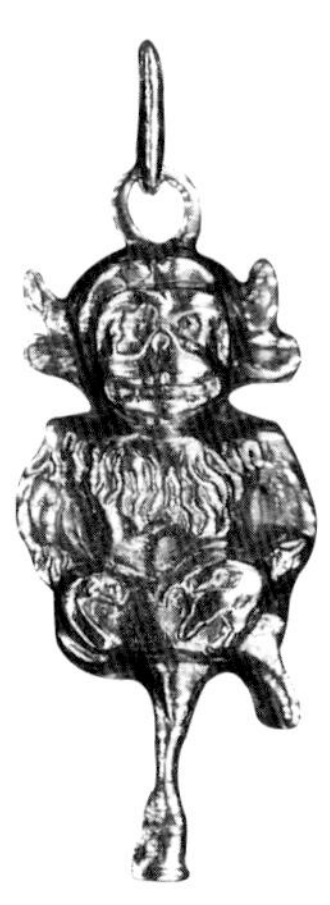

2. *Gold Devil Charm* (a replica of the Imp of Lincoln Cathedral) given to Granirer by her parents. She was to use it later as a recurrent symbol in many of her works.

3. Pnina, age three

her illustrative work and calligraphy were assumed to be subordinate to an accompanying text and outline.

Works of art that must "stand alone" are another matter. They are governed by totally visual standards, rules and theory that comprise a dominant consensus, the theoretical rationale in an accumulated history of development. Rapid and radical change in 20th-century Western art-thinking, for instance, dispensed with Symbolism as a relic of a 19th-century romantic attitude.

Although Granirer could never feel comfortable with total abstraction (solutions to art-making that for her were too similar to art school design problems) she has long since abandoned the narrative for the mythic. She has based her work on personal experience, intuition and the long evolution of a belief system that has crystallized itself (sometimes whimsically or enigmatically) in her work.

The insistence on meaning-as-content carries with it its own philosophical perplexities. Granirer could settle for nothing less than projecting her individual world view through a comprehensive distillation of "world meaning". This is a staggering order, but she has arrived at some personally valuable solutions. She has also, after years of plying the most intricate linear draftsmanship and graphic technique, become a painter in the most classic sense.

What can be the perspective of a sixty-year-old, Romanian-born, Jewish, twice-immigrant artist, who is also a traditional wife-and-mother? One might immediately conclude it would be complex, perhaps even culture-shocked, as this perspective metamorphosed through five languages and at least as many time-frames.

Granirer has staunchly refused to be slowed down or put off by any of these challenges: her outlook is lucid, life-affirming and extraordinarily resourceful, although many of her generation would have every reason to be filled with nihilism.

While not attempting to place an individual woman artist in confrontation with the deficiencies of "Western Civ", one finds in her work a growing awareness of having maintained, as she puts it, her "two secret lives": the contradiction (and perhaps reconciliation) of two vital roles — those of "wife and mother" and "artist", which over a forty-year period have progressively surfaced in her self-styled visual language.

As her life unfolds, Granirer—illustrator/draftswoman/printmaker/painter — contemplates the causality and significance of her career. Her recurring angels and devils puckishly leer, smile and mug for the camera, but are otherwise non-committal.

Romania, 1935–1950

Pnina Granirer in no way considers her perilous youth, restless migrations or protean mandates as ordeals or victimizations (a word she feels is constantly trivialized, in light of real abominations such as the Holocaust). Nevertheless, she has come under the shadow of catastrophe at several points in her life.

She was born of Jewish parents, in the Danube port-city of Braila, Romania, in 1935: not an auspicious time and place for one of her ethnic heritage. Her first language, surprisingly, was German because her constant companion was Fräulein Mina, a nanny from Germany. Later, during the Nazi occupation of Romania, she refused to speak German and adopted Romanian, her family's native language.

Granirer remembers the illustrations in Grimm's fairy tales, with its text in Gothic script, as being her first exposure to art. Even here, one could incautiously infer the influence of heavy-handed children's parables on a little girl. Their stress on "good" and "evil" — transgression and retribution — would be of later symbolic importance to her artistic production, running like a unifying thread through her work. But what we see in an early photograph is a trusting child, oblivious to life's more overpowering riddles, with a white hair-bow the size of a large hat.

Her parents, Lascar and Carola Solomon, were not particularly involved in the arts. Her father, a certified accountant who worked in his father's hardware and drygoods store, considered himself a philosophical Socialist. He was, however, an accomplished amateur pianist, with a natural talent for music, who played mostly by ear. When still a young man he accompanied silent movies in the local cinema. After Pnina learned to play the accordion, they provided the family with pleasant musical evenings. Both her parents were always very supportive and proud of her

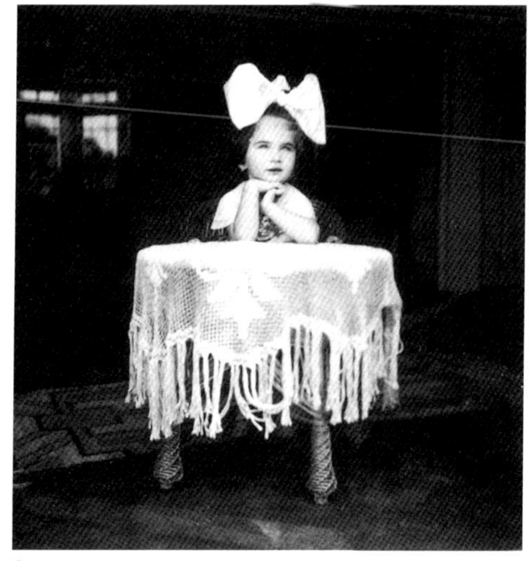

3

artistic talents and creativity.

Pnina was always drawing, tracing, or colouring things (she remembers with deep pleasure the smell of Pelikan coloured pencils). These activities automatically made her the family "artist". As she recalls:

There were no art galleries or museums in our town, but after the war, we visited the Royal Palace in Bucharest, which had become the National Art Gallery. This was my first experience of a fine art museum.

The large, dark and heroic paintings of battle scenes, landscapes and portraits made a big impression on me. However, I most fondly remember the two thick volumes of the French Larousse encyclopedias in our house, their covers graced by an image of a beautiful young woman blowing dandelion seeds into the wind. There were many (mostly black and white) reproductions of classical paintings in these books, over which I spent long hours. Sometimes I copied the ones I liked most, particularly the French artists Gericault and Delacroix. My early art education consisted of these rather poor reproductions which introduced me to painters such as Rubens, Poussin, Ingres, Michelangelo, Raphael and many others. Years later, when I went to the Louvre and saw the real paintings, it was like greeting old and familiar friends.

Pnina spent most of the war years in a Catholic girls' school, the only one which accepted Jewish students. Here she was clearly the class "artist", always called upon to draw the most fastidious maps and compelling posters. Original creativity was discouraged, but there were art classes where copying of old Dutch and classical paintings took place. This emulation helped to acquaint Pnina intimately with the Old Masters, a knowledge which is impossible to acquire by merely viewing. Once she did a portrait drawing of a favourite nun, to whom she gave the finished work — only to see it glanced at and torn up before her bewildered eyes. This nun could not be party to what she saw only as conceit and self absorption, and Pnina remembers the pain of this incident as the first lesson in rejection for a would-be artist.

At home, together with a close friend who loved drawing as much as she, the girls would choose a story, illustrate it and then have "exhibitions" in various rooms of the house.

She put together a rather large collection of shiny pictures of cherubs and other attractive images. Acquisitions were limited by the modest proportions of her pocket money, so she traced pictures out of fairy tale books, hand-coloured and sold them at school for pennies.

When her mother discovered this, she was very upset and stopped it right away, thinking it an improper and mercantile activity for a child of seven or eight.

In spite of the pestilence of Naziism (already spreading through Europe at the time of her birth) the family remained relatively safe throughout the war years. Romania was an ally of Germany and wanted to prove it could run its own show. Many of the Romanian Christians were actively anti-Semitic, but they were also sometimes easily bribed. In Braila, Pnina's town, the relationship was tolerable between the Christians and the Jews and there were no life-threatening situations. There were relatively small indignities: Jewish families were not allowed to have a telephone or a radio and Jewish children were not accepted in public schools. Jewish men had to work out on the streets shovelling snow, but they did not always have to wear the Star of David. Security was often purchased through bribes. There were some friendships between the two camps, but in other parts of Romania, such as the neighbouring port of Galatsi, where the German High Command was installed, conditions were much worse.

Pnina was too young to realize this fully. She was aware that something sinister was happening, remembering how, every night, she knelt by her bed and prayed that the Allies would win the war. She recalls:

I was five years old at the onset of the war and my memories are a haze of some ominous cloud hanging over our heads. However, our town was spared the more brutal happenings. My family, who lived in part of a large, rented house owned by an absentee Greek owner, had a Romanian officer and his family billeted in some of the rooms. This officer was very kind to us, trying to protect us as much as he could.

Only more than 30 years later was I to find out the extent of the destruction of the Romanian Jews. While having experienced first-hand the rampant antisemitism, I had not been aware how intense the virulence and the brutality displayed by the Romanians was. They had developed one of the most extreme forms of antisemitism, beginning already in the 12th century. Independent of Nazi Germany, they introduced the same draconian exclusion laws and initiated the mass destruction and plunder of the Jews, particularly in the annexed territories of Bessarabia, Bucovina and Moldavia.

The numbers are staggering: out of a population of 750,000 Jews, over 400,000 were murdered in the most savage and sadistic way.

Only now do I understand how very lucky we had been to escape the camps and the death trains. But I remember quite clearly the last days of the war, the fear and uncertainty, the frightening rumours of deportations and the sight of the nearby city of Galati going up in flames. At the station there were trains ready to take the Jews away, towards Poland and Germany, in a last frenzied attempt at more killings.

At the same time the Russian advance was rolling along with great speed, and when they entered our town we greeted them with immense relief and joy. King Mihai of Romania and the Fascist Romanian Führer, Ion Antonescu, signed the armistice with the Russsians on August 23, 1944. We were free at last, but for the rest of Europe the war went on until May 9, 1945, swallowing the Jews of Hungary and other countries in the flames of Auschwitz.

Pnina was ten years old when her parents threw open the gates of their yard to a Russian communications unit which rolled in with jeeps and equipment. The soldiers were dusty and tired, their heads shaven and smelling of DDT delousing powder. Everyone was smiling as her family welcomed them as liberators. They had no inkling of the new hardships and problems which would follow. Later, they befriended a Russian officer, incredibly named "Berliner", who candidly advised them to leave Romania as soon as possible. He knew that the new order would bring the curtailing of freedom of movement and a continuing anti-Semitism under a Stalinist regime. It was during this time that her family changed their name from "Solomon" to "Savin".

Under the new political regime there was great pressure for all adults to join the Communist Party. Those who refused were persecuted for their stubbornness. In 1949, Pnina's father, who served on the Board of Directors of a large cooperative store, narrowly escaped arrest when the store's Socialist board members were deposed by the Communists. Warned in time, he went into hiding until the family smuggled him out of Romania aboard a Yugoslav freighter. He succeeded in making his way to Israel with the uncertain hope that his family would eventually join him.

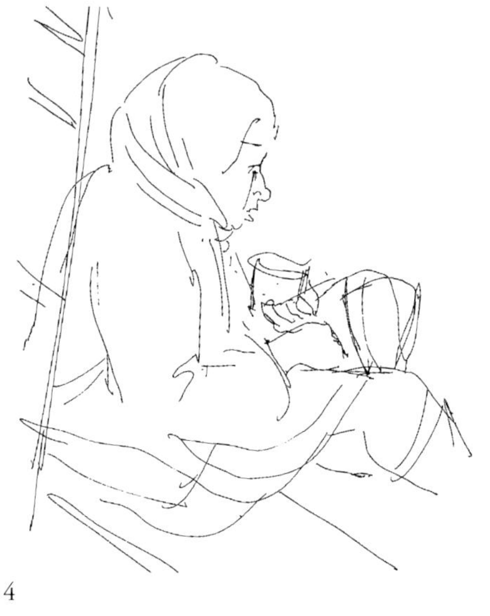

4

4. *Beggar,* 1959
17 x 12 cm (6 3/4 x 4 3/4 in)
pen & ink on paper

Israel 1950–1962

After her husband's escape, Pnina's mother was forced to give up her house and the two moved in with her elderly father, who died soon after. Being the wife of an accused fugitive was dangerous. It was necessary for Carola to divorce her husband in absentia, in order to distance herself from his "counter-revolutionary" ideas. Life as they had known it became only a memory. Emigrating to Israel by obtaining passports and exit permits, seemed an impossible dream. At school, Pnina felt the chill of a Communist "re-education". On one occasion she was called upon to paint a large copy of the standard, adulatory portrait of Josef Stalin, a task she performed reluctantly.

In 1950, due to a sudden and unexpected shift in official policy, a great number of Romanian Jews were issued passports to Israel. It is now known that the Jewish Agency (JOINT) had paid the Romanian government large ransoms for these exit permits. Pnina and her mother were among the lucky ones selected and in August 1950 were able to join her father in Israel.

Arriving in her new country, Pnina, then fifteen, was filled with hope and idealism. By now, as more and more details of the Holocaust were made public, she understood the magnitude of the sheer chance which had somehow preserved her family. It was exhilarating to be in a place where she could feel at home and without fear of discrimination and persecution. Israel was a small country suddenly coping with a huge influx of refugees: bewildered and exhausted people, most of them remnants of now-destroyed communities. Temporary tent towns sprouted all over the country. People lived as well as they could under Spartan conditions in a difficult climate.

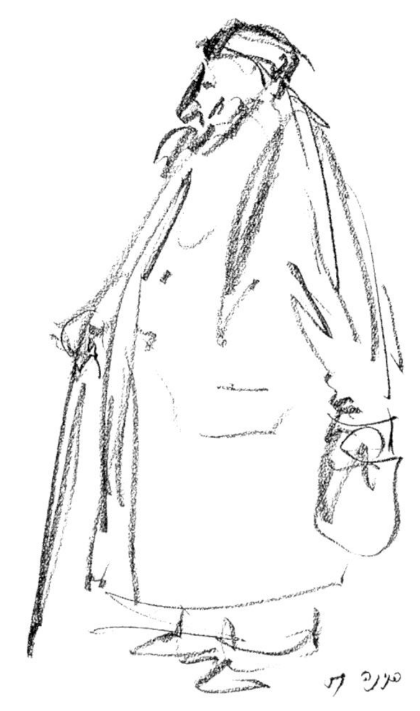

5

5. *Old Man,* 1959
25 x 16 cm (9 1/2 x 6 1/2 in)
conté on paper

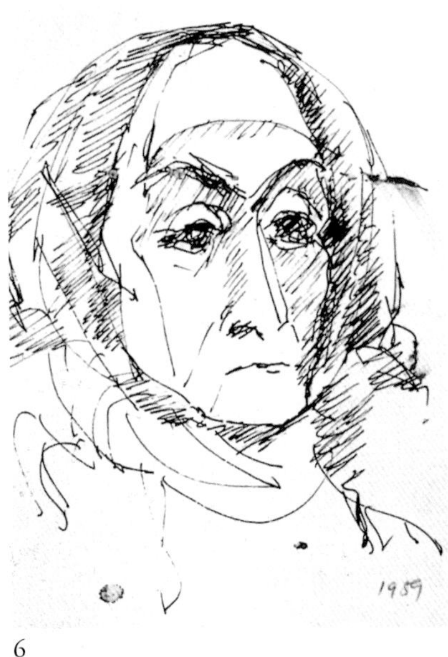

6

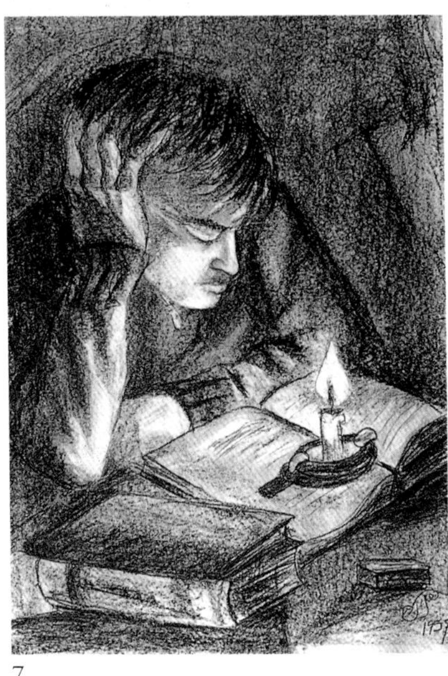

7

6. *Arab Woman,* 1959
17 x 12 cm (6 3/4 x 4 3/4 in)
pen & ink on paper

7. *Power Failure,* 1959
60 x 46 cm (23 5/8 x 17 3/4 in)
charcoal on paper
portrait of her husband

Pnina's small family was fortunate enough to obtain a shikun, a small studio flat with kitchenette and shower, in a cheaply built, prefabricated building located in a settlement near Haifa called Gav-Yam Ghimel, created almost overnight on the sand dunes by the sea. This community comprised a mix of people, not only of European origin, but from Arab countries as well. There was, despite the privations, a feeling of revival in the air, a sense that a great historical event was in the making.

In many ways, adjustment to this new world was more difficult for Pnina's parents than for her. Although not always pleasant considering the cramped living conditions, life for a fifteen-year-old was an adventure. For the next three years, food continued to be rationed, and money scarce. Her father drove a truck for some time, unable to find work as an accountant. Later he was unemployed, which was extremely stressful both financially and emotionally. Her mother took up sewing to supplement their income, and Pnina began piece-work, painting Walt Disney images on cuckoo-clocks and lampshades for children's rooms — her first real job using her natural skills.

Here in Israel, as a young immigrant in a new country with a new language, she adopted her present first name: "Pnina". Her given name had been Paula, but she wished to have a Hebrew name. Since she had been named after her grandmother, whose name was "Paula-Pearl", she chose "Pnina" which means "pearl" in Hebrew, and was a name popular in Israel at that time.

Although Pnina had taken private reading and writing Hebrew lessons while still in Romania, her vocabulary was limited. She had arrived in Israel in August and was determined to start school in September. Studying a new language was hard work, but she was accepted in school although put back a year because of her still-limited Hebrew. All subjects were taught in Hebrew, and one of the main subjects, the Tanach (the Pentateuch), was read directly from the original text. She studied English and Arabic as well. Her memories of that first year are a haze of memorizing lists of new words and trying to keep the three new languages separate in her mind. But the effort paid off. The following year she took the necessary exams and was advanced a grade rejoining her own age group.

In Grade Eleven, the students had to make a choice in their studies between the sciences and the humanities. Following her natural inclination, Pnina might have opted for the latter, but she was aware that Israel's difficult economic situation meant that attempting to support herself as an artist might prove to be a luxury she could not afford. Consequently, she chose a path in the sciences which would prepare her for future studies in architecture and a greater possibility for employment.

After graduation from high school, like all young Israelis, she was conscripted into the army where, after basic training, she worked as a clerk. One of the officers at her base, who was a technical draftsman by profession, offered a course in perspective drawing. From him she acquired the knowledge of drawing objects in space, linear and colour perspective and the uses of light and shadow. This, she initially thought would be useful to her aspirations to become an architect.

In a few months she was transferred to Nazareth where her new base was one of the police fortresses built by the British during the Mandate. She was assigned to office work, but found herself temperamentally unsuited to coping with an unfamiliar filing system. After weeks of confused frustration, she collapsed in total exhaustion trying to repair the damage of her own awkward bungling. She was sent to hospital and on her release was re-assigned to a mapping department, which gave her a chance to apply her more natural skills.

On weekends, when she had no leave to go home, she would sketch and paint in the Old City of Nazareth. The small stone houses perched on hillsides, the minarets and the wonderful light were ideal subjects for numerous drawings and watercolours.

In 1954, after a year in the army, Pnina married a fellow Romanian, Eddy Granirer, and was demobilised. She took a job in a ceramics factory, hoping to decorate and glaze the various objects produced there, but this was not to be. Rather, she was relegated to painting endless stripes on plates, boring and deadening routine work which haunted her dreams at night. Three months later she left the factory, learned to type and began work as a secretary. Her goal was to earn enough money to study architecture at the Technion Institute in Haifa. But once again, fate intervened.

When my husband's military duty ended, he planned to study at the Hebrew University in Jerusalem. However, the only art school in the country, the Bezalel School of Art (named for the craftsman who built the original Ark of the Covenant, and now an accredited Academy) happened to be in Jerusalem. I happily changed my plans, believing that fate, after all, had led me to the right path.

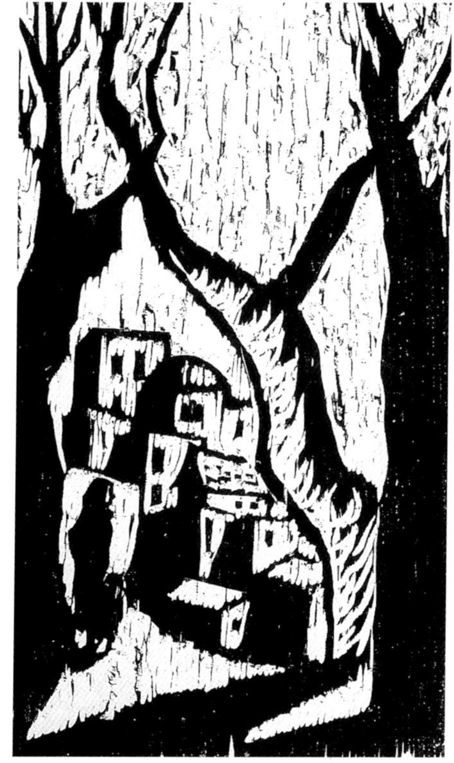

8

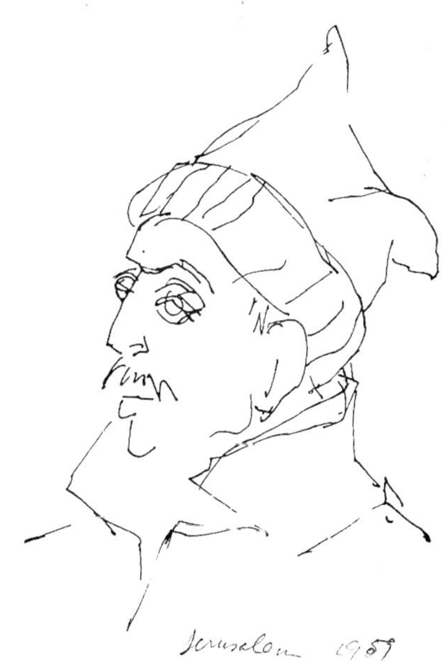

9

8. *Ein Karem,* 1959
36 x 25 cm (14 1/4 x 9 3/4)
woodblock print

9. *Man with Wool Toque,* 1959
17 x 12 cm (6 3/4 x 4 3/4 in)
pencil on paper

At the time, Bezalel taught mainly Applied and Commercial Art in three main departments: Graphics, Metalwork (such as jewellery and sculpture) and Weaving. The Graphics Department offered drawing, illustration, poster design, as well as some painting and printmaking. Granirer hoped that her studies would at least prepare her to make a living by doing illustration and commercial art work. An older artist friend from Haifa, Yehoshua Grossbard (who supported himself as a housepainter), gave her much moral support and encouragement.

Granirer and her husband concentrated on their studies, worked part time and ate mostly spaghetti. Not having a great deal of money didn't really mean much. They were happy and excited about what they were doing. As for many young Israelis, life was difficult, but extremely auspicious and satisfying.

For a while the young couple lived in an old house with marvelous vaulted ceilings. In her free time, Granirer went out and sketched in the narrow streets near her house, or in and around the market of Mahane Yehouda. Curious child-onlookers virtually perched on her shoulders and superstitious "models" shielded their faces from the evil eye. For the last two years of studies, they moved again to an old stone house on Samuel the Prophet street, on the border between Israel and Jordan. There was a wall protecting the street from snipers but they lived behind it, adjacent to no-man's-land. A barbed-wire fence ran behind the house. When Granirer's parents came to visit, they were horrified. A sign on the fence ominously warned: "BORDER! BEWARE!"

The teaching staff at the Bezalel Art School were all European immigrants, most of whom had escaped Germany in the 30's. Those with the greatest influence on Granirer taught painting and drawing. However, she found herself frequently at loggerheads with Mr. Eisenscher, a painting instructor. She loved drawing and line, while Mr. Eisenscher stressed the Cezanne technique of creating line only through the visual illusion resulting from abutting colour masses. To the young student, this concept seemed unreasonable. She preferred Picasso and Matisse to Cezanne, painters who used line as an important component in their paintings. At this point she realized how much she disliked hard and fast rules, particularly in art. How could one be creative and original if one obeyed arbitrary rules? Ironically, for the graduation show, Mr. Eisenscher chose one of her paintings in which lines were very prominent. He wanted to keep it for the school collection, but when the exhibition was over, she took it back.

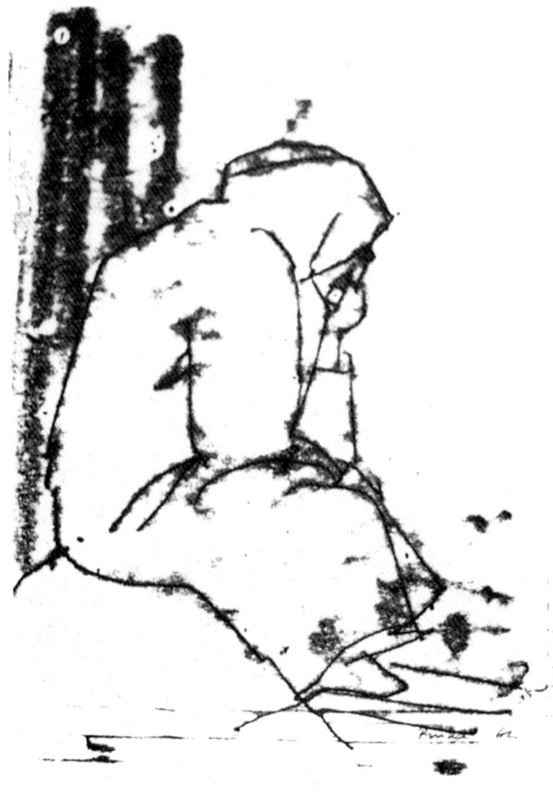

10

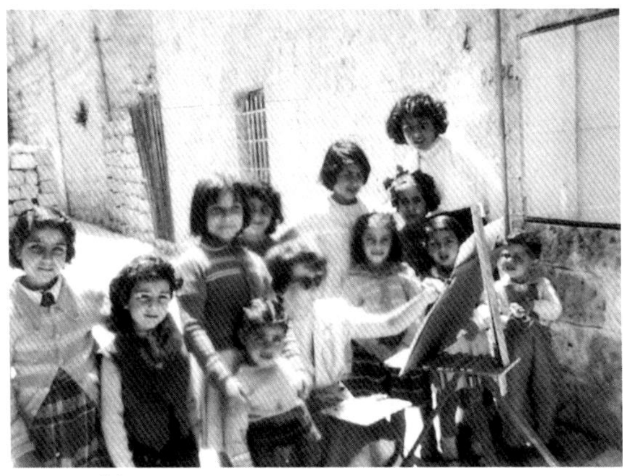

11

10. *Old Woman,* 1962
18 x 17 cm (7 1/8 x 6 1/2 in)
monotype

11. Granirer sketching in Jerusalem alley, 1959

Another one of Granirer's teachers, Isadore Ashheim, who had come from Germany, instilled in her an undying love for drawing. His life-drawing classes were her favourite ones. From him she learned the pleasure of capturing movement in a few quick strokes and an appreciation for the style we now call "magic realism". Jacob Pines, who invited his students to his studio from time to time, taught her woodblock printing in the Japanese tradition. He owned a large collection of beautiful Japanese prints, the first Ukyio-e she had ever seen. For a long time, woodblock was her preferred medium.

Yehouda Bacon was a survivor from Auschwitz, a gentle man who taught etching and lithography. The drawings he had made while in the death camps have been included in a book by prisoner-artists. Yossi Stern, a teacher of illustration, had come to Israel with the illegal "children's transports" from Hungary. These were mainly orphans who had been pried out of the Nazi clutches. Everybody had a story, everybody had been uprooted and had experienced the trauma of war. She took art history from Mordechai Ardon, who later went to Paris and became prominent in Europe. Like most artists who do not live in large metropolitan centres like New York, Paris or London, none of these

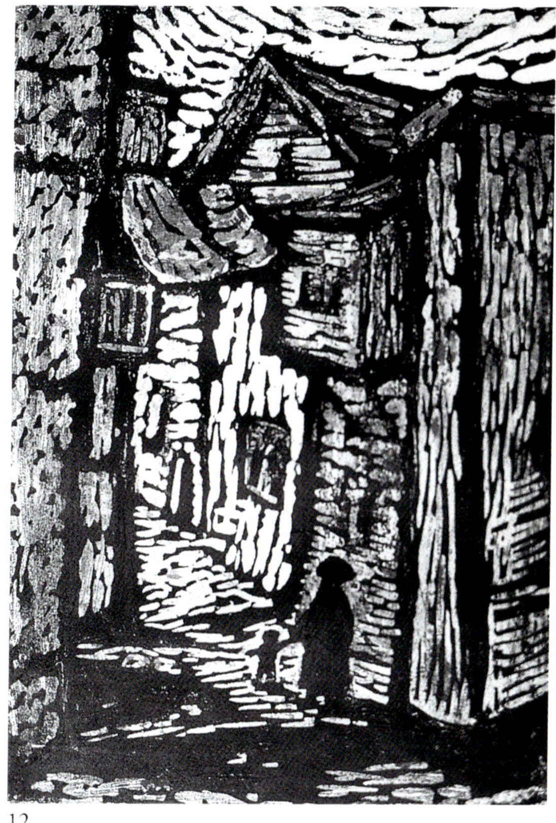

12

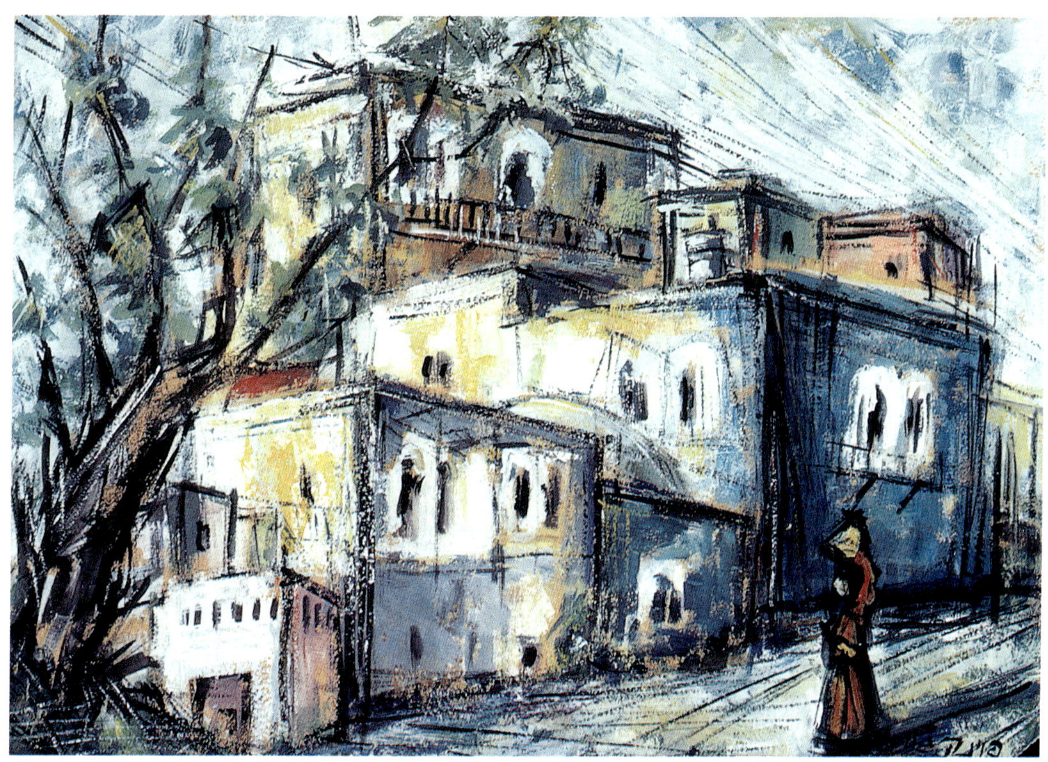

13

12. *Alley in Jerusalem,* 1959
21.5 x 15,5 cm (8 1/2 x 6 in)
colour woodblock print

13. *Ein Karem,* 1959
48 x 69 cm (18 7/8 x 27 1/4 in)
oil on board
This was Granirer's graduation painting, which she removed from the school collection

names became known in North America. Only Mordechai Ardon achieved some degree of recognition due to his stay in Paris.

Throughout Granirer's four years at Bezalel, there was no teaching of abstraction, although there were a few artists in Israel who were painting abstract works.

Granirer's first son, David Eran, was born in 1960. By then, she had graduated and found it convenient to be able to work at home, while taking care of the baby. She worked regularly illustrating books and making educational filmstrips for schools. She loved this work, particularly the colour filmstrips based on fairy tales, which transported her to the happier moments of her childhood. Most of the illustrations were for children's books. The methods were simple and straightforward: there were no computers and very few aids. It was mostly hands-on work.

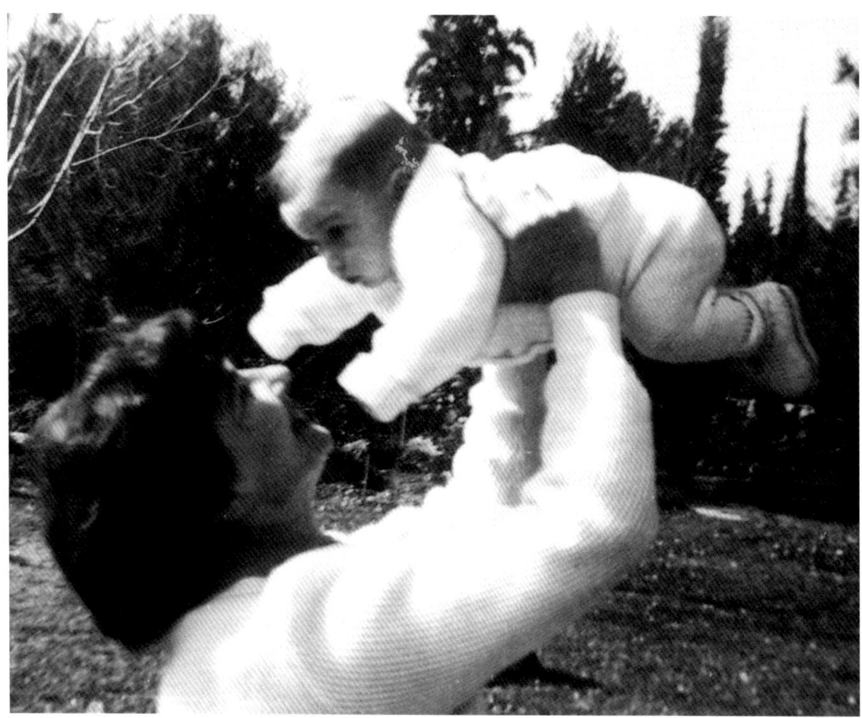
14

14. Enjoying her son David, 1960

Urbana, Illinois & Ithaca, NY, USA, 1962–1965

In 1962, the Granirers moved to Urbana, Illinois, where Eddy had obtained a teaching position at the University and two years later they went to Cornell University, in Ithaca, N.Y. As her visa did not permit her to work, Granirer turned from commercial art to something she was to find more rewarding: woodblock prints and drawings, and later, watercolours and mixed-media compositions. For the first time, she was free to do "art for art's sake". She felt somewhat bereft of subject matter in Urbana, in contrast to Jerusalem, where the content present in her work had been the old streets and buildings, people in the marketplace, the children and beggars on the street. Everything was, in her words, "too neat and pretty" in Urbana, the detached houses in a row with their green, manicured lawns stretched out like welcome mats.

For a while she drew from memory or from sketches she had brought from Israel. Eventually she met Vera, a black woman who ran a second-hand store, selling items she liked to call "antiques", and who grandly called herself Lulu Belle. She had a face like an ebony carving and would sit motionless in her shop, among the old lamps and grandfather clocks, almost like an exotic piece of sculpture herself. Granirer did numerous studies and paintings of Lulu Belle, some of which were exhibited in Urbana, at the University's Student Union Building. She was "honoured" at this time with an unexpected compliment: one of her works was stolen from the show, "hopefully," she muses, "by a poor art lover." She took part in several other shows, entered competitions and art fairs, and "other things one does when one is young."

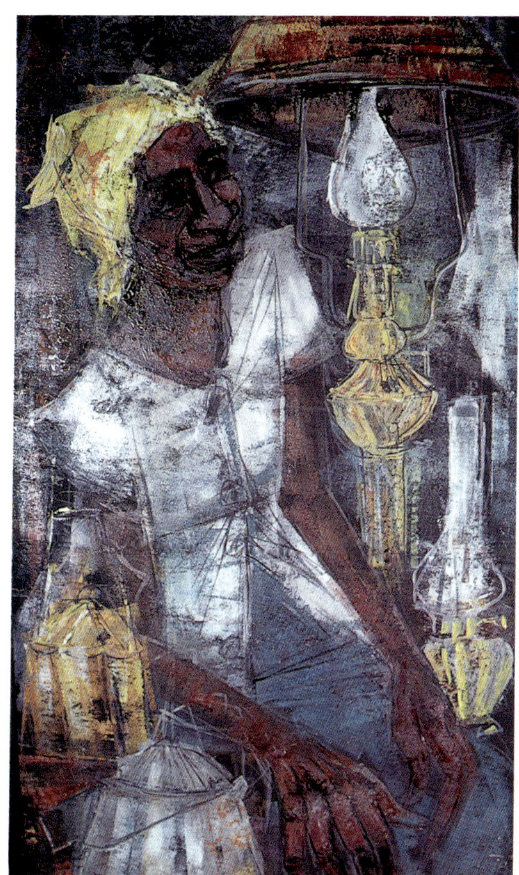

15

15. *Lulu Belle,* 1964
71.1x40.7 cm (28x16 in)
water-based printing inks on card

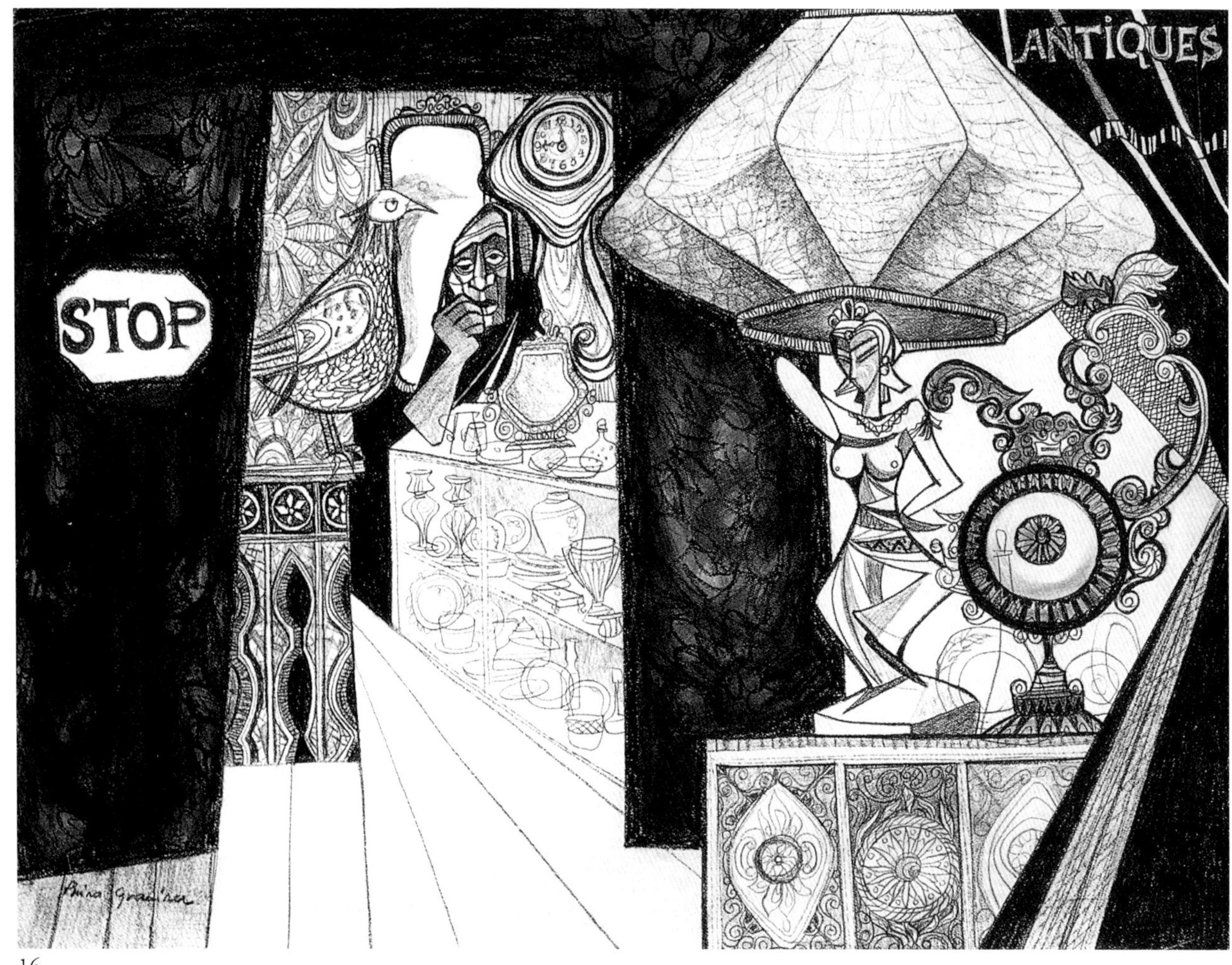

16

16. *Antiques*, 1964
61x81.5 cm (24x32 in)
conté on paper

This was also the time for exploring a new technique, which was a direct outcome of the monotypes she was working on. This technique consisted of rolling water-based printing inks directly on paper board. There was almost no brushwork. She liked the transparency of the colours as they overlapped, lending, she felt, an air of mystery to the work. Then she added small objects such as feathers, lace, broken toy telephones and other found materials, which were inked and then printed individually on the painted surface. These gave greater richness to the composition, much like a tapestry of texture and colour (ill. 15, 44, 50). Years later, when she settled in Vancouver, British Columbia and met the senior artist, Maxwell Bates, she was elated to see that he had used exactly the same technique in his *Secrets of the Grand Hotel* series. It was also in Urbana that Granirer became aware of the huge gap between the training she had received and what was being taught in North America.

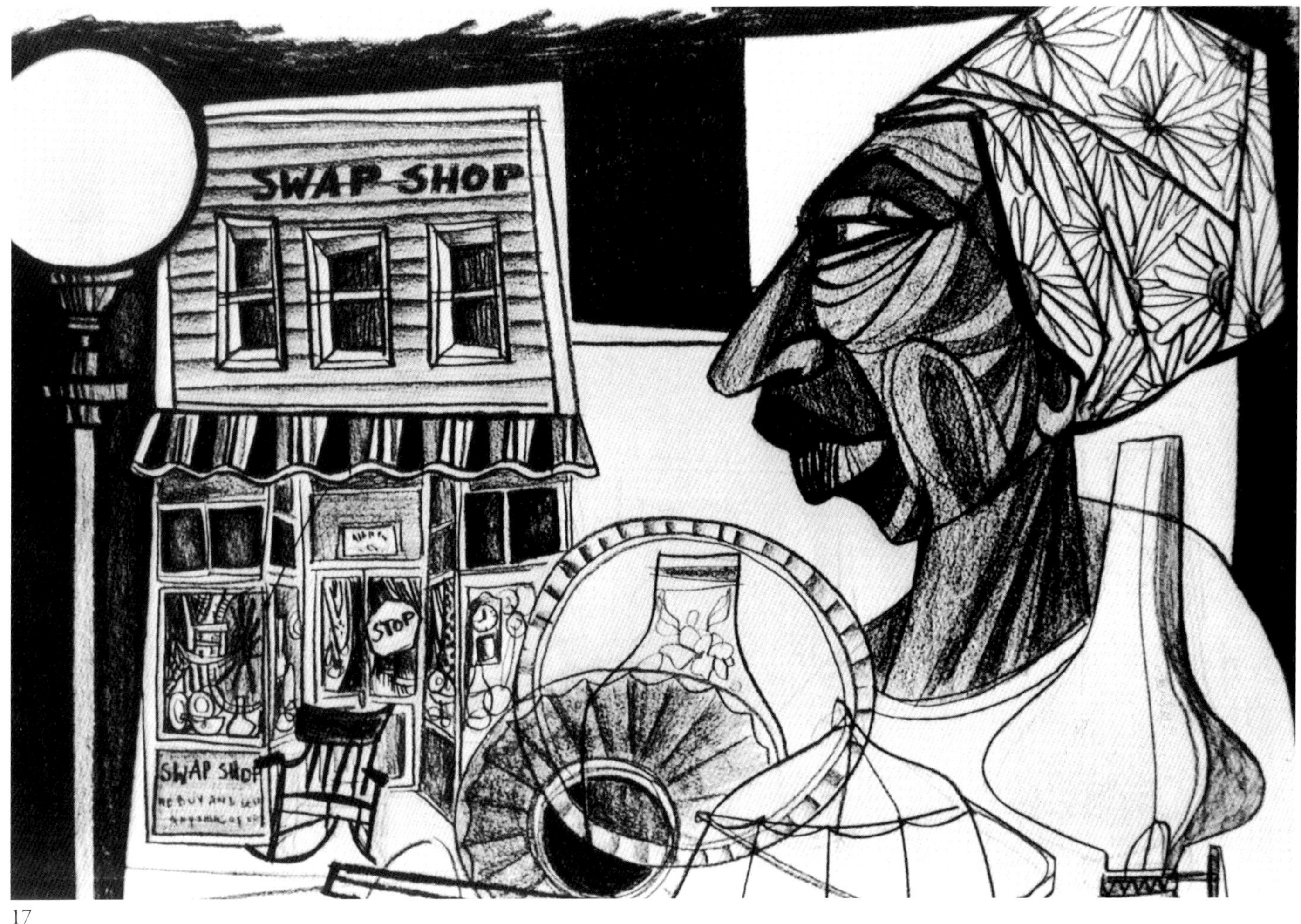

17

She felt increasingly estranged from what had become the heyday for non-objective art in centres such as New York, Los Angeles and San Francisco. She writes:

I remember my surprise, having just arrived in North America, that one could get a Master of Fine Arts degree. I could not understand why a working artist would need a degree at all. I felt then, as I still do, that art belonged in separate schools or academies, and not in universities. In fact, I am convinced that the intellectualization of art has drained it of its soul. The dry, didactic, sparse and text-oriented objects which are so tirelessly promoted by curators with university degrees fail to move the viewers, who have been voting with their feet — by avoiding these much touted exhibitions. It is another phenomenon of spiritual alienation which perhaps reflects society, but also perpetuates and deepens its emptiness. Theory has replaced passion.

17. *Swap Shop*, 1964
61 x 81.5 cm (24 x 32 in)
conté on paper

Some of her most successful gestures are to be found in the sobriety of black and white, as in Lulu Belle's Swapshop.
– David Watmough, *The Vancouver Sun*
March 3, 1966

With her arrival in the United States, Granirer's life as an artist had changed. She continued to work, producing prints and exhibiting on occasion, but there was no sure monetary reward as when she was doing illustration work in Israel. Like most women of her generation, family came first. Daycare for children was almost impossible to be had, unless one was prepared to pay a great deal. She was not earning any money, and could not afford the luxury of daycare. In spite of her husband's support and interest in her art, her perception of her own creativity at this time in her life was that it did not count as an important enough occupation. It was the issue of taking herself seriously as a woman who was an artist. With the perspective of time, she feels that she now understands this more adequately:

It was the feeling of guilt for taking time away from the baby; the obligation to run a "perfect house"; the knowledge that I was not contributing financially — everything came before the art. And yet, I plodded on.

18. *Child with Doll,* 1964
62 x 46 cm (24 1/2 x 18 in)
monotype on paper
Private collection

19. *Friends,* 1963
61 x 46 cm (24 x 18 in)
charcoal on newsprint

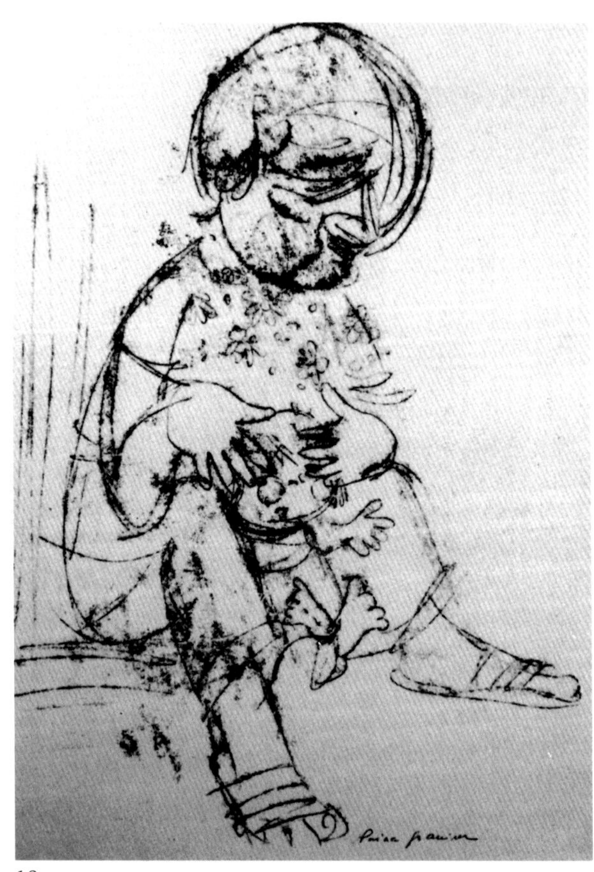

18

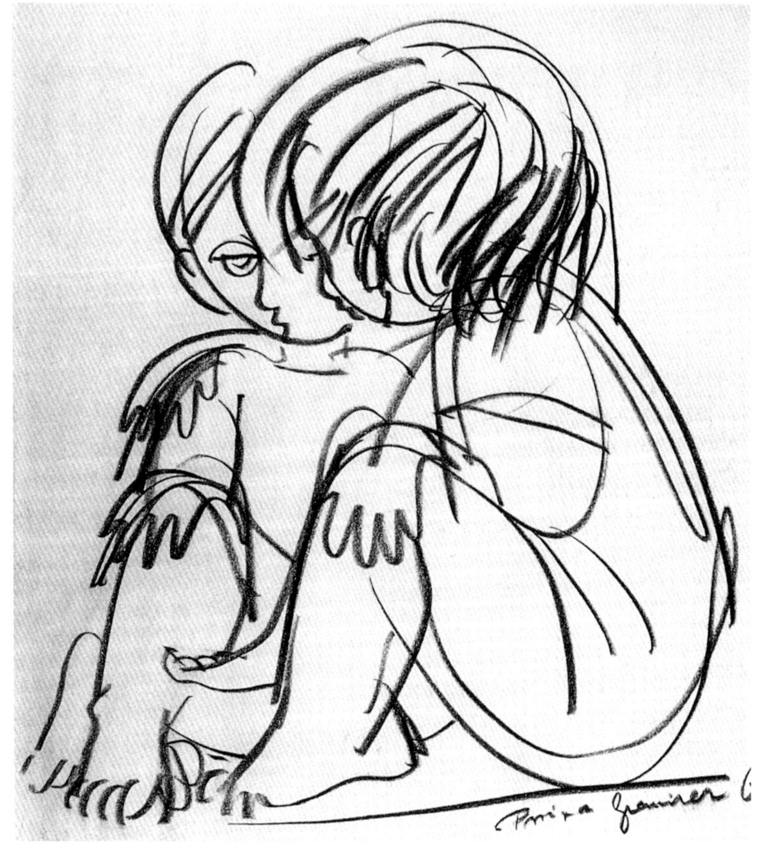

19

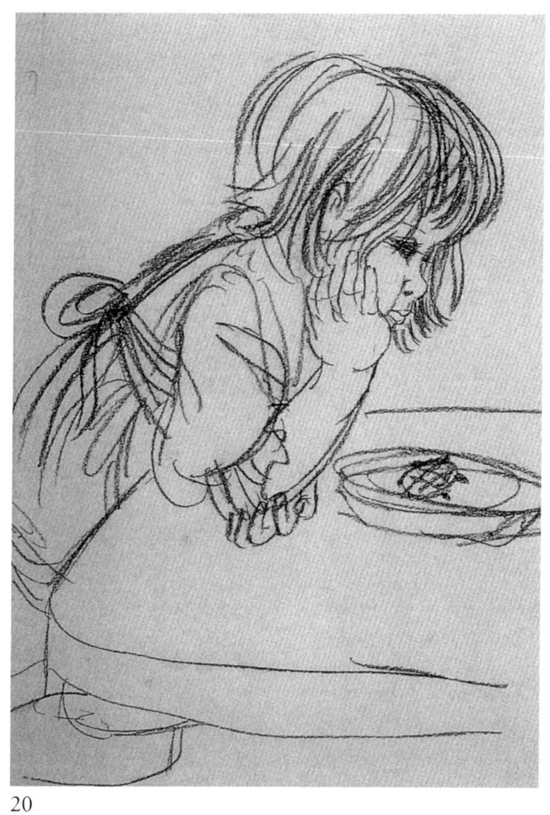
20

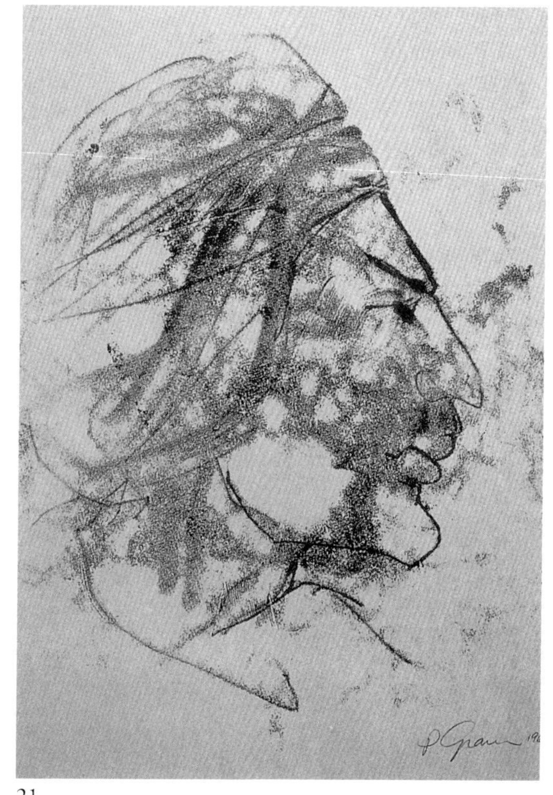
21

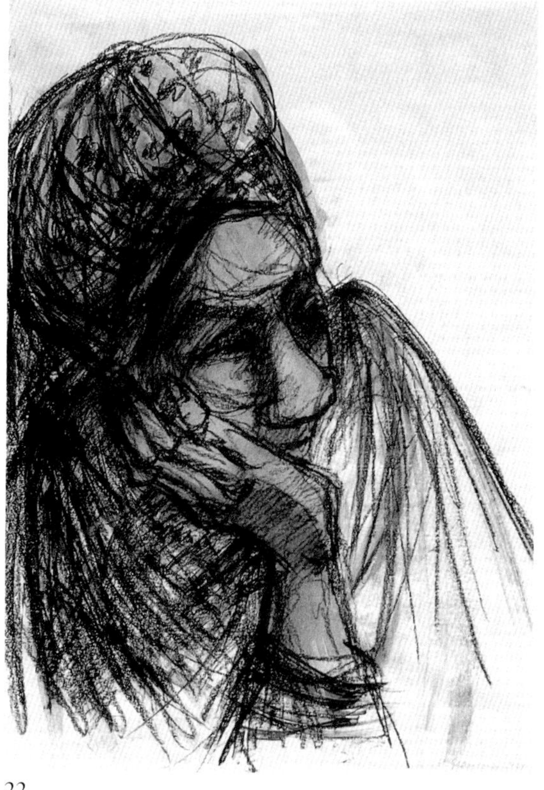
22

23

20. *Mary Jo with Turtle,* 1965
61.5 x 46 cm
(24 x 18 in)
charcoal on paper

21. *Man with Turban,* 1963
50 x 35.5 cm
(19 3/4 x 14 in)
monotype on paper

22. *Vera,* 1964
61 x 46 cm
(24 x 18 in)
charcoal and watercolour on paper

23. *Lulu Belle,* 1963
61 x 46 cm
(24 x 18 in)
felt pen on paper

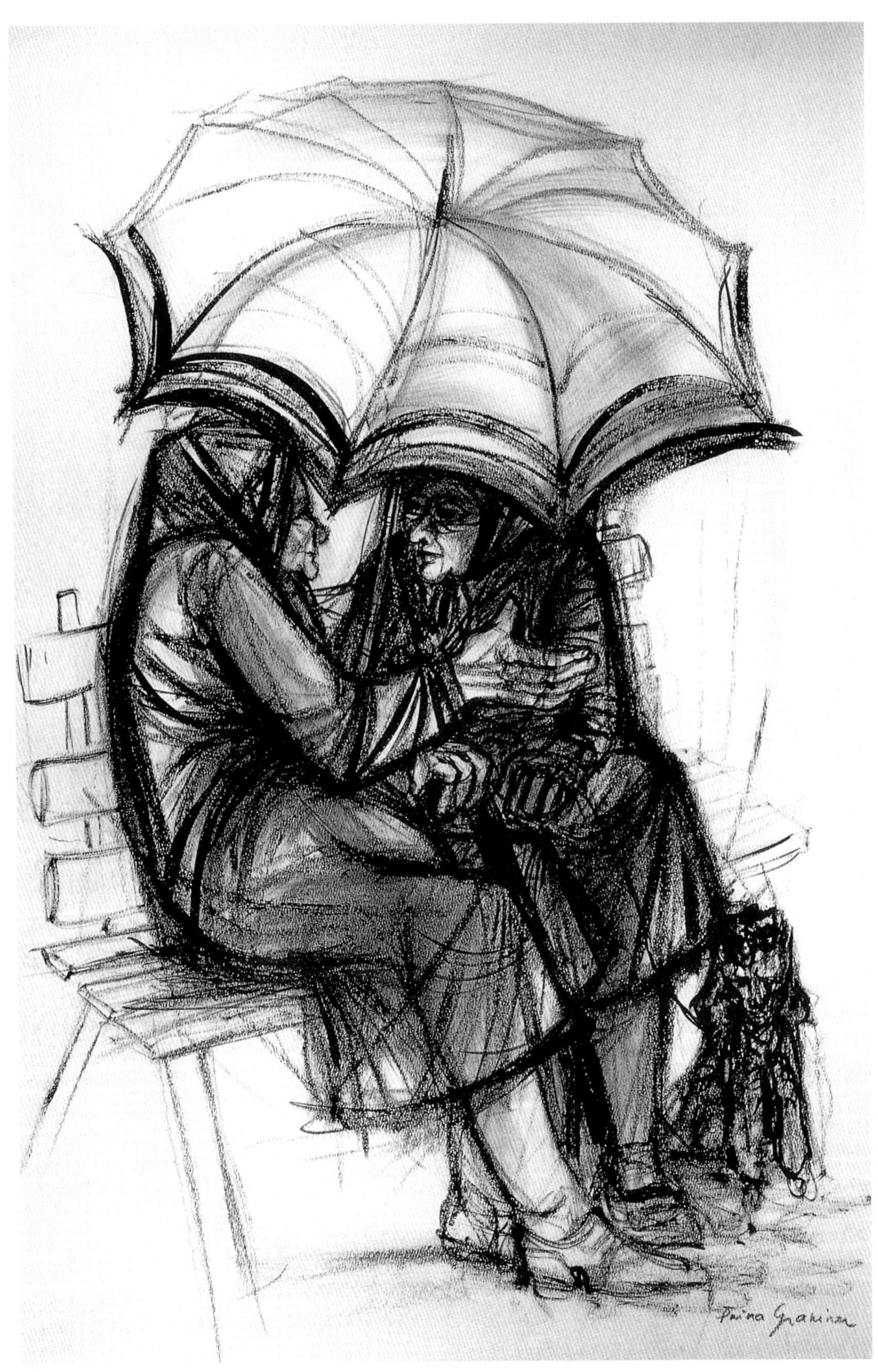

24. *The Chat,* 1965
81x57cm (32x22 1/2 in)
charcoal and wash on paper

24

Vancouver & Montreal 1965–1966

In 1965, Granirer's husband was offered a position at the University of British Columbia. The Granirers rented an old, rambling house in the Kitsilano district, where there was a spare room which Granirer transformed into a studio — her first. Here, she continued with her woodblock prints, drawings and mixed media painting. However, having a small child and no extended family to help, her productivity was limited. She nonetheless produced enough work for an exhibition at the Danish Art Gallery in 1966. It was was reviewed by Max Wyman in *The Vancouver Sun* and Granirer felt it was well received.

Later that year, during the summer, she exhibited at Pandora's Box, a progressive gallery in Victoria, B.C. Granirer was surprised and excited when all of the Limners, a collegial group of contemporary professional artists, came to the opening. This was perhaps the first professional artists' acknowledgement of her existence and she was thankful for their support. Until this moment, she had felt very much a stranger in Vancouver, having little contact with local artists and no connection with the "art scene". Maxwell Bates, an architect and painter formerly from Calgary, Alberta, bought one of her prints and invited the Granirers to his house the following day. Perhaps because Bates' bitingly sardonic work was most often likened to German Expressionism, and Granirer's teachers had been Europeans, his work greatly appealed to her. Bates had his own problems, however. She was amazed when he opened a large store-room full of paintings and bitterly said, *"Do you see these? Nobody wants them."* Fortunately, not long after this meeting he was

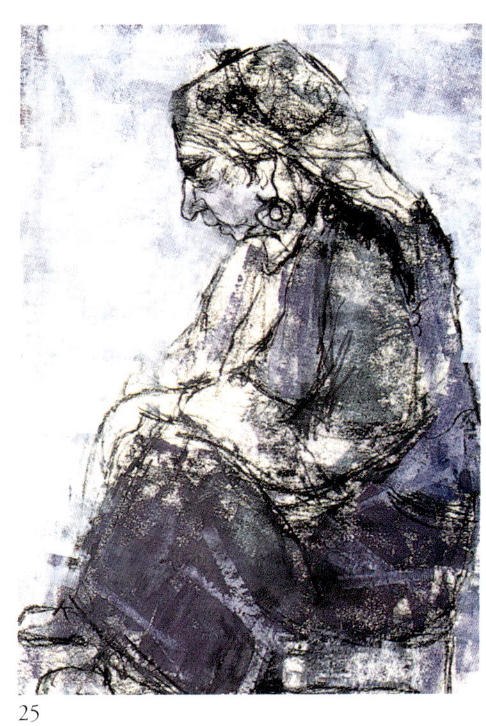
25

25. *Seated Woman,* 1964
56 x 38 cm (22 x 15 in)
monotype and roller, printing inks on paper

One of the most outstanding paintings is not for sale — a collage called The Leader.

Mrs. Granirer has used this painting to show children at play. When you walk away afterwards you feel as though you've just looked through the window of a child's mind and seen that child at play.

Mrs. Granirer knows her subject. In this painting at any rate she has entirely succeeded in communicating with the children depicted in the work, as though the viewer didn't really matter. Only in this case the viewer comes along for the whole ride.

— Jerry Boultbee, *Victoria Daily Colonist,* July 1966

taken on by the Vancouver Bau-Xi Gallery, which opened a branch in Victoria. He was thus "discovered" in the last years of his life in British Columbia.

The first year Granirer spent in Vancouver was an unsettled one, a time of uncertainty for the future. She was an outsider who might soon be gone, a visitor in transit. Her life concentrated within the family and the friends made through the University. Her imagery explored the world of children, as in *The Leader,* which she took back from a prospective buyer due to her small son's disappointment at its disappearance.

In this work, a group of boys with paper hats and wooden swords is spilling forward in the hunting game, unaware of the lion hiding in the tall grass. This is the first time that Granirer explores the juxtaposition of light and dark, of the joys and pleasure of innocence and the dangers lurking in hidden places. This theme will return in later years through the use of symbols such as the angel and the devil in the *Childhood Series,* nature versus culture in the *Carved Stone Series* and good and evil in the *Alhambra Suite.*

During this time she received her first commission, a mural for the *Tree Island* nail factory. It was to be her first large work. In general she worked mainly on paper, keeping in mind the transitory nature of her situation, paper being much easier to store and transport than canvas. One of her favourite techniques was the monotype, or monoprint and

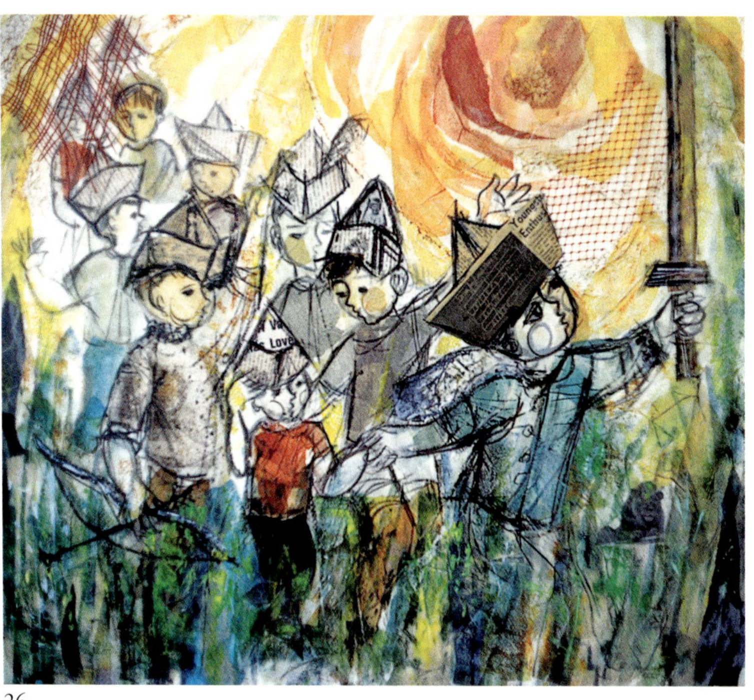

26

26. *The Leader,* 1965
68.5 x 75 cm (27 x 29 1/2 in)
watercolour and collage on paper

lift-drawing, although these works were not, at the time, accepted in any competitions or exhibitions. This did not bother Granirer, whose main interest was in the work itself.

The monoprint is a very direct and spontaneous technique. The image is painted with oil paint or printing inks on a smooth surface. The paper is carefully and lightly laid on top and then pressed onto the surface by hand. The paint is thus transferred from the smooth surface of the glass or plexi onto the paper placed over it. The brush marks are clearly visible, creating a texture unique to this technique. The lift-drawing is done in a similar manner. Here, the ink is rolled onto the glass until it reaches the right consistency. The paper is laid on top and the drawing made on the back. Wherever the pencil touches the glass, there is a mark, a fuzzy, beautiful line, characteristic of this medium. Later, in the 90's, this technique was to be expanded to the use of watercolour and printing presses.

Granirer and her family moved again in 1966, this time to Montreal. This was the year when the decision to settle permanently in Canada was taken — a productive one for her. She produced an increasing amount of work and had an exhibition at the Art Den on Rue de la Montagne. By now, she was experimenting even more widely and showed everything she produced. During the Art Den exhibition, one visitor inquired whether this was a group show, so unfashionably broad was her range of styles and technique.

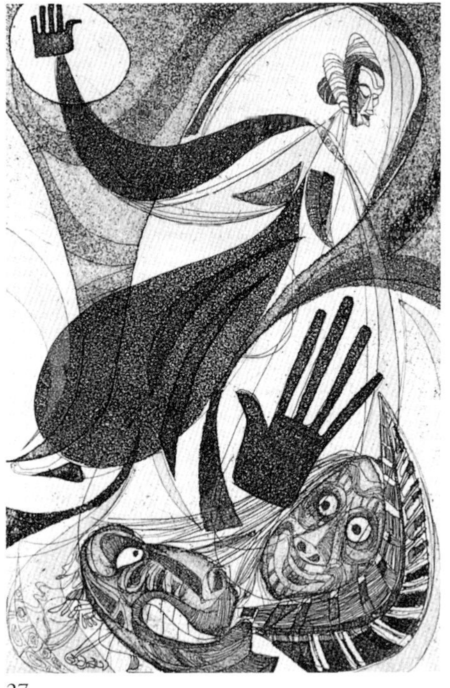
27

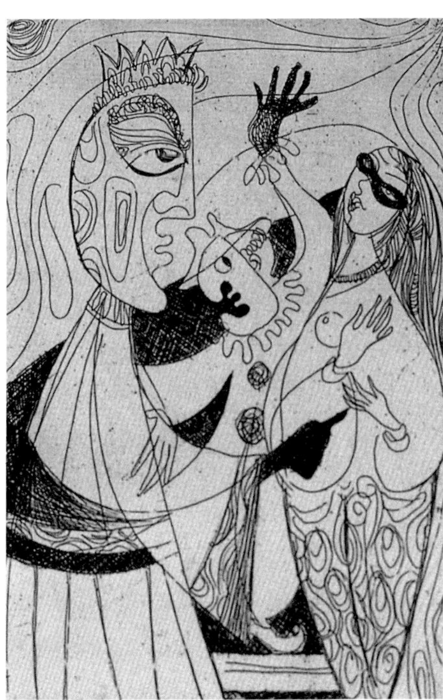
28

27. *Incantation,* 1967
22 x 15.2 cm (8 3/4 x 6 in)
etching

28. *Masquerade,* 1967
15.2 x 10.2 cm (6 x 4 in)
etching

These etchings were done at the Atelier Pierre Ayot, in Montreal. The influence of African masks, seen by the artist at Le Petit Musée on Sherbrooke Street, is visible in these works.

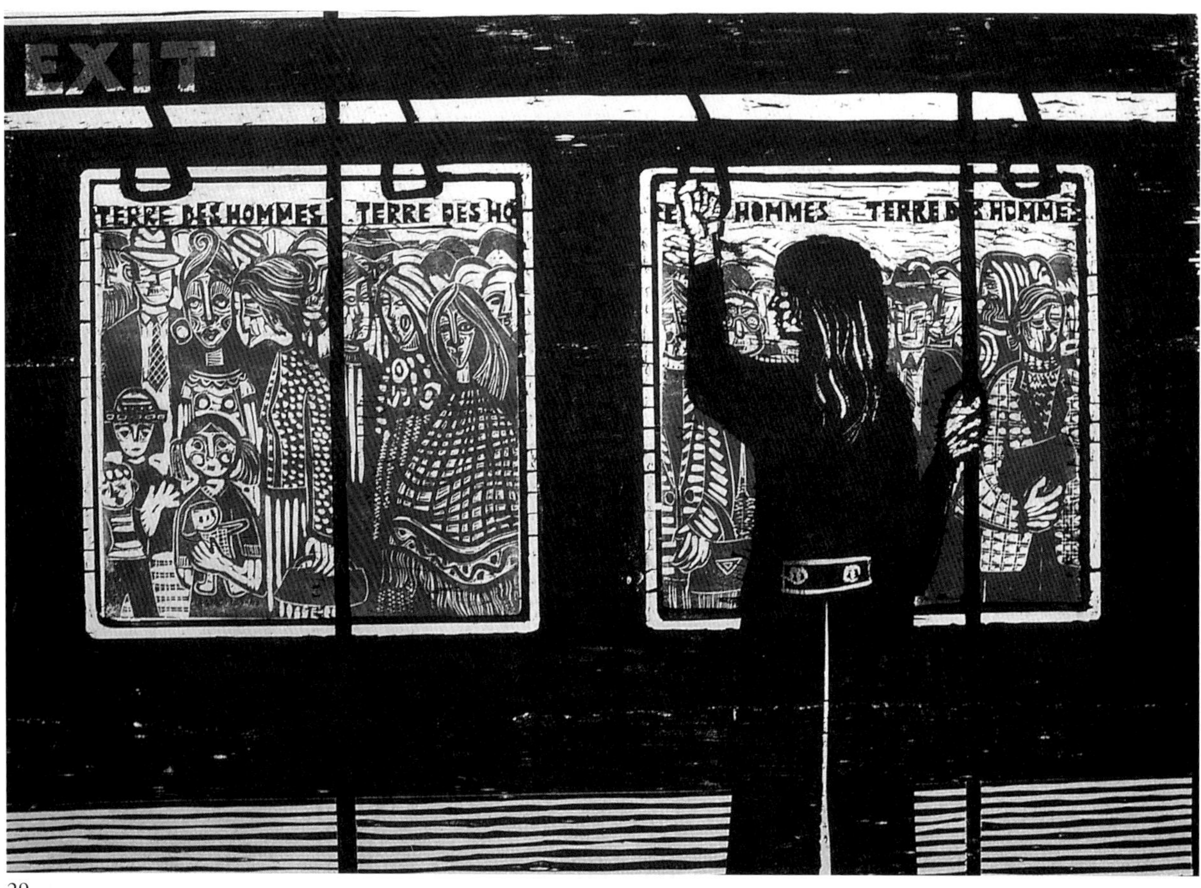

29

During this same year she worked at Pierre Ayot's Guilde Graphique, where her knowledge of French helped, since Ayot spoke no English. He maintained a well-equipped studio in the Old City, where artists could engage in any printmaking technique. He and his wife lived in the studio, Granirer's first encounter with a de facto vie bohème life style. Sometimes, arriving early in the morning, she would find them still asleep on a mattress under the etching press. Ayot did large, erotic paintings which made her somewhat uncomfortable, since the images were unmistakably taken from projected photographic images of himself and his wife in various poses.

In Montreal, her artistic confidence grew. Her son started school, which allowed more time for work and experimentation. Her work was still essentially figurative, with some early-Picassoesque influences, definitely outside mainstream Abstract Expressionism. Without substantive contact and discourse with other artists, she relied solely on her own devices.

In 1967, the Granirers decided to settled permanently in Vancouver, putting down roots for good.

29. *Exit–Terre des Hommes,* 1967
46 x 66 cm (18 x 26 in)
woodblock and linocut

30. The artist with her new son, Dan Michael, 1968

31. Granirer with her two sons, David and Dan, 1972

Vancouver, British Columbia

At this juncture, the migration and insecurity ended. At thirty-two, Granirer could at last settle and experience a sense of permanence. This could be disquieting as well as comforting, however. The family would grow and mature, safely and confidently, but what of her "secret life" as an artist? She felt no resentment about her husband's academic success and steady career advancement, and he was loving and supportive. But there was the implicit division of responsibilities, something that women in traditional relationships know too well. Granirer relates:

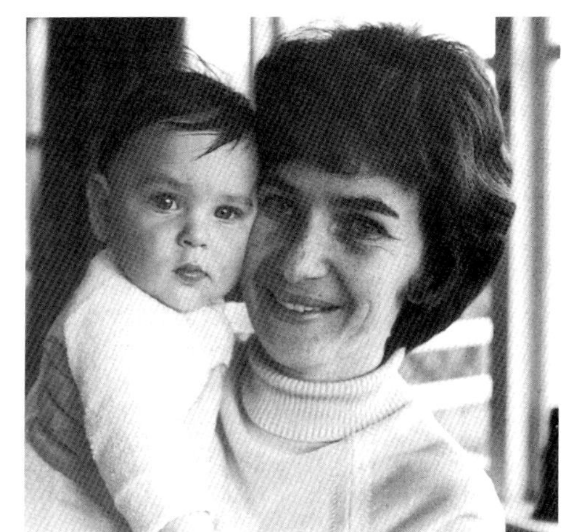

30

We bought the house in Point Grey. Our second son, Dan Michael, was born there in 1968. In retrospect, when I look back at those times, I realize that I wasn't aware of what was going on with the Western Front or Metro Media [younger, avant-garde groups]. I was never part of the Vancouver "avant-garde", never felt that what I was doing had any relevance to their activities. I lived in a different world, the world of academia; I had very little free time since now I had to look after my younger son, who was not in day-care. This is something which, I think, many women experienced: "family comes first". There is little time left for professional socializing and particularly for making art-world connections. On the other hand, since my personal experience has always been reflected in my work, this time in my life found expression in the Kite Series. I used the kite as a symbol of the yearning to fly, to break free and soar, while in reality, it is held down and tied fast by an almost invisible, but sturdy string.

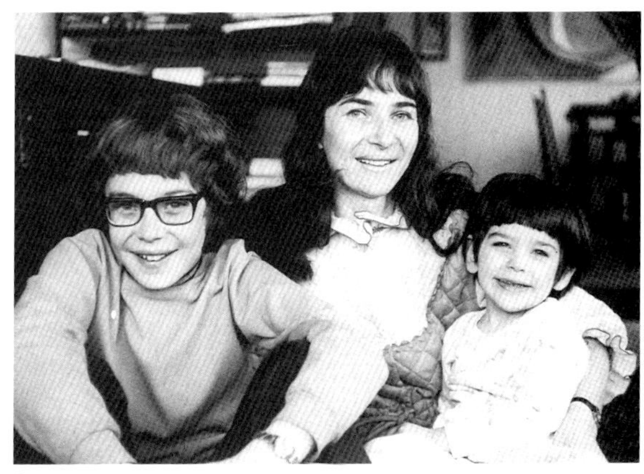

31

32. *Birth,* 1969
60 x 43.5 cm (23 5/8 x 17 1/8 in)
India ink on paper

33. *Blue Spirit,* 1969
122 x 91.5 cm (48 x 36 in)
Oil on canvas
Collection of Crispin Sion

Making art and having a family amounted to living the "Super Woman" syndrome. She noticed that the few successful women artists in the region never publicly discussed their husbands or children. She relates:

In 1974 I was invited to participate in an exhibition of women artists organized by the Art Gallery of the Students' Union Building at the University of British Columbia. There was a reception and a panel discussion for the participants. On the panel there were artists such as Pat Martin Bates and P.K. Page, among others. One of the panelists made the remark that she never ever mentioned her family when discussing art-related topics with people in the field. I still remember how saddened I was by this remark. The perception was that, somehow, having children was a shameful thing, to be hidden away like the proverbial skeletons in the closet. It was as if women artists had to conceal one of the most vital and creative aspect of their lives, in fear that otherwise they would be labelled "housewives" rather than artists. Unfortunately, I was to experience this myself, later on. However, my family being of utmost importance in my life, I have never played this game. If these two aspects of a woman artist's life are not accepted as a creative whole, it is a sad comment, indeed, on the way the art world operates.

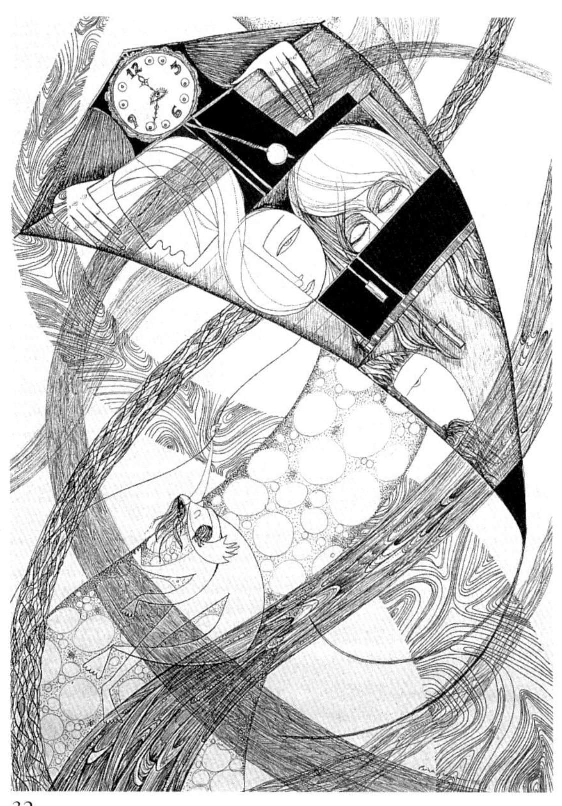

32

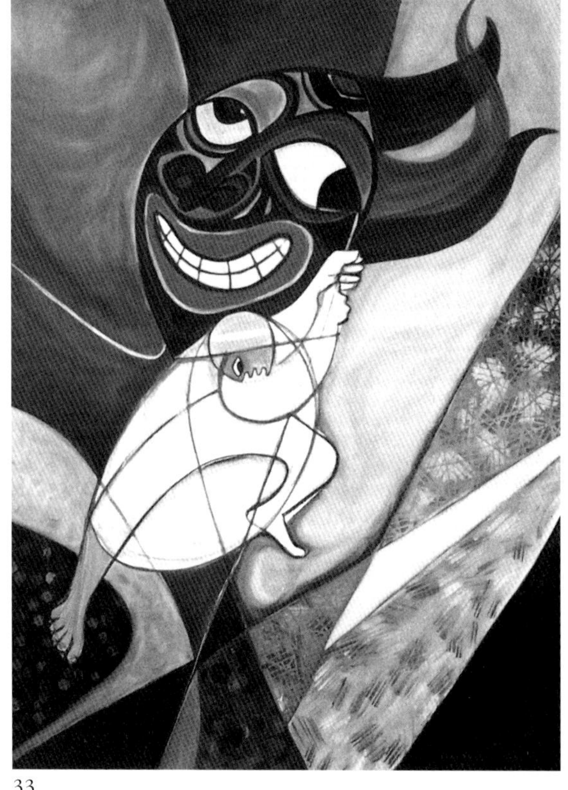

33

With her own background and conditioning, it was impossible for her to see her family as not deserving her whole attention. She entirely enjoyed the all too brief growing up of her sons and insisted on being there for them. Her art, after all, was something she was doing for herself, or so she thought. Looking back at this period, she now has a different insight: that by being an artist, she, in fact, enriched the family's life.

By the late 1960s, Granirer's level of frustration and anxiety concerning the dichotomy of art-versus-life became intense. She reasoned that the only alternative was to work less, bide her time and wait until her second child was older. Although she reflected that she could not (to this day) tread water in a swimming pool, this is precisely what she learned to do with her art. The secret recipe was *"never to stop, but to lower the flame and let it simmer"*. A number of her women friends gave up their art altogether, finding the rewards too meagre and time for art simply too difficult to combine with family life.

In fact, she came to realize that her children were a great source of inspiration for her. Understandably, her focus at this time was on small children, their ephemeral, rounded beauty and innocence. She observed the development of her two sons from moment to moment, their inherent, magical qualities. A monoprint drawing of her older son, David, expertly conjuring the essence of the universal child, was chosen for the cover of the 1969 UNICEF calendar and is part of the UNICEF collection. A chance remark by her younger son, Dan, then four years old and fascinated with "magic tricks" *("Grown-ups know nothing about magic!")*

34. David at play, 1964

35. Cover of 1969 UNICEF Calendar.
Building a Dream, 1966
This monotype is in the collection of UNESCO, New York

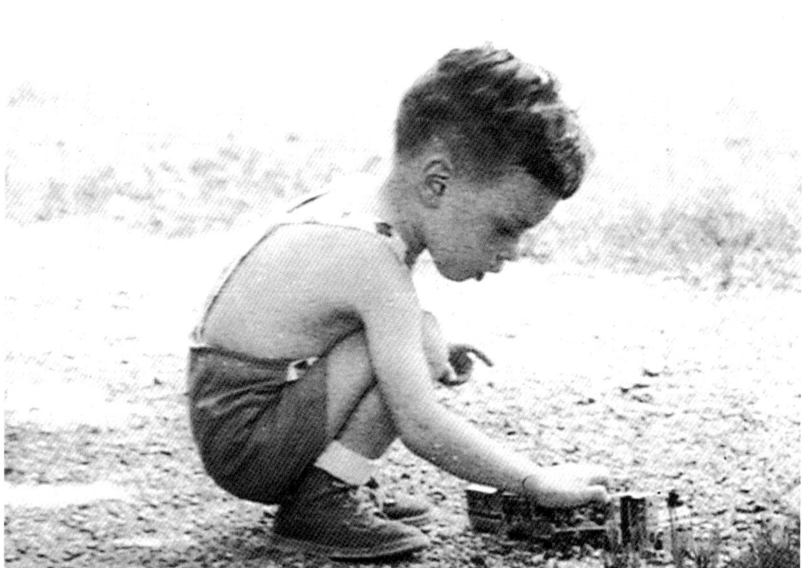

34

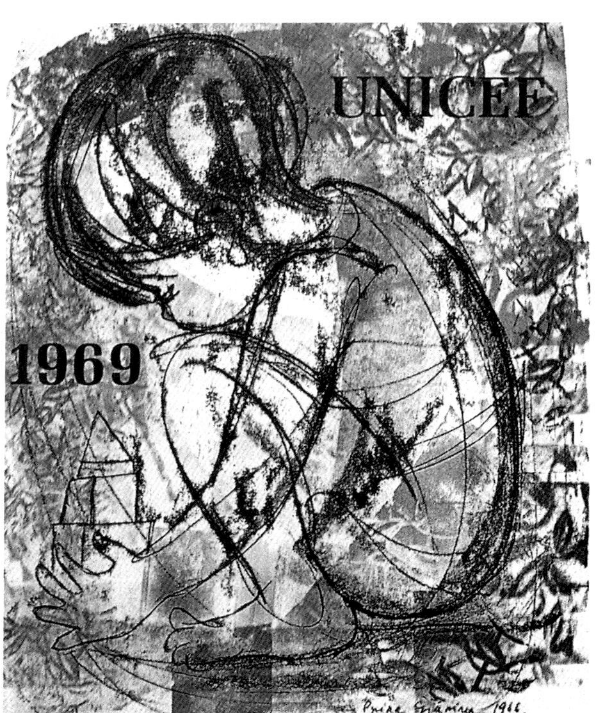

35

36. *The Magic Flute,* 1967
91.5 x 61 cm (36 x 24 in)
Oil on masonite

37. *The White Mouse,* 1967
102 x 76 cm (40 x 30 in)
Oil on canvas
Private collection

launched an entire *Childhood Series,* which were among the first works displayed at the Bau-Xi Gallery in 1972.

Being both mother and artist, Granirer was constantly aware of the value of educating young people in the enjoyment and appreciation of art. She would often invite her sons' classmates to her exhibitions, using this opportunity to introduce them to the life of a working artist. For most of them, this was their first encounter with art. On a few occasions she was instrumental in developing an "art day" at school, bringing in other artists who worked and talked with the children. Even today, she occasionally has the unexpected pleasure of meeting a young person who approaches her with recollections of what became memorable school experiences.

Up to this time, Granirer's work consisted of figurative depictions of children and quiescent, sometimes alienated, older people. Her oil painting, *The White Mouse,* 1967, is a strangely affecting portrait of a young girl holding a caged white mouse. The winsome child has dark hair, wears a rust-coloured jumper, a white blouse and black stockings.

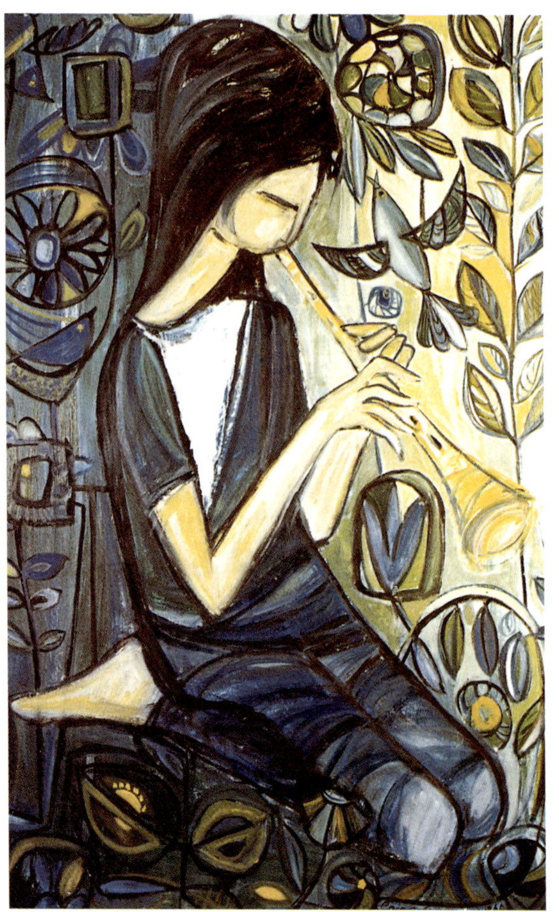

36

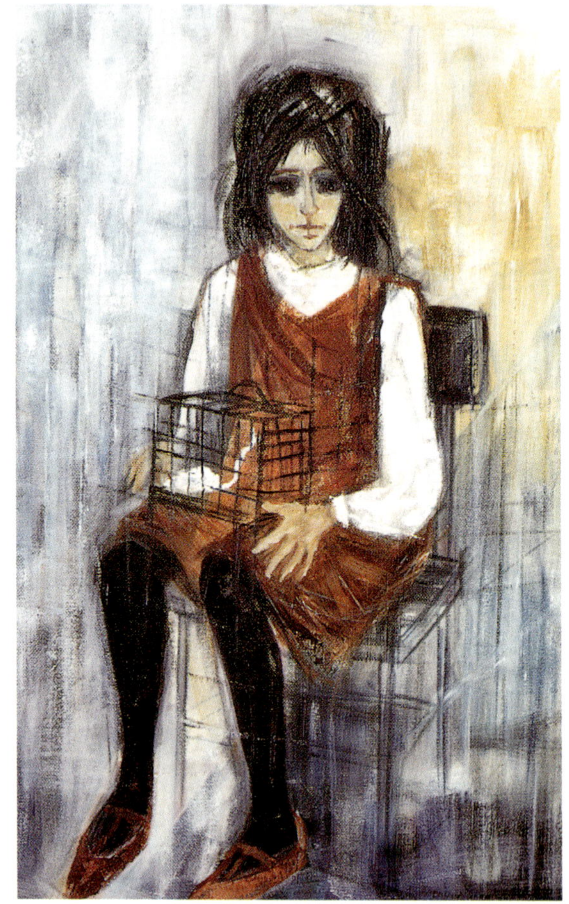

37

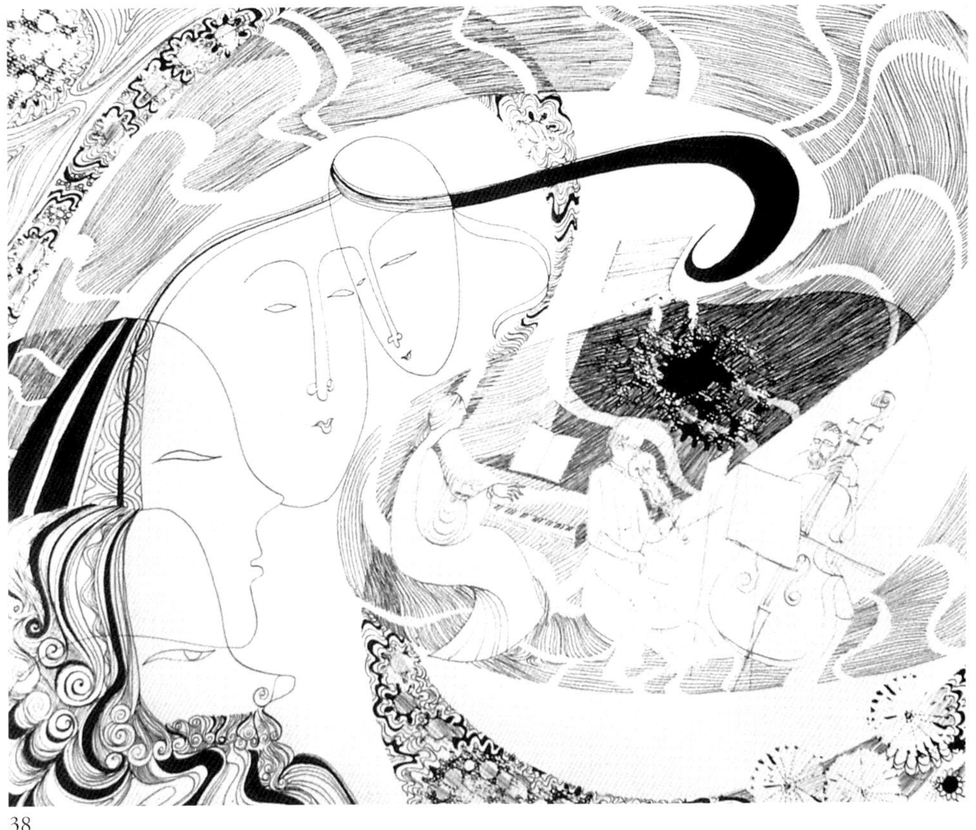

38

Her darkly shadowed eyes appear almost sightless. She sits in a straight geometric chair (reminiscent of Lionel Feininger's rectilinearity) and the space surrounding her suggests a "white perspective", as in "white noise" — there, but not there. The dichotomy of a caged animal under the control of a child — the concept of freedom and restraint — is one which is consistently posed, creating tension, in Granirer's work.

Vancouver Sun art critic Joan Lowndes, in a December 9, 1971 review of a group show at the H&S Canvas Art Gallery, commends Granirer's *"finesse of line and a removed, inward quality"* and suggests she is creating *"fairy tales for grown ups — crammed with exuberant color and movement."* A year later, Lowndes reviewed her *Kite Series,* begun when Granirer was pregnant with her second child — works that are metaphors for a tethered spirit — and lauds her *"swirling Art Nouveau bands . . . rich effects in mixed-media"* [James Cowan Theatre at Burnaby Arts Centre]. Granirer, by 1972, was successfully breaking away from literal, illustrative content, although still based on a central idea.

Whether this break resulted from the effort to describe the pressures and demands of child-rearing, or whether she was instinctively recognizing the substance of imagination and ambiguity in a composi-

Pnina Granirer brings an experience of life in the near east to her work and it is evident in everything she does. Her silk banners are richly coloured and replete with exotic human and vegetable forms. Her colours tend toward the gold of sunlight and the mysterious hues of the evening sky. There is a ripe beauty about these pieces that gives great pleasure.

— Christopher Dafoe, *The Vancouver Sun,* June 11, 1970 in a review of Granirer's work at the H&S Canvas Art Gallery

38. *Trio,* 1974
30.5 x 37 cm (13 x 14 1/2 in)
India inks on paper
Collection of Sherry and Eugene Wilson

39. *Child's Dream with Caesar,* 1975
56 x 75 cm (22 x 28 1/2 in)
India inks and printing inks on Arches
Collection of Doris Ludwig

Pnina Granirer has reached a new level of fantasy in her drawings, beyond mere charm and decorativeness. Her mythic Egyptian cat, her child with the paper crown, her puppets, are executed in sinuously interwoven bands of line and dramatic pure white highlights. It seems as though someone should write a story for these drawings. Why must a book always start the other way round?
— Joan Lowndes, *The Vancouver Sun,* Sept. 4, 1974

40. *Freedom on a String,* 1976
101.5 x 76 cm (40 x 30 in)
mixed media on paper
Private collection

tion of lasting power — she was on her way as a serious artist.

Granirer's drafting skills, particularly the penned employment of exquisitely flowing fine lines, afforded her new subjects and levels of expressiveness. In a drawing titled *Music,* 1974, she turns from children to attempt the graphic equivalent of the spell and ennoblement created through closely shared and performed music — faces, figures, instruments, wrapped in a unity of fluid, vortex-like lines.

Trio, 1974 (ill. 38), a similar composition incorporating a trio of musician friends from the University of British Columbia, alternates thick and thin black lines in an almost calligraphic bravura.

Child's Dream with Caesar, 1975, is an excellent example of the fine, gravure-like drawing with colour that had begun to emerge in the early 70's. The family cat, Caesar, in the child's dream, is rather sinister. He clutches to him a scroll of fanciful images: sleeping children and puppet kings. His claws are prominent and sharp, his eyes display a vague derangement. Granirer has aptly conveyed the mixed emotions small children experience with even benign, familiar creatures.

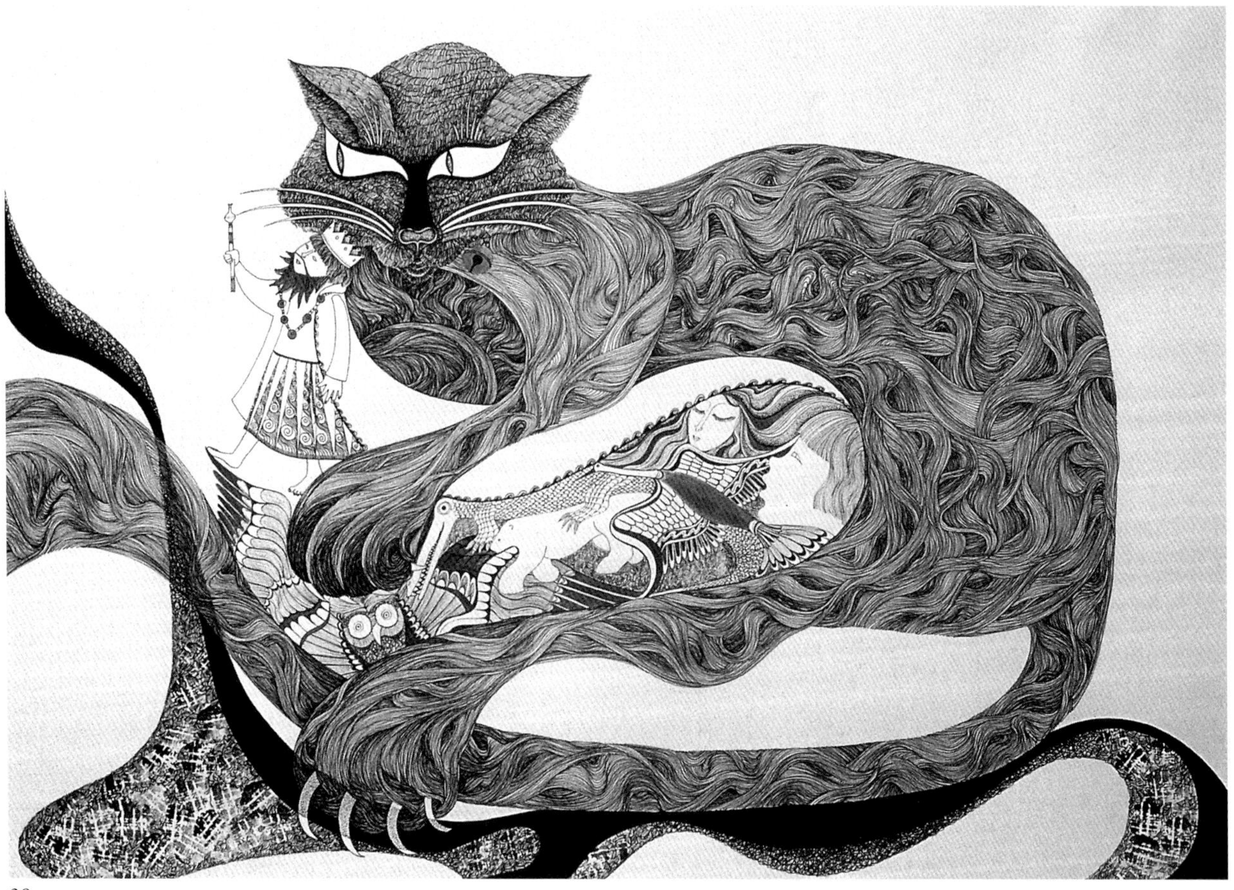

39

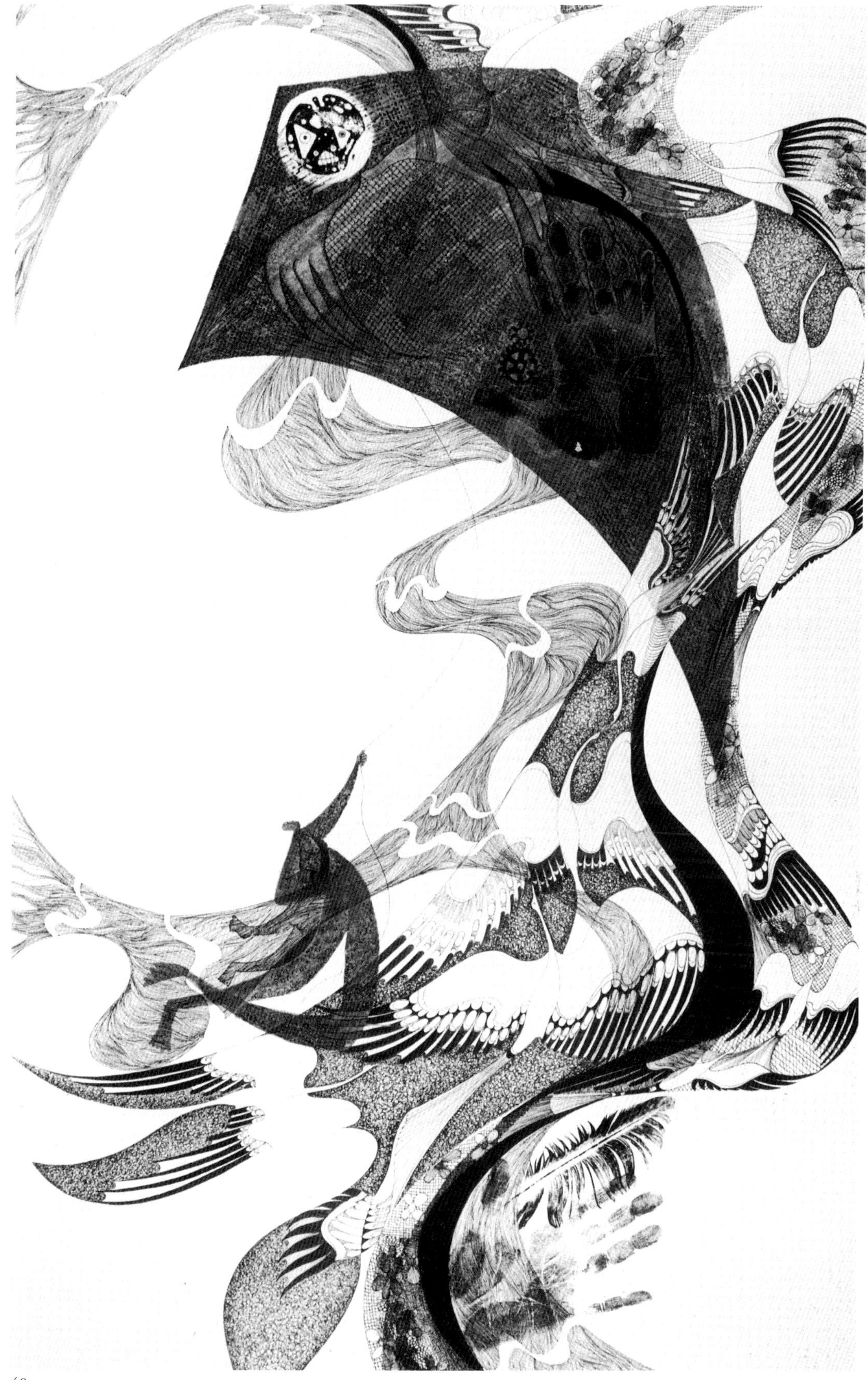

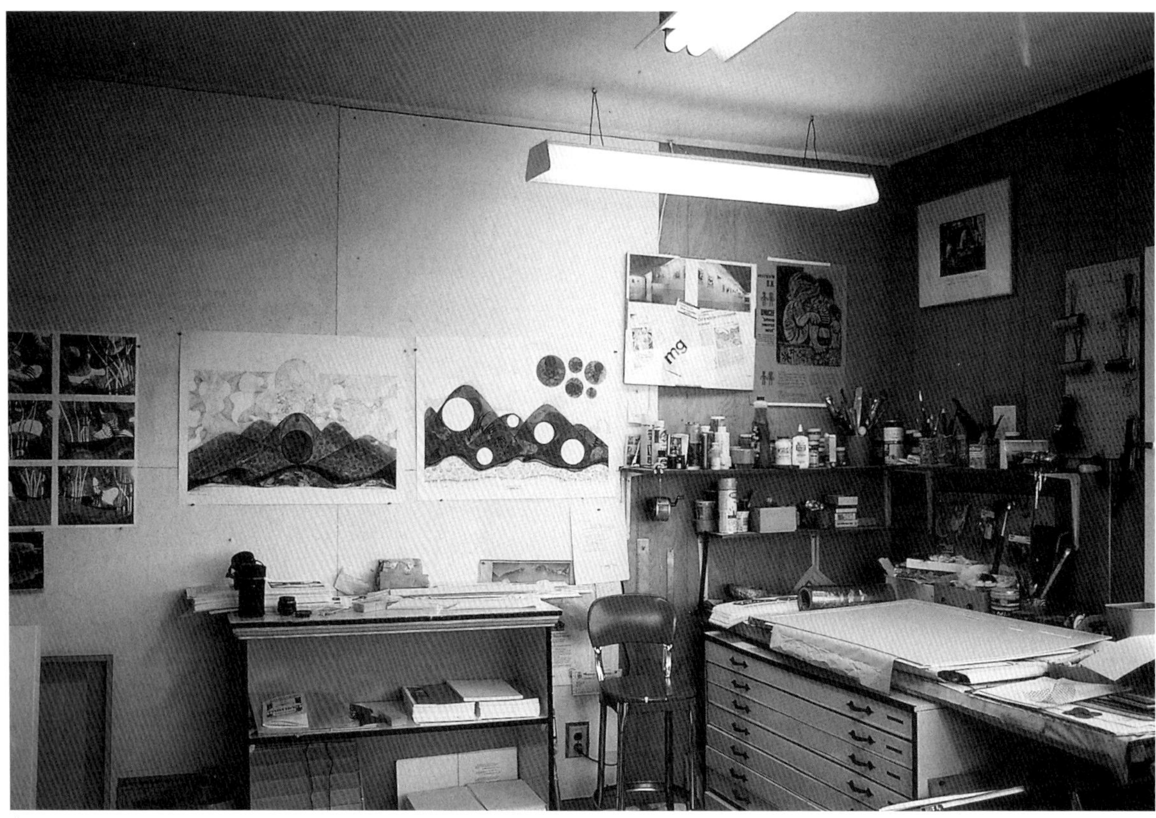

41

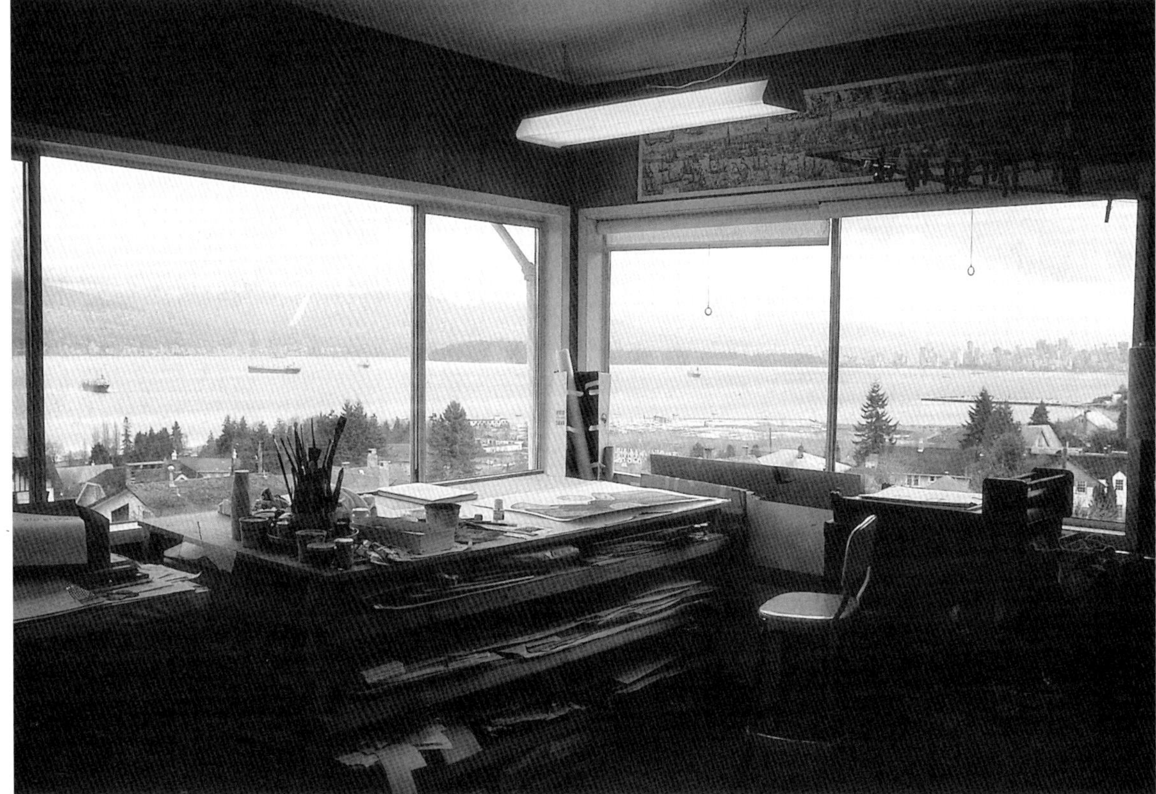

42

41–42. Two views of Granirer's studio in her house in Vancouver

The Childhood Series

The next distinctive series to appear in Granirer's work, the *Childhood Series,* derives not from Granirer's children, but from growing recollections of her own childhood. It is in this series that she introduces the symbolic imagery of two souvenirs from that time: an embroidered angel and a gold devil charm that is dented with her childish toothmarks. These two images are to figure prominently in much of her subsequent work. As she comments:

In the month of March there was a holiday in Romania originating probably from pagan times, when people gave one another good luck charms. It was the time of the year when the snow melted and the air was sweet with the promise of spring. Young gypsy girls sold small bouquets of snowdrops and perfumed hyacinths on the street corners, and the jewelry shops displayed windows laden with gold and silver charms of all sorts. I had been given many charms when I was a child, but my favourite one was a small golden devil standing on one leg.

When Granirer began working on the *Childhood Series,* she became interested in the exploration of the sense of magic and wonder children possess, but is seemingly lost with adulthood. When she searched for objects which would provide the link with her own childhood, she came across the lace angel and the gold devil charm. And finally, a random observation by her son Dan, then four years old, was the key which unlocked the door to this exploration. She put his words into a poem which appeared on the invitation to the exhibition at the Bau-Xi Gallery in Vancouver, in 1975.

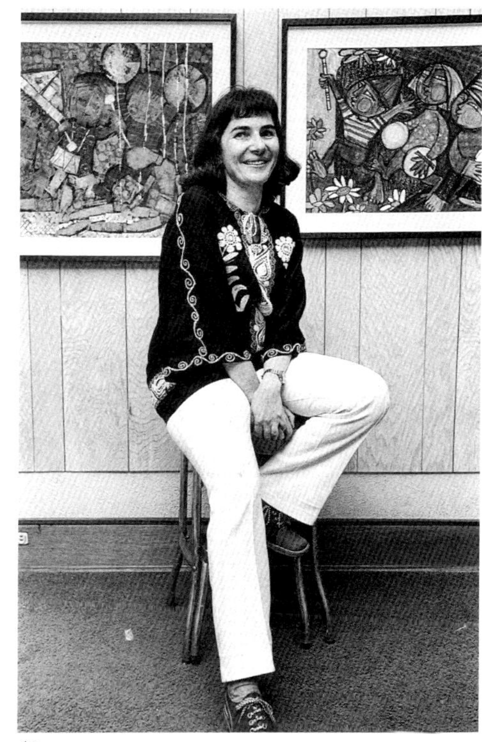

43

43. Granirer as featured in a review by Joan Lowndes in *The Vancouver Sun,* 1973

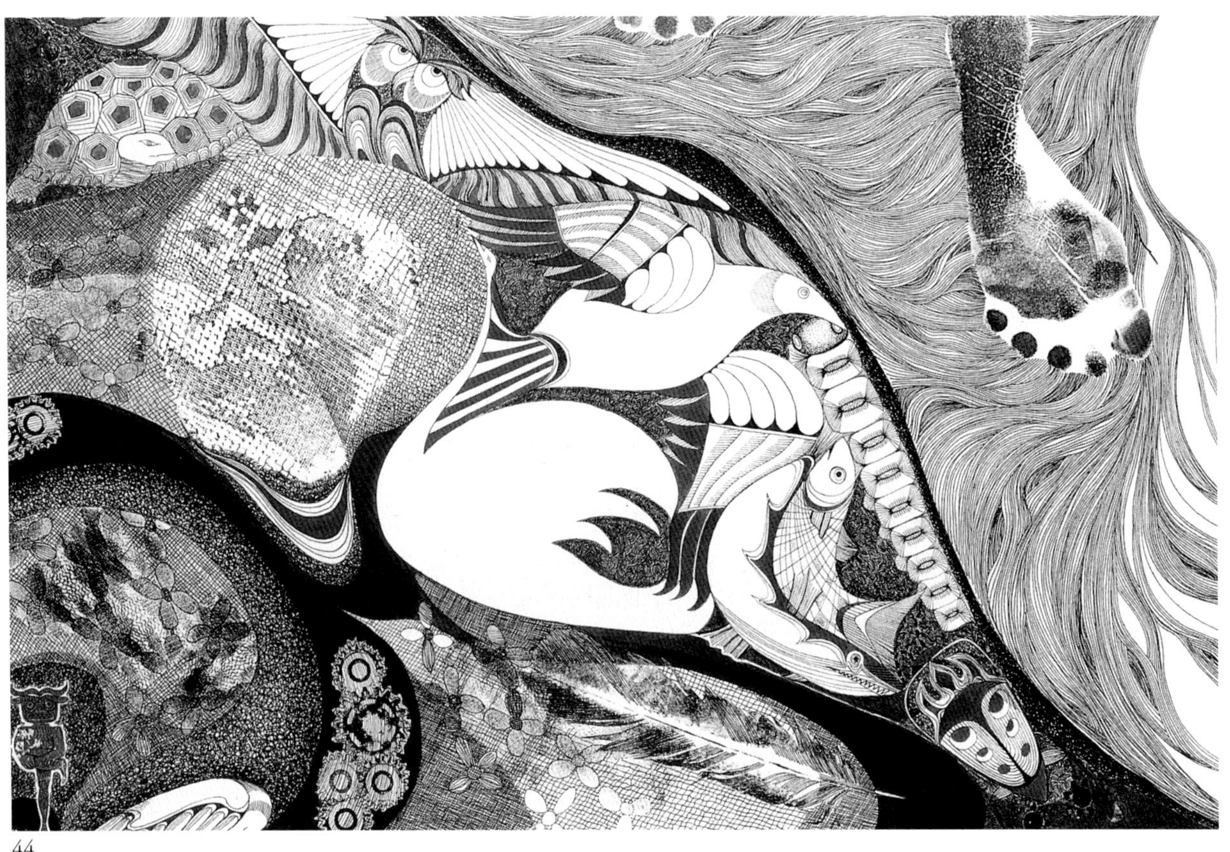

44

"Only little children can do magic," said
my small son.
"and when you are a grown-up
you cannot make it
anymore. "
I asked
"can you explain?"
"You grown-ups do not understand . . .
I am made of magic . . ."
SO —
I set about trying to go back in time
searching for things long forgotten.
The wonder of those years
I could not return
BUT —
I tried to stretch my hand
and capture
a spark of the magic.
And here it is.

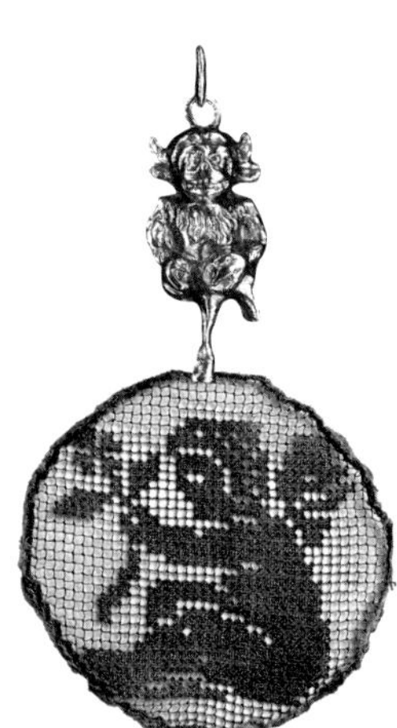

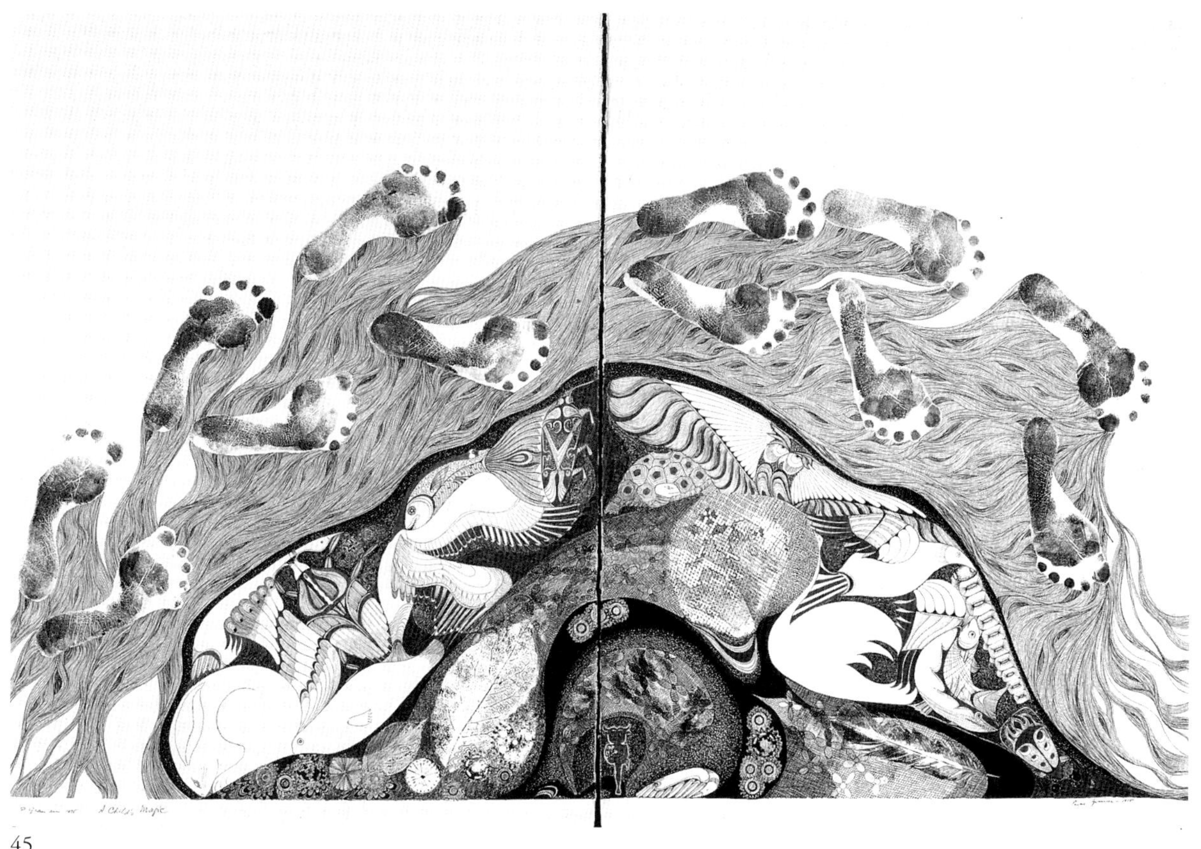

45

Child's Magic is typical of this group of works. Beneath the child's footprints, unseen by adult eyes, a small universe is unfolding. Birds and insects, fish, rabbits and turtles, intertwine Escher-like among printed leaves and feathers. The lace angel is present, resting against the swan's neck, while the little devil lurks deep in the bowels of the earth, repeating the pattern of the lion in the grass, as in *The Leader* (ill. 26).

Alistair Bell, artist and printmaker, writes about these works:

Pnina Granirer's preoccupation is with an evocation of the innocent vision and imagination of childhood, which she expresses through her own highly personal vocabulary of images and symbols.

The works which are the outcome of this preoccupation are handsome indeed. In each work a great primary form dominates, with other, smaller, images embedded in the surrounding spaces, while the whole design seems to grow from her pen in a richly articulated artwork.

The way in which she employs delicately printed impressions of real objects and substances in certain parts of her designs creates a special intensification of the texture. Although these inkings of feathers, leaves, small hands and feet, and patterned textiles are marvellous and beautiful in themselves, I

44. *Child's Magic,* 1974
detail

45. *Child's Magic,* 1974
diptych, 2(75 x 56 cm) 2(28 1/2 x 22 in)
coloured India inks, printing inks on Arches
The footprints are Dan's, the artist's younger son

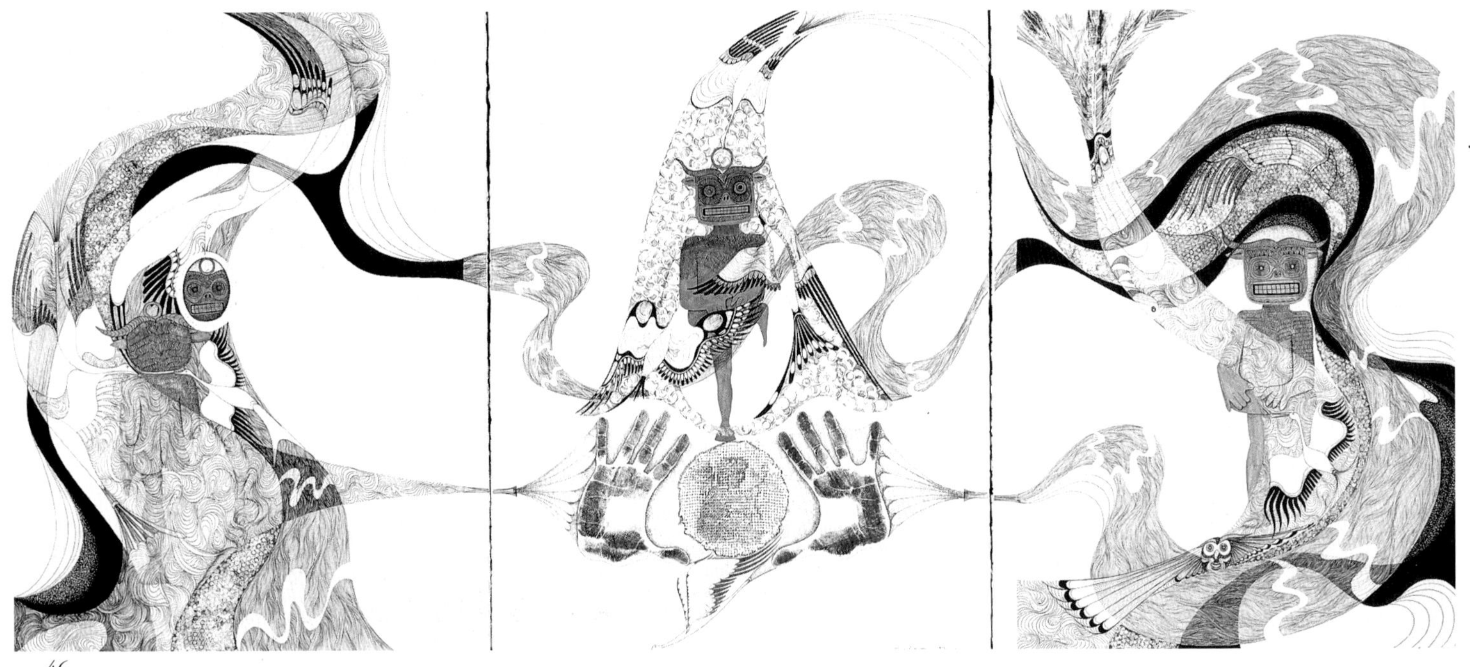

46

think the excitement comes from their being actual, existing things suddenly different from the penwork with which they are surrounded.

These designs glow with a richness of colour wholly out of proportion to the actually very restricted range of black and coloured inks she uses.

The two small mementoes carried from Romania to Israel and later to Canada, the little golden devil and the lace cherub from the embroidered edge of an old handmade sheet, were two potent images to work with: the devil and the angel. These become constant themes in her work during the ensuing years — the two opposites — the yin and yang, the light and dark.

After Granirer joined the Bau-Xi Gallery in Vancouver (1974), her work started selling consistently, contributing a great deal to her sense of self-esteem and the perception of herself as an artist. This financial aspect has always been an important issue for women who are artists. She writes:

Unfortunately, our society values people according to their monetary worth. Although women have now achieved a measure of success on the economic scene, art is different. As a whole, it is generally less valued in North America than in Europe, unless the artist is successful in selling his or her art well.

46. *Angel Waiting to be Born,* 1975
triptych, 3(76 x 56 cm) 3(30 x 22 in)
India inks, printing inks on Arches

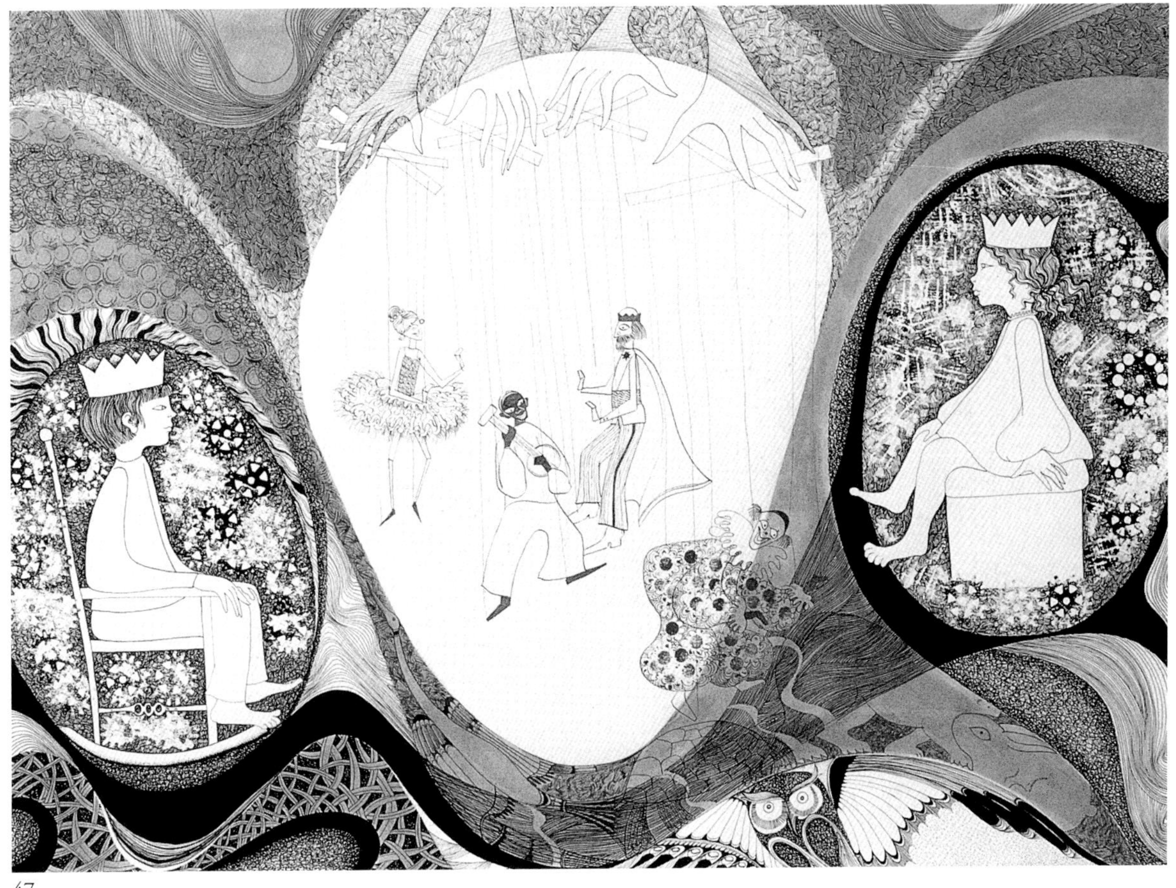

47

The higher the prices, the higher the esteem. But even here there are important differences between men and women artists. Male artists, even if they are poor, are usually taken more seriously than their female counterparts. The situation has improved slightly as far as representation is concerned. But when one looks at the number of women artists at large – and the number of exhibitions of their works in museums and public galleries, it is evident that still very few women artists are represented.

In 1981, Judy Chicago, the American feminist artist, said in a workshop she conducted in Vancouver that no woman artist could achieve recognition if she had a family. At the time this remark upset me, but now I recognize that, unfortunately, there is a great deal of truth in it. The image of the artist as a totally dedicated and obsessed individual who eliminates everything in life not relating to his art is usually one of a male artist. Often there is a woman behind such a man, who sees to his daily needs, makes sure he is fed, raises his children and quite often promotes his art. The only instance of such a support towards a woman artist that I can think of is that of Alfred

47. *Make Believe,* 1975
56x76 cm (22x30 in)
India inks and printing inks on Arches
Private collection

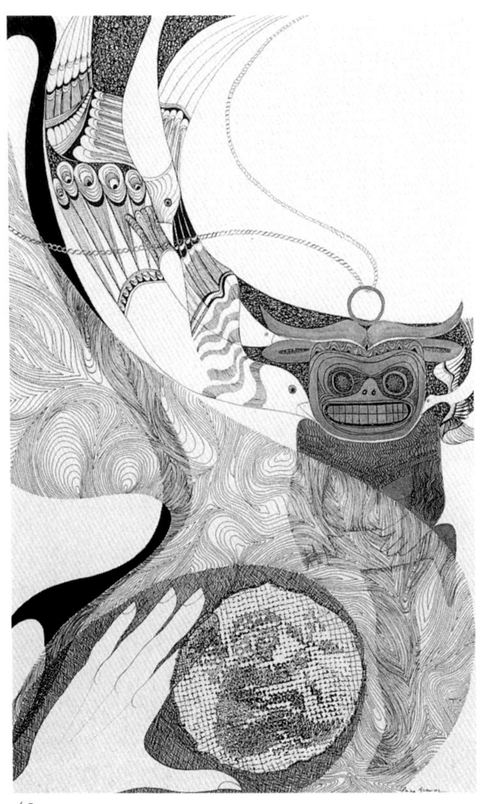

48

Stieglitz, who supported Georgia O'Keeffe and helped start her career as a painter. But even in this case, although the couple was childless, O'Keeffe eventually left Stieglitz and continued her way alone. As far as I know, most women who achieved national or international recognition in the visual arts have been single or have lived unconventional lives.

One makes choices in life, although not all of them are free choices. Most often they are determined by who we are, how we are brought up, the times we live in and even, quite simply, where we live. Getting married and having children was the natural thing for me to do. I did not even consider other possibilities. Life is not a dress rehearsal and the spool cannot be unwound in order to start all over again, not that I would even want to.

But these choices had far-reaching implications on my professional career. There were times of despair, when I thought I would never be able to paint again, times when I would rush into the studio the minute my children left for school, only to remember that I had a load of wash to do, or to plan the family dinner. There were times when I was resentful of the interruptions, frustrated by the lack of time and opportunity to keep in touch with the art community. But there were also times of great joy when the work was going well, or when I felt that, in spite of everything, I was working, producing and creating new worlds: surviving as an artist. This is what we call "living". It was also, although I did not know it at the time, living the syndrome of the "Super Woman".

48. *Devil Charm,* 1974
56x38 cm (22x15 in)
India inks on Arches

49. *Memories of Impending Doom,* 1974
56x75 cm (22x28 1/2 in)
coloured India inks, printing inks on Arches

This drawing was based on an incident from Granirer's childhood. A hawk descended one day and snatched away one of the pigeons which populated the family's yard. The bereaved mate grieved for a while and then died of a broken heart. This event imprinted itself vividly on the artist's memory.

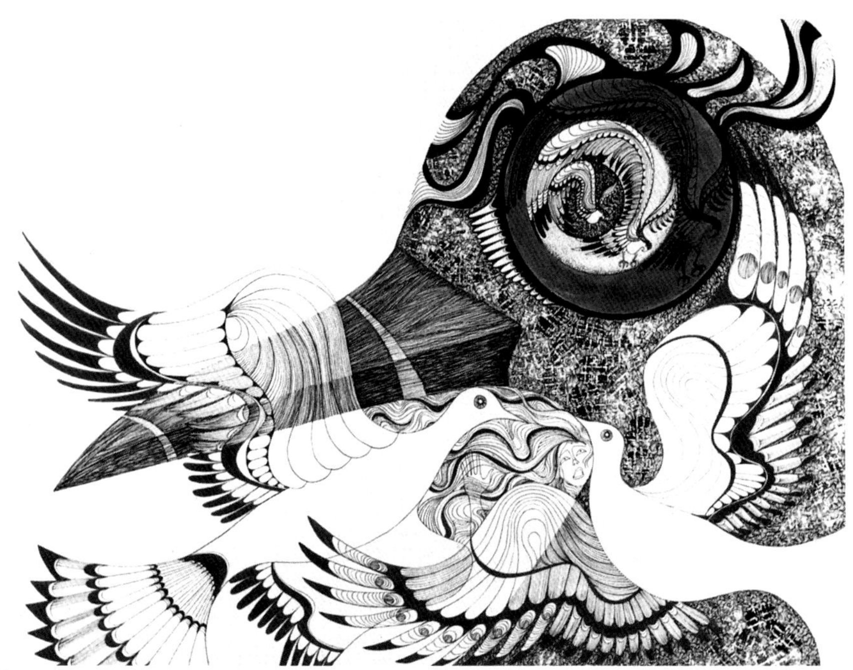

49

50. *The Little King*, 1972
58.5 x 32 cm (23 x 12 1/2 in)
printing inks on black card

51. The artist's younger son, Dan, was the inspiration for this work. He wore a foil crown for quite a while, after using it for Halloween.

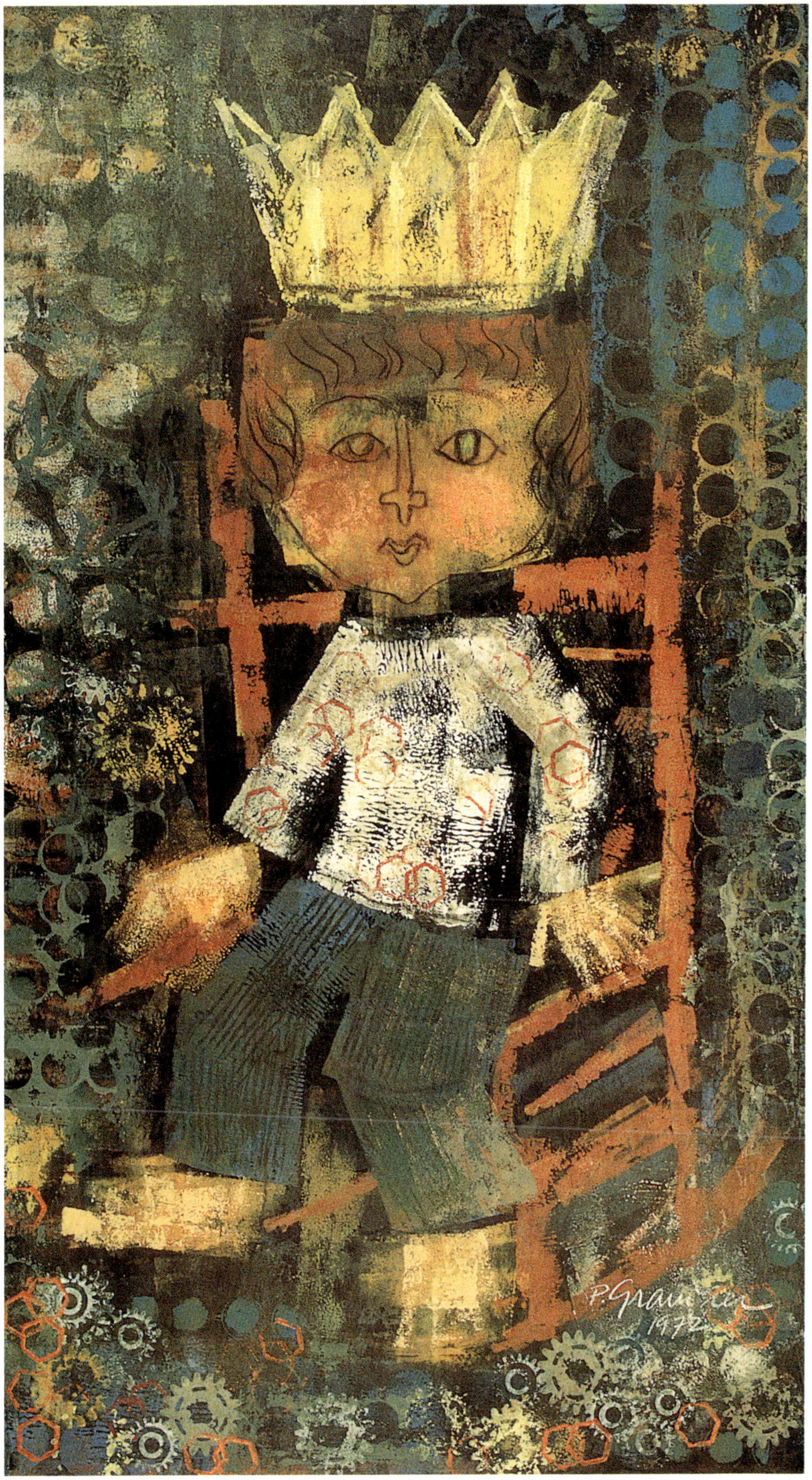

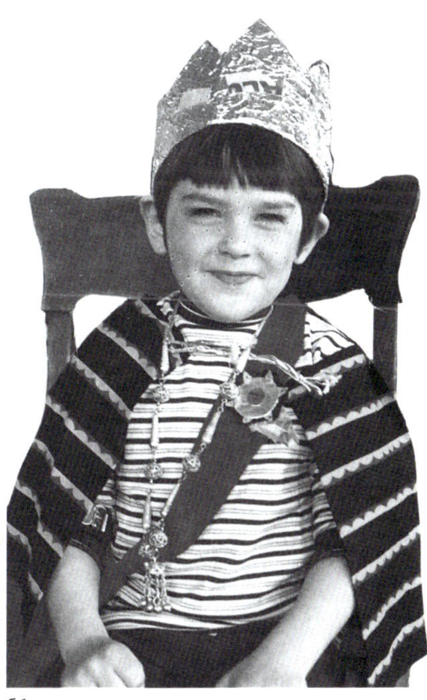

50

51

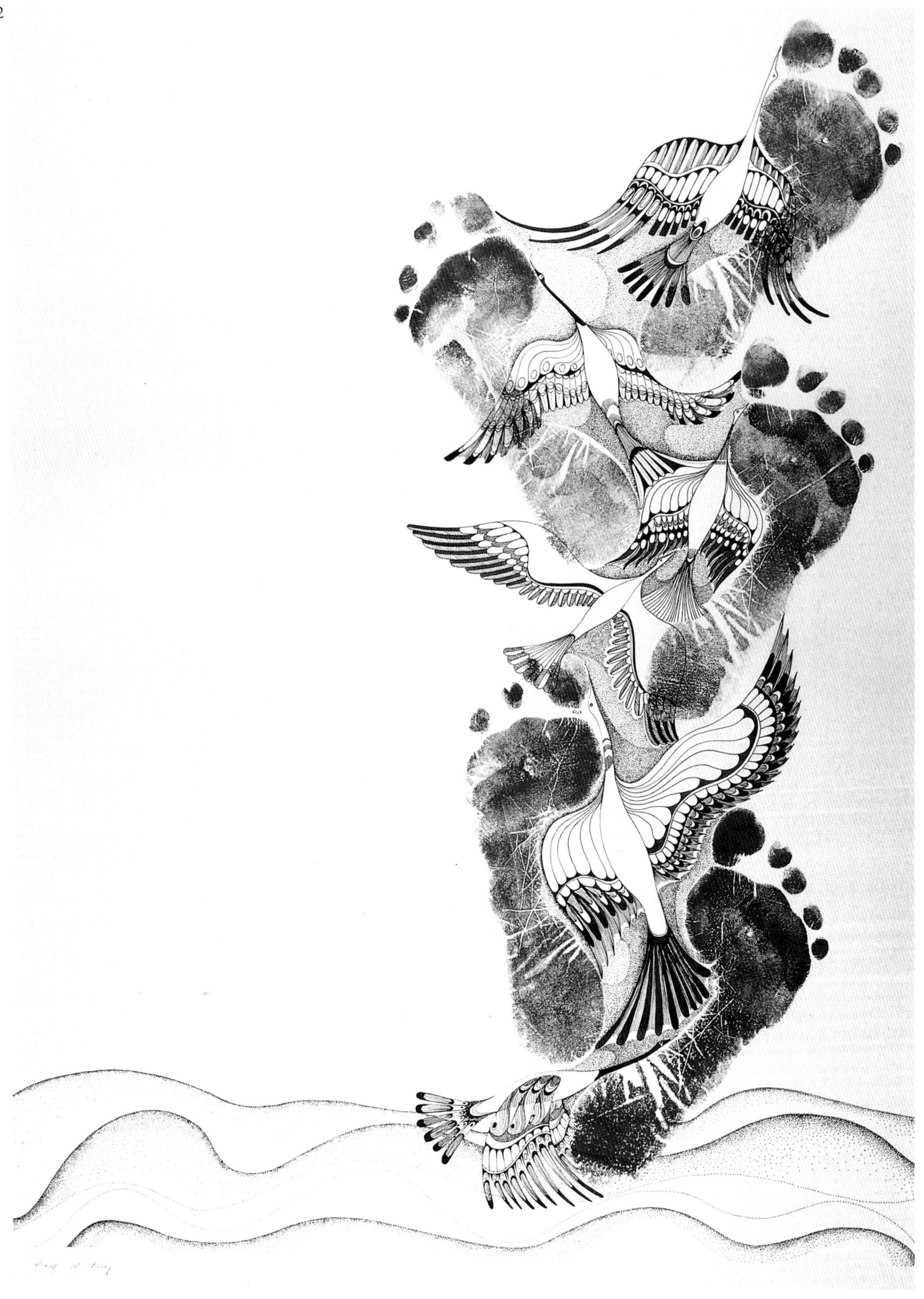

Devil Charm, 1975 (ill. 48), is one of the first instances where Granirer melds the devil charm with the cherub in a vortex, almost a fabric of fine lines and stylized bird-forms. A white hand smooths the egg-shaped embroidery, holding it up in approximation to the leering imp.

In his review of "Dawn," an exhibition of fifty B.C. women artists at the Student Union Building Gallery, at the University of British Columbia, Robert Diotte writes:

One of the more startingly vital of the works at the exhibit is Pnina Granirer's Proof of Being *(mixed media drawing). Her images of geese grow vertically in the composition and ascend against the background of footprints. This is a fine expression of the imagination at work in the mundane world of commonplace.*

The symbol of the goose is, of course, central to the Canadian consciousness. Ms Granirer is showing herself an important force in distinguishing new regions of the Canadian imagination.

52. *Proof of Being,* 1975
76 x 56 cm (30 x 22 in)
India inks, printing inks on Arches
The footprints are the artist's own
Private collection

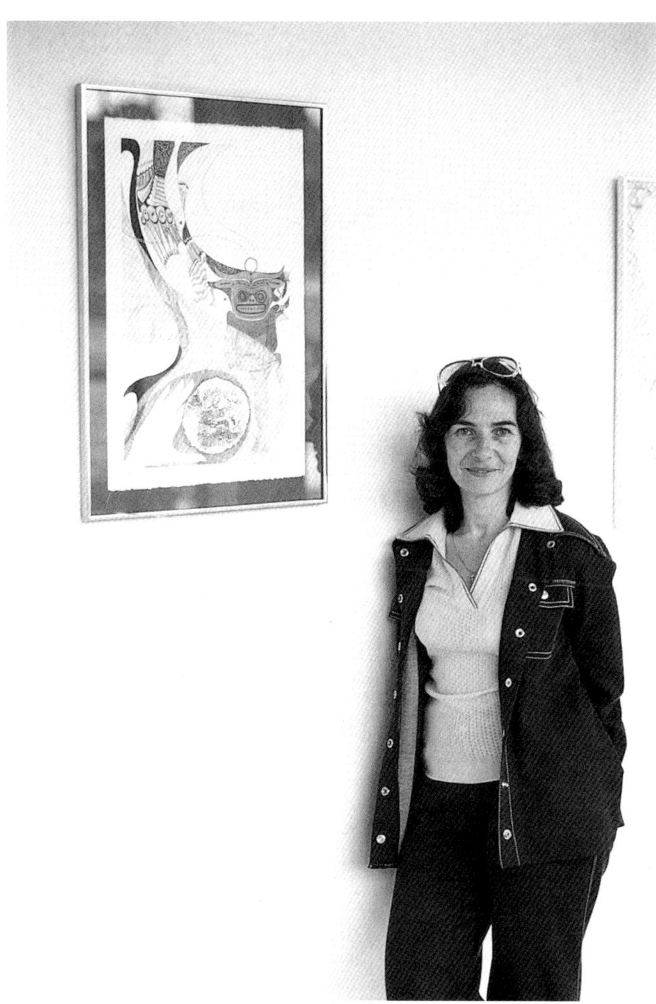

53

53. Granirer at her exhibition at
the Bau-Xi Gallery in Vancouver, 1974

54

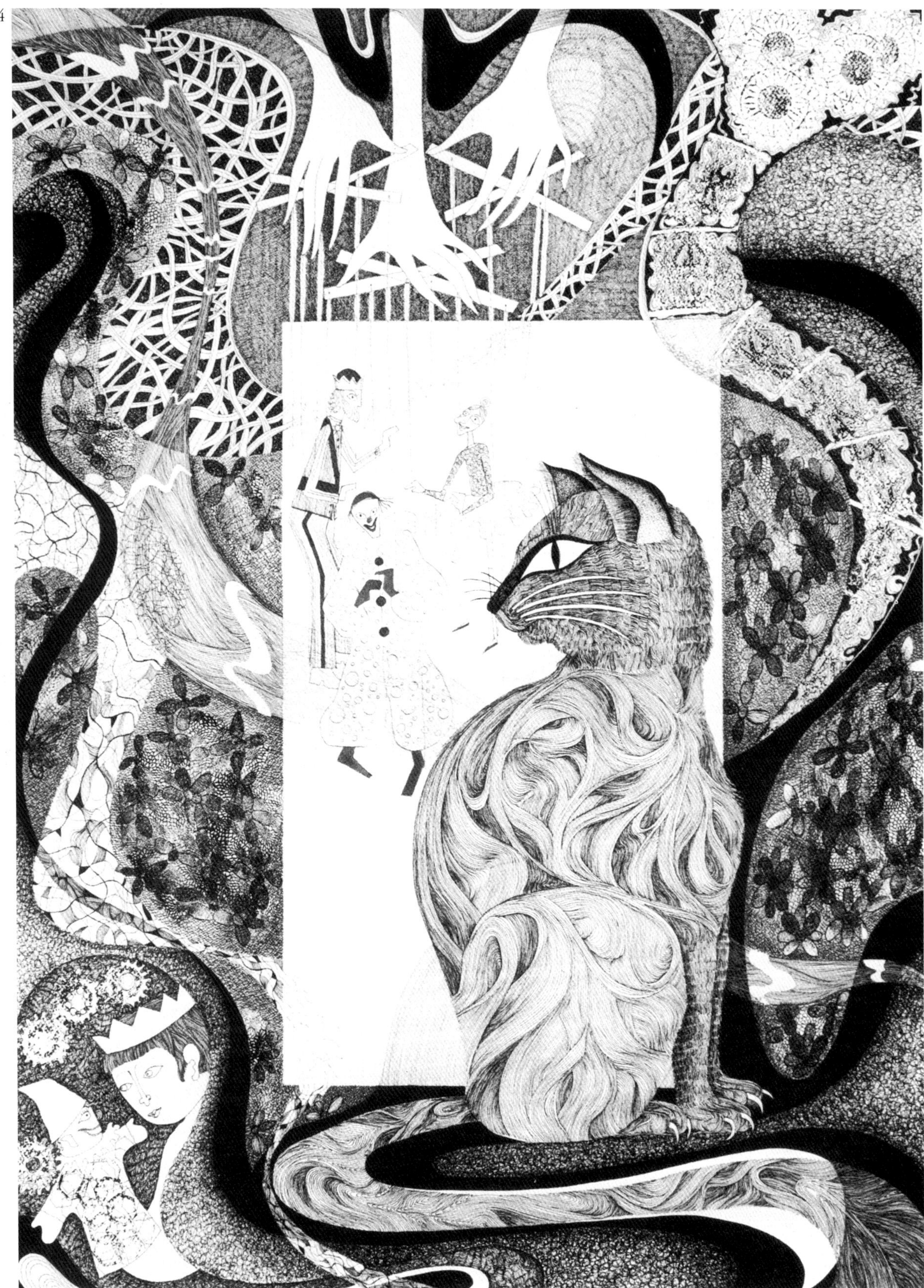

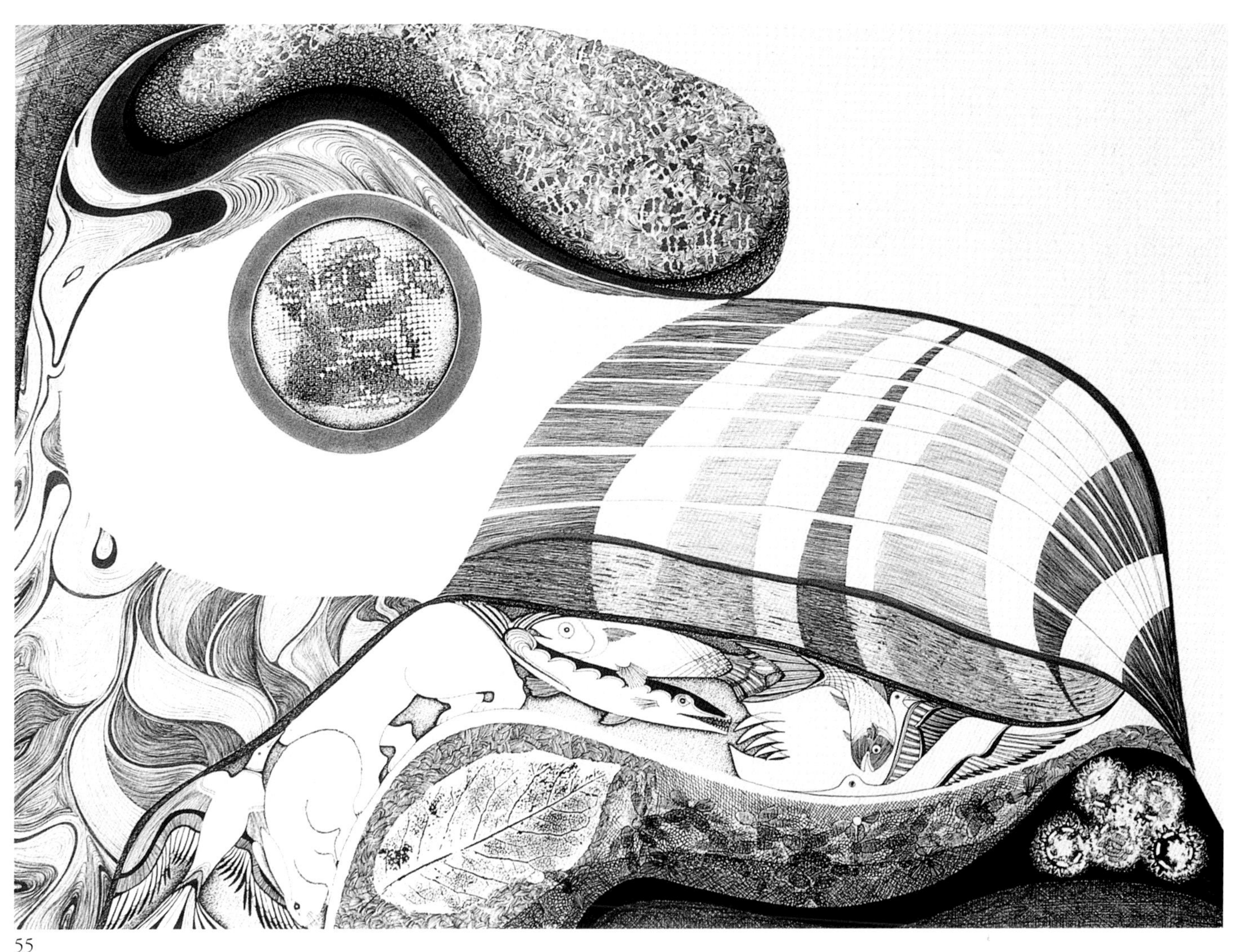

55

54. *Fantasy with Caesar,* 1975
76 x 56 cm (30 x 22 in)
India inks, printing inks on Arches
Collection of Dan and Adeena Amir, Israel

55. *Fantasmagoria,* 1974
56 x 76 cm (22 x 30 in)
India inks, printing inks on Arches

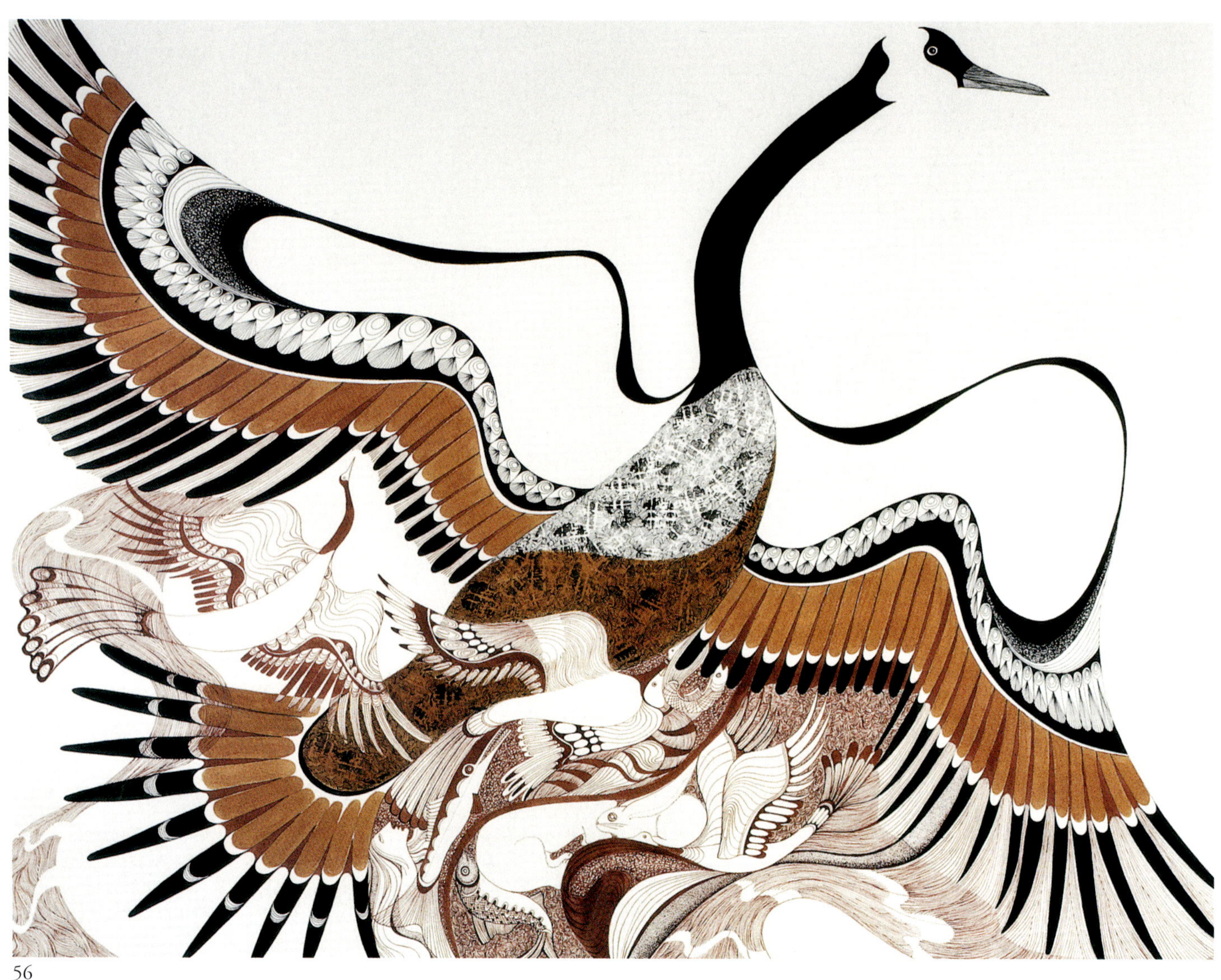

56

56. *Song of Freedom,* 1974
55.5 x 72.4 cm (21 7/8 x 28 1/2 in)
Coloured inks on Arches
Private collection

Despite all of the intelligent documentation, it is the birds we will remember. It is the artist's understanding of these, the way she stops them in time and flight, the way she closes the distance between them and us, that is the major attraction of this collection. After the birds, it is Pnina Granirer's ability to interpret in her own terms the traditional art of the West Coast Indians, and use it without plagiarization, that stands out as remarkable in the work.

— Laura Anne Holden, *The Tribune,* October 10, 1979, Winnipeg, Manitoba

Wild Goose Series, The Musical Suite, In the Beginning Series

In 1974 the secondary bird images became central, as reflected in the *Wild Goose Series.* Bird forms appeared more often, their wings creating linear rhythms. Or, when using images of birds of prey, such as eagles and hawks, Granirer introduced an ominous note, while at the same time revelling in her control of the fine, undulating line, the pleasure of pattern and decoration. She was unaware, in her relative isolation, that a minor movement called Pattern and Decoration had emerged in the U.S., mainly as a counter to Minimalism but also as a feminist concern for woman-made crafts such as quilts and Navajo blankets. More likely,

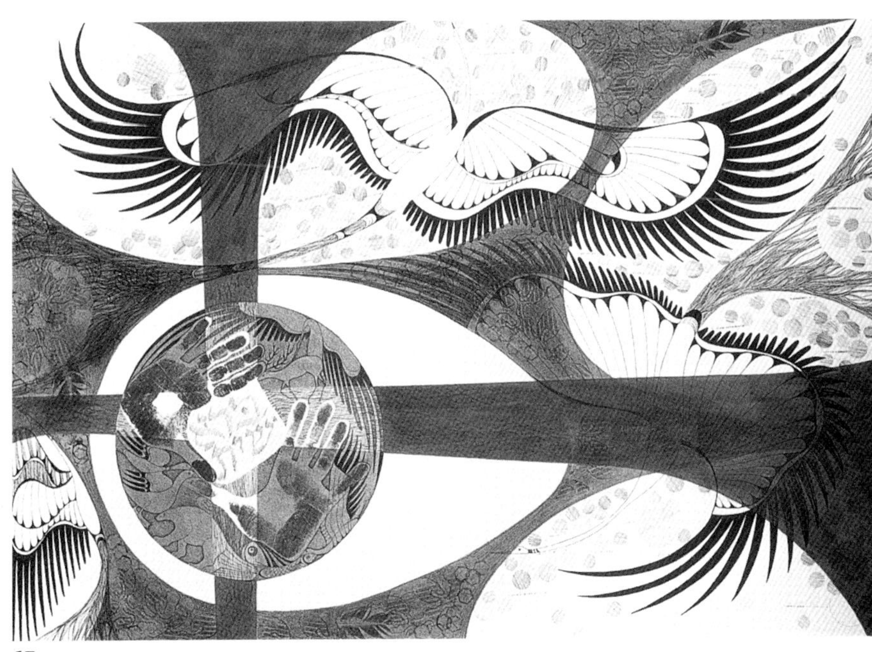

57

57. *B'reshit — In the Beginning,* 1976
69.8 x 94 cm (25 1/2 x 37 in)
India inks and graphite on paper
Collection of Lynne and Mitchell Gropper

In *B'reshit — In the Beginning,* three concepts, used by Granirer in other works, converge: the wild geese as the spiritual creation out of the void, the egg as life source and the yolk as the magic circle which contains the first Hebrew word in the Bible, framed by the hands of the Creator.

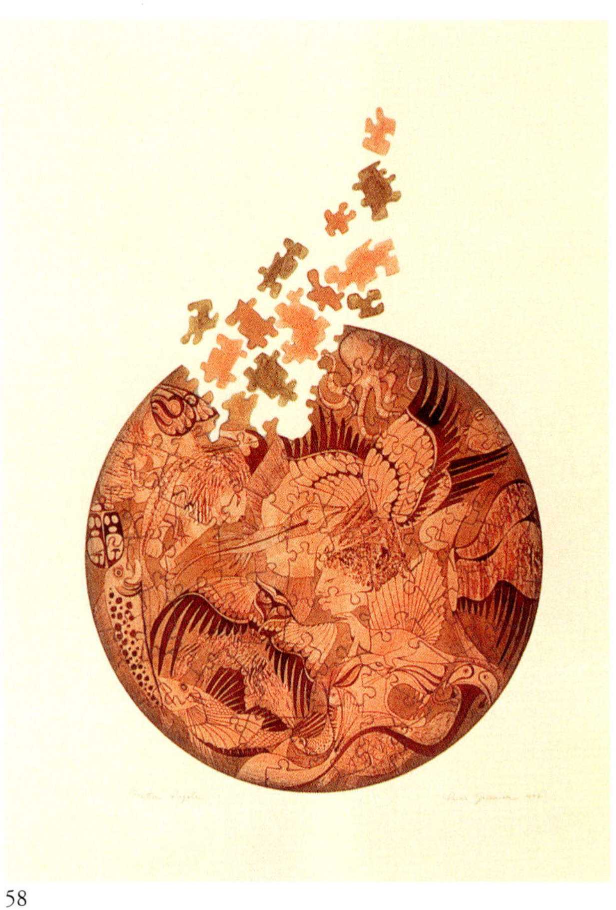

58

58. *Creation Puzzle,* 1977
76 x 56 cm (30 x 22 in)
India inks, printing inks,
graphite, grease pencil, on Fabriano

59. *Rhapsody in Blue,* 1975
54.6 x 68.5 cm (21 1/2 x 27 in)
India inks, printing inks on Arches
Private collection

This drawing is important for the introduction of pencil to Granirer's work. The decorative technique is otherwise the same, but has been softened by the nature of the graphite. Here the eagle in menacing pose, swoops down toward a rather gentle goose. The narrative contrast is strong, and is re-enforced by the combination of pencil and ink.
— Melanie Gold, *Arts West* May-June, 1978

60. *Requiem,* 1976
56 x 76 cm (22 x 30 in)
India inks, printing inks,
graphite on paper
Collection of Judith and Moshe Mastai

Granirer was unconsciously looking back to the complex and sophisticated patterning of Byzantine and Islamic art.

A few years later, Melanie Gold in *Arts West* (May-June 1978) sees Granirer's bird and feather motifs as being informed by Eastern Art, although this is difficult to rationalize, her original instruction coming from exclusively Euro-émigré teachers, the only exception being Hebrew calligraphy. Gold also characterizes Granirer's "ideistic symbols": birds and wings as they relate to the concepts of freedom, harmony, endurance, and motion; the goose and eagle epitomizing the beauty and strength of those concepts; while the *"oval and circle are elements of totality and continuity which she relates to the evolutionary process of the womb, birth and life cycles."*

Technically, these drawings were conceived with the idea of achieving the greatest possible richness of texture through intricate line and pattern, in spite of very sparing use of colour. Granirer used India inks, mostly monochrome earth tones, supplemented by pencil drawing and printed textures of lace, leaves and other patterns. During a trip to

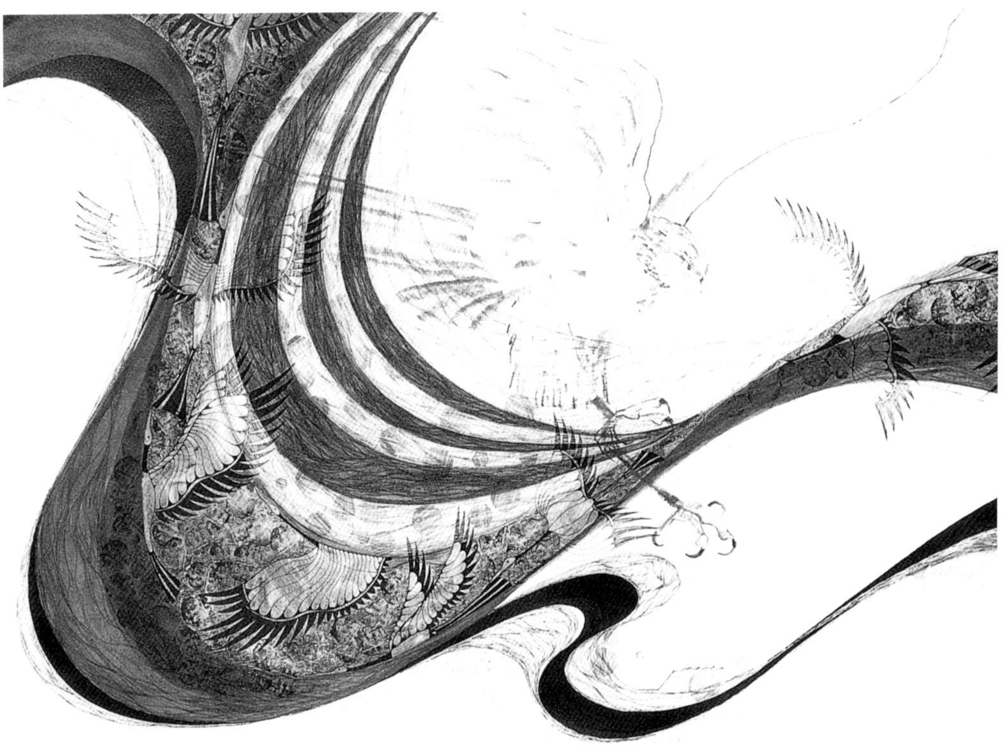

59

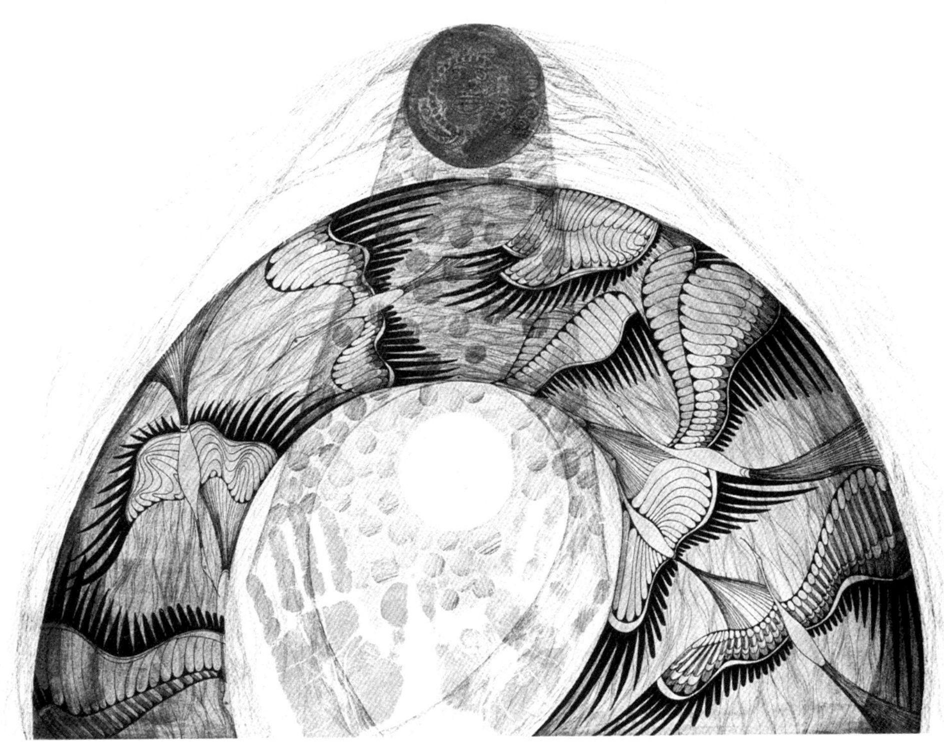

60

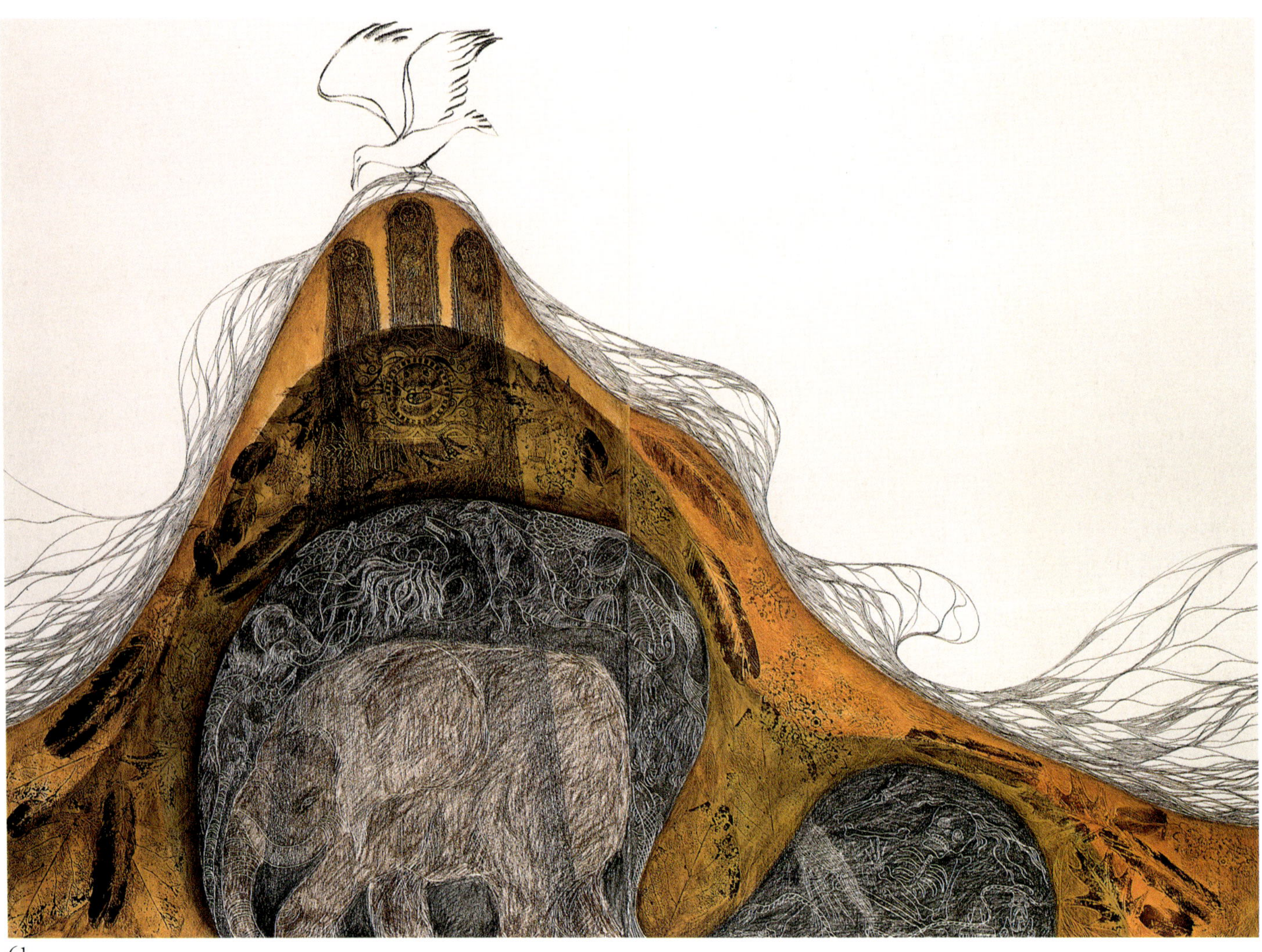

61

61. *In the Beginning — Traces,* 1977
From the Human Landscapes Series
diptych, 2(72.4 x 53 cm) 2(28 1/2 x 20 7/8 in)
India inks, coloured pencils, graphite
on Fabriano

She is not a landscape painter. She feels that "an artist has a lot to say and should say it." The statement she is making through the drawings is that we should keep what we have that is beautiful in the world, not destroy it; less a pretentious stance, in her case, than a sincere desire to keep life intact.
— Deanna Levis, *Artmagazine,* Oct/Nov, 1977

Rome she discovered the wonderful Fabriano paper, which became her favourite, replacing the French-made Arches paper she had used before.

Creation Puzzle, 1977 (ill. 58), which approaches the complexity of some of M. C. Escher's fantastic structures, is a continuation of Granirer's further absorption in cosmic procreation. Like a round, red/orange Mayan stele, it abounds with animistic and patterned metamorphoses, alludes to a diversity of creation myths, and suggests that the "pieces" of mankind's eternal riddle might be coming together.

Reviewing Granirer's three suites, *The Musical Suite, In The Beginning,* and *Human Landscapes,* in a Bau-Xi Gallery exhibition, *Province* art critic Art Perry acknowledged her *"Precise line . . . detailed decoration,"* but felt she was less successful in her *". . . attempts to give substance and meaning to the overplay of visual rhythms that, at first glance, dominate*

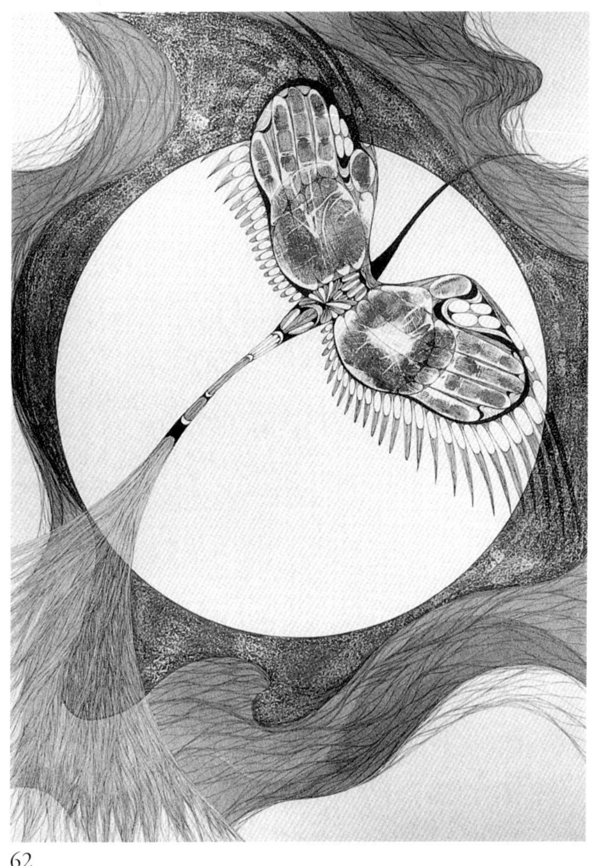

62

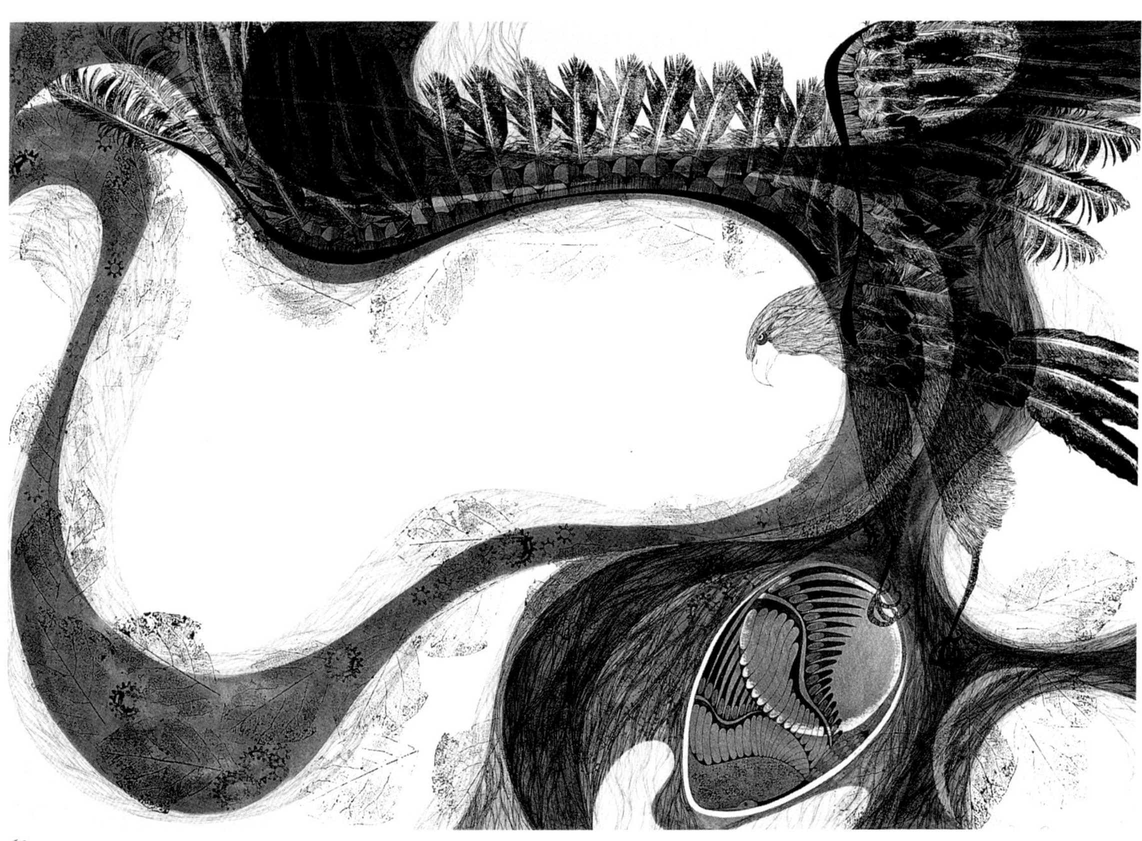

63

62. *Solo,* 1977
76 x 56 cm (30 x 22 in)
India inks, printing inks on Arches

63. *Sonata for Eagle and Golden Egg in Green Minor,* 1977
70.5 x 100.2 cm (27 3/4 x 39 1/2 in)
India inks, printing inks on Arches

In an *Artmagazine* review of Granirer's exhibition at the Bau-Xi Gallery in Vancouver in 1977, Deanna Levis writes:

A departure from the more metaphysical concepts of the rest of the exhibition, and my personal favourite, is the Musical Suite. *A dazzling equation of form and content, these works fairly sing with rhythm and movement. Here, the abstract form displays to the full Granirer's ability as a graphic designer. Even the titles are rich in lyrical cadence, like* Sonata for Feathers in Gold Flat, *or* Symphony #1 in Wings Major. *Listening to her poetic manner of speaking, one wonders if she might also have made a mark as a writer.*

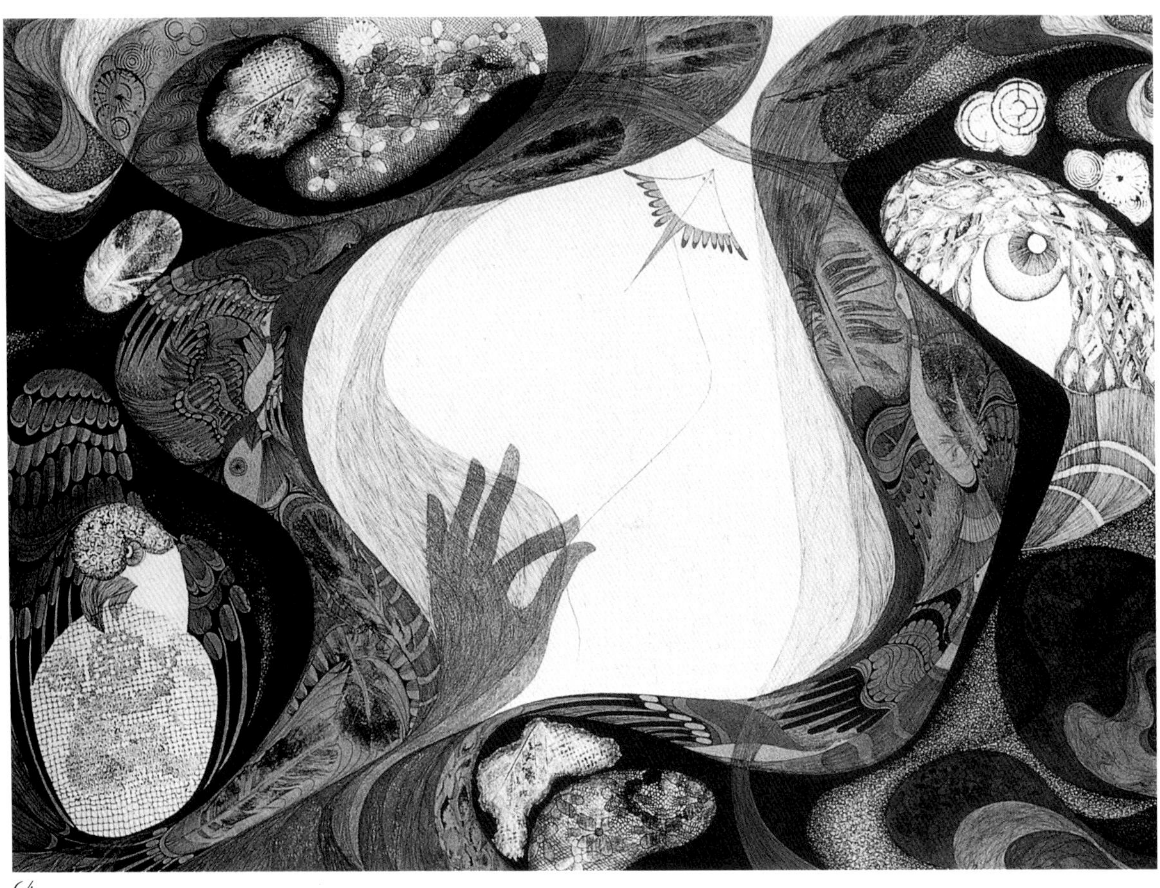

64

her works." Perry, less than tolerant, chided and paraphrased her written wall-statement *("Now, the oval has slowly turned into an egg — the centre of all creation, the Beginning — the life-giving starting point for everything — the mystery of it all will never cease to overwhelm me . . .")* but offered nothing in the way of a metaphysical rebuttal, since formal criticism of the day did not extend to spiritual concerns. Wayne Edmonstone reviewed the same show, for *The Vancouver Sun*, describing the work as *"airy, intense, and decorative drawings . . . soaring eagles and geese, cosmic eggs,"* but Deanna Levis, reviewing in *Artmagazine* (Oct/Nov '77), had the grace and empathy to include Granirer's verbatim rationalization for these themes and was much more understanding of the rising tide of women's sensibilities in art, praising her "visual delights".

The circle appears in many of these works during the seventies. It usually acts as a central artistic device, enclosing complex forms of birds, printed textures and images of fantastic fauna. It is almost as if Granirer is seeking the security and stillness associated with this perfect shape.

Granirer's recurring symbolism for her perceived personal constraints, the *Kite Series,* 1975–79, works in and out of other operative

64. *Mystère au Cerf-Volant,* 1975
56 x 76 cm (22 x 30 in)
India inks, printing inks on Arches

65. *Worship of the Magic Circle,* 1976
76 x 56 cm (30 x 22 in)
India inks, printing inks on paper
Collection of Dan Granirer

66. *Magic Circle 4,* 1976
76 x 56 cm (30 x 22 in)
India inks, printing inks on paper

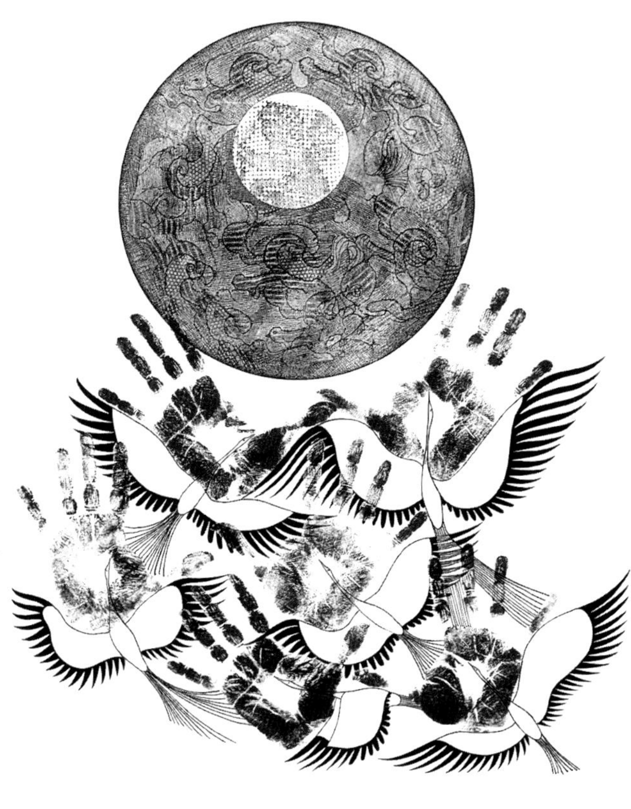

65

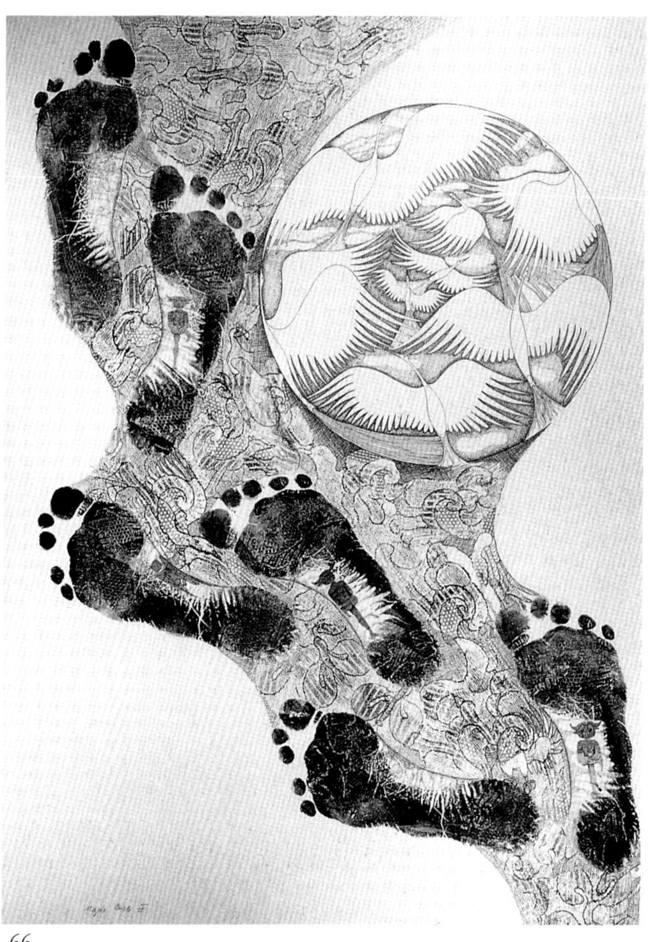

66

themes of the 70's. *Mystère au Cerf-Volant (Mystery of the Paper Kite)*, 1975, reiterates this feeling of inquietude. A grey hand (her conscience? sense of duty?) holds an almost invisible line to a distant bird/kite flying high outside a biomorphic "nest" filled with Paisley birds and egg-like forms. She does not angrily decry her situation; rather, she sounds a whimsical, ironic note.

In 1976, local dealer Estika Hunning, who was the first to exhibit the Yugoslav prizewinning printmakers in her Kerrisdale gallery, the H&S Canvas Art Gallery, initiated an exhibition of four Canadian artists at the Moderna Galerjia in Ljubljana, which also travelled to the Museums in Zagreb and Maribor in Yugoslavia. This exhibition was made possible by the interest of Zoran Krzisnik, secretary of the International Biennial of Graphic Art and the Director of the Moderna Galerjia Ljubljana, in introducing Canadian artists to the Yugoslav public. The four artists were Wayne Eastcott, James Felter, Pnina Granirer and Arnold Shives.

INCANTATION FOR A MAGIC CIRCLE

The wind is howling through the branches
a man is killing man somewhere
each one of us lives in a circle —
we just don't know it's there

I'll hide my head under my pillow
when thunder shakes my bed at night
I'll step into the perfect circle
and will be safe inside.

No evil will befall me
the devil cannot reach me
the circle will enclose me
safe forever.

Pnina Granirer, 1974

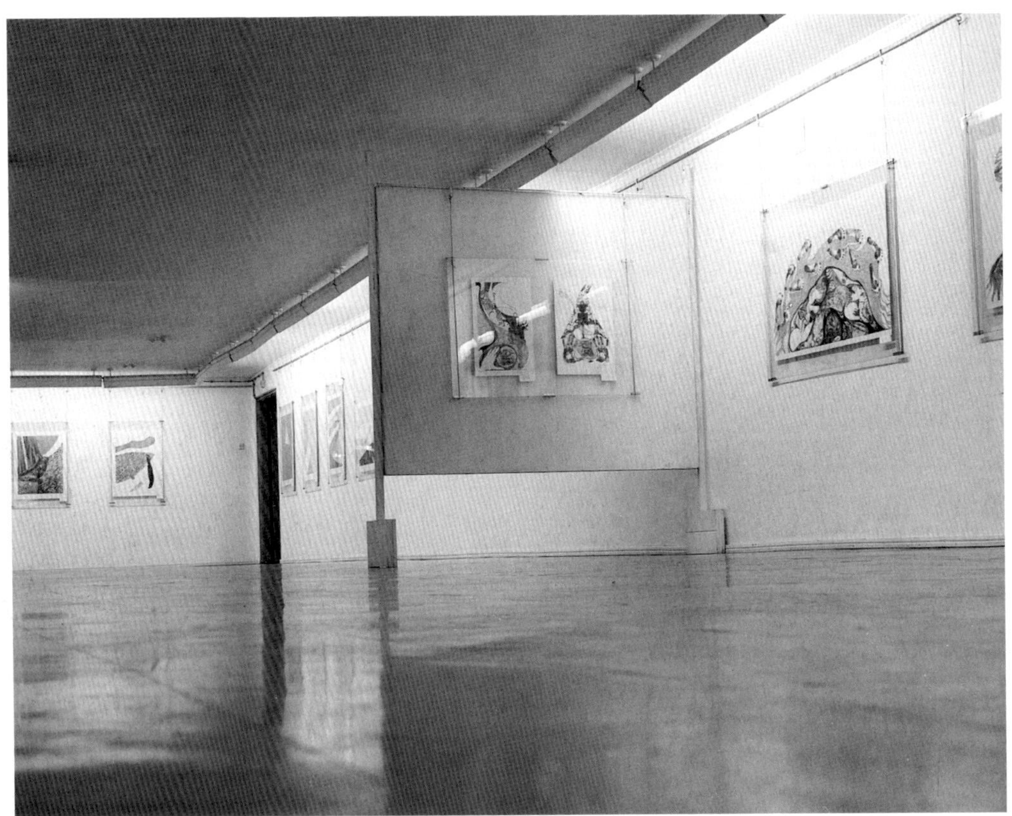

67

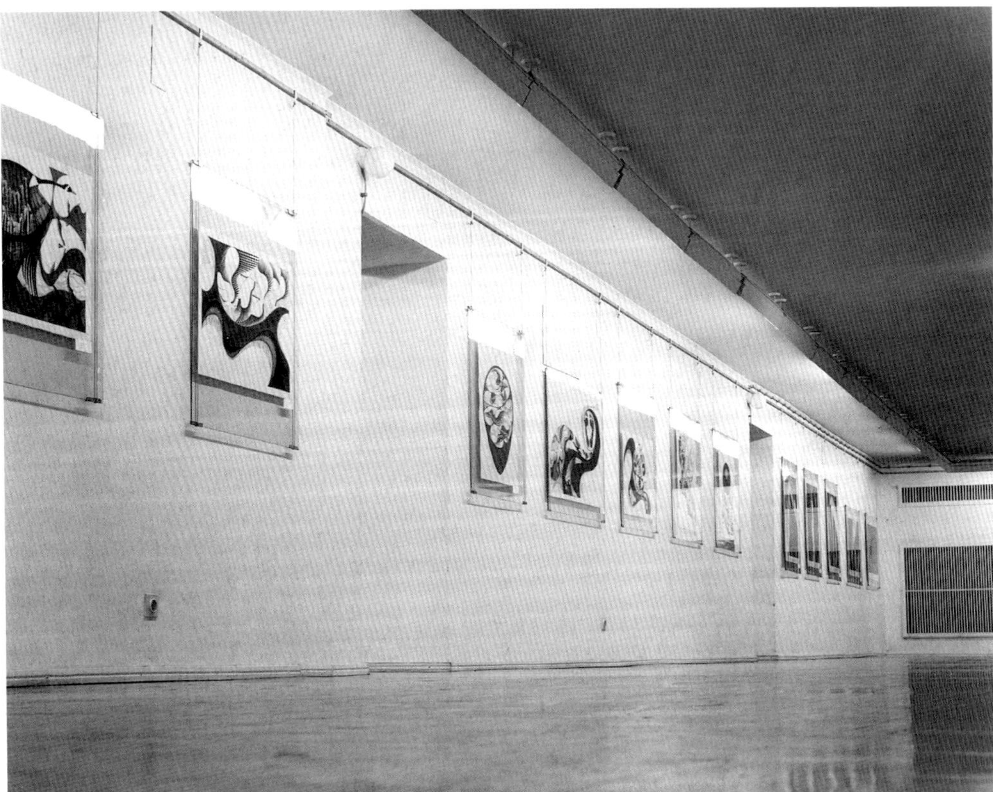

68

67–68. Installation views of Granirer's works from the exhibition *Four Canadian Artists,* at the Moderna Galerija, Ljubljana, Yugoslavia, 1976

69. *When the Earth was Young and Fertility was a Goddess,* 1977
70.5 x 99.3 cm (27 3/4 x 39 1/4 in)
India inks, printing inks,
pencil on paper

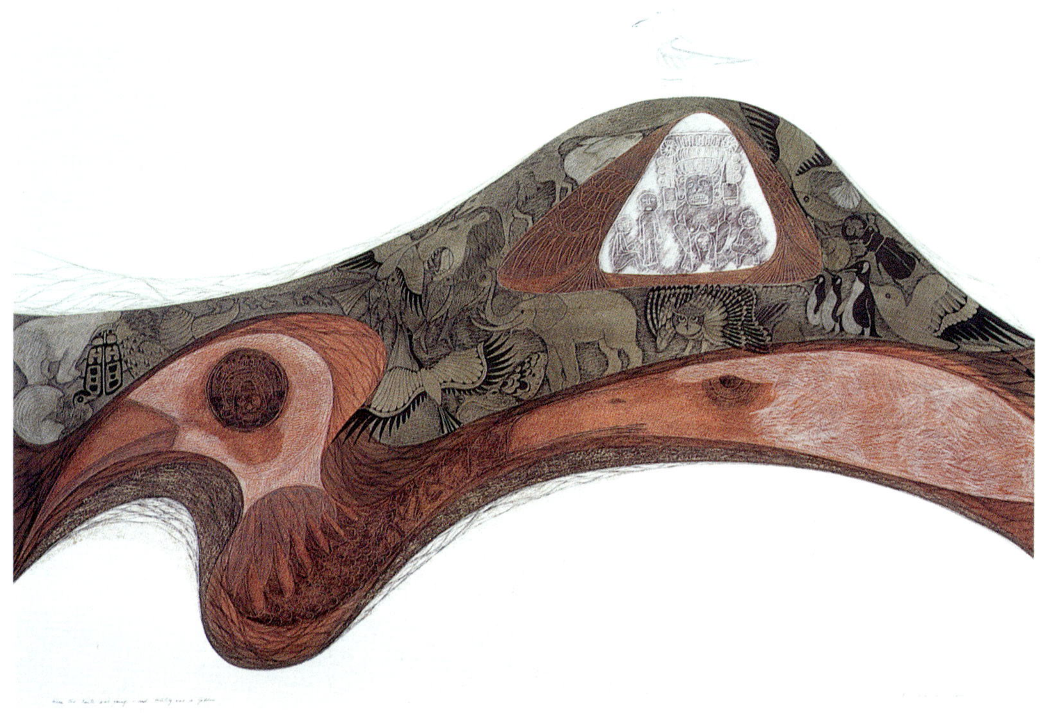

69

Referring to Granirer's work, Glen Allison, curator at the Fine Art Gallery, University of British Columbia, writes in the introduction to the catalogue, *Four Canadian Artists:*

In mature motherhood, Pnina Granirer has become obsessed with the visual melodies of childhood. Renderings of souvenirs, tiny relics which represent vast remembrances of her own childhood are delicately mingled in her work with images she witnesses surrounding her youngest child.

The Imp of Lincoln Cathedral, a talismanic charm given to her by her parents over thirty-five years ago, takes on properties of Eden's serpent, frequenting her pages with a premonition of evil. Its counterpart, a winged cherub which hovers in a hermetic circle of lace, was saved from her own cradle linen.

These fragments of personal history are combined with inkings of actual leaves, feathers, fabrics and mechanical toy parts, then blended with penwork creatures of a private mythology: cats, beetles, fish, griffins, turtles, owls and wolves have all been corraled in enchanted ribbons of space. Magical metamorphosis is literally tangible. Kites become birds when they leave the ground. The restricted colour range, acting as a filter of nostalgia, nurtures gently the evocation of innocence.

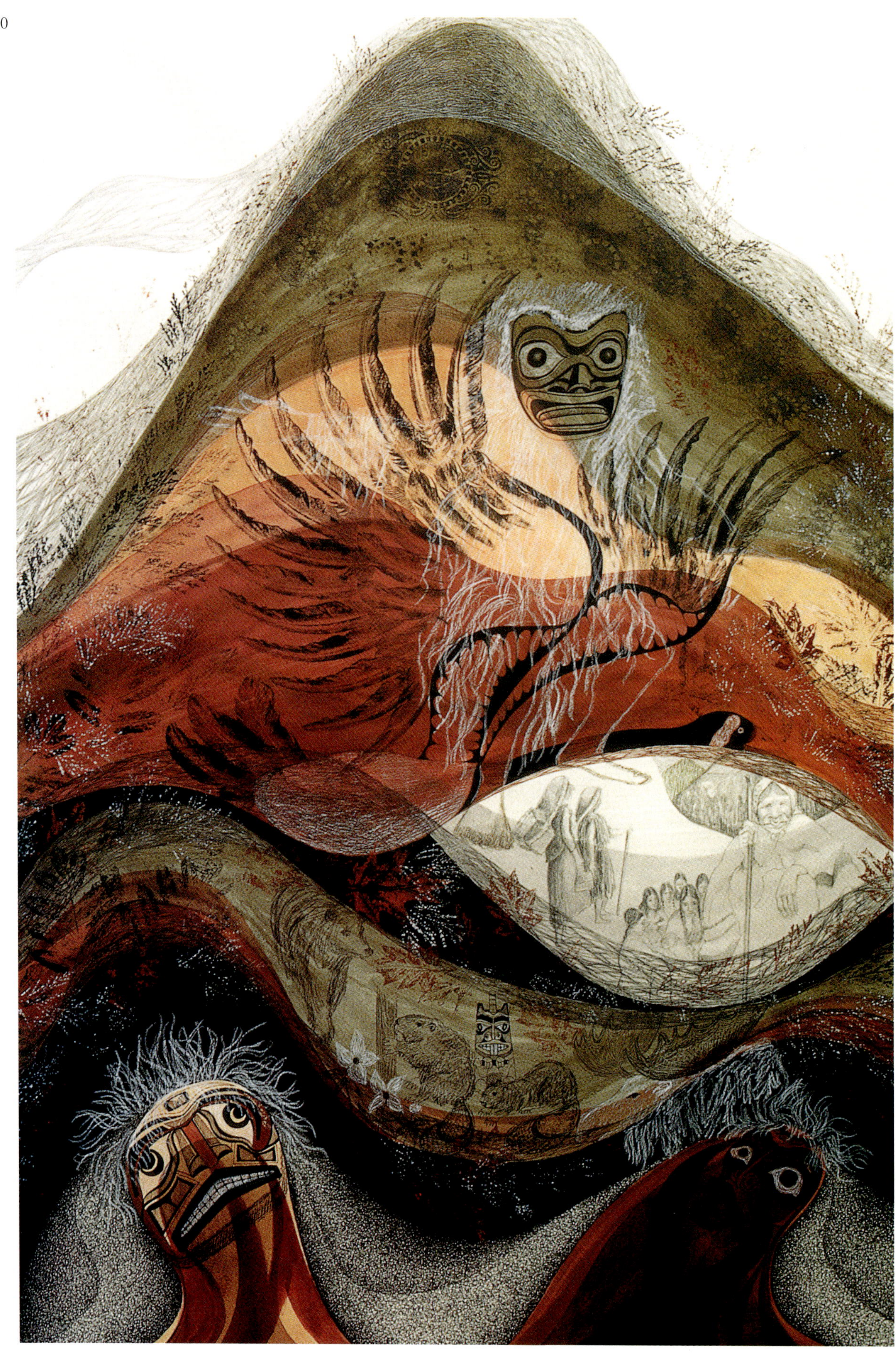

West Coast Series

Granirer believes that there are universal forms that some individuals are attuned to, which surface regardless of time and geography. Since these observations of stylistic similarity continued, she started paying closer attention to native art. She became more interested in the landscape of the West Coast — not from a realistic standpoint — but rather from an inner perception. She felt strongly that the native element was an important part of that landscape and ought somehow to be integrated into it. This is how the salmon, the loon, masks, leaves and feathers found their way into her work.

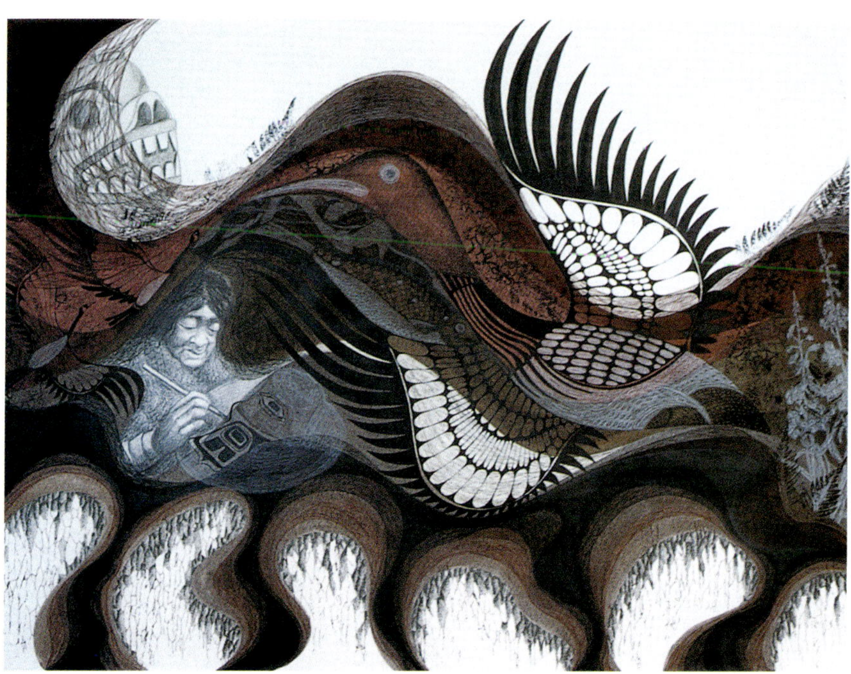

71

70. *Legend of Forbidden Plateau,* 1978
triptych, 3(96.2 x 71cm) 3(38 x 28 in) left panel
mixed media on Arches

71. *Homage to an Unknown Kwagiutl Artist,* 1978
56 x 76 cm (22 x 30 in)
India inks, printing inks, graphite on Arches
Collection Imperial Oil of Canada Ltd., Calgary

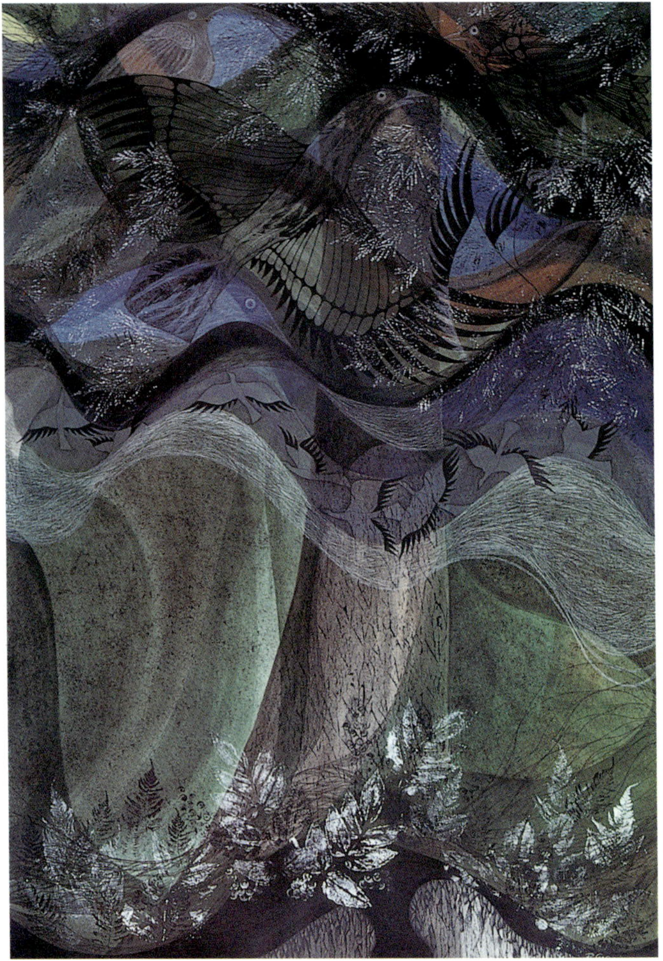

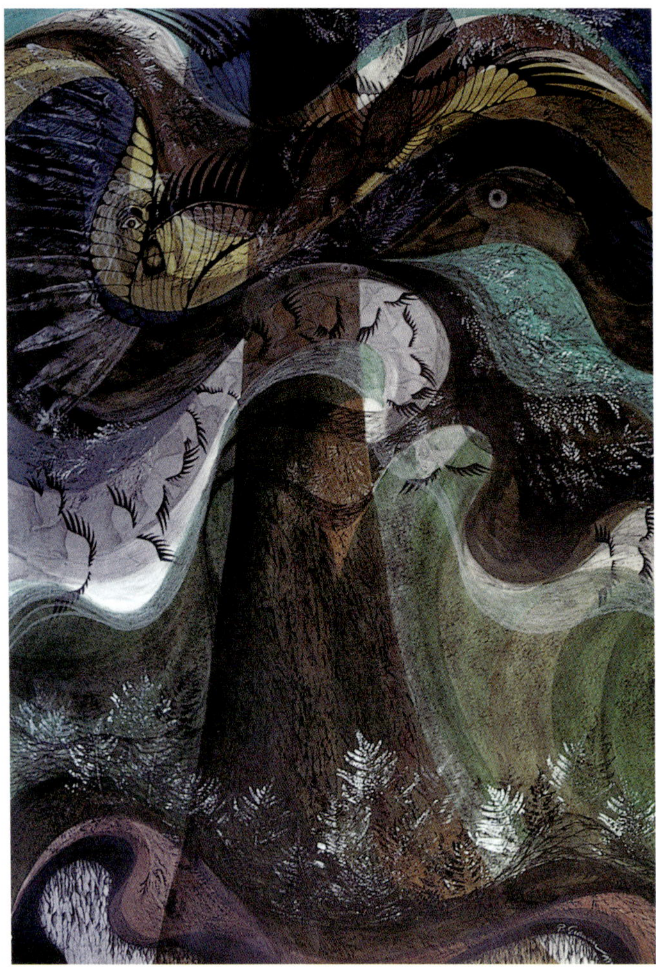

72

Although Granirer points out that Caucasian appropriation of West Coast Native images would no longer be "politically correct", she is but one among many British Columbia artists (such as Emily Carr and Jack Shadbolt) who have been affected by the directness and purity of Coast Indian art in expressing the essence of place and a recognized evolutionary kinship with all living things. This may be seen as a response to other modernist art forms that seemed unequal to the task of expressing these deeply intuited, primordial intimations.

Even before I began working on the West Coast Series, people interpreted my work as being influenced by native imagery. In fact, looking at some of my student drawings, one can see even then that the flowing decorative lines so characteristic of West Coast native art were in my work long before I was aware of this North American indigenous art.

Legend of Forbidden Plateau, 1978 (ill. 70), is a prime example of Granirer's intuitive meld of figuration and landscape, layers and currents of history, imagery and graphic stylization which convey her impressions of an endless continuity from the far removed past and into the present. Her linear embellishment is countered by bold bands of earthy colours. Finely detailed patterns of elegant birds, salmon, animals, faces and

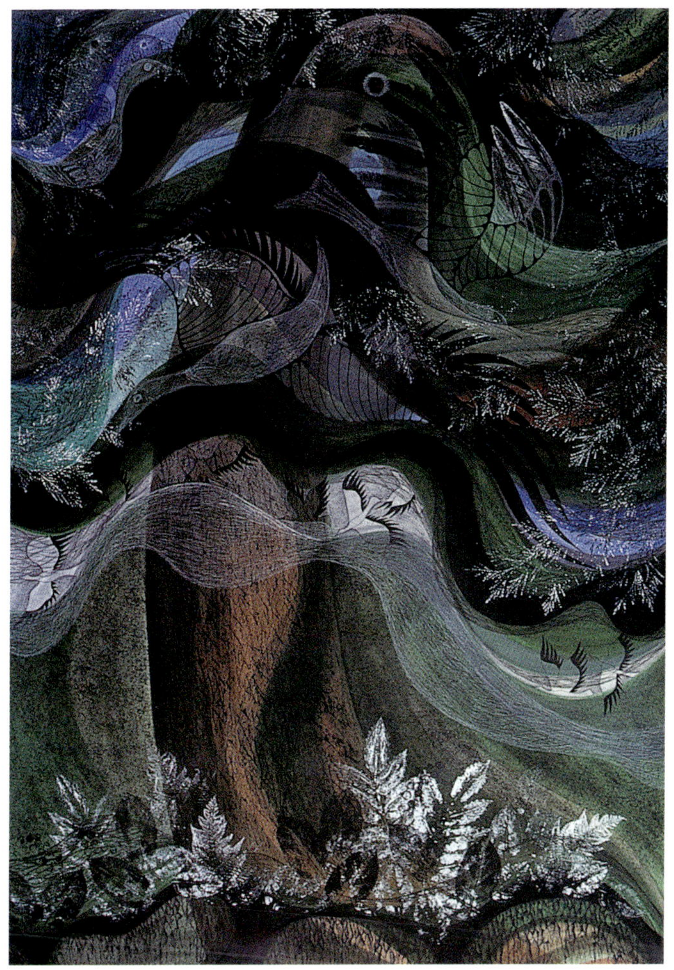

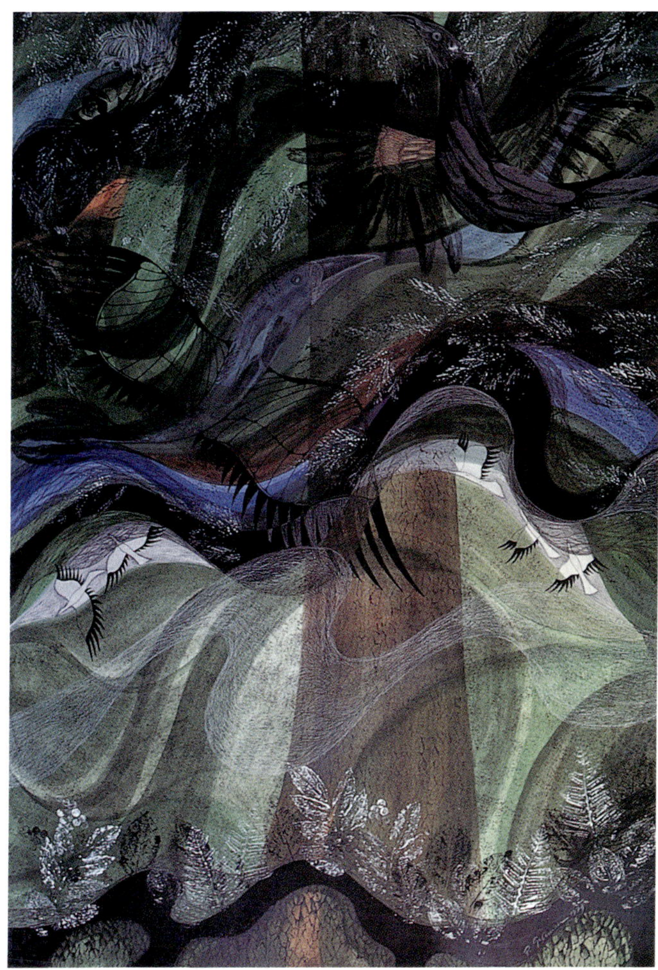

native animistic symbols are juxtaposed with the inexorable flow of time — an artistic device which alludes to native presence but also abstracts it into a larger evolutionary quotient.

Writing in *Art Magazine,* Ed Varney comments:

Several of the paintings in this exhibition are three, four and five panel works and, as such, are the largest works Granirer has done. Although many of them share common concerns, there is a progression of thought and, therefore, image, which explores different aspects or visions drawn from the same source. This exhibition represents a major artistic statement by Granirer which is developed and amplified by a high level of craftsmanship and commitment. With this work, she has shown herself capable of using her excellent graphic sensitivity and her skilled manipulation of colour as the means to a coherent and satisfying whole.

72. *Whispering Forest,* 1979
four out of five panels, 5(96.5 x 71 cm)
5(38 x 28 in)
mixed media on Fabriano
Private collection

In *Homage to an Unknown Kwagiutl Artist,* 1978 (ill. 71), Granirer makes the logical transition from the use of figuration, childhood associations, bird and animal devices to a concerted effort to comprehend and evoke the pantheistic culture of a nearly destroyed people. She sees their history in waves and strata of intermingled, largely unrecorded phenomena, which have been nonetheless distilled into the Native American's remaining (often impermanent) art. Above all else, she specifically focuses on the image of an anonymous native woman and suggests another, entirely new, level of speculation — possibly a contemporary woman's perspective on the prehistoric obsession with fertility. What more significant, shared knowledge could women possess over the eons that separate them?

With respect to Granirer's West Coast landscapes, it is clear that she remains a studio artist, not a *plein air* painter. Whatever imagery she uses, whether sketch, photo, or reproduction, is brought back to the studio for the rendering of an entire scene or vista.

She was doing some etching at the time, at the Print Studio on West 4th Avenue in Vancouver, doing more "landscapey" work. An artist

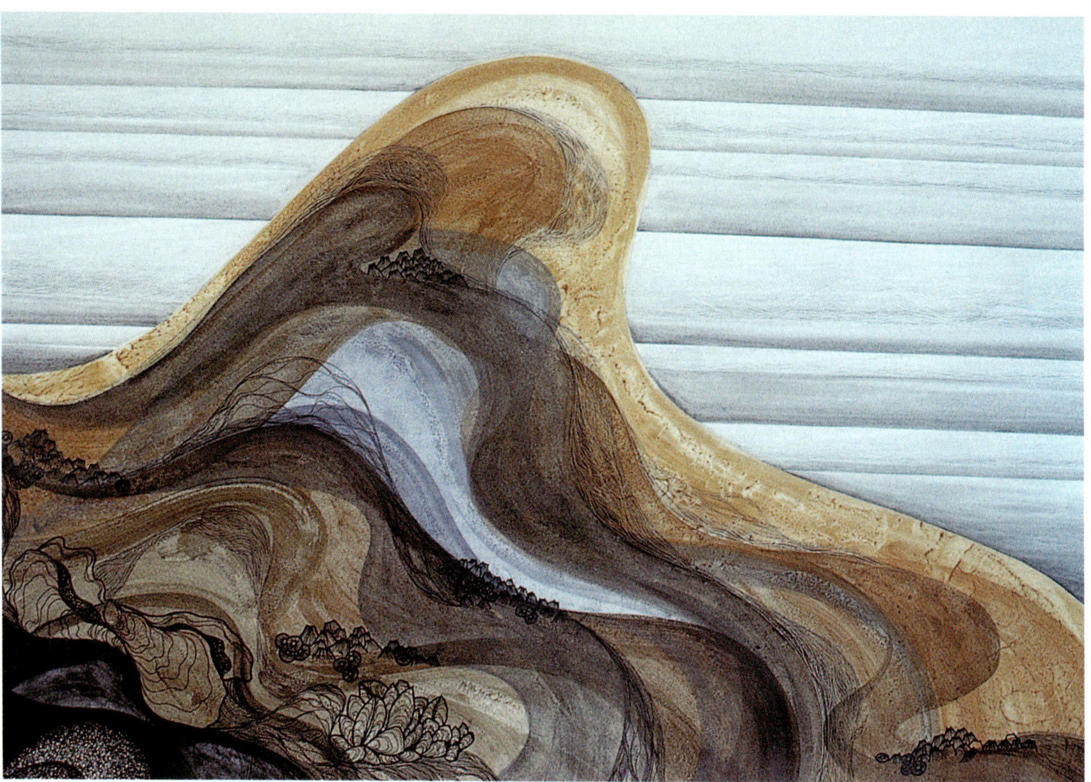

73

73. *Beach,* 1981
56x76 cm (22x30 in)
mixed media on Fabriano
Collection of Peter Dodek
and Hela Lee

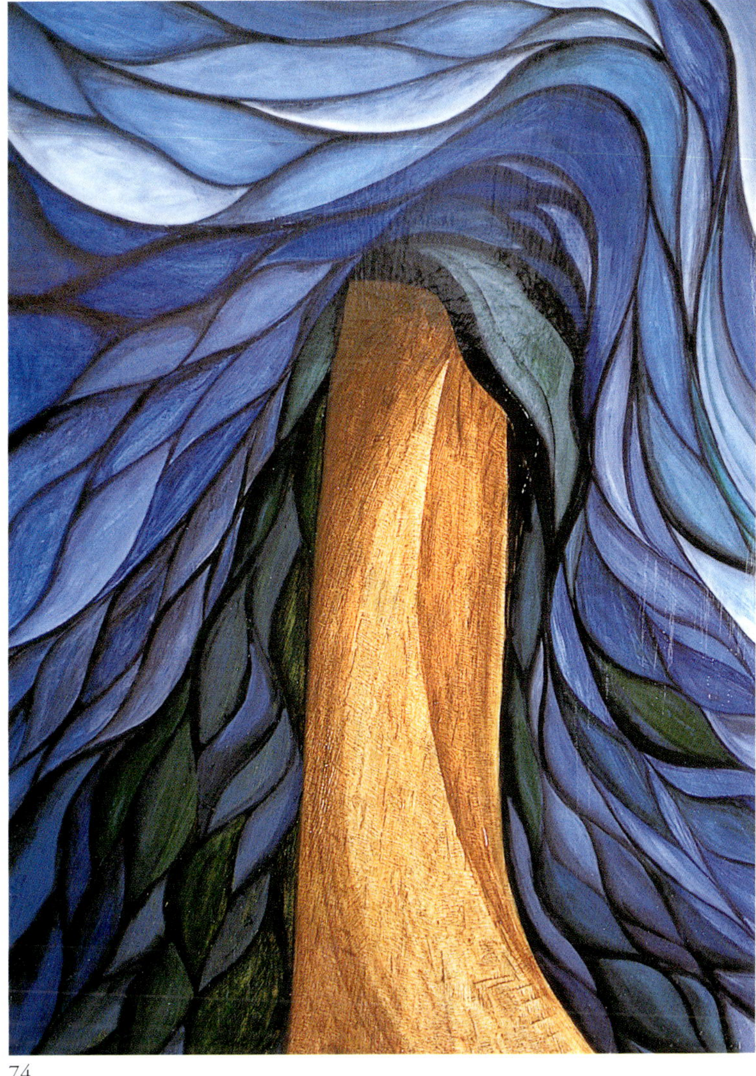

74

74. *Blue Cedar,* 1979
acrylic on particle board
62 x 43 cm (24 1/2 x 17 in)
Collection of Jane Baker

75. *Forest Ghosts,* 1981
diptych, 2(101.5 x 70.5 cm) 2(40 x 27 3/4 in)
mixed media on Fabriano
Private collection

working next to her said, *"Oh, now you're a real Canadian."* When Granirer asked her what she meant, she explained that there were no longer any figures in her work. Coming from a figurative tradition, Granirer found it rather shocking to realize that's what it meant to be a Canadian artist. It had, in fact, taken ten years for the landscape to insinuate itself in her work, albeit not in a conventional, realistic guise.

Forest Ghosts, 1979 (ill. 75), suggests a feathery, lyrical apparition, the undulating grey wraiths echo the time-strata of the Native homages. In this landscape mode, Granirer's work has occasionally been compared with Emily Carr's — a comparison that is unfortunate because it is almost impossible (at least in British Columbia) to treat such content without drawing this parallel. The same association may be invited

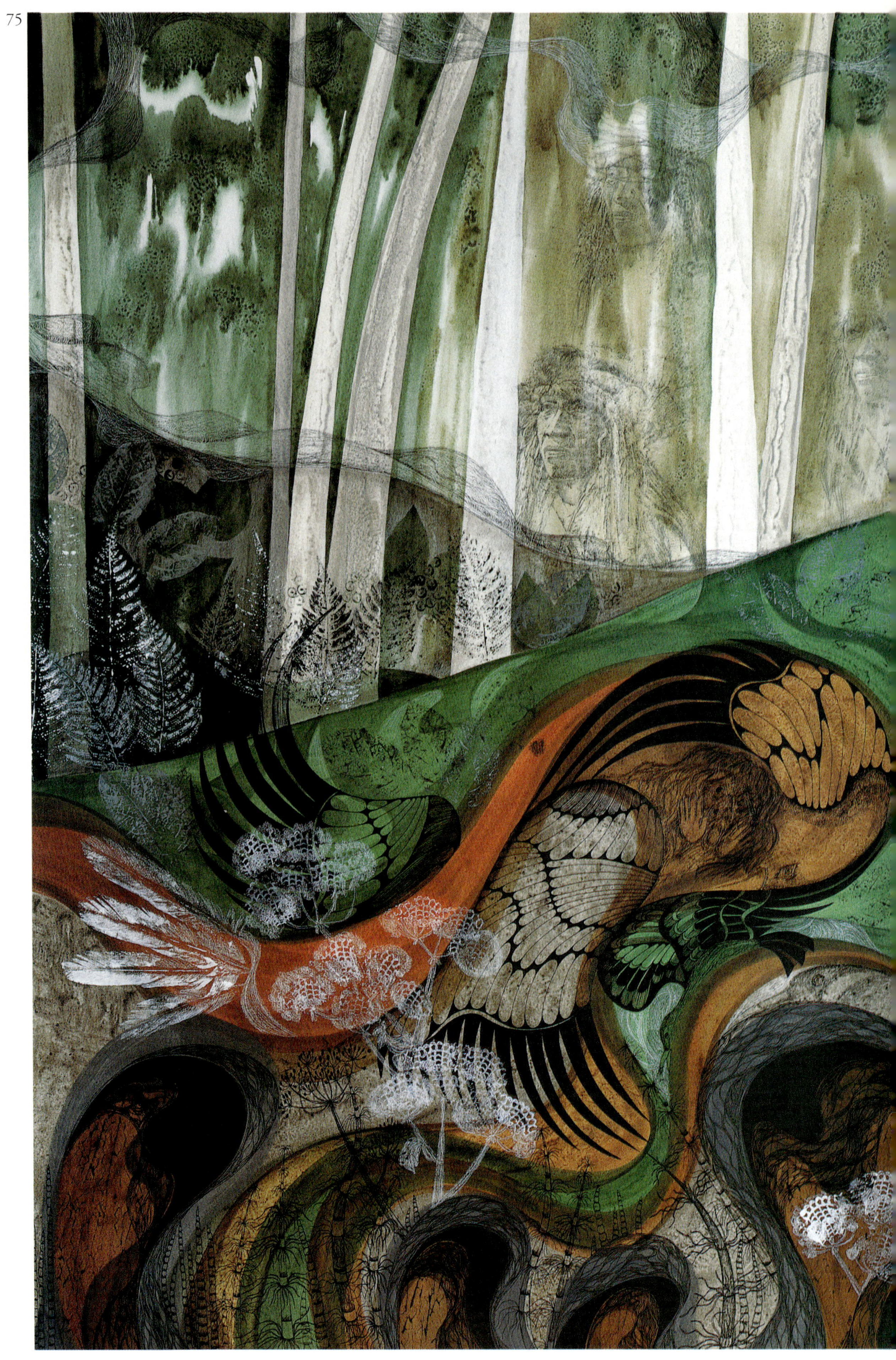

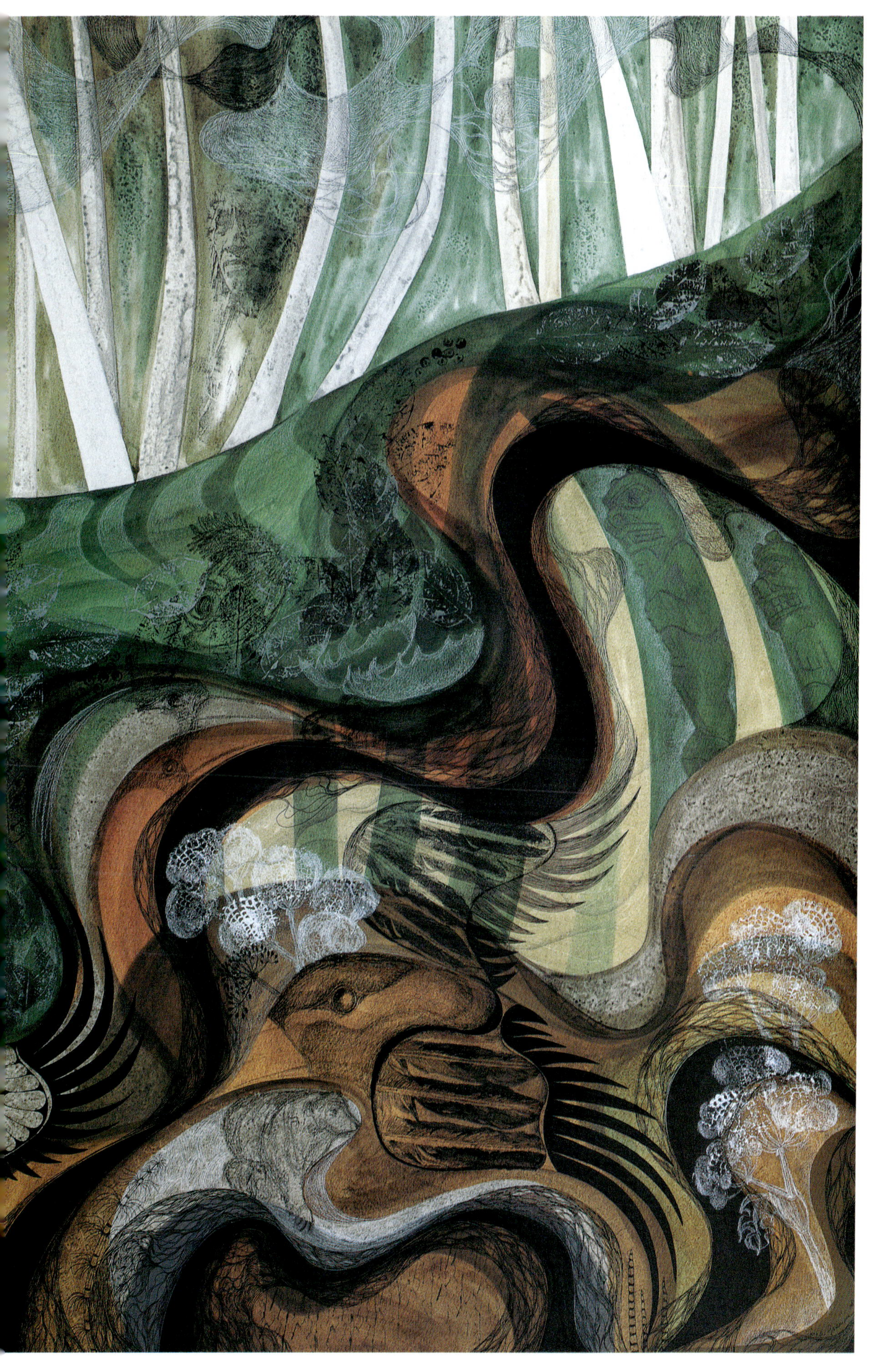

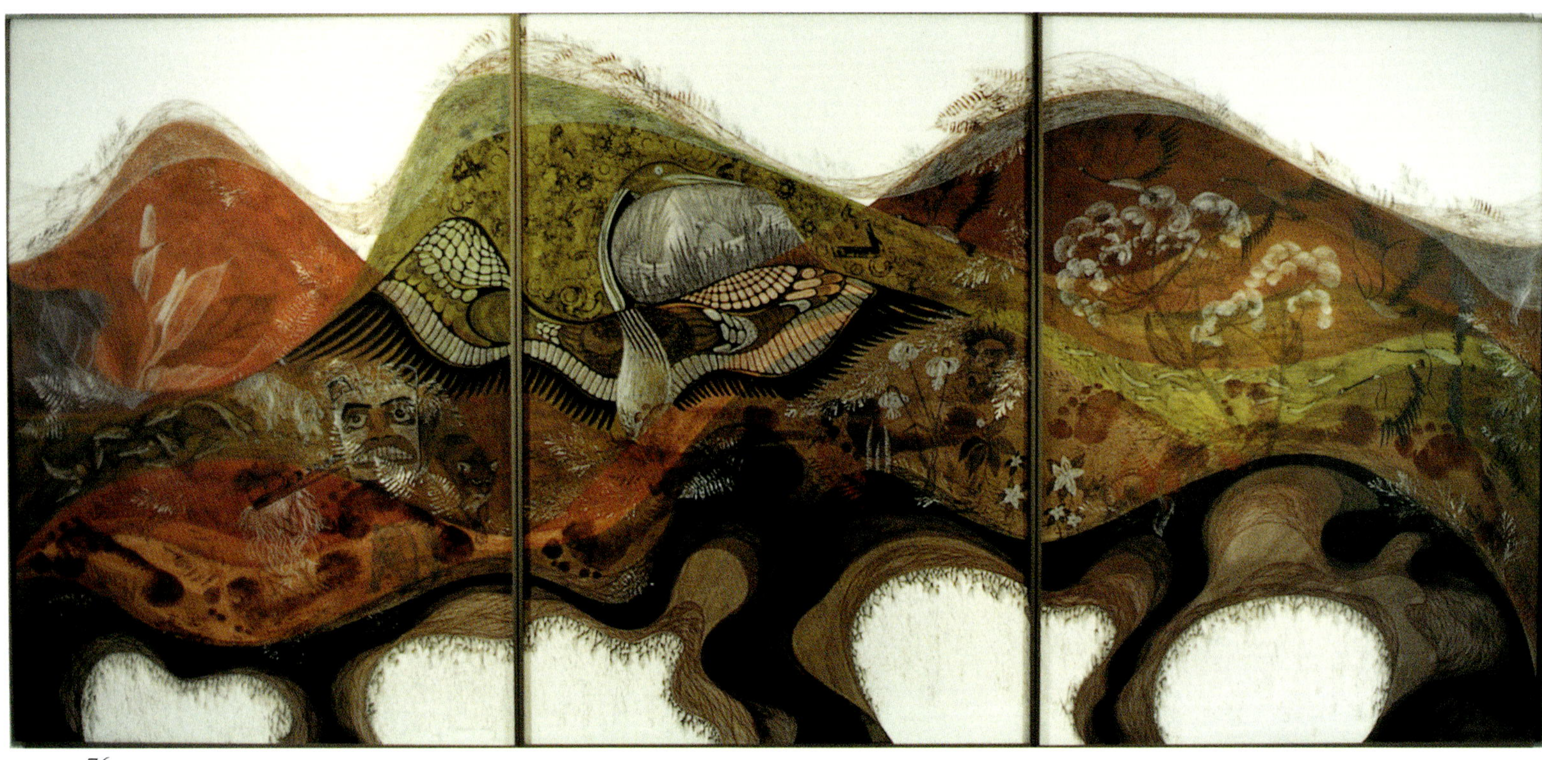

76

76. *Silent Roots beneath the Mountains,* 1978
triptych, 3(99 x 68.5 cm) 3(39 x 27 in)
mixed media on Fabriano
Private collection

77. *Portrait of an old Kwagiutl Man,* 1978
56 x 76 cm (22 x 30 in)
mixed media on paper

78. *The Great White Father Comes to Paris – or, How to use a Soulcatcher,* 1989
56 x 76 cm (22 x 30 in)
mixed media on paper

I was living in Paris in 1980, when the city was honoured with a Papal visit. Whenever one turned on the television, there was the Pope. With the imagery of West Coast Native art from British Columbia still fresh in my mind, I could not help the association with the shamanistic soulcatcher, which kept running through my head. Hence the title of this work, a gentle pun aimed at the ritual of the white, "advanced civilization".

in *Blue Cedar,* 1979 (ill. 74), with its red heart reaching deep into the soil, but Carr seldom, if ever, brought herself to project graphically the interiors of trees or the sustaining earth they penetrate.

Possibly to sidestep further similarities to Carr, Granirer found other formats and design solutions, groupings of poplars and continuous canopies of trees, for instance — or natural assemblages framed by white window sash and mullions. As always, Granirer worked a thematic series until she felt it was exhausted for her — regardless of its market currency.

A review in *Le Nouvel Alsacien,* entitled "When the Canadians distinguish themselves by their seriousness and originality", says:

Canada, certainly with its fauna, but mainly with its mysterious aspect, this depth of magic surging from the night of time, is celebrated in these works with mythical abandon. The rhythm of these works is, somehow, like the pulsations of a great, generous heart. Here, then, are the components of a work whose power and strength we are happy to salute.

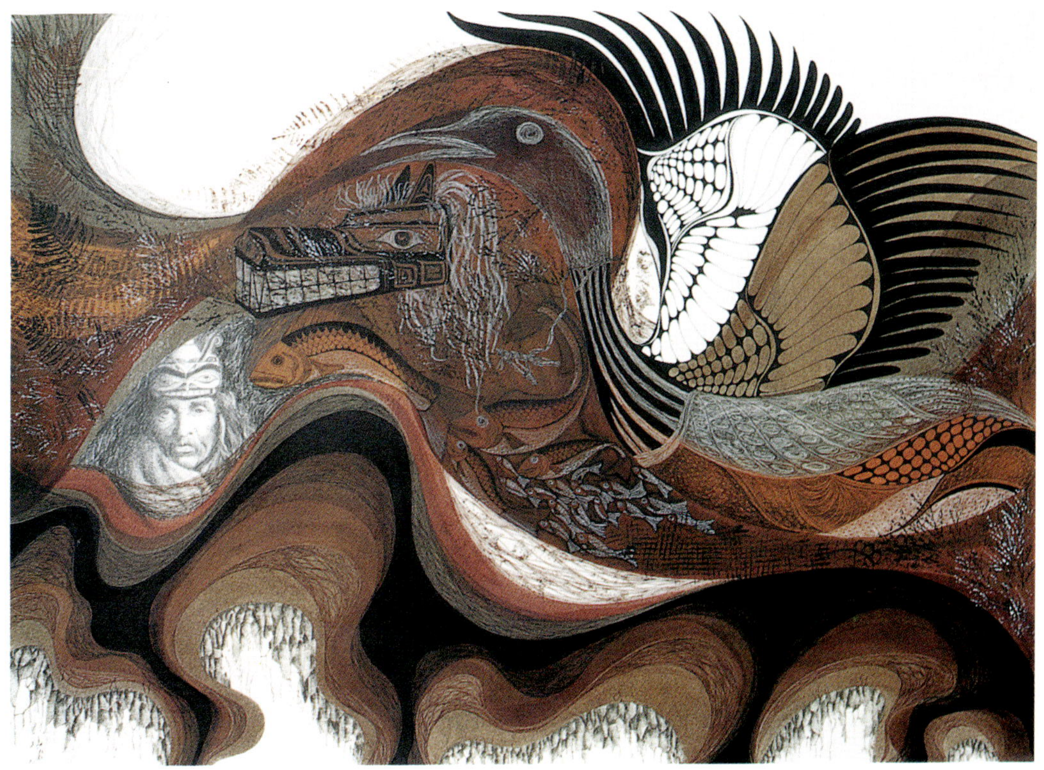

77

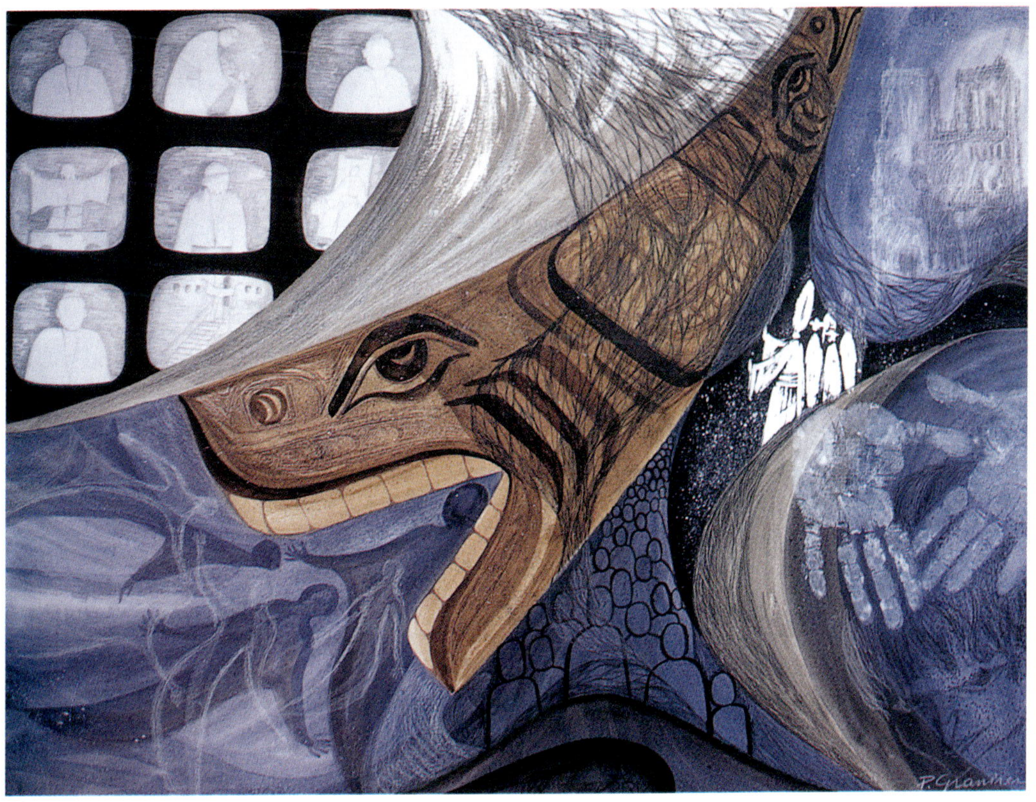

78

For the past year I have been working on themes of Creation/ Beginnings/Human Landscapes. These ideas seemed to develop from one to the other, continually changing from more linear forms into larger colour areas, reminiscent of layers going deeper and deeper, containing the wealth of our past — for us to discover. This brought me in a most natural way into the exploration of our own past. I deliberately used some native design elements, as well as images of things vital to the life of the Coast People, who lived here from time immemorial. The animals, the boat, the fishhook, the fern and leaves printed directly on the paper are there to pay homage to the ancient West Coast People's culture and to the hope of its survival in our times.

— From a statement to the exhibition of the *West Coast Series*.

A bird market is held each Sunday morning in Paris, on Ile-de-la-Cité. Hundreds of birds of all colours and sizes, from tiny canaries to large, exotic parakeets, are tightly packed into small cages waiting for prospective buyers. On some cages signs such as "Bons Chanteurs" (Good Singers) were posted, proclaiming the worth of the merchandise, an added bait for Parisians searching for a token of nature for their own cage-like apartments. I felt sorry for these fragile prisoners and longed for the free birdsong in my Vancouver garden.

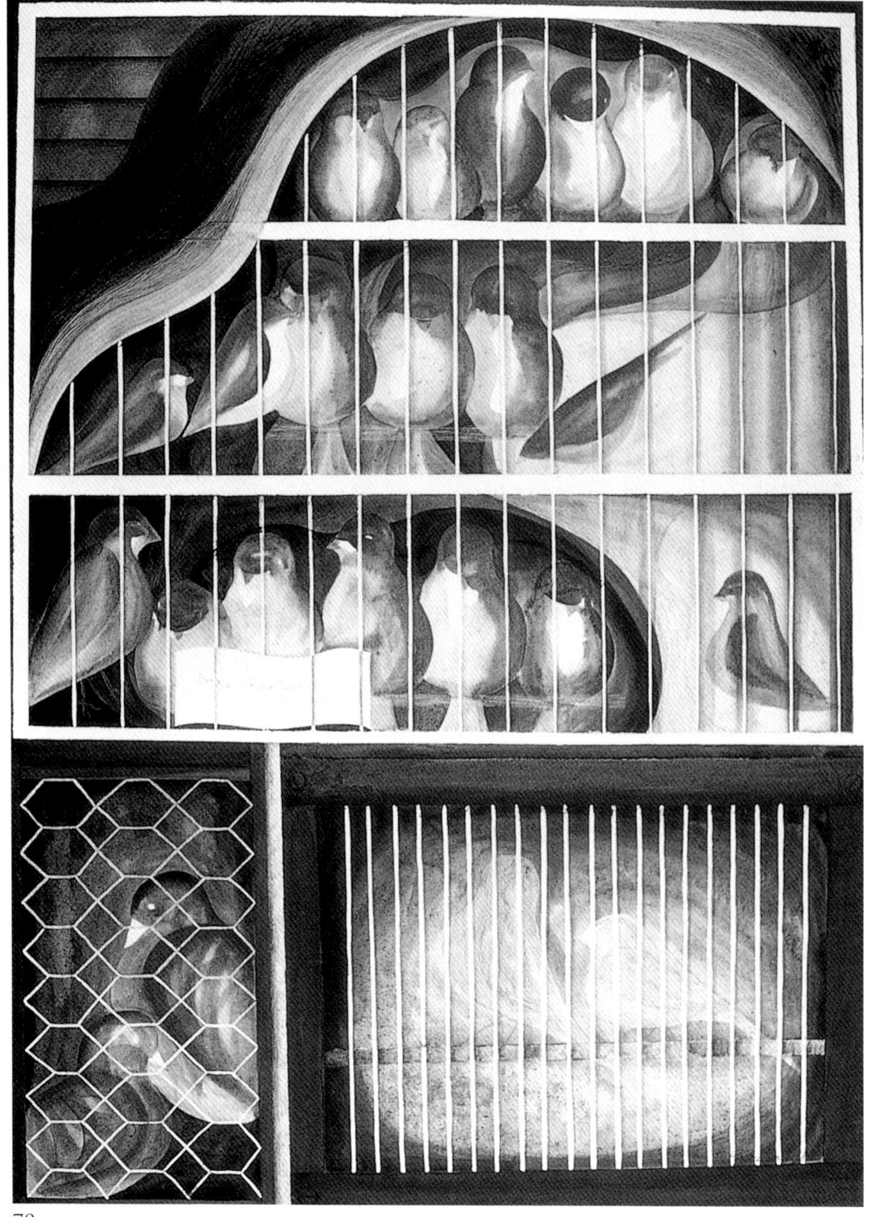

79

A sub-series on caged birds resulted from a 1980 stay in Paris, where Granirer saw great numbers of birds offered for sale in banked stacks of cages. To her, there was something unnerving about the birds' confinement as commodities. In *Bons Chanteurs,* 1980, nature is metaphorically caged (or framed, as her trees seen through window sash and mullions) in a further meditation on freedom versus constraint. As a design element, the grids and hexagonal chicken wire provide pictorial enhancement, but their meaning remains ominous.

79. *Bons Chanteurs,* 1980
from the *Prisoner Birds Series*
76 x 56 cm (30 x 22 in)
mixed media on paper

During her stay in France, Granirer showed some works from the *Canada Geese Series* at the Galerie Artal, in Strasbourg. A review in *Les Affiches-Moniteur* ends by saying:

The beauty of the works and the scrupulous care for detail, are the secret powers which constitute their particular attraction, as if the artist, like the bird, places herself between sky and earth, where all the dreams of humanity meet together.

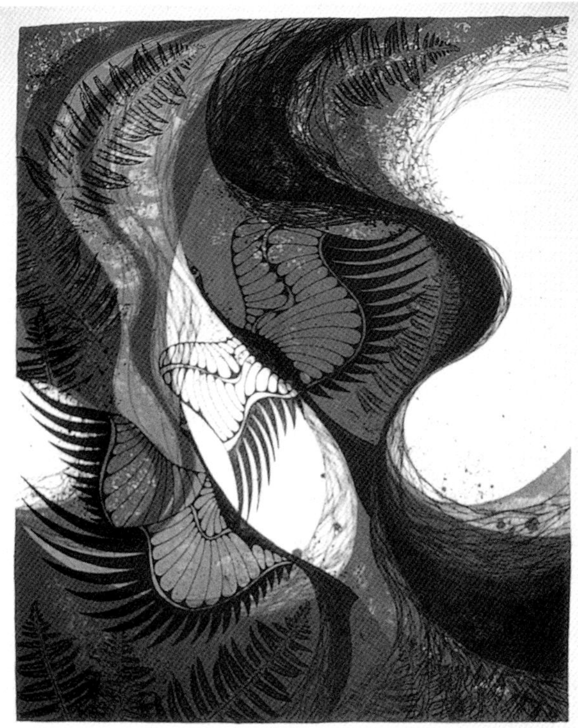

80

80. Lithographed poster for the first Strasbourg exhibition. The image is *Pas-de-Deux,* originally an edition of 100, pulled on Arches by master printer Yann Samson.
52 x 43 cm (20 1/2 x 17 in)

On her return from Paris, Granirer called up her close friend, the painter Dorothy Manning, only to learn the terrible news: Dorothy had been recently killed in a car accident, leaving her husband, artist Ed Varney and their five children behind. Shaken by this news, Granirer created a few works in Dorothy's memory, which were exhibited at the Bau-Xi Gallery.

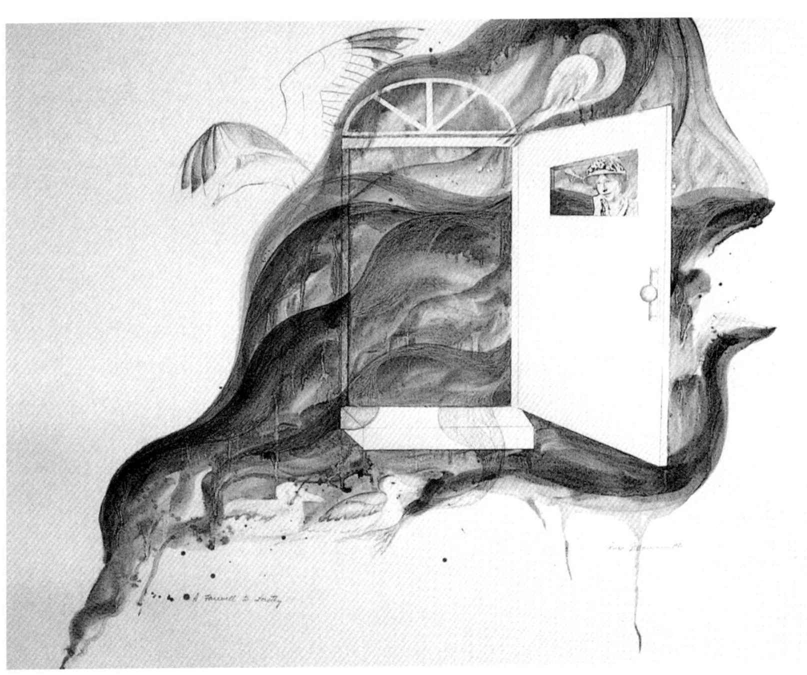

81

81. *A Farewell to Dorothy,* 1980
56 x 76 cm (22 x 30 in)
acrylic, collage, graphite, transfer on paper

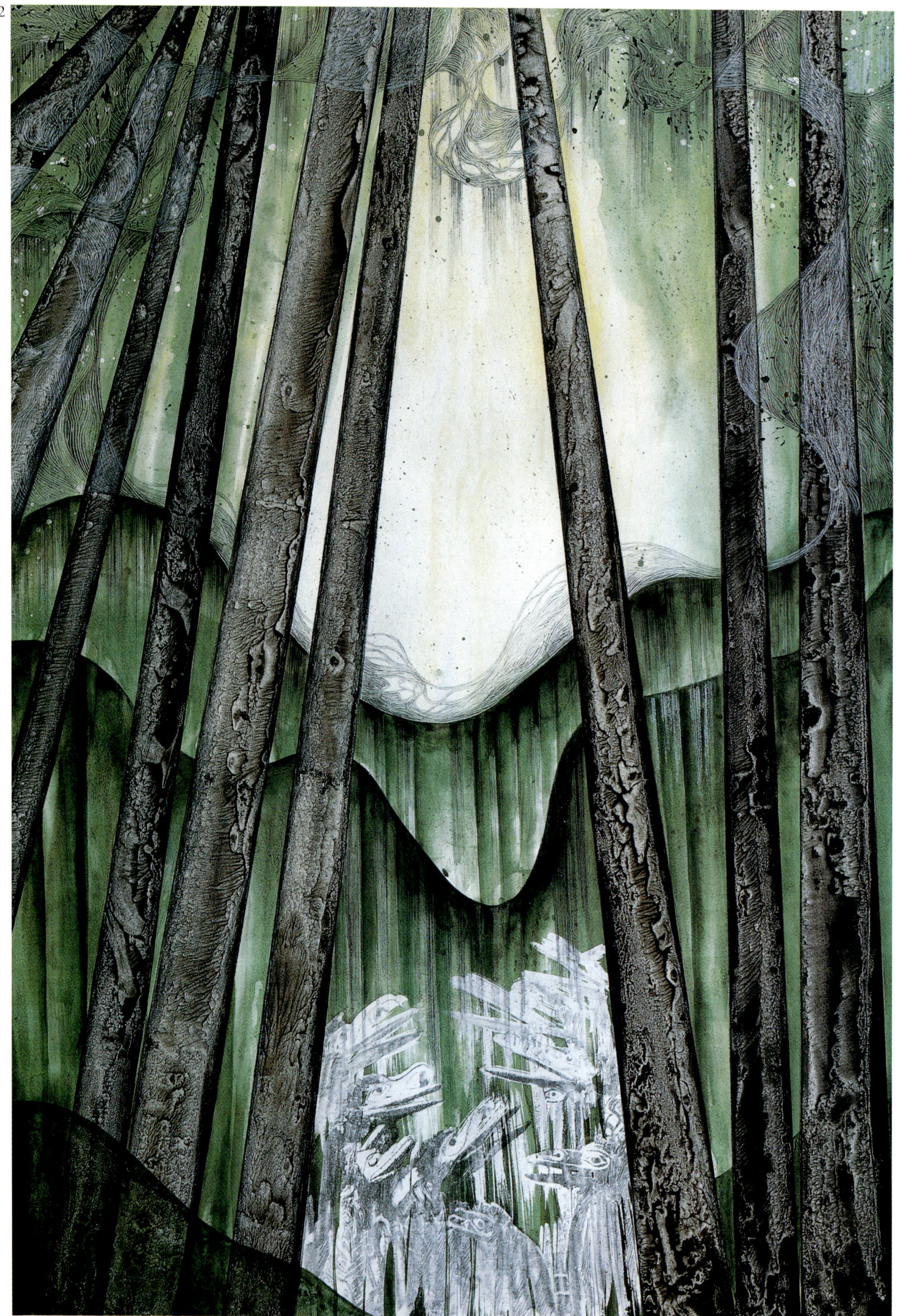

The Cannibal Bird Suite

After a visit to the rain forests of the Queen Charlotte Islands, the elements of longing for liberation, forest canopies, Indian mythology and vertical bars came together in Granirer's *The Cannibal Bird Suite,* 1981. The Coast Indian initiatory custom of sending un-provisioned young men into the dark, haunted forest interior as a rite of passage contained powerful associations with the universal need to come to terms with nature. The Cannibal Bird, an ancient Coastal figure who lived at the ends of the earth and ate its victims whole, represented unimaginable terror and fear of the unknown and of one's inner self. The initiate could defeat the Cannibal Bird by metaphorically embracing it (rather than running from it) and, in effect, becoming the Cannibal Bird, himself. He could then return to his people as a "wild man", but one who had found his song (or true self).

This scenario becomes a vehicle for virtually all this series of Granirer's mixed-media graphic devices based in asymmetry, linearity and flowing organic structure: the filigree of birds' wings and lacy ferns, the strata of earth and rich verdure, the spiritual wraiths and sustained visual rhythms.

Similar to her self-imposed restraints on colour while working on the *Childhood Series,* Granirer put certain limits on her treatment of the *Cannibal Bird Suite.* She chose to use two constant elements in these works: the vertical pattern of tree trunks, a symbolic cage of the inner self, and the cannibal birds themselves, the hidden demons which have to be confronted and dealt with at unexpected times and places.

82. *Dawn,* 1981
76 x 56 cm (30 x 22 in)
mixed media on paper
Collection of Dianne and Pierre Faber

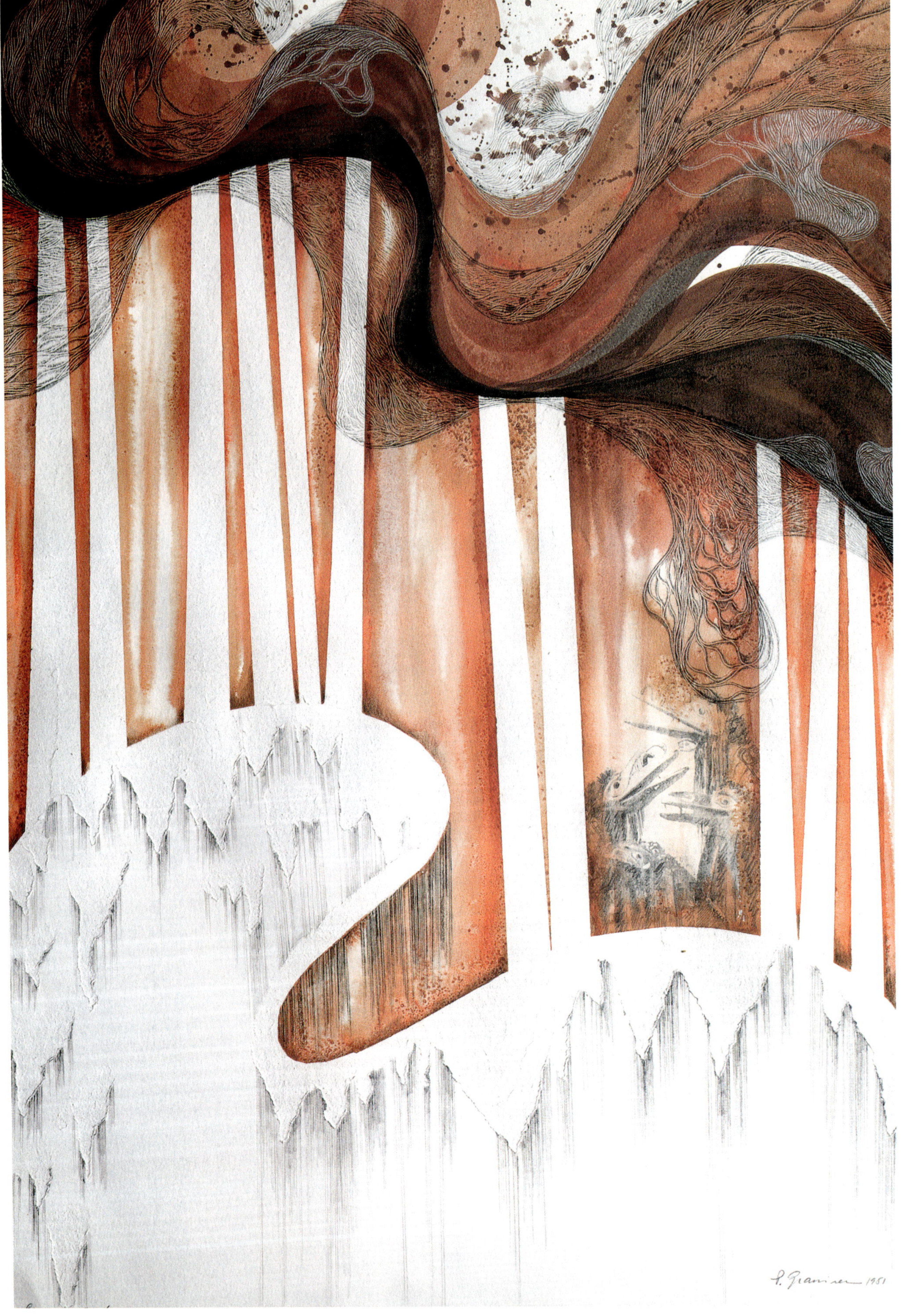

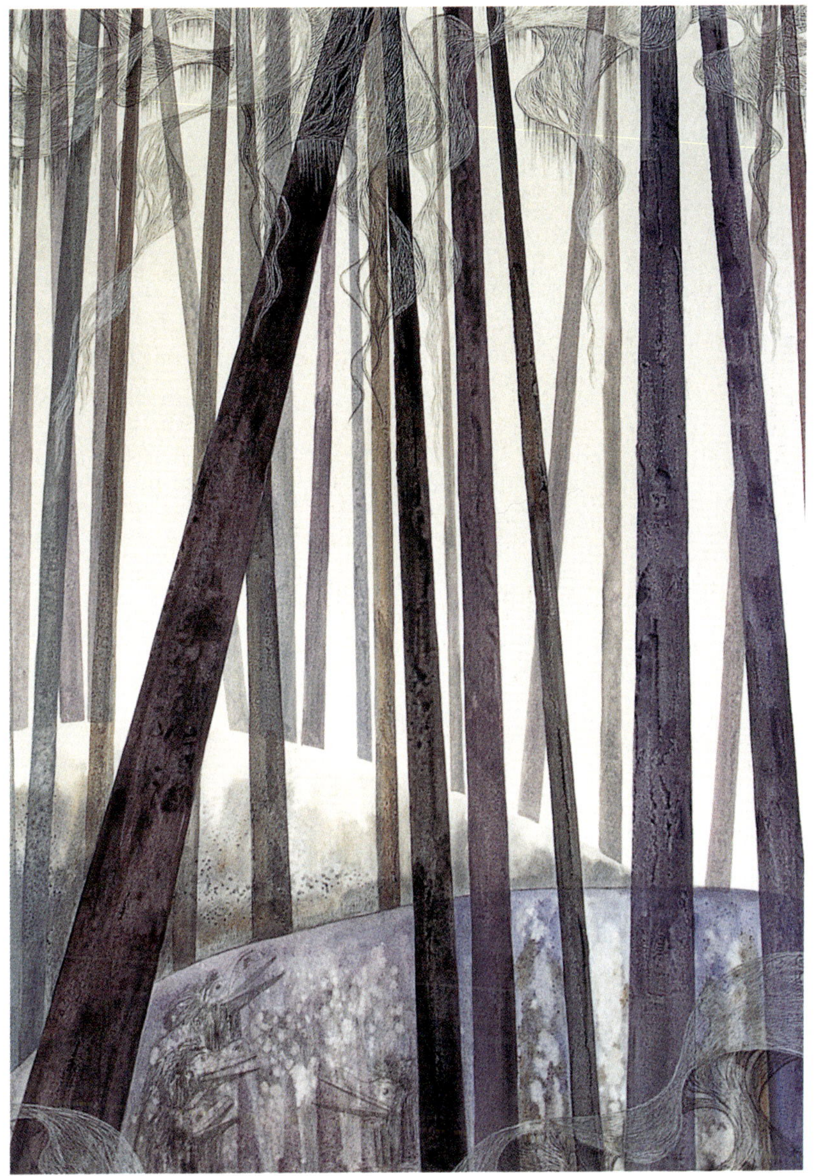

84

Our passage through Pnina Granirer's Cannibal Bird *series is her interpretation of an old Indian initiation, whereby young men would be sent into the forest to find their "song". The paintings portray a metaphorical search for identity, with the "cannibal birds" symbolizing doubts, fears and hesitations. Amidst the dark forests, there are beautiful clear openings and verticals, but the cannibal birds are always lurking in the shadows.*

Viewing the work is not easy: it requires silence and meditation. But I found the results to be enormously rewarding – an almost religious experience. There is a potential for inner peace in this series that moves far beyond the legend, beyond the "mixed media", and beyond decorativeness. At moments like this, the heartbreaking comments of visitors rushing through the gallery – "Not my cup of tea", "A bunch of birds with beaks" – makes me wonder whether people deserve art.

Watch out for the cannibal birds.

— Mia Johnson, July 29, 1982, *The West Ender*

In 1983, Granirer had a second show in Strasbourg, exhibiting her new *Cannibal Bird Suite.* The response of the press, as before, was positive and showed a genuine interest in following her work. *Les Affiches-Moniteur* writes:

Pnina Granirer's art is most fascinating, casting a real spell through the intensity and the concentration of a graphic approach which is wonderfully coherent in its rhythm, through the subtlety of the shading and the transparent use of colour, as well as through the steady thrust towards the essential.

83. *Consumed Forest,* 1981
70.8 x 56.2 cm (27 7/8 x 22 1/8 in)
mixed media on paper
Private collection

84. *Blue Forest with Cannibal Birds,* 1976
73.7 x 53.4 cm (29 x 21)
mixed media on Arches
Collection of Ronald and Veronica Hatch

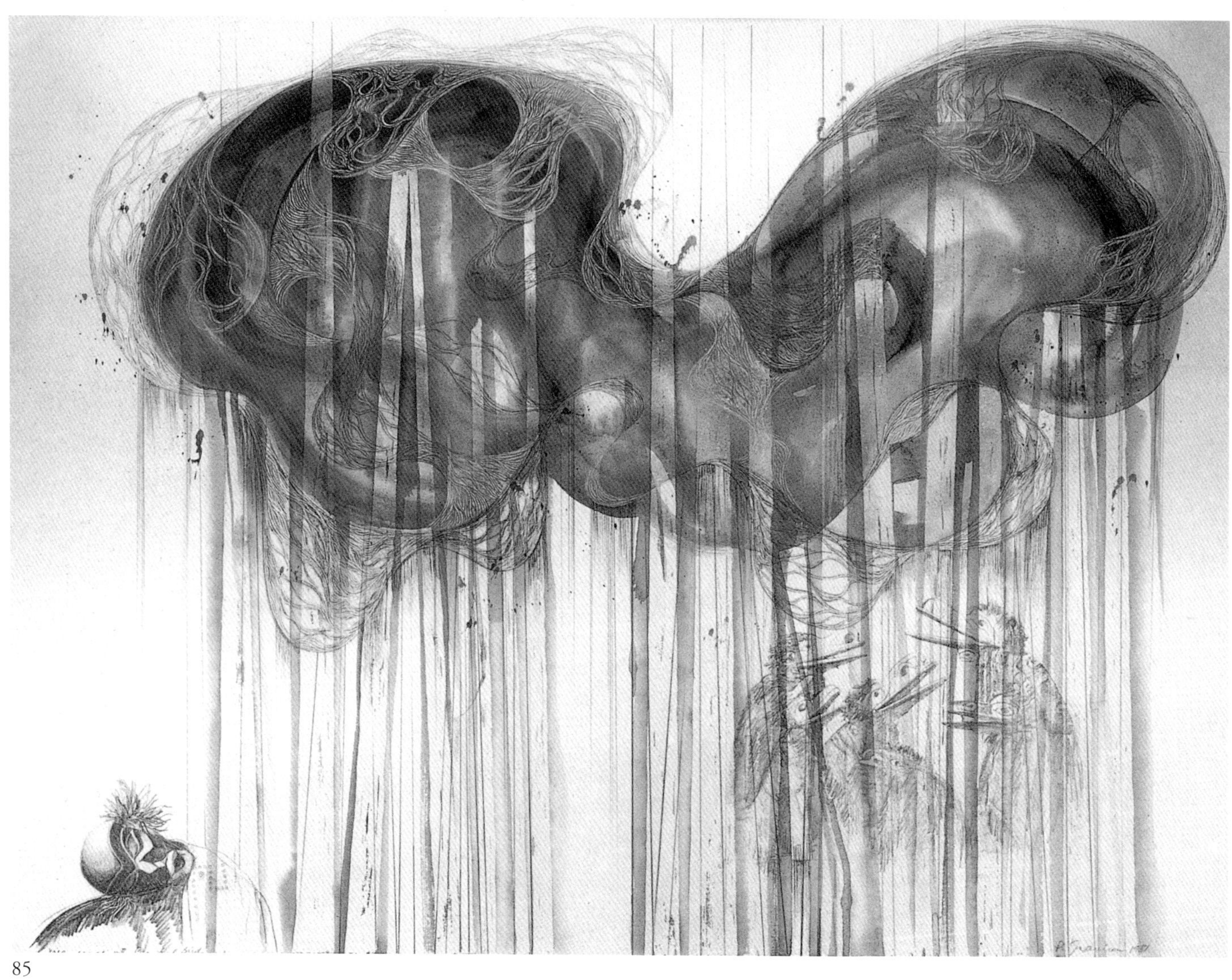

85

Le Nouvel Alsacien delves deeper into the images:

It is the self search, the utterly personal experience, which the artist turns into a universal one, the very quest of man for himself. There is an inevitable and powerful rhythm which penetrates the works. The stable element, the immovable vertical of the forest, and the unstable element, man's life within nature, expressed through lines and curved surfaces, blend in perfect unity.

Here is a profoundly thoughtful and at the same time exceptionally passionate art.

85. *Dreamscape with Cannibal Birds,* 1981
56 x 76 cm (22 x 30 in)
acrylic, graphite, resist, grease pencil on Arches

86. *The Search,* 1981
79.2 x 56.2 cm (31 1/8 x 22 1/8 in)
mixed media on paper
Collection of Lynn Hayes

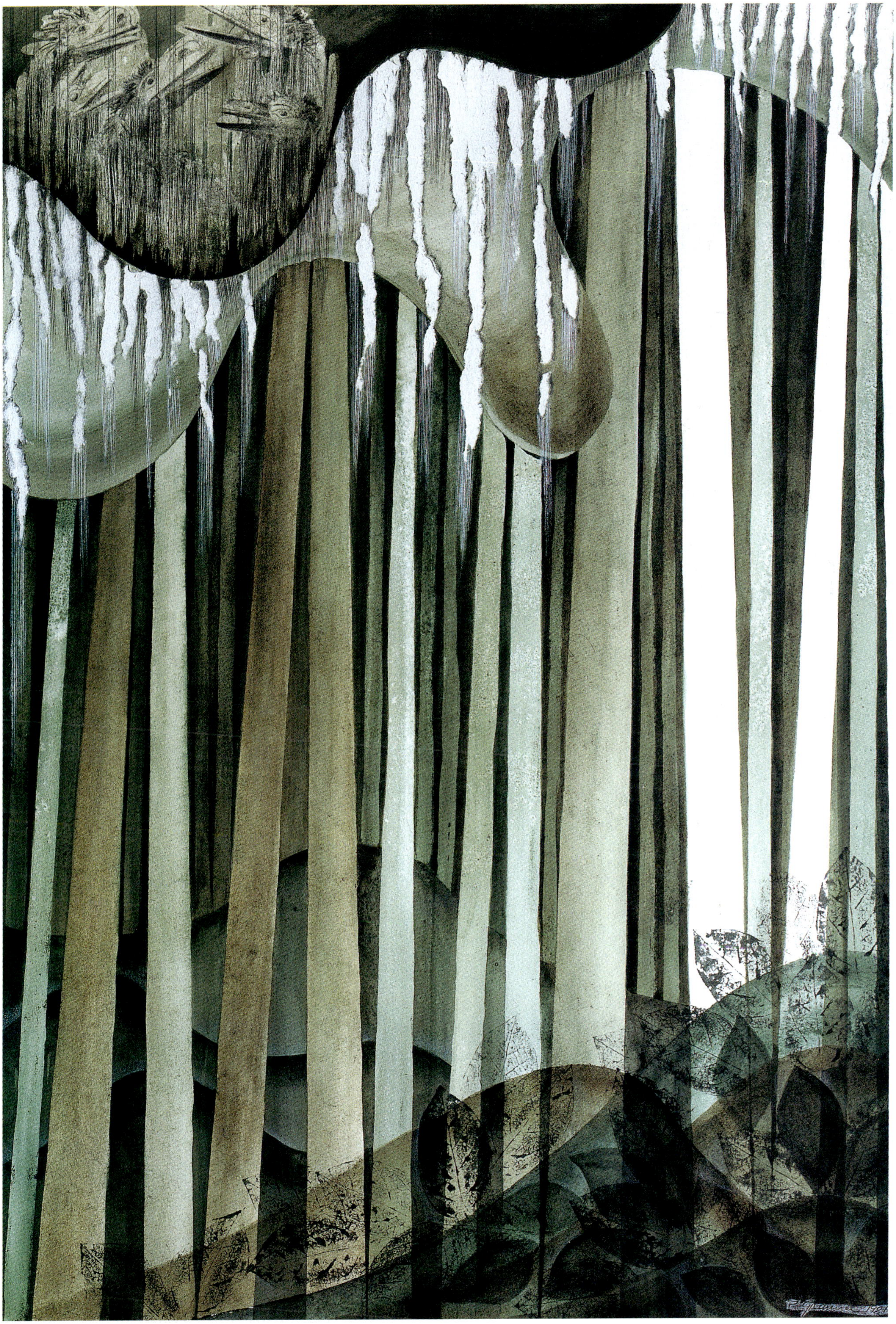

ADAM AND EVE TEMPTED BY CANNIBAL BIRDS

No snake from the outside
but a devouring will to know
bursting from within

Cannibal Birds tearing at the mind
temptation
to discover
the innermost secrets of God.

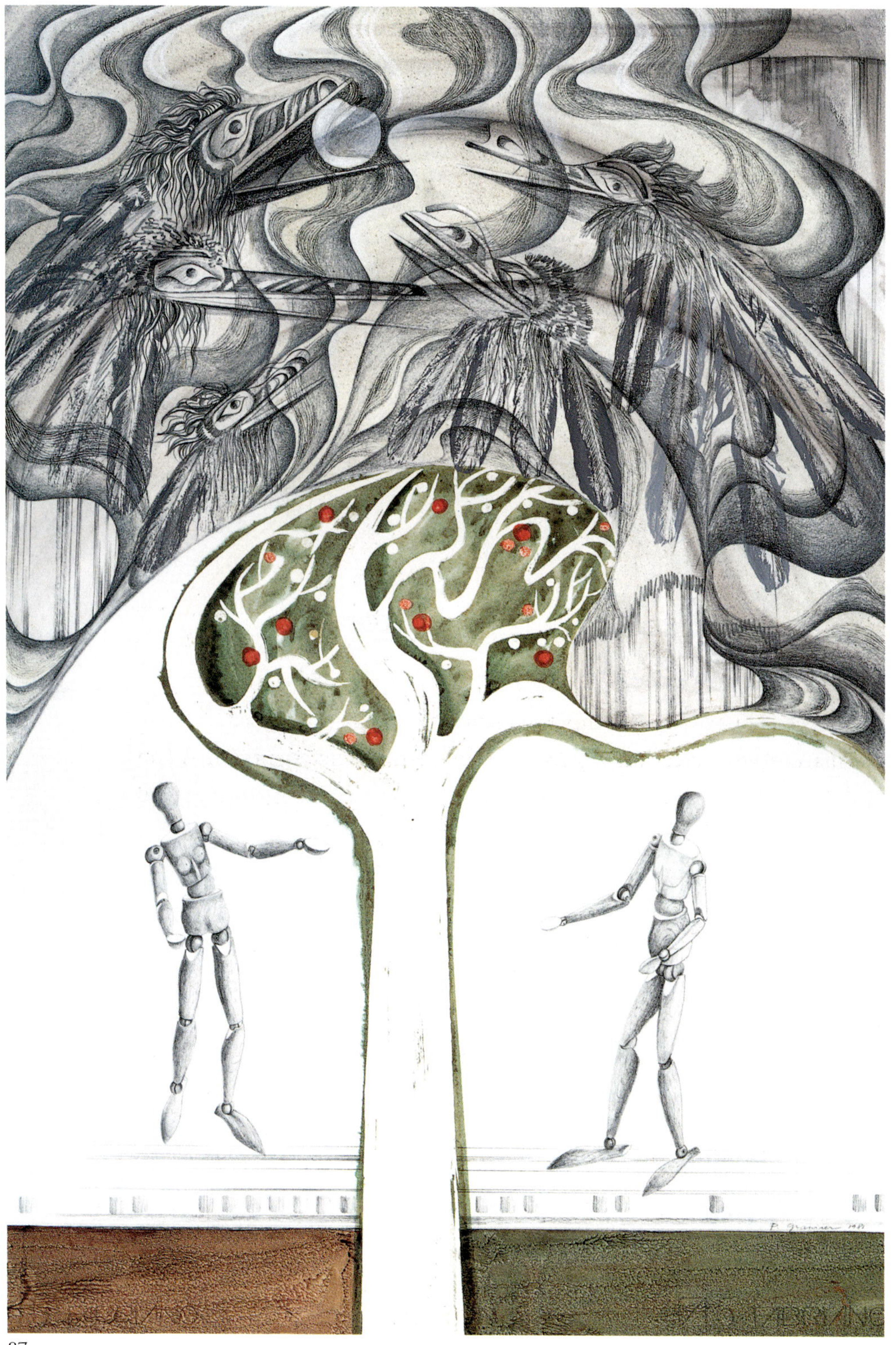

87

87. *Adam and Eve Tempted by Cannibal Birds,* 1981
70.8 x 49.8 cm (28 x 19 3/4 in)
mixed media on paper

The Trials of Eve Suite

Following closely on, and strongly influenced by the Judy Chicago film about her collaborative making of *The Dinner Party* (a colossal installation piece honouring a host of historically uncelebrated women in the arts and sciences), Granirer developed another narrative series which she titled *The Trials of Eve Suite* (1980–81). Looking for subjects to express her growing comprehension of feminism and her ongoing fascination with creation myths, Granirer trained her sights on Adam and Eve: Eve as a sinner and scapegoat, Adam as an unwitting and feckless accomplice.

In an uncommon meld of Old Testament and Coast Indian symbolism, Granirer places Adam and Eve (depicted as articulated artist's mannequins to establish their universality) in a series of vignettes reminiscent of the works of William Blake. The Satanic serpent becomes a Cannibal Bird; the rainforest is simplified to the Trees of Life and Knowledge; Eve's punishment is the objectification and segregation of women throughout history and art. Only at the conclusion does the parable become conciliatory, suggesting, in a jig-saw pattern, that the puzzle can be reassembled if only the less-than-complete Adam can, as it were, re-define himself. Meanwhile, the almost-complete Eve defiantly brandishes the Forbidden Fruit — which now possibly signifies her liberation from Biblical stigma. Perhaps the most satisfying reverberation from this work is Granirer's ultimate retort to the age-old (male) Jewish prayer, which begins, "Thank you, Lord, for not making me a woman. . . ."

After this suite had been exhibited a number of times, Granirer wrote twelve accompanying poems. Each time the work was exhibited, viewers suggested to her that it ought to be published as a book. With the support of two friends, *The Trials of Eve Suite* was published in December, 1989 by Gaea Press and received the 1990 Alcuin Design Award. A film with the same title, based on Granirer's drawings, was produced by filmmaker Gretchen Jordan-Bastow and shown at the 1991 UNESCO International Film Festival in Paris. Granirer writes:

> *The making of* The Trials of Eve *was the first time my art reflected my beliefs without holding back. I was taking chances I had never taken before: taking a stand as a woman and as an artist. In the process, I learned a great deal about what it meant to be a woman in a Judeo-Christian-Moslem society; I also learned a lot about myself and the various parts I had been playing as wife, mother, an always-available nurturer, and ultimately — an artist. This work changed my outlook on many issues, but particularly toward myself, my family and my work. I became more confident, valuing my work more and feeling thankful for the creativity I possess.*

Over time, *The Trials of Eve* seemed to acquire a life of its own. In 1985 all twelve panels were exhibited at the Art Gallery of Greater Victoria, in an invitational show celebrating 100 years of British Columbia women artists, curated by Nicholas Tuele.

The limited edition of the book did well, making the publication of a new softcover edition possible. For over twelve years this work generated activities and interest, such as panel discussions, lectures, book launches and exhibitions of the original drawings.

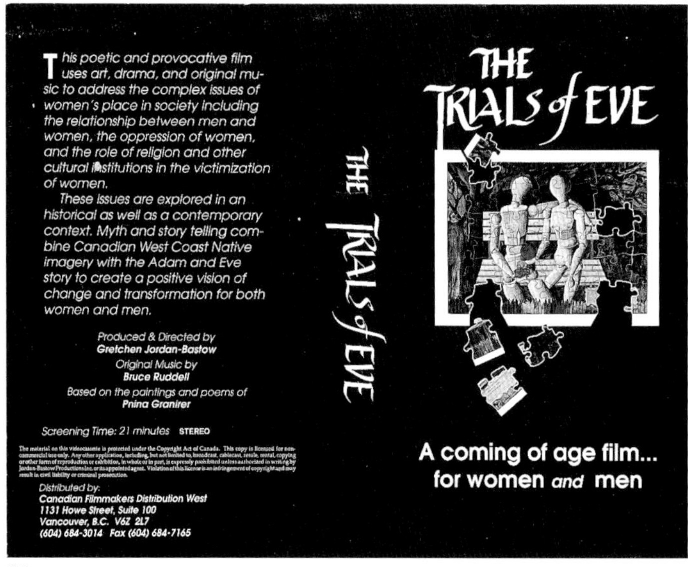

88

88. Jacket of video *The Trials of Eve* produced and directed by *Gretchen Jordan-Bastow* with original music by *Bruce Ruddell,* based on Granirer's paintings and poems.

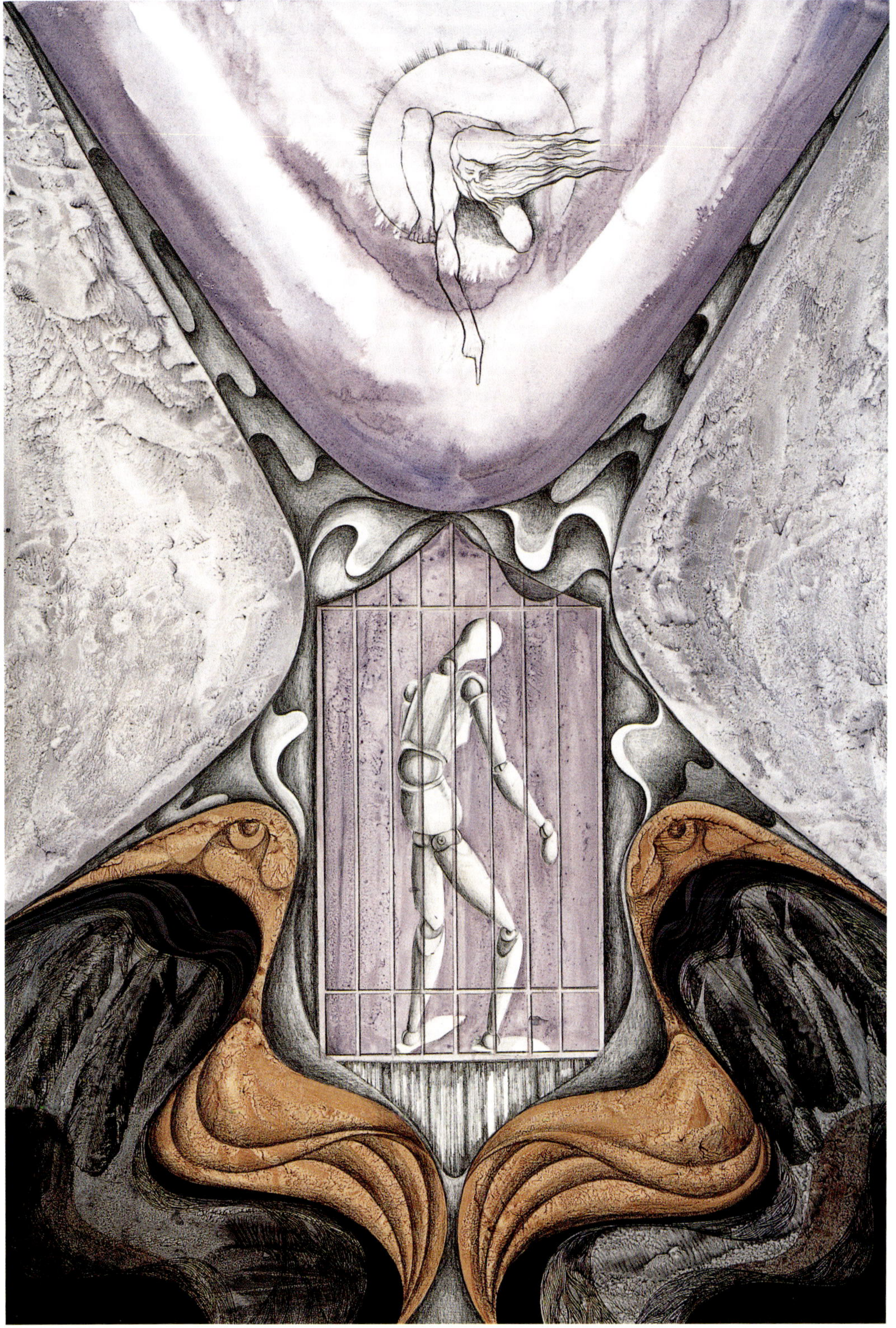

89

THE TRIAL

A Sin
great enough
for God Himself to judge
ominous prelude
to fiery witch hunts yet to come.

Eve
stands prisoner
behind the rigid bars.
The softness of life-giving womb
is cursed now
a painful duty
and not
the joy of life created.

89. *The Trial,* 1981
70.8 x 50.2 cm (28 x 19 1/2 in)
mixed media on paper

For The Sentence *I adopted an image which had profoundly affected me when I first saw it. This was a medieval stained glass window from Strasbourg Cathedral in France, showing the seemingly innocent scene of Mary Magdalene washing Christ's feet and drying them with her hair. I was shocked to see that the craftsman who had designed the window chose to portray Mary Magdalene lying flat on her belly at His feet. Unlike other representations of similar scenes showing Christ Himself, or His apostles washing feet (an old Middle Eastern hospitality custom), kneeling in a dignified posture, here the woman was depicted in a totally subservient position. Quoting the old marriage vows, used until not too long ago, I felt that this image expressed the idea of the sentence passed on women for centuries: "to love and to obey."*

— From Granirer's essay for the soft-cover edition of *The Trials of Eve.*

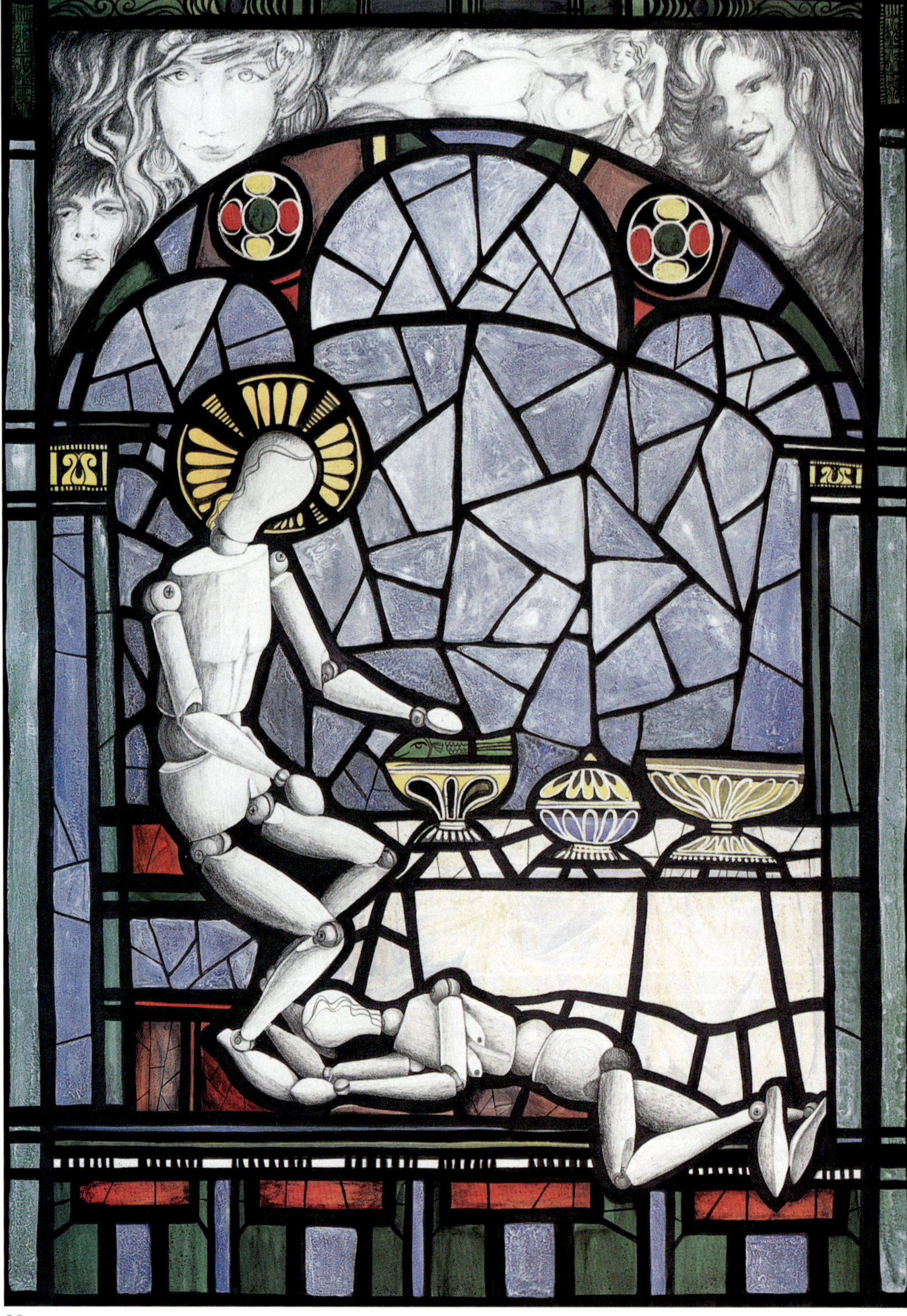

90

90. *The Sentence,* 1981
70.2 x 56.5 cm. (27 1/8 x 22 1/4 in)
mixed media on paper

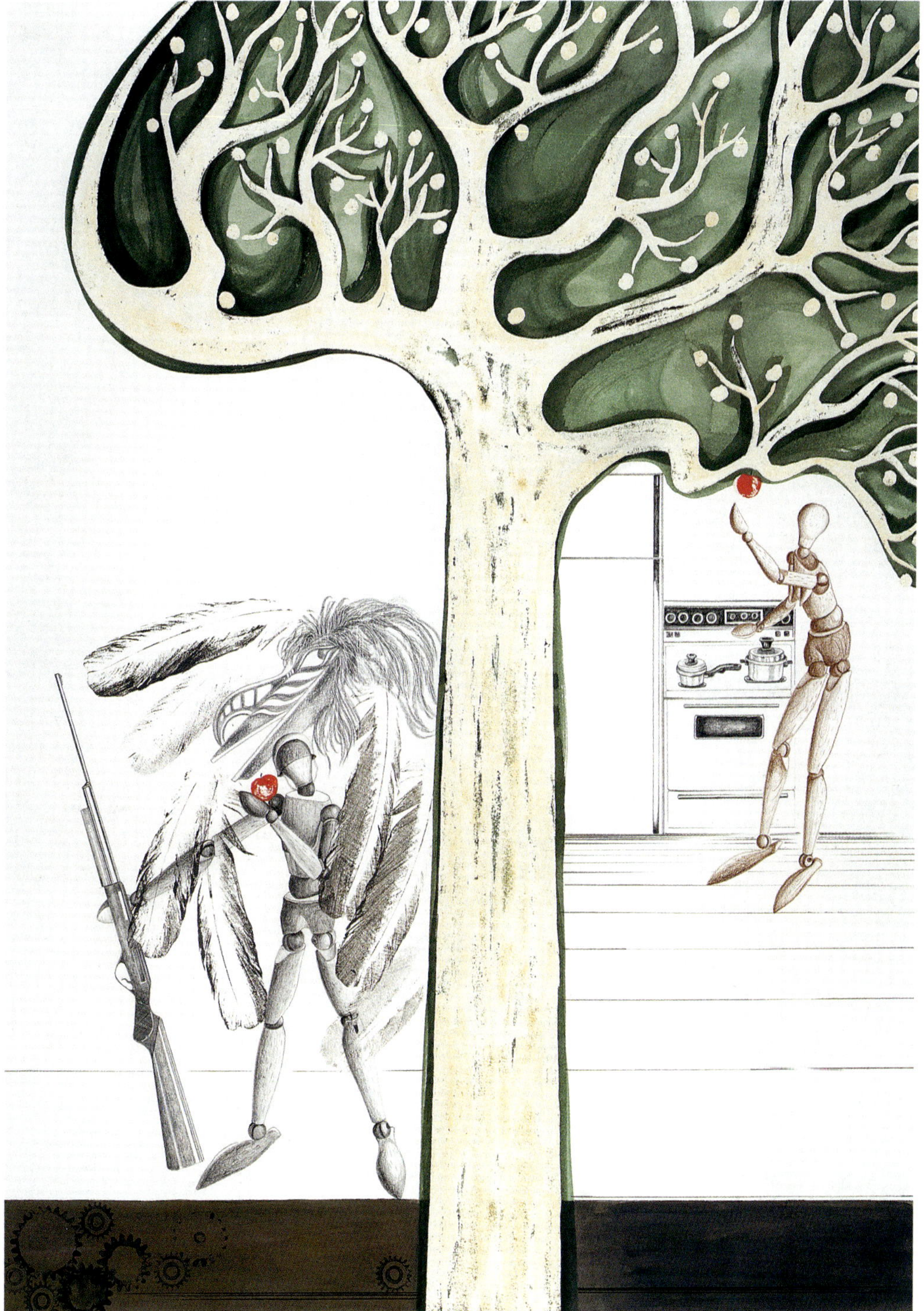

91

EVE TRIES AGAIN

Centuries
like stones sunk in the sea
have come and gone

The giant mirror
of a millennium about to die
throws back reflections
of shattered dreams.

Out on parole
Eve tries again.

In Adam's hand
the apple has turned sour
the tree has borne destruction
guns
bombs
missiles
great poverty and wealth,
a plundered Earth.

Too much for only half the human race
to handle.
The time is ripe:
Eve tries again.

91. *Eve Tries Again,* 1981
76.8 x 56.5 cm (30 1/8 x 22 1/4 in)
mixed media on paper

ADAM & EVE PUZZLE: TO BE ASSEMBLED WITH LOVE

So much to lose
much more to gain.
Forgotten pieces of a broken puzzle
falling into place.

Two halves of one whole
one needing the other.

A silent sound of fear
has reached the Heavens.
The Earth cries out in pain.

The time has come
to reassemble
and to complete the puzzle.

Shall we begin anew and

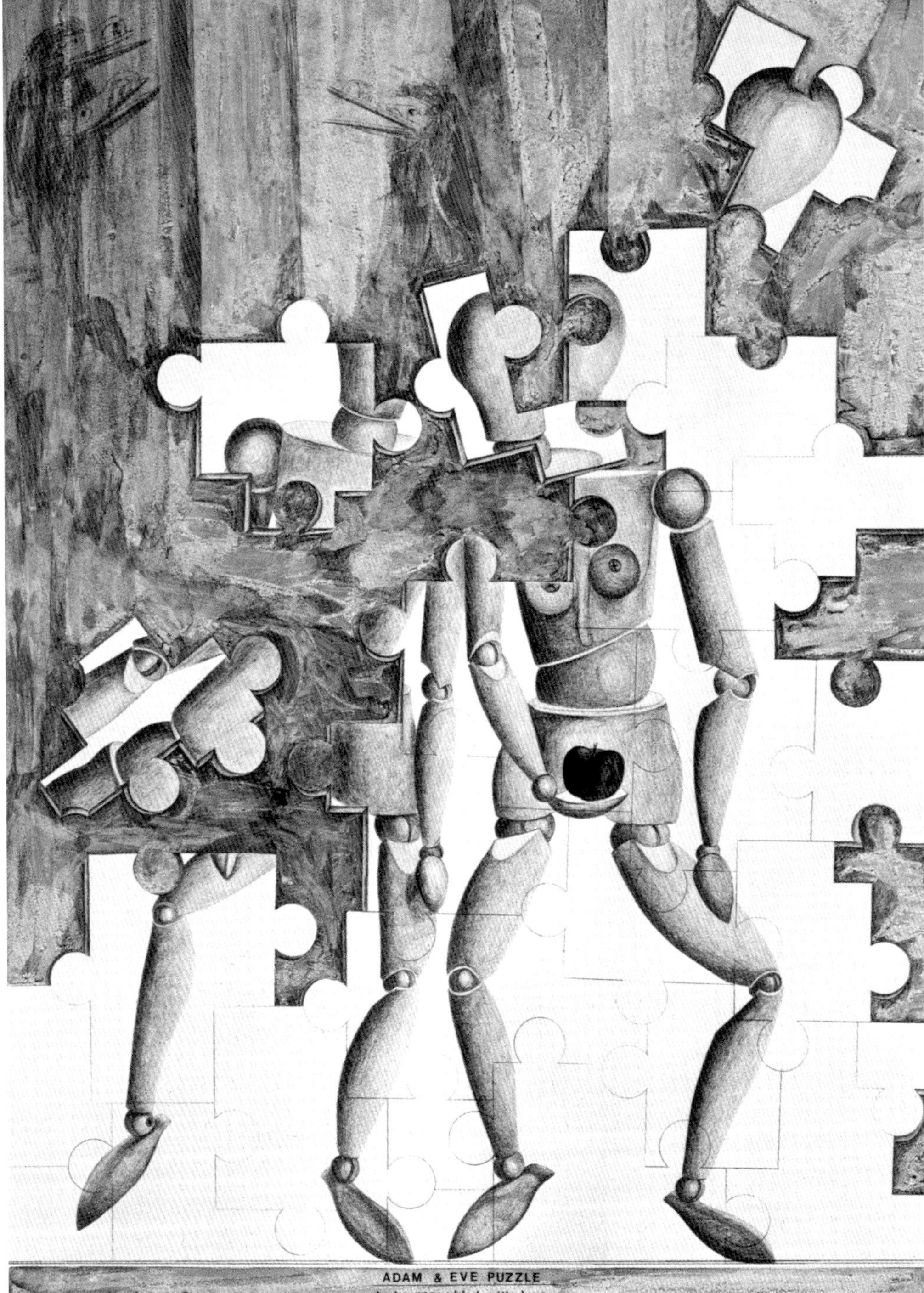

92

92. *Adam & Eve Puzzle: To Be Assembled With Love,* 1981
76.5 x 56.2 cm (30 1/4 x 22 1/8 in)
mixed media on paper

Stage Series, Family Album Suite

With the *Stage Series* in 1983, Granirer continued in the dramatic tone which had been established in *The Cannibal Bird* and *The Trials of Eve* suites: settings, vignettes, theoretical *mise-en-scènes* which grew out of the work she had done with the Shakespeare in the Park Festival company in Vancouver. For them, she had designed backdrops, banners and props such as a Chagall-esque donkey's head for a production of *A Midsummer Night's Dream.*

At the close of her collaboration with the Shakespeare Festival, she extended the idea of theatre to a series of surreal prosceniums that

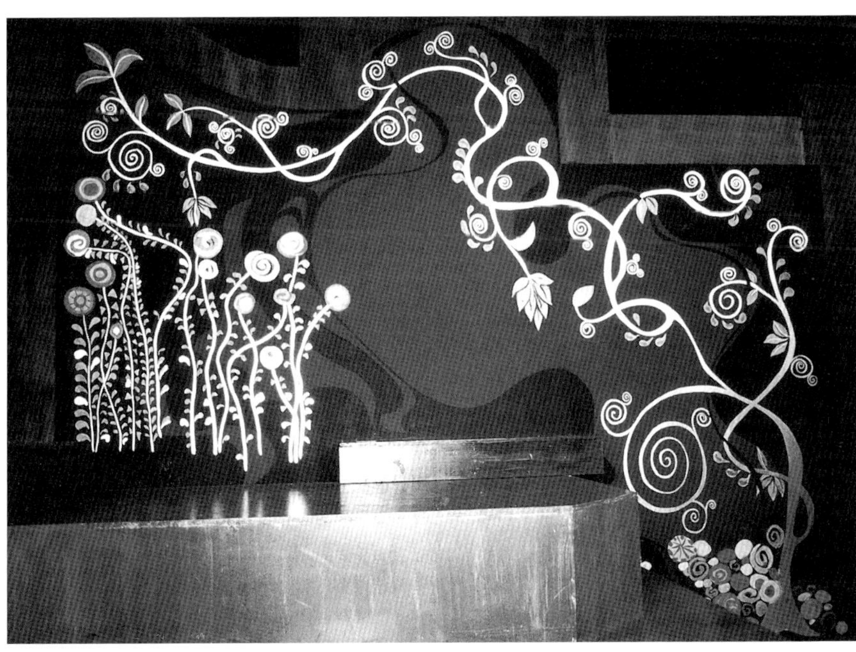

93

93. View of sets for *A Midsummer Night's Dream,* 1983 Shakespeare Festival at Vanier Park, in Vancouver, British Columbia

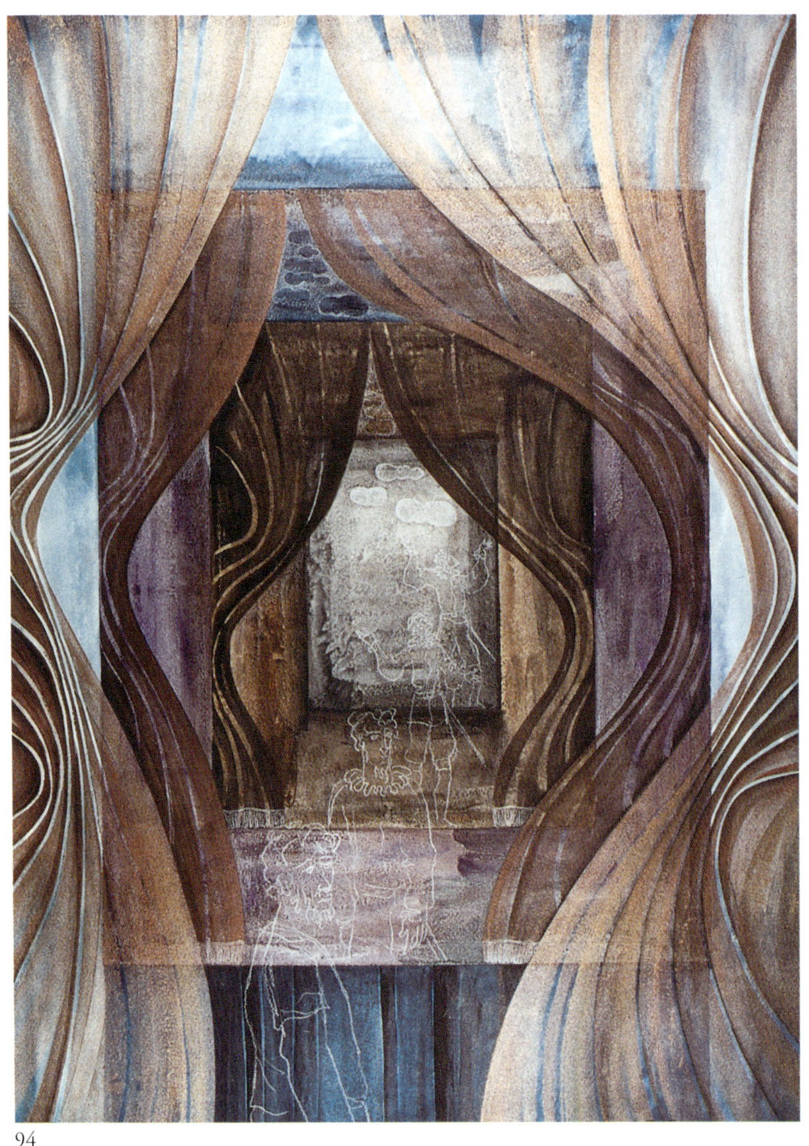

94

would frame life's actual *dramatis personae:* the human race. The difference between a framed picture and a theatrical proscenium was the living, breathing human element that proceeded through a succession of stages in time — very like "real life".

94. *Transformation,* 1983
76 x 56 cm (30 x 22 in)
acrylic, resist, grease pencil on paper

The curtain appears as a symbol of time passing. It reveals the present, but hides the future and sometimes conceals the past.

Here, again, as in the early pen and ink drawings, Granirer set herself a specific technical task. Limiting herself to a few images, such as the rectangle of the stage, the curtains, and sometimes the figure, she achieved endless variations on one theme.

In *Transformation,* 1983, a mixed-media work, Granirer suggests a sequence of Art Nouveau curtained stages, diminishing through perspec-

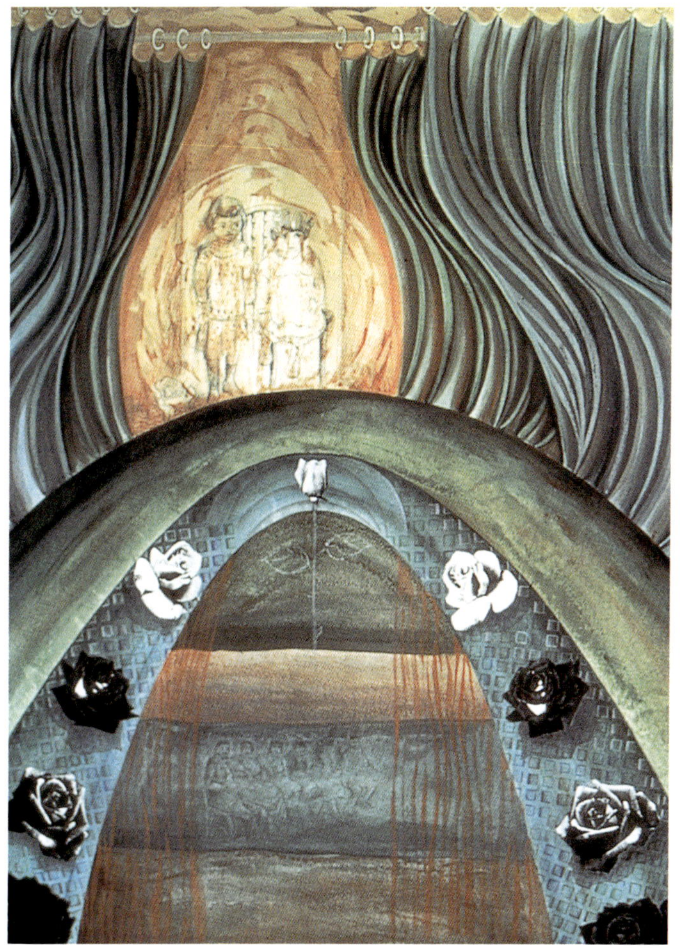

95

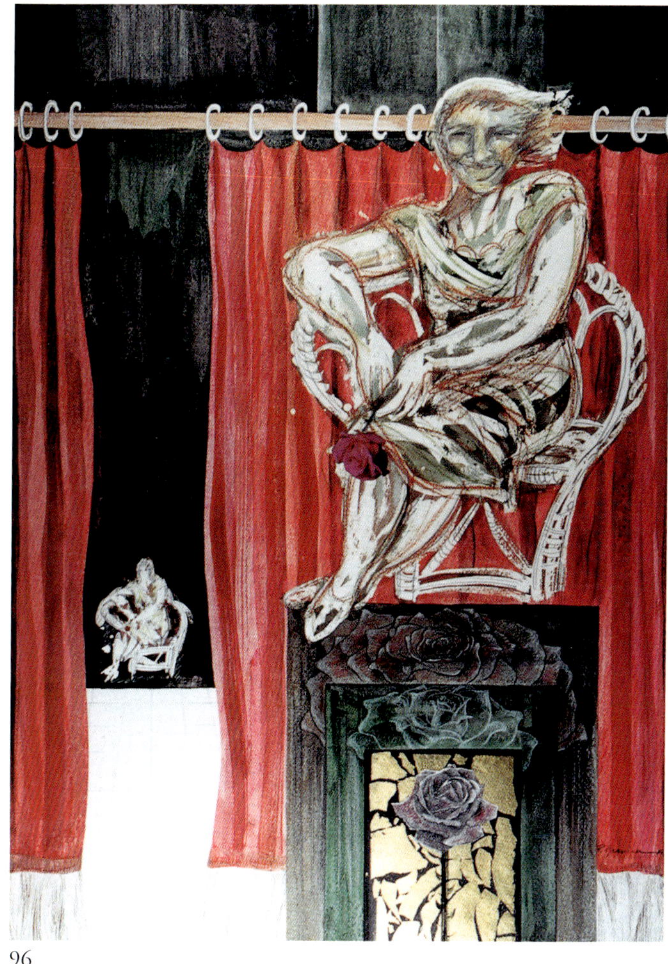

96

tive into a pale, indistinct horizon. Through these stages, ghostly actors, delineated in white line, advance toward an uncertain "end", echoing Shakespeare's ironic observation on man's fate — his time completed on the boards, *is heard no more.*

The Ghost, 1983, visualizes a forest-like setting in maroon, brown, and greys with undulating lines surrounding another white-line figure in a long gown responding to spectral, applauding hands. The "ghost" perhaps symbolizes the expended energy of human action or activity, and indeed, the stilled reverberation of grateful applause. "Where has it gone? What did it mean?" the work seems to question.

95. *Two Sisters,* 1983
76 x 56 cm (30 x 22 in)
acrylic, resist, grease pencil, graphite on paper

Granirer's mother and her sister are the subject of this work.

96. *Monument to Happy Days,* 1984
76 x 56 cm (30 x 22 in)
acrylic, resist, grease and coloured pencil collage and graphite on paper

Collectively, a painter's works are a time tunnel. A life's work, stacked in a row, front to back, also reaches into a kind of infinity that poses the same questions: where has it gone? What did it mean?

The seriousness of such investigations deepened in 1984 when Granirer took another tack toward understanding and articulating life's enigmas and possible meanings. Inspired by the rediscovery of an old family picture album, she was taken back through the inevitable meditations on images known and unknown, dear and dim, beautiful and uncomely.

For this new body of work, *The Family Album Suite,* Granirer developed a different way of working, harking back to the time when she had explored the technique of batik in the late 60's. She put down thin washes of acrylic paint, almost like watercolour in their transparency, and covered areas with paint resist. When the paint dried, she would put down another layer, cover it with resist and thus continue working in negative. At a certain point the surface was almost completely covered with an opaque film of rubbery material, the colours unrecognizable. But when the resist was completely dry, she would rub it off and the colours would magically appear, one below the other, rather than one on top of another.

Two Sisters, 1984 (ill. 95), is also set in a proscenium format, bracketed by flowing green curtains and layered through successions of arches and variegated strata, again suggesting the passage of time. Above the arches Granirer has photo-transferred the images of two young girls in a sun-like halo of shimmering gold; below the arches, and framed by collaged, photocopied images of black and white roses, is another photo-transfer of a group of adults, so indistinct and shadowy that one learns nothing about them. They are ghosts, fading by the minute into greater and greater insubstantiality.

Granirer seems, here, to be contemplating not only the living and unliving, but the ghosts of childhood that belong to the adult. She seems to be reminding us that psychically, memory and reality have similar qualities.

Other works in this series appear to allude to the strangeness of the photographic process itself: its ability to transform ordinary portrait subjects into quirkish, ungainly caricatures, especially in informal snapshots. Granirer's family album proved a rich source of images to be used in mixed-media collage and experimentation, but perhaps it was too personal for an audience accustomed to her more lyrical and decorative, nature-derived compositions. In a *Vanguard* (summer, 1984) review of

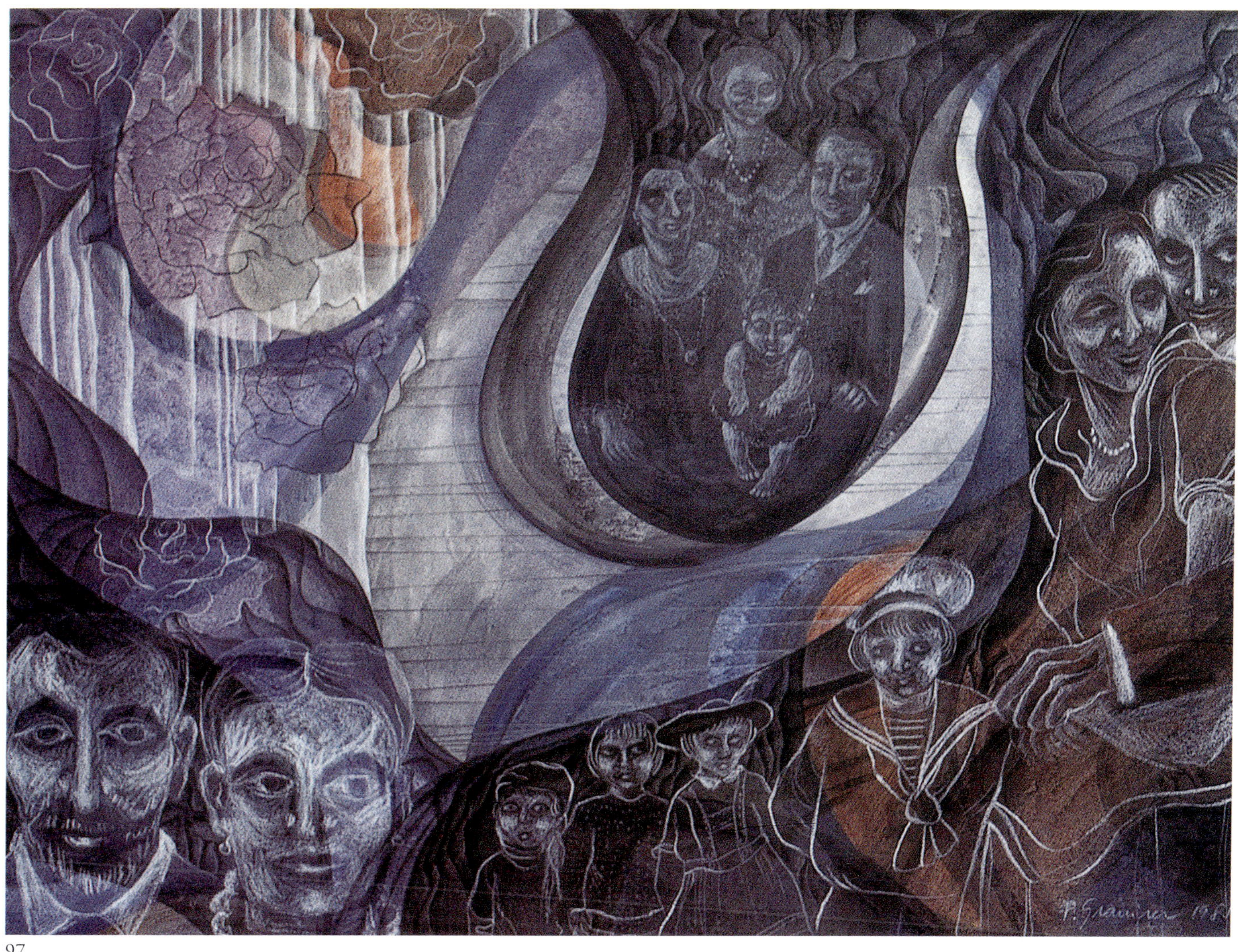

97

Family Series, Jill Pollack was unenthusiastic about the personal, hermetic qualities of the subject matter and felt Granirer had become lost in her attempt *"to resolve certain technical and aesthetic problems simultaneously."* Conversely, Jerry Szymanski in the *Bellingham Herald,* (Oct 5, 1984) pronounced the work *"just plain good"* and warily avoided any discussion of essentially feminist issues.

At a time when virtually no Vancouver artists were doing figurative work, the Bau-Xi Gallery (which had regularly exhibited Granirer's work) found this series "too personal" and "unsaleable", starting a process which, two years later, was to bring to an end a relationship of some thirteen years, just as Granirer's art became, if anything, more serious.

97. *Family,* 1984
56 x 76 cm (22 x 30 in)
acrylic, transfer, grease pencil, graphite on paper
Collection of Paul and Lesley Lambert

The family in the centre is the artist's own: her grandparents with two of their children. The boy dressed in a sailor's suit is her father.

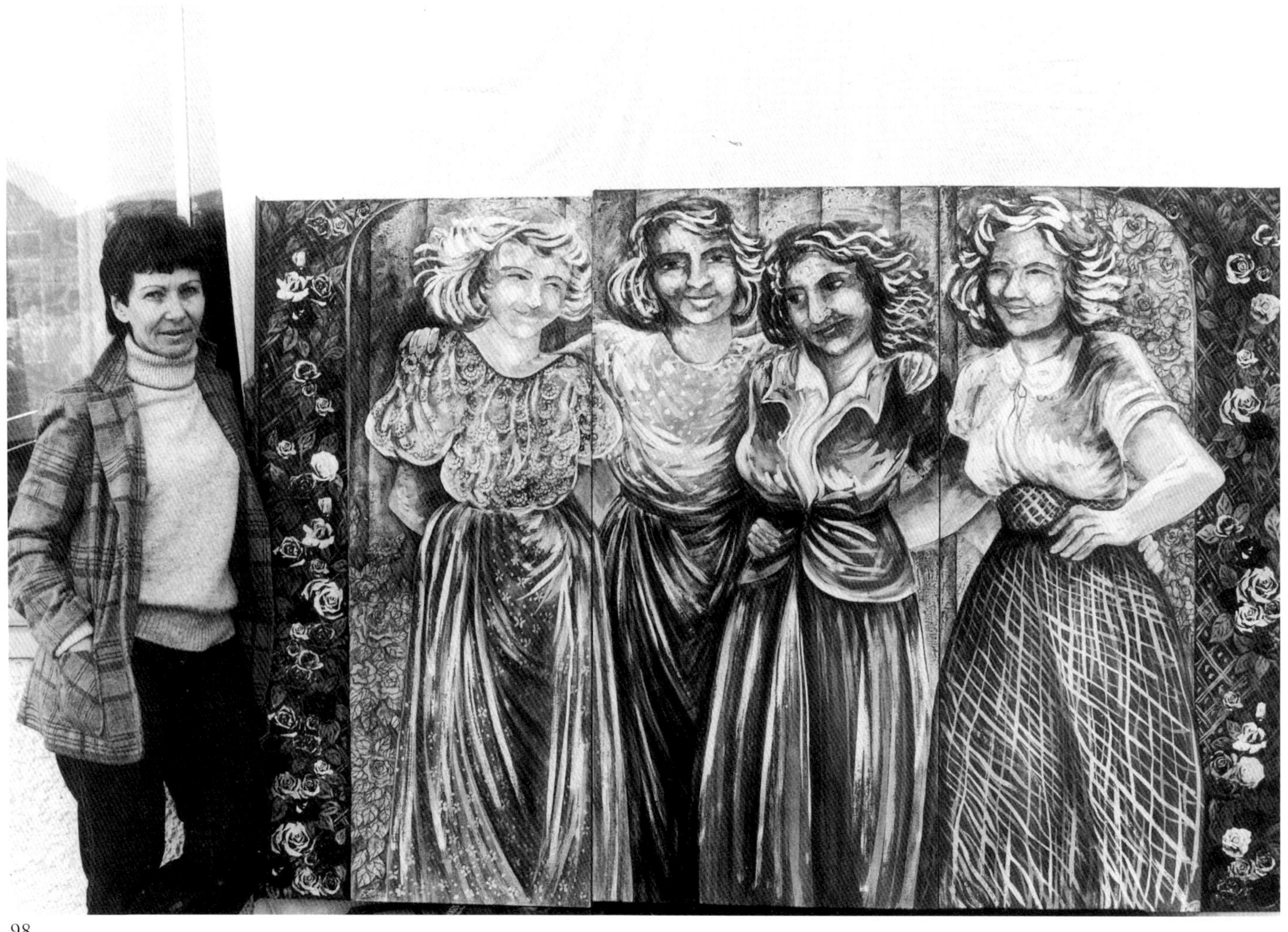

98

98. Granirer with her painting *In the Garden,* 1985
triptych, 3(122 x 61 cm) 3(48 x 24 in)
acrylic, resist on canvas

Roses are used by Granirer in much of her work to signify middle age, a time when the decay of expectations and hope is as much a certainty as bodily degeneration.

The black roses fulfill their function well, and most effectively in In the Garden. *They seem to place the viewer in the uncomfortable position of joining the artist in knowing the future before the young subjects of the painting will. The effect is to temper the gaiety of the young women and the painting with a touch of melancholy; one wishes he could keep these girls locked into their current time, yet knows he cannot.*

— Jerry Szymanski, *The Bellingham Herald,* reviewing Granirer's exhibition at the Chrysalis Gallery, at Western Washington University.

Granirer was unrepentant about this turn of events. She had never hung onto a style or content simply because it sold, and she was not about to discontinue her progressive explorations. She concluded her *Family Series* only when she felt she had exhausted the subject and the phenomena that surrounded it.

In what had become a well established pattern in her working habits, Granirer would work and expand on a certain idea for a number of years and then move on towards a new phase. She always felt the need for renewal. As she is fond of saying: "The only thing which does not change is death. If I don't explore new ideas I should die as an artist."

The Carved Stones Series

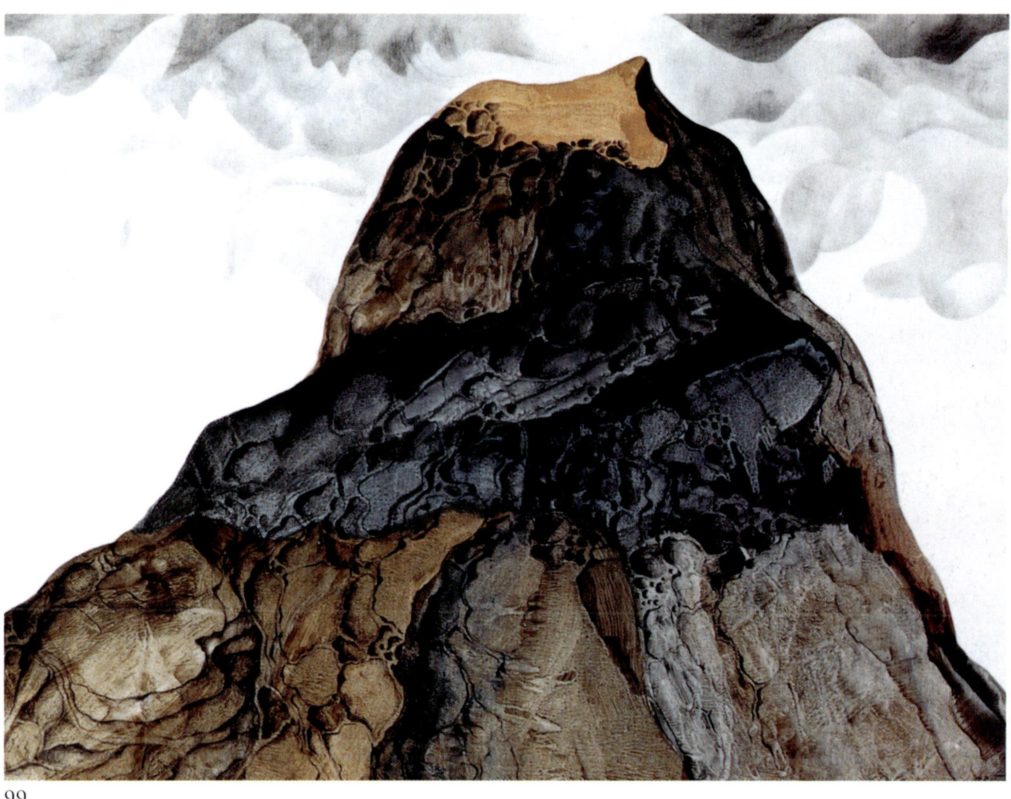

99

While still exploring the *Family Album Suite,* something occurred which diverted Granirer's interest in a totally different and unexpected direction. It was a strange experience: a rare and unusual insight. She recalls:

This experience led me into a totally new direction, that of the Stone Series. I have never been interested in stones before. It's one of those things one is almost embarrassed to talk about, which falls into the realm of revelation — but it really happened.

99. *Sandstone #1,* 1985
56 x 76 cm (22 x 30 in)
acrylic, grease pencil and graphite on paper

BEACH

Black shadows
hide
    in black, smooth holes
    carved deeply in the stoney flesh.

The beach,
a battlefield of light and darkness.
Eerie sight of rocks
    becoming
        bleached bones
        shapes fit for dreams.

I walk upon the backs of silent creatures
turned to stone
        by a malevolent magician.

Pnina Granirer, 1985

In the summer of 1985 we were visiting friends at Roberts Creek, on the Sunshine Coast. I went down to the beach and walked slowly, carefully stepping on the rounded, polished stones. It was late afternoon. Low sun brilliantly reflected in the small waves moving back and forth in the gentle breeze. The tide was just starting to come in, accompanied by the piercing cries of the seagulls. I climbed upon a huge black boulder and sat on its warm, dark surface. All of a sudden, out of nowhere, a powerful feeling swept over me and my heart raced at the sound of the waves. I understood that this rock upon which I was sitting had been there from time immemorial; it was older than history and had perhaps witnessed events which we will never know. It held mysteries in its silent, stony bosom, stories never to be revealed. I had the extraordinary feeling of a curtain being lifted, allowing me to see the universe unfolding.

Until that moment, as I have mentioned before, I had never had the slightest interest in rocks of any kind, but from that moment on stones were the subject of numerous paintings and poems.

MEDITATION

The brown rock I sit on
glistens with sparks of silver chips.

Voluptuous lump of stone carved by the sea,
condemned forever
        to listen
        to the perpetuum mobilae
        of waves breaking.

Close to my hand,
two green flies warmed by the sun
buzz lustily amid the barnacles
intent on madly making love.

Pnina Granirer, 1986

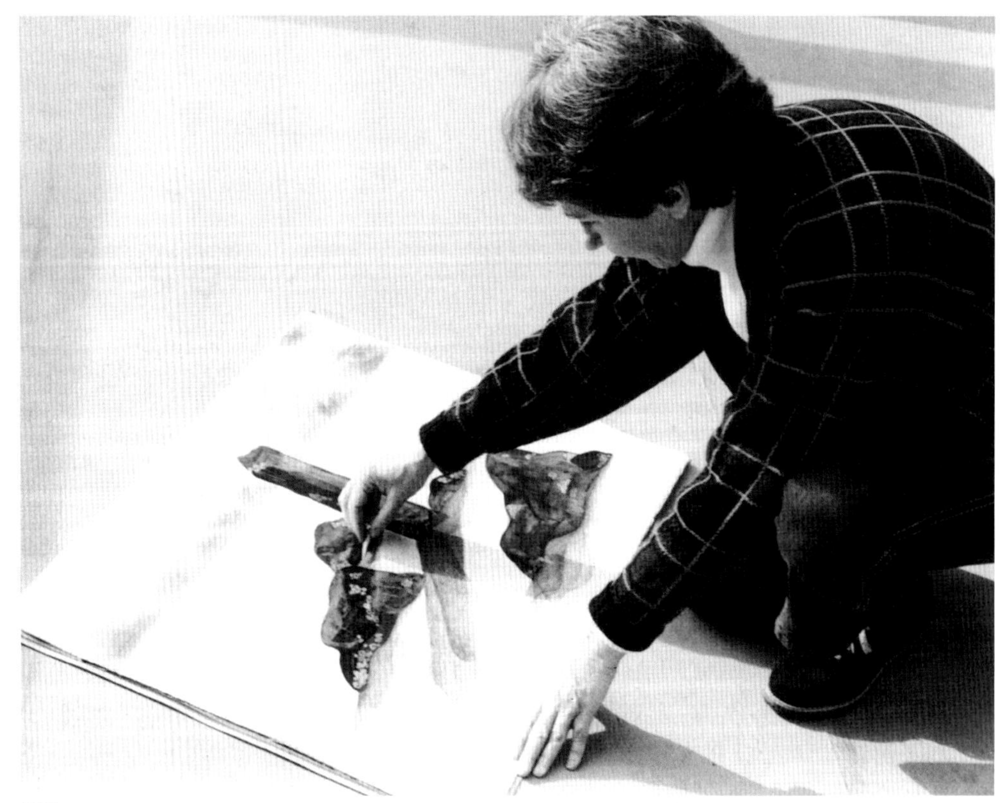

100

100. The artist at work, 1986

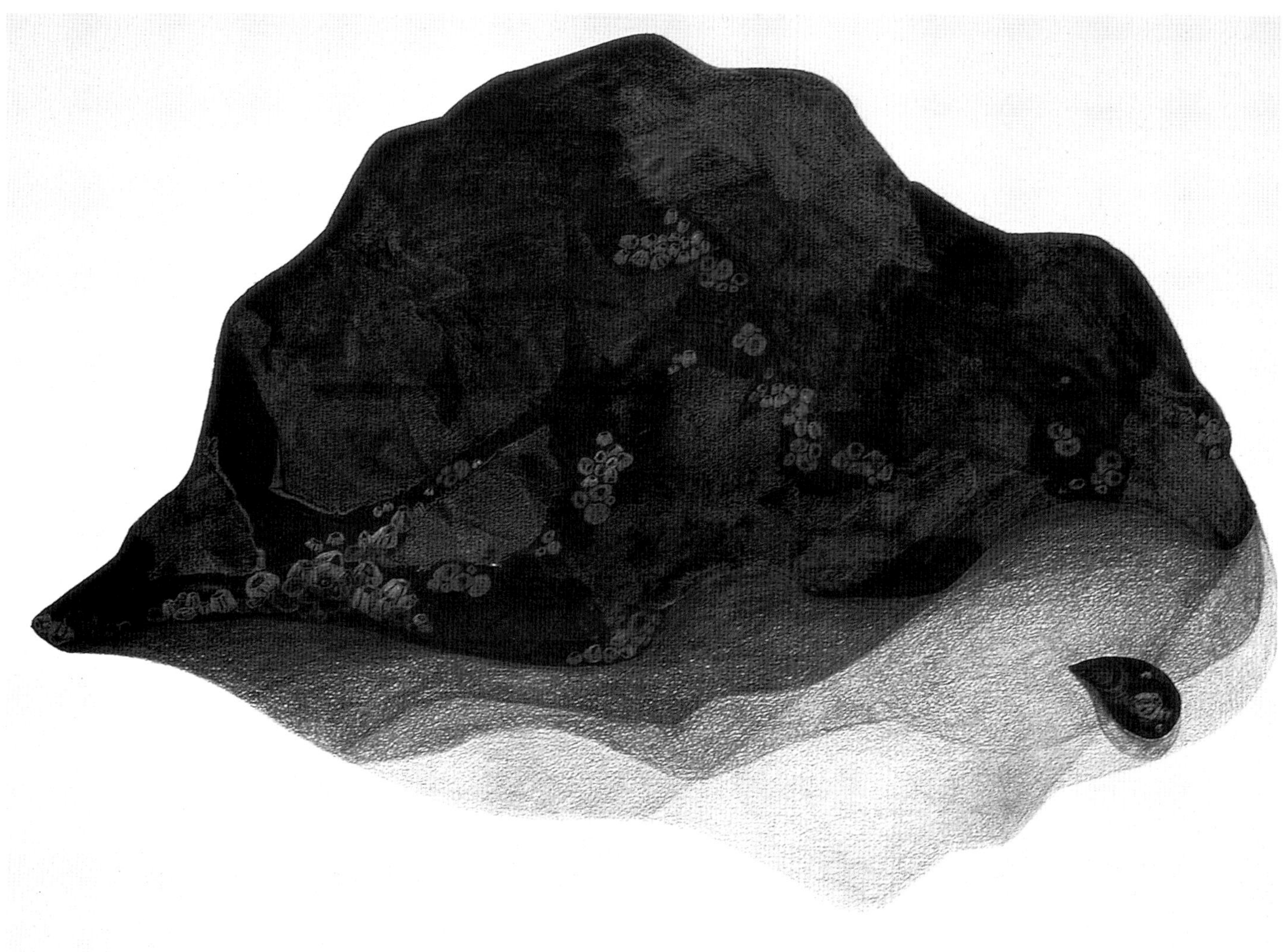

101

The first work was a blue rock on paper. These mixed media drawings and paintings were very Japanese in style, very simple, shades of blue with white barnacles on them.

Granirer was fascinated by their monumentality, their silence, their sculptural presence. As time went by more colour came into the paintings and they became more complex in texture and composition.

101. *Blue Rock Opus 3,* 1985
75 x 105 cm (29 1/2 x 41 1/4 in)
acrylic, grease pencil, graphite on paper

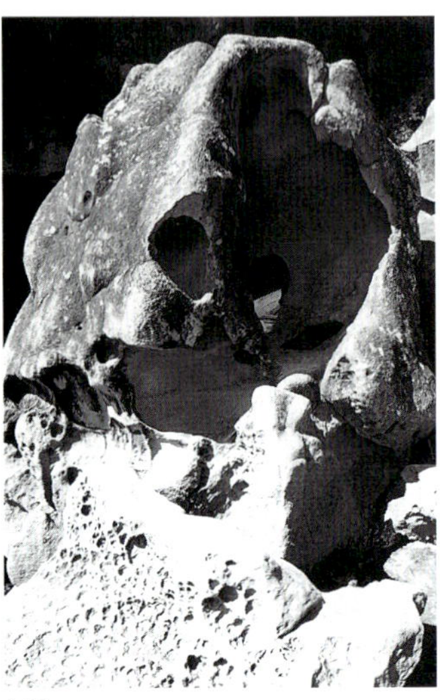

102

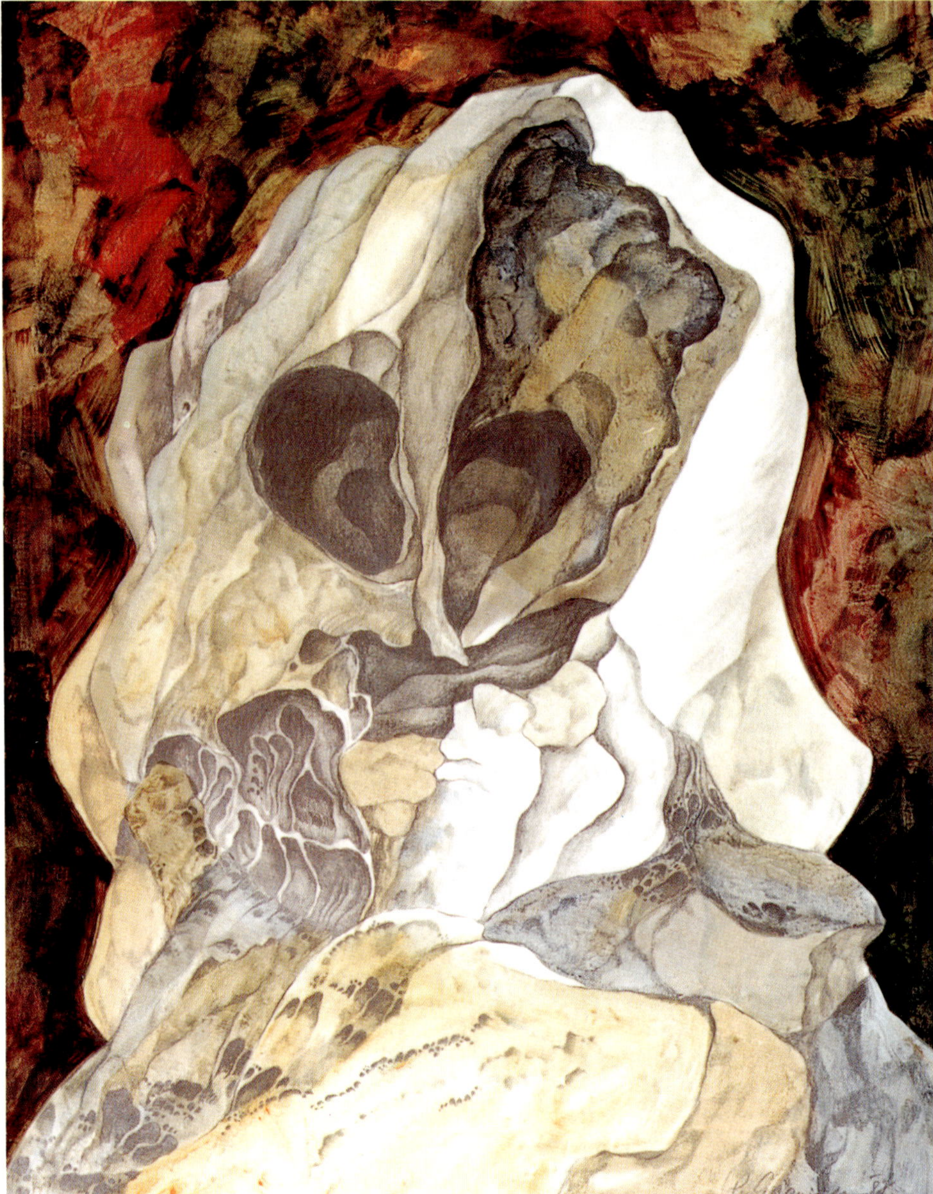

103

102. Rock formation on Gabriola Island, British Columbia, nicknamed The Head by the artist

103. *Portrait of a Rock,* 1988
70.7 x 56 cm (27 7/8 x 22 1/8 in)
acrylic, graphite on paper

The Stone Series, which extended for a sustained period after 1985, is another example of Granirer's selecting single elements in nature for attention, rather than constructing more broadly literal "landscape" paintings. Rocks on wet sand, rocks in fog, rocks with sea and sky, rocks with stormy sky, rocks with stranded logs and seaweed: all are treated with the intimacy normally lavished on still lifes.

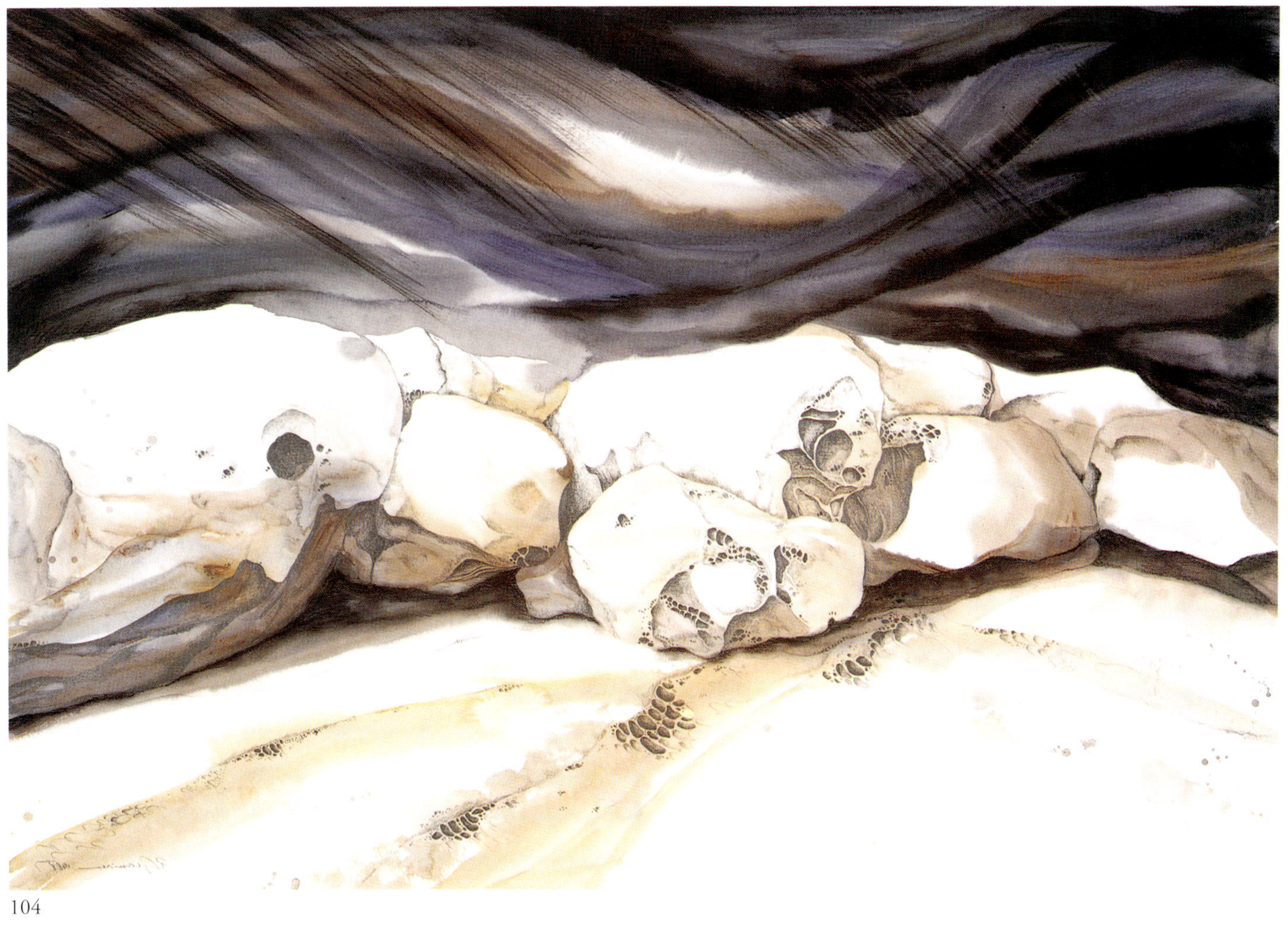

104

These works have been created in the studio, with reflective thought and planning. Local colour has given way, in many instances, to Granirer's innate colour sense: an endless array of blues and greys and violets. Granirer has collected her sentinel rocks from Saturna and Gabriola Islands, as well as Spanish Banks, the beach which lies below Granirer's Point Grey home. In works such as *Two Logs on the Beach,* 1986, she turns to warmer colours — tans, yellows, with white sand — and a forest backdrop in dark greens and black shadows.

104. *Barrier,* 1988
76.2 x 111.8 cm (30 x 44 in)
acrylic, charcoal and graphite on paper
Collection of Mary and French Tickner

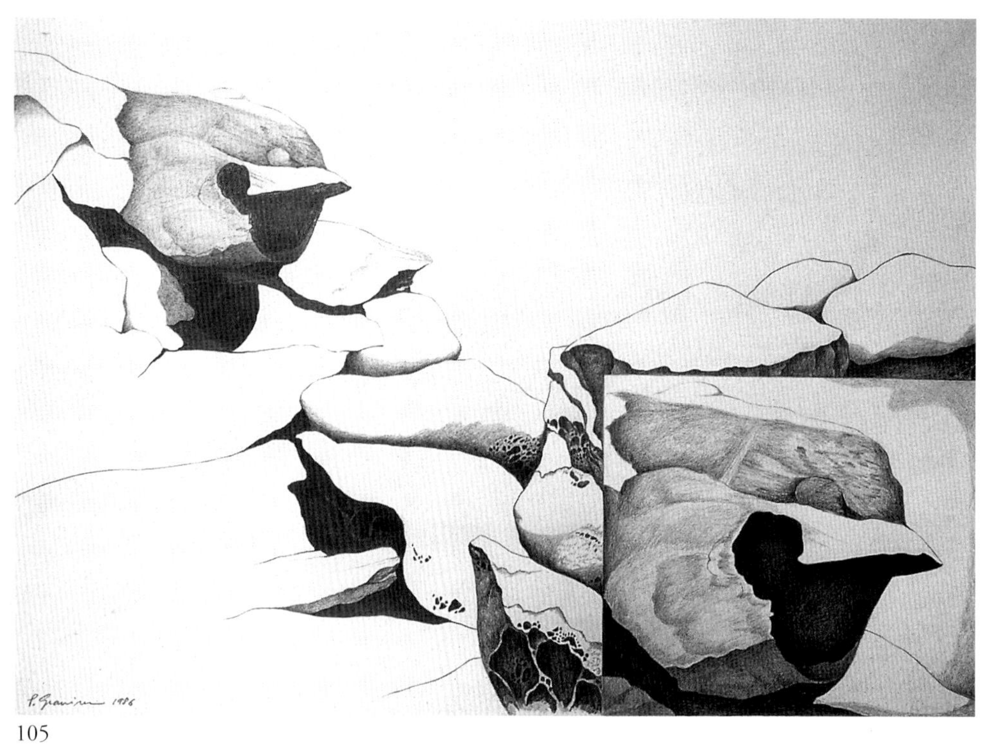
105

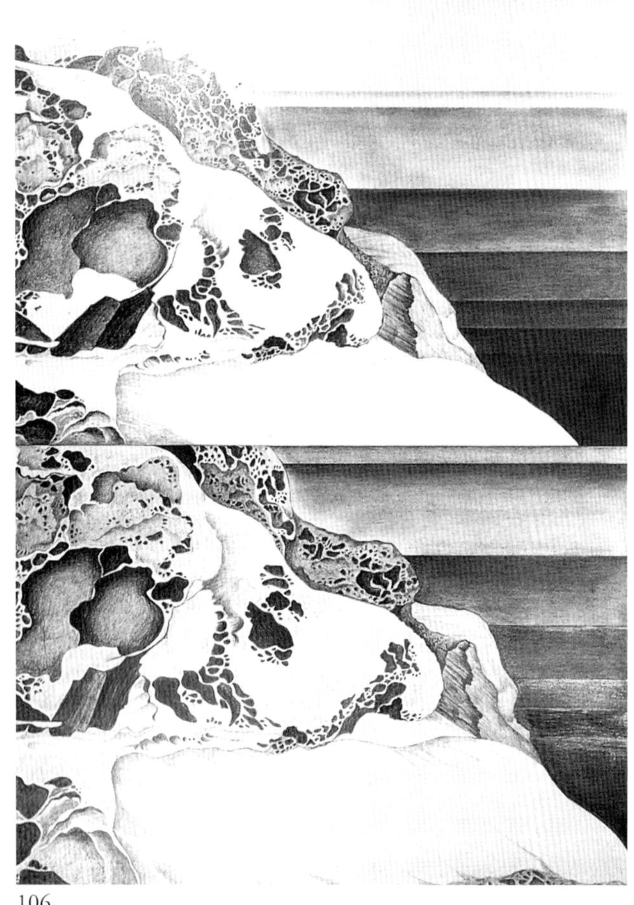
106

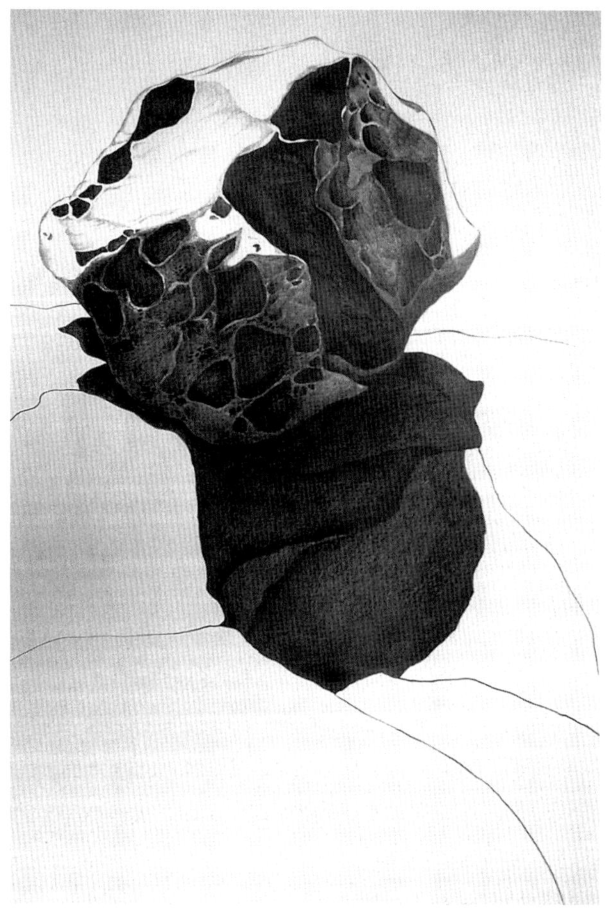
107

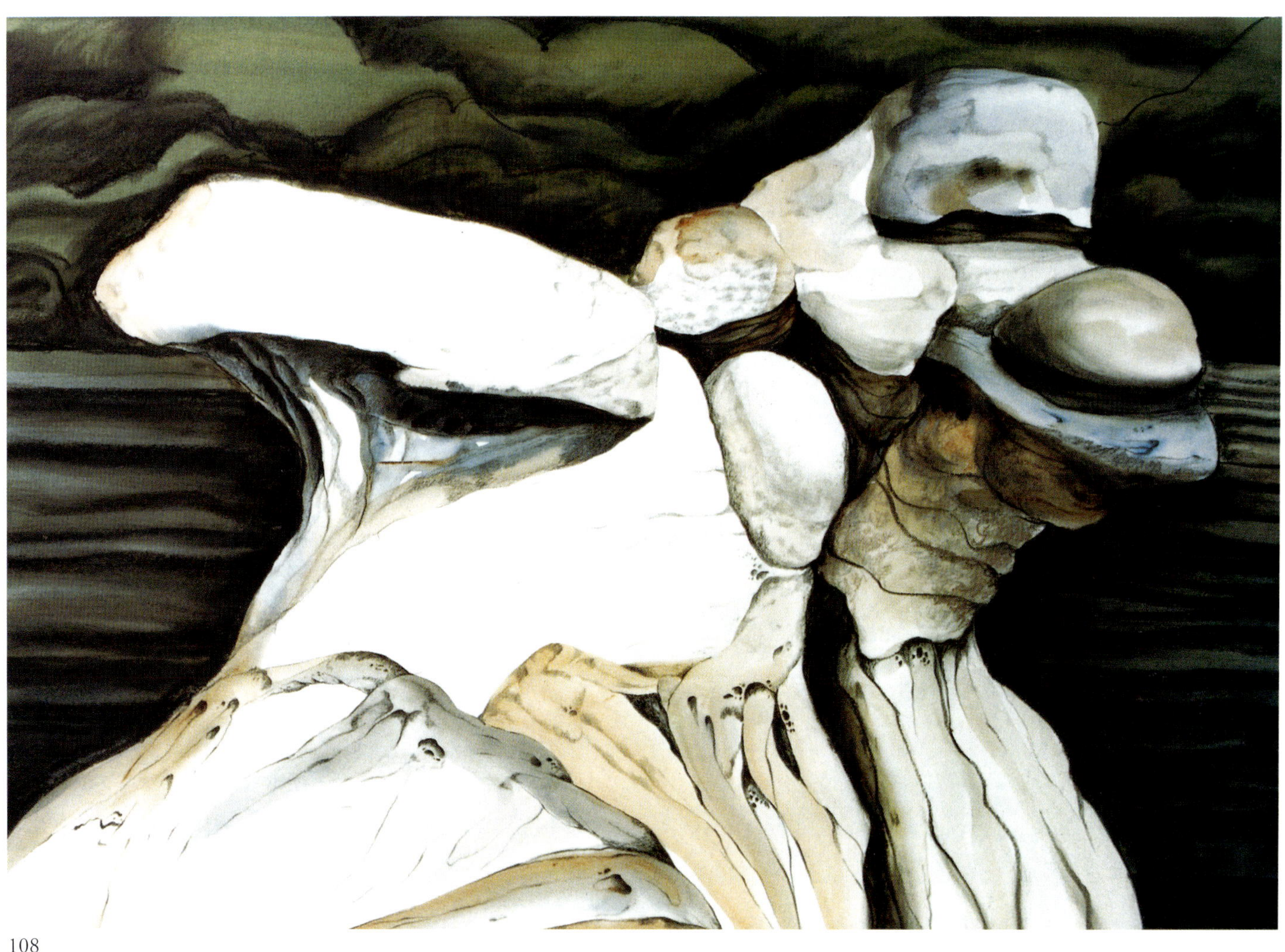

108

Reviewing Granirer's solo exhibition *Carved Stones* (July, 1989) at the Art Gallery of the South Okanagan, in Penticton, British Columbia, P. M. Ritchie has this to say in *The Penticton Herald:*

> *These are not paintings of purely visual interest. They are paintings that require concentration, for there are underlying meanings in each one.*
>
> *Granirer's strength is in her drawing. This is seen in her pencil and charcoal drawing, one called* Rock on Beach *and another* Salmon Rock with Head *which illustrate her ability to interpret the shoreline. They are firm drawings and simply done.*

105. *Stone Bird,* 1986
56 x 76 cm (22 x 30 in)
graphite on coloured pencil on paper

106. *Double Exposure,* 1986
76 x 56 cm (30 x 22 in)
graphite and coloured pencil on paper

107. *Rock & Shadow,* 1987
76 x 56 cm (30 x 22 in)
graphite and coloured pencil on paper

108. *Sculpture by the Sea,* 1988
56 x 76 cm (22 x 30 in)
acrylic, graphite, charcoal on Fabriano
Collection of Graham Good

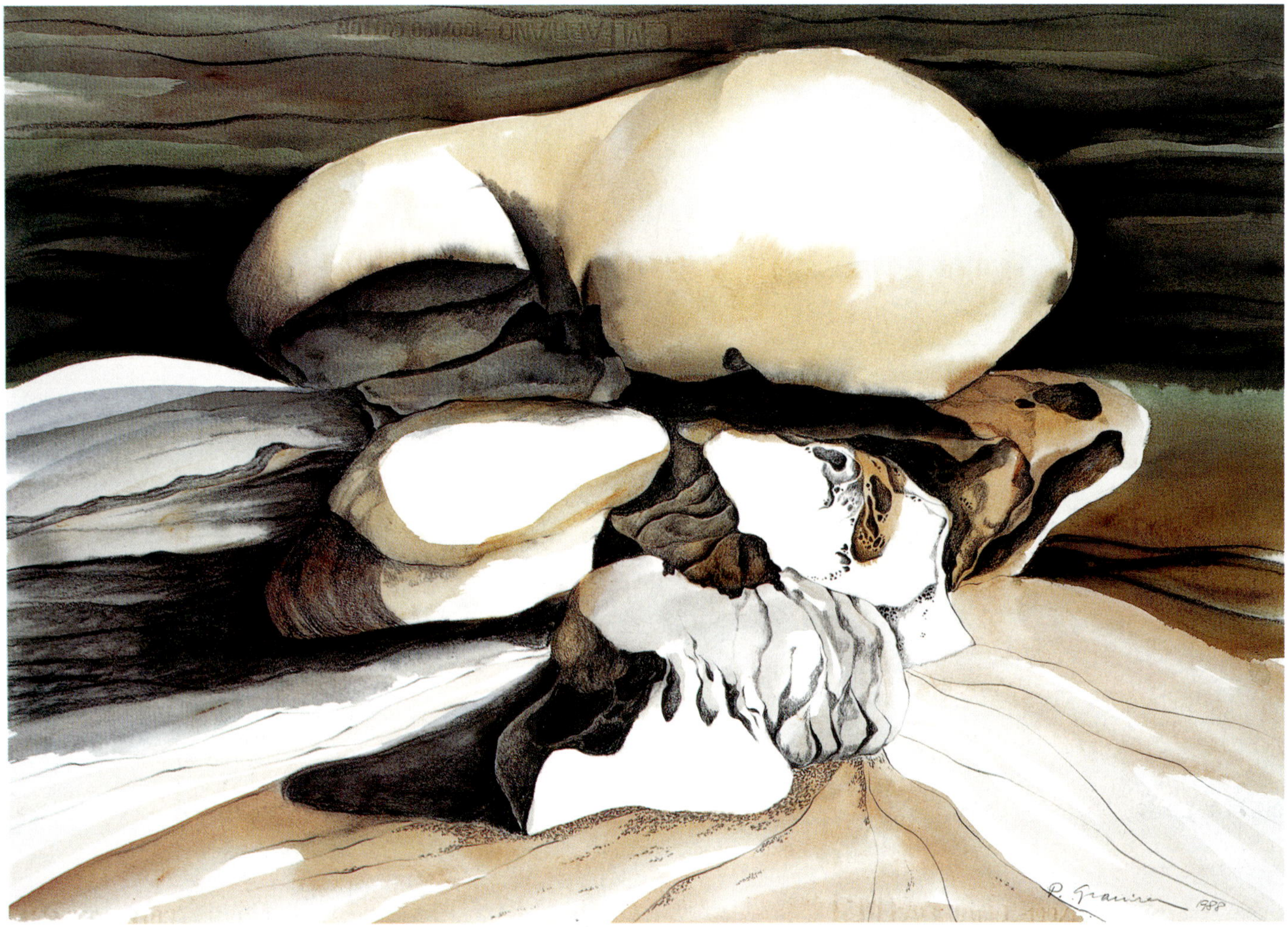

109

109. *Sculptor Unknown,* 1988
56.5 x 76 cm (22 1/4 x 29 7/8 in)
acrylic, charcoal, graphite on Fabriano

110. Rock on Gabriola Island, British Columbia

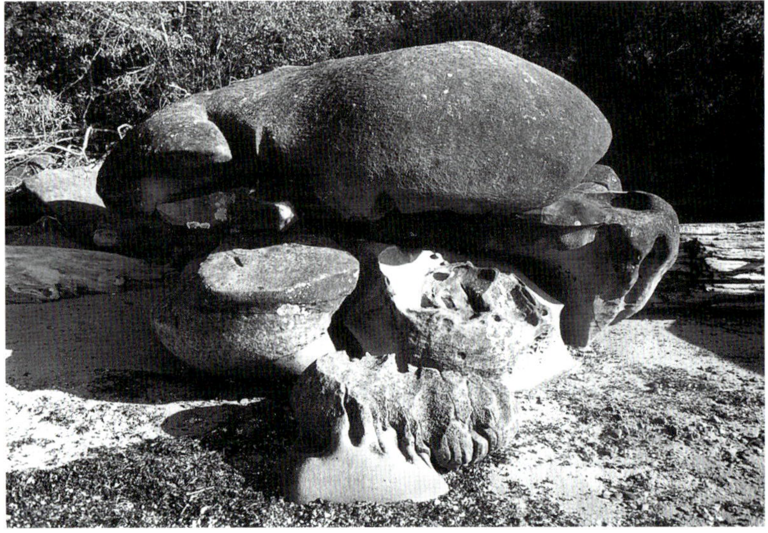

110

The Millstone Quarry

One of the most fruitful "sub-series" of this period became known as *The Millstones Series.* In 1986, Granirer was taken by friends to a unique site on Gabriola Island. She found a sandstone floor receding

111. *Discovery at Gabriola,* 1987
56 x 76 cm (22 x 30 in)
acrylic, graphite on paper
Collection of Lila and David Quastel

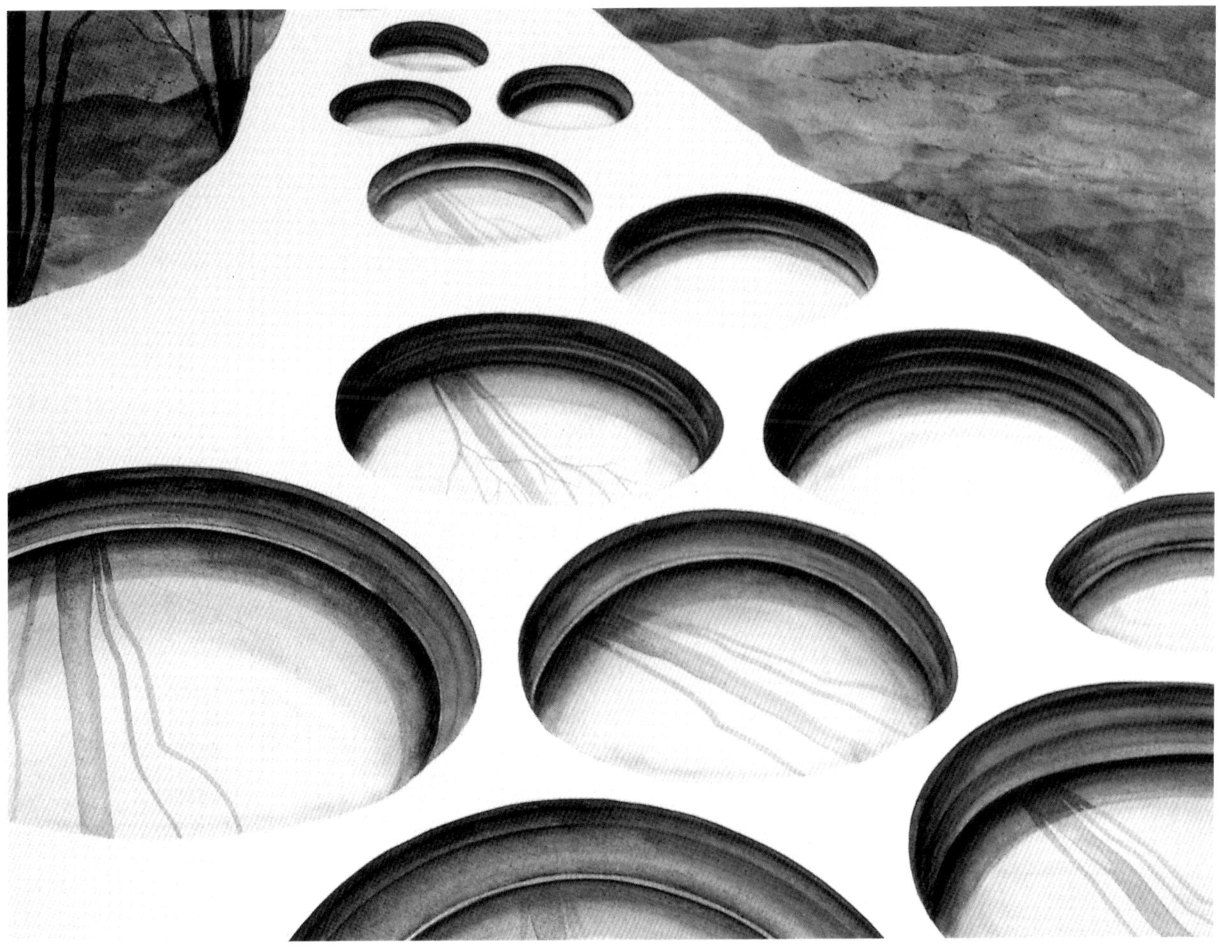

111

Pnina Granirer created a marvelous suite out of these secret places, entitled "Discovery at Gabriola", putting her own personal stamp on the whole exhibition. Even though the artist has already exhibited twice before in Strasbourg and thus is not a stranger to us, she still surprised us by this new height, which more than justifies the international reputation she has developed for quite a few years now. Moreover, far from repeating herself, she treats the most original themes with beautiful control and sobriety, suggesting the silence of the space, disturbed at most by the rumbling of the ocean and the piercing cries of the seagulls. And also by an overwhelming poetry.

— Jean Christian, *Les Affiches-Moniteur d'Alsace et de Lorraine,* February 10, 1987

in the natural landscape, into which wide, deep holes had been cut, as if by a giant cookie-cutter. In the mid-30's, millstones for a pioneer society had been cut from the living sandstone, separated and lifted from the soft strata and exported as far as California and Finland. The eerie voids, suggesting moon-craters or impressions left by extra-terrestrial spacecraft landings, had over time filled with earth, water and rushes. The landscape had been perforated with symmetrical forms totally out of character with everything around them — yet for once, man's exploitation of the land had unintentionally created something utterly strange and beautiful. Granirer rendered these phenomena in mixed-media works, altering the light, perspective and colour, not always bothering, in title, to indicate their origin, as if the mystery was too delightful to explain away.

To better understand the visual and emotional impact of the Millstone Quarry on Granirer's work, it is best to quote the short essay she wrote as an introduction to the paintings inspired by this site:

A few years ago my husband and I went to Gabriola for the first time. Our friends, Jane and Bob, had bought a little cabin there and had given us enthusiastic descriptions of a West Coast Garden of Eden well worth a four

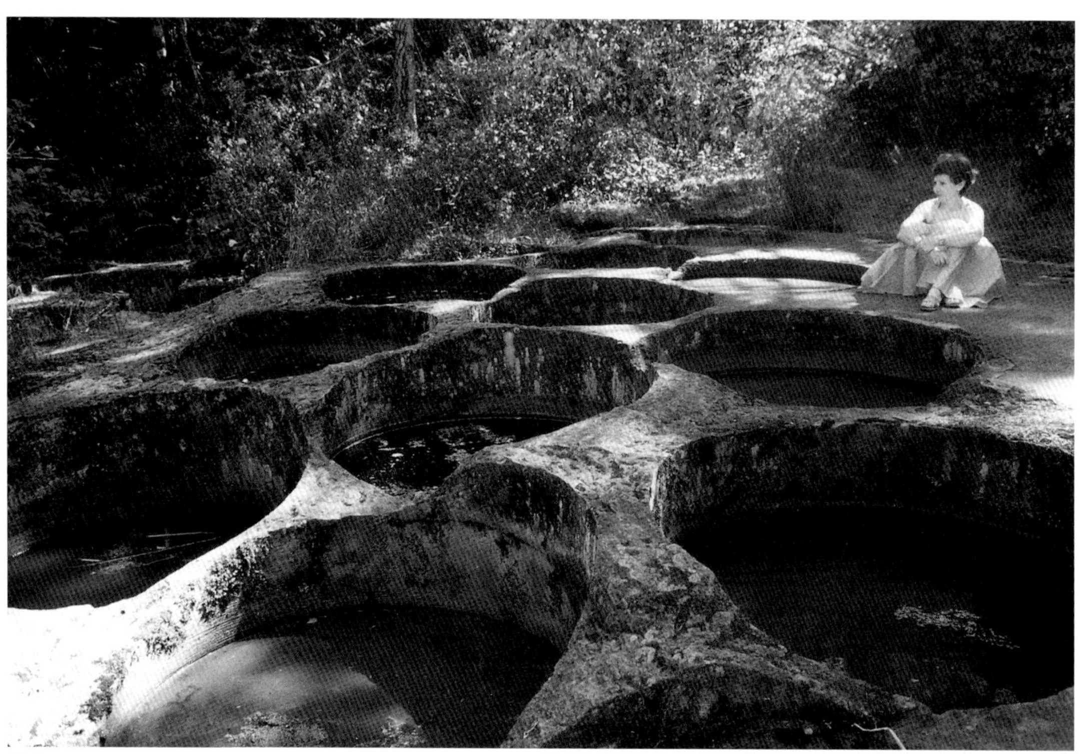

112

112. Abandoned millstone quarry on Gabriola Island, British Columbia. This quarry was operational 1931–36.

113. *Mystery at Gabriola,* 1987
triptych, 3(98 x 71 cm)
3(38 1/2 x 28 in)
acrylic, resist, pastel on paper

hours' trip from Vancouver. They were right. Not only was this visit a most pleasurable experience; such was its visual impact on me, that soon after it was to become a rich source of inspiration for many paintings, photographs and poems.

Our friends took us on a grand tour of the most unusual and beautiful spots on the island. They gave me the first introduction to the sculptural stones on the beaches and to the spectacular Malaspina Galleries, the wave shaped overhang of sandstone high over the still waters of a protected bay. And at the end of the day, they brought us to the most enchanting place of all, the strange and mysterious Millstone Quarry.

There are no signs or directions by the roadside. Just a small clearing between the forest and the road, which gives no indication about the unusual place hidden among the trees.

We park the car and follow the narrow trail, stepping over gnarled roots snaking their way across the path. The sun does not easily penetrate the thick growth; its rays find slim passages through the green branches, creating lacy patterns of light. Here and there one ray breaks through, a slanted line of brilliance connecting the treetops with the soft ground; tiny insects flit up and down this bright path of sunshine like dancers in the spotlight.

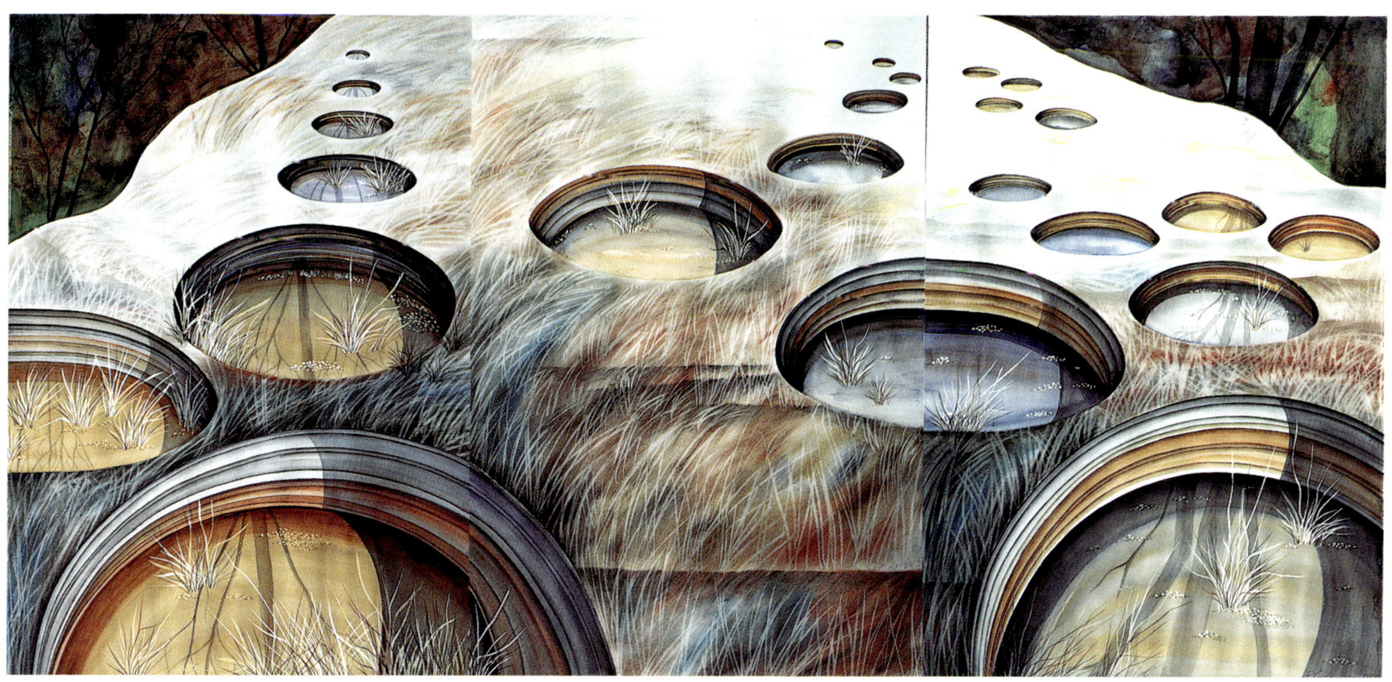

113

114. *Mystery at Gabriola 2*, 1987
111.8 x 76 cm (44 x 30 in)
acrylic, pastel, resist on paper

The trail ends abruptly. I stand at the edge of a clearing. In front of me, a strange sight of deep, round holes carved directly into the bedrock. They are filled with rainwater and thin, sharp blades of wild grasses grow from their depths, like fine drawings reflected back into the liquid mirror. What is this place, this moonscape invaded by rich life forms, and what are these unusual shapes? Has a giant, carrying a huge cookie cutter, been hollowing out these forms for a banquet of sweet giant food? Is this a real place, or is it only a vision?

It is quiet, like in a cathedral; only a bird breaks the silence once in a while with its song. The round holes are empty eyes staring at the sky, drawing the Universe into their depths. A Monarch butterfly tests the weeds briefly, adding a splash of colour. Then it is gone.

In another century people will wonder at the civilisation which left behind these bizarre holes and will try to guess their purpose. Will they think that an unusual religious sect carved these holes for worshipping strange gods? Or imagine, perhaps, that unusual ceremonies of baptism were carried on here, in these round pools? They will probably be just as curious as I in their guessing game.

The magic of the Millstone Quarry has inspired me to produce a series of paintings, some of which were exhibited in Strasbourg, France. At the opening, a woman asked me what these strange holes were and went on to tell me that she had seen similar ones on her hikes through the Vosges mountains, which were thought to be ancient Celtic libation holes.

The truth, unfortunately, is much more prosaic than most of these imaginative answers. With the help of circular saws and small explosives, large cylinders were extracted from the bedrock, to be used as millstones for grinding pulp. In the early thirties they were exported to Finland, to Prince George and elsewhere. But after five years the quarry was closed down; and a wondrous, mysterious place, just off the beaten track, a refuge of heavenly peace was left behind to be discovered by the casual visitor, like an unexpected gift.

114

Culture / Nature Series, & Stones of Worship

The combination of Pnina Granirer's new interest in expressing a feminist redress through *The Trials of Eve Suite* and her sustained preoccupation with an animistic reading of ancient stones, led her to a re-evaluation of culture and nature as it might apply to art.

Paris (ten months in 1986–1987) had provided her not only with the stimulus for *The Caged Birds Series,* but a new opportunity to visit the Louvre and re-experience her favourite works of art through a modified vision conditioned by her growing feminist perspective. Her

115. *From Milo to Saturna,* 1987
56 x 129.5 cm (22 x 51 in)
acrylic, pastel, on torn paper

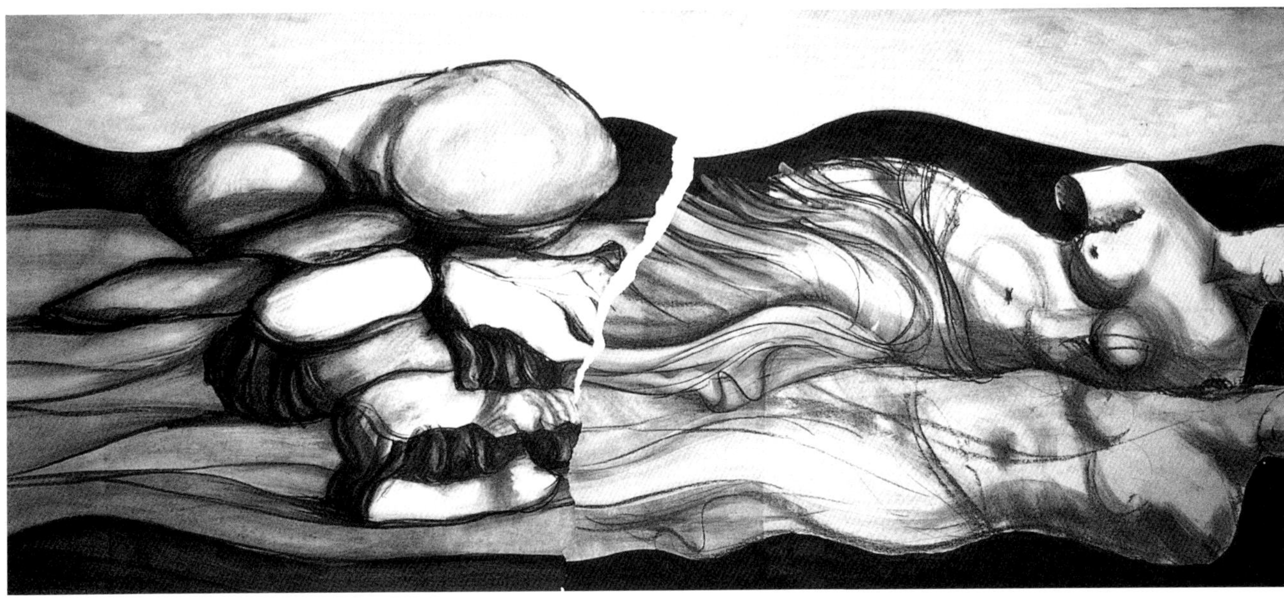

115

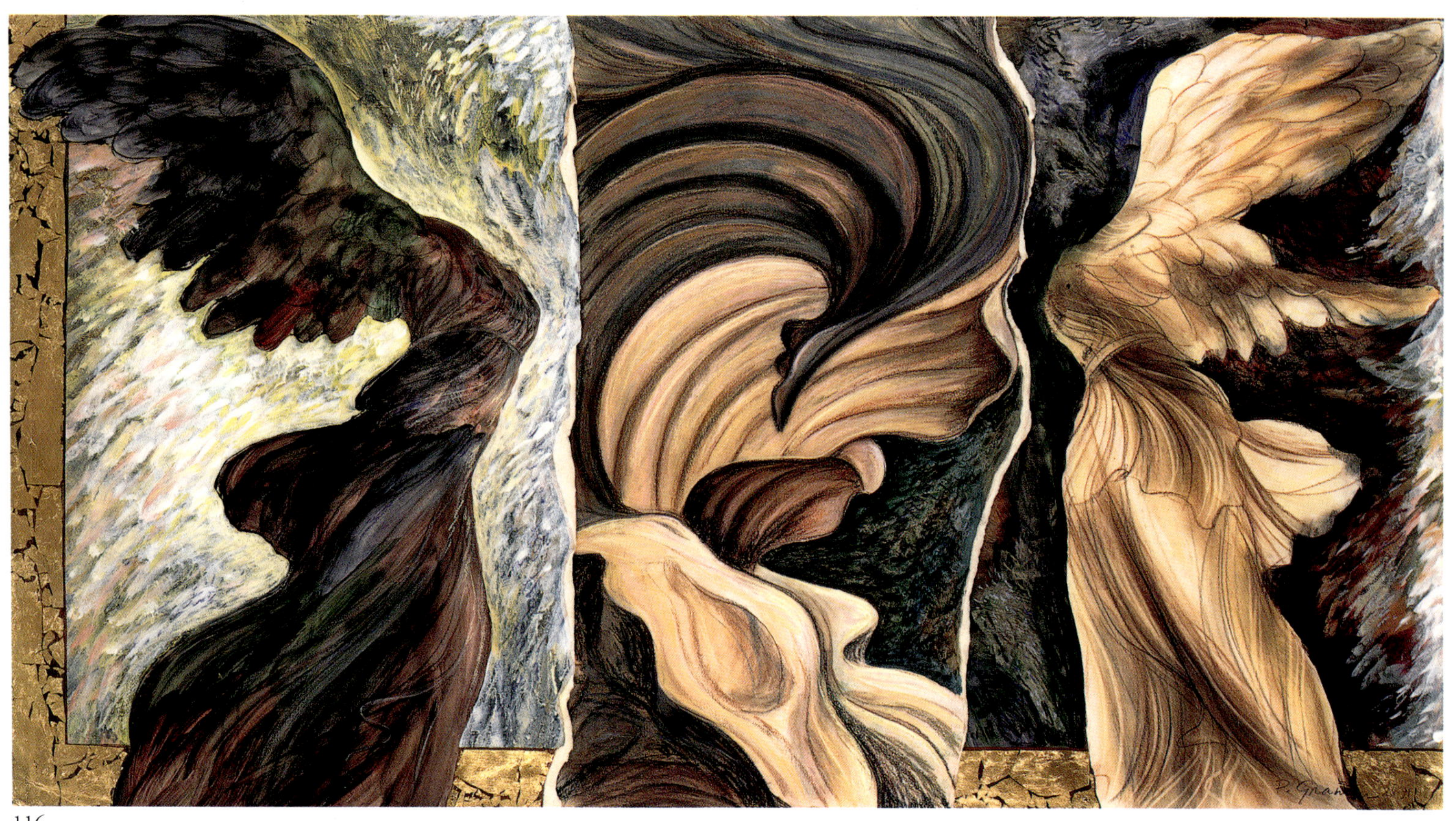

116

most profound experience was in a revelatory reconsideration of the Louvre's dominating Nike (the Greek Goddess of Victory, circa 190 BC, found on Samothrace, an island in the north-east Aegean sea). She realized that Nike possessed qualities unlike any other female figure in ancient art, such as Venus or Aphrodite. Not only was Nike winged, resonating compatibly with Granirer's life-long predilection for angels, but (even headless) was strong, erect and triumphant in a way few other female figures were portrayed in Hellenistic art. There was nothing traditionally soft, sensual or passive in this Nike, alighting from the skies in the prow of a ship, who had stood through the centuries proud and implacable against the sea-winds.

It was also in Paris, with centuries of stone monuments and heroic sculpture at every hand, that she dreamed of British Columbia and its

116. *From Samothrace to Gabriola,* 1988–92
76 x 139.7 cm (30 x 55in)
acrylic, pastel collage on paper

117. *Nike,* 1991
91.5 x 61 cm (36 x 24 in)
acrylic on canvas

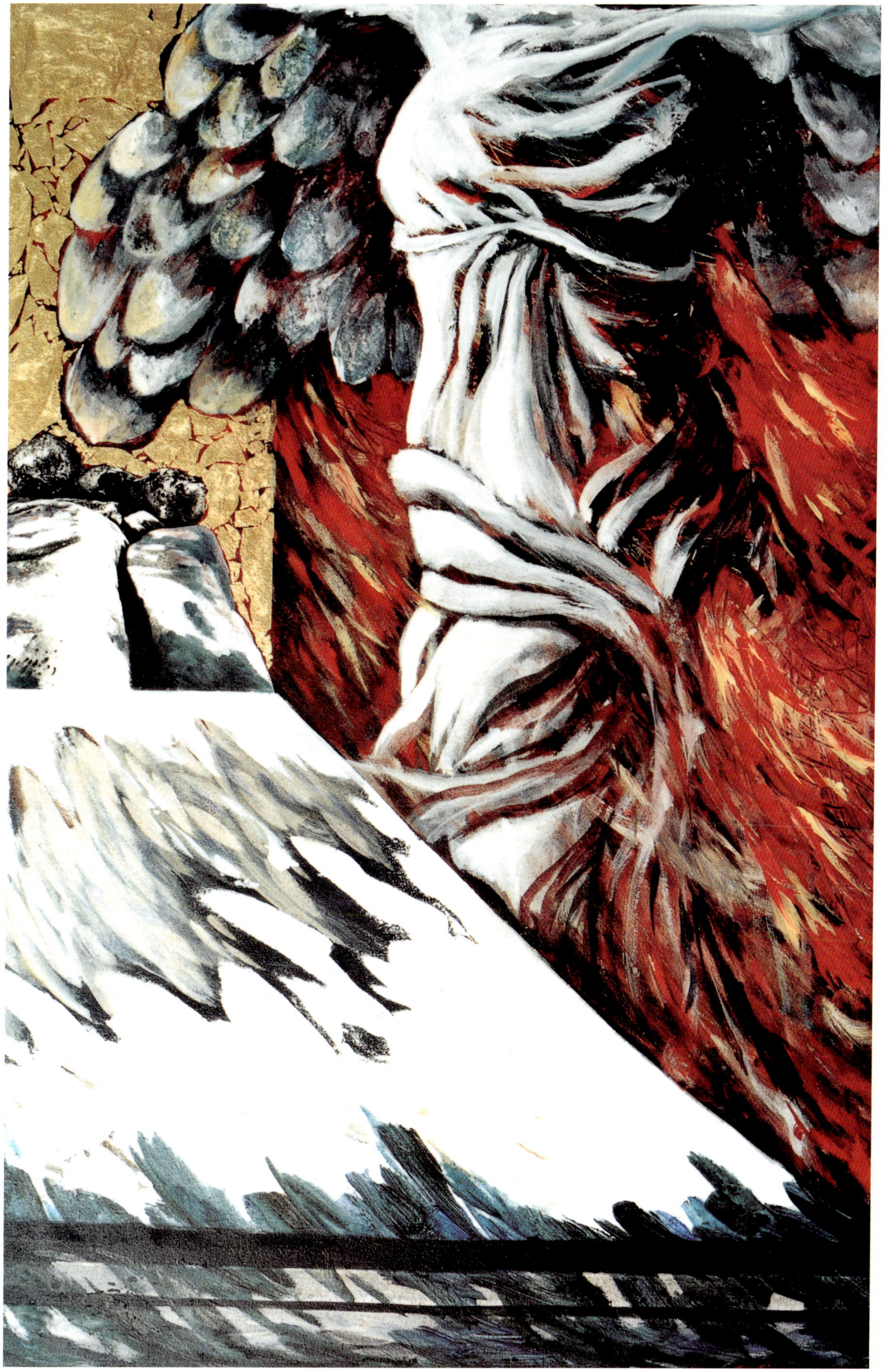

118. *Landscape with Inuit Sculpture,* 1988
triptych, 3(76 x 56 cm) 3(30 x 22 in)
acrylic, pastel, charcoal on paper

119. *Visions of Nike on Gabriola,* 1988
101.5 x 76 cm (40 x 30 in)
acrylic, pastel, collage on paper

nameless rock formations — and began to formulate a comparative theory concerning the overlapping worlds of nature and culture, which developed into the *Culture/Nature Series.* In metaphoric terms, Granirer thought of stone as the common denominator between the two — whether it was carved by man, or by countless eons of wind and water. In her own words:

Although I had seen the sculptures in Paris before, I had never been so aware of them as now, while working on my Carved Stones series. These sculptures were made from stone, the same material as our islands. Here, stone carved by man represented culture, considered in our civilization as superior to nature, which, in turn, is seen as female. Nature was to be dominated, exploited and raped by the (mostly male) culture, which was extolled and admired for its spiritual qualities.

I felt compelled to bring these stone symbols of culture back into the stone landscape from whence they had come, back to the source which gave them life. The arrogance of culture towards nature, its need to dominate and

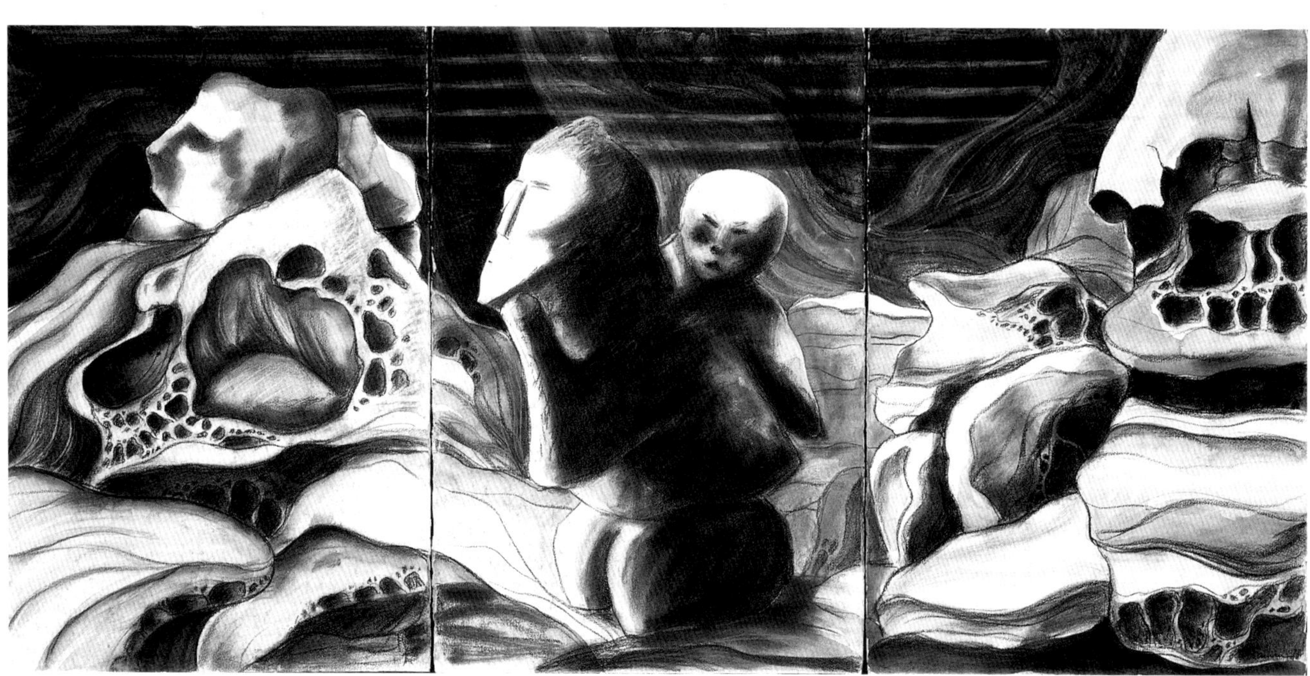

118

enslave, has diminished the human race and is destroying the very source which nurtured it. My wish was to integrate the two. The thread which has been running through my work for a very long time — as the angel and the devil— the dark and the light— culture versus nature— was surfacing again.

In a 1988 mixed-media work, *Visions of Nike on Gabriola,* these Paris threads are brought together. Granirer has installed Nike figures in her Gabriola millstone cavities, wedding the Old World to the New, as if this had been preordained through the millennia, waiting for a catalyst such as her to complete the act. As Granirer comments:

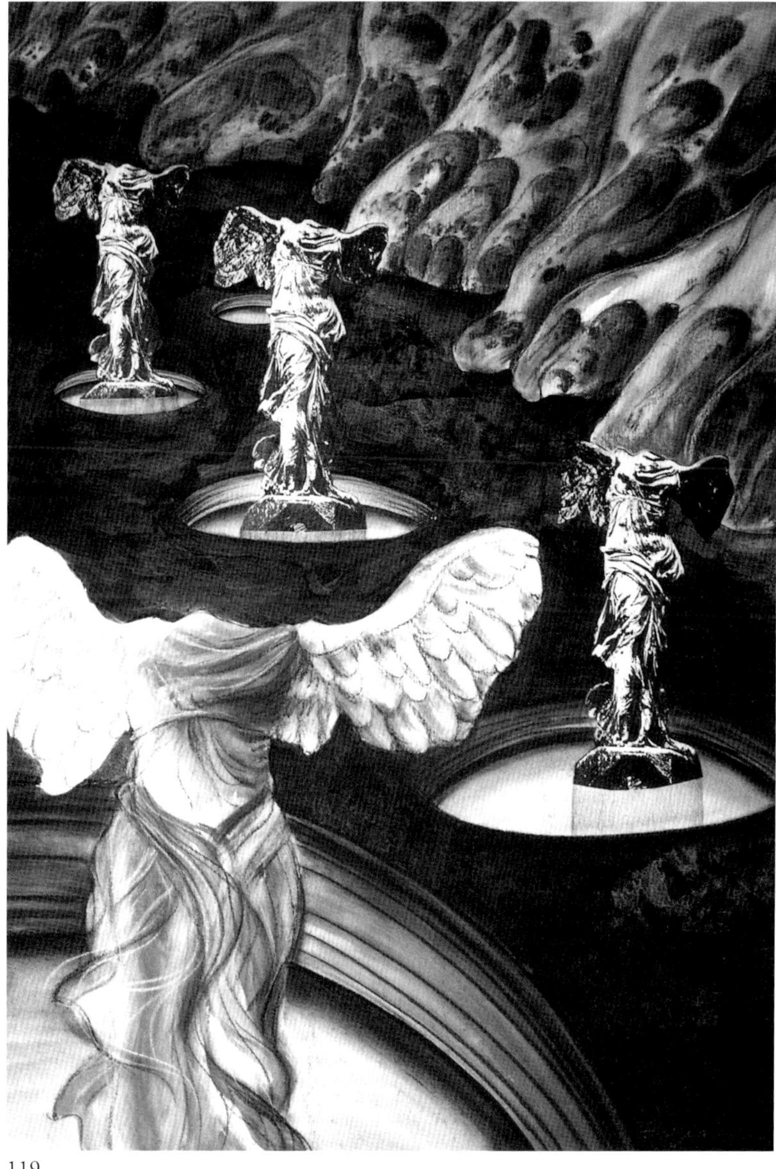

119

This exhibition represents one of many stages in the development of Pnina Granirer's Carved Stones Series. *As Granirer states, "there is a thread through my work, linking the past with the present." Granirer explores this link by superimposing the ancient stone carvings that chart the history of civilization with the natural stone carvings that chart the history of the earth. She interprets history as people moving through the landscape, presenting us with a visual link between centuries and across continents.*

Early exploration began as Granirer was growing up in Romania, and continued as she was studying and living in Israel, France and Canada. She participated in and absorbed the spiritual, social, psychological and aesthetic aspects of these cultures. What resulted was artistic brainstorming out of which the Carved Stones Series emerged.

Granirer chooses stone as a universal medium. She sees ancient stone carvings as transformations of a natural element that individualize cultures and in her words "provide historical references for the journey of humankind." The stones carved by both humanity and nature are silent witnesses to what has gone before.

After living in Canada for several years, Granirer has come to see our ancient monuments as the stone formations carved by nature. The Canadian landscape, still so much a part of our artistic culture, is what connects us to the universal experience and to other artistic cultures.

Granirer believes that artistic culture is humanity's personal reaction to nature and she explores the struggle for integration and separation that exists between the two. Her integration of drawings of the sculpted rock formations along with the stone carvings of ancient and primitive cultures, places the relationship between nature and culture in an historical context. In a time when technology and environmental change place us in competition with nature, Granirer reminds us of the creative potential for a positive relationship with nature.

She also explores the masculine and feminine forces in both nature and humanity. Visually, the carved and textured surfaces of stone represent the qualities of vulnerability and power inherent in both the feminine and masculine aspects of humanity and nature.

Granirer is an optimist and through her work emphasizes the regenerative powers of harmony, richness of spirit rather than destructive powers of conflict, and the depletion of spirit.

We are very pleased to be representing the work of Pnina Granirer at the Art Gallery of the South Okanagan. The Carved Stones Series *represents an important stage in the development of Granirer's imagery and acknowledges her place in contemporary Canadian Art.*

— Jane Clark, Director/Curator

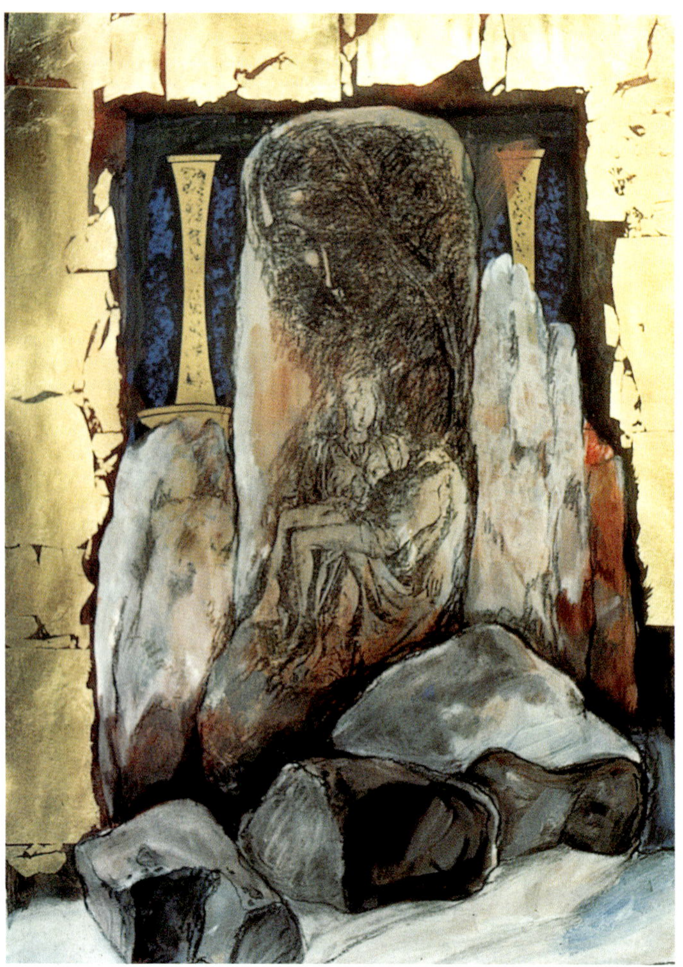

120

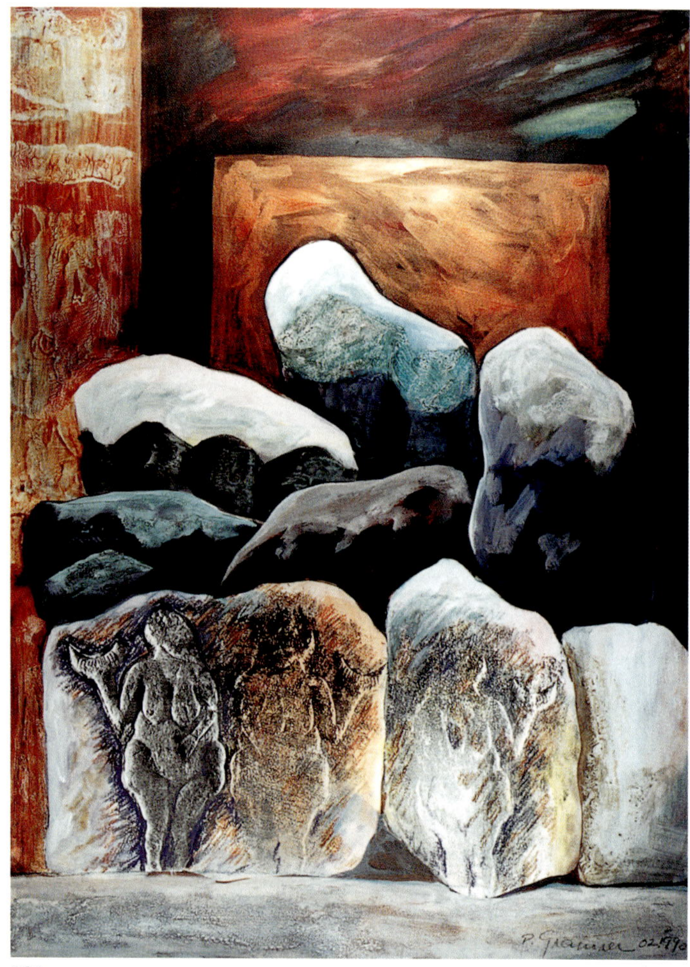

121

The image of Nike became a catalyst for expressing my feelings of liberation and personal freedom. She is different from the many other female sculptures of antiquity. Her wings about to take flight, she boldly strides forward, her gown billowing in the wind. I painted her again and again, not realizing how much I wanted to be her. At one point I painted her rising from the flames like a Phoenix — and was fulfilled (ill. 117).

120. *Pietà,* 1990
from the *Stones of Worship Series*
76 x 56 cm (30 x 22 in)
acrylic, transfer, pastel, grease pencil on silkscreen
Collection of Kirsten Skov

121. *Testimony,* 1990
from the *Stones of Worship Series*
76 x 56 cm (30 x 22 in)
acrylic, pastel, transfer, collage on paper

In 1989, and with equal alacrity, Granirer employs line and pastel subtleties in another nature/culture exercise, *Headless Stone,* reiterating her infatuation for insinuating classicist sculpture into the glacial stone carvings and pitted sandstone strata of the Gulf Islands. Beyond the seeming contradiction of time and geography, there is a strong argument for the universality of a human spirit in congruence with a much older, unknowable, earth-history.

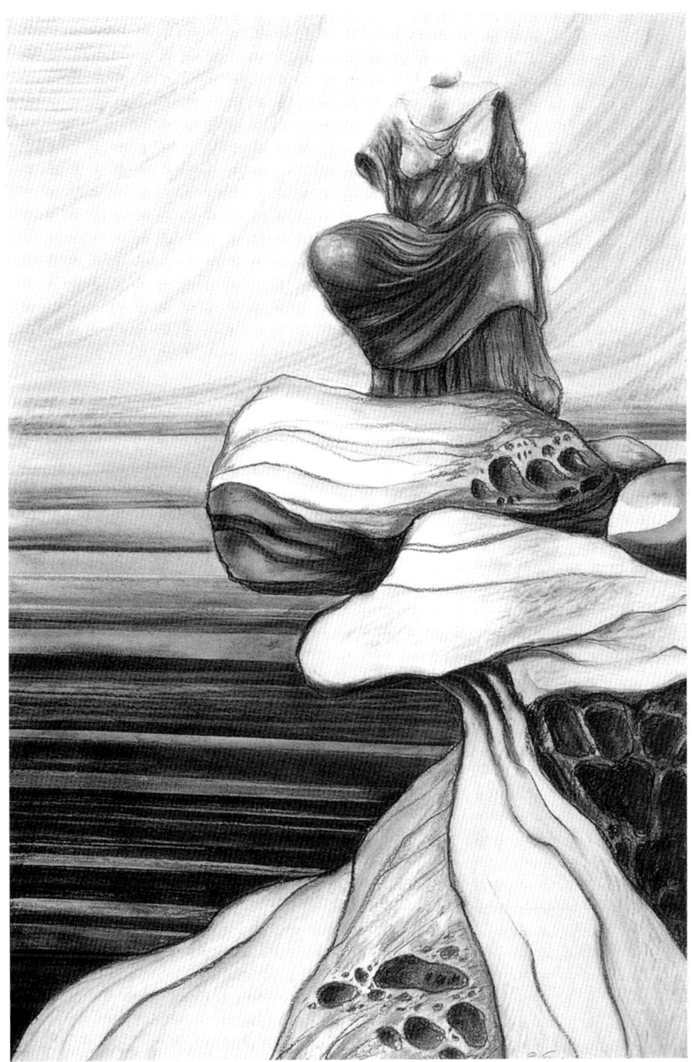

122

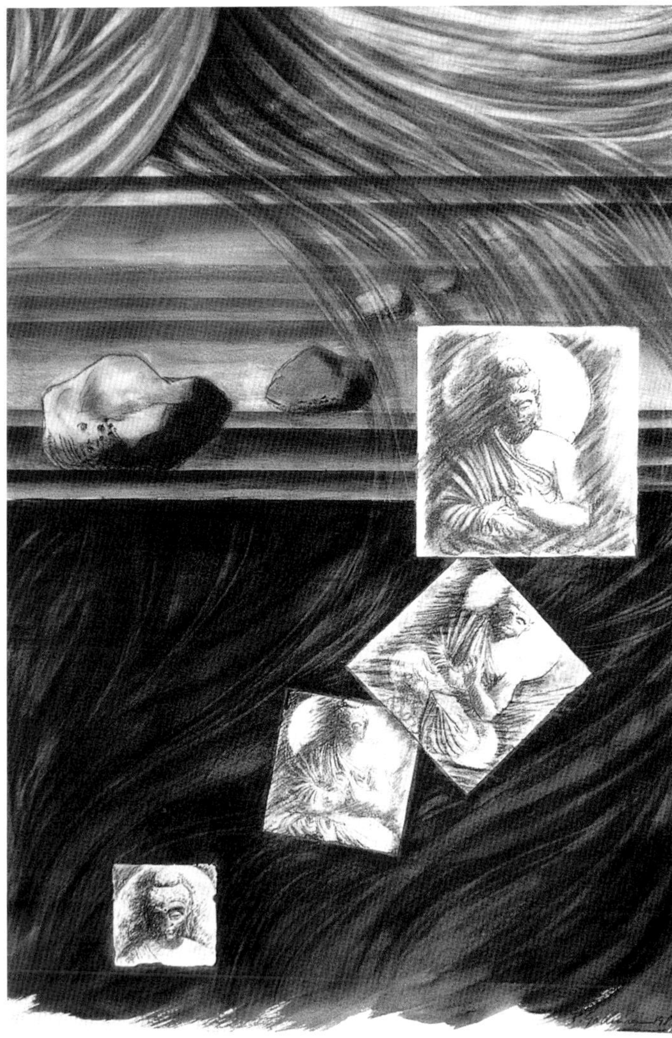

123

Titles such as *Conversation With Venus, Apparitions on Gabriola, Victory in Stone, Beach Sculpture* and *Stone Face* punctuate her 1988–1991 passion for altering natural sculptural qualities of stone into "stones of worship", "stones in the sky" (à la René Magritte), pyramids, stone temples, and numerous stages and evocations of stone figuration. Paintings like *Pietà, Testimony* and *Meditation with Buddha,* form part of a sub-series entitled *Stones of Worship*. They all include sculptural images made of stone and designed to be worshipped. This is a comment on the universal attempt by human beings to appease and control nature, through prayer or magic incantation, by carving natural elements such as stone into various godlike shapes. Used in this fashion, stone becomes the common denominator between nature and culture.

122. *Headless Stone,* 1989
111.8 x 76 cm (44 x 30 in)
acrylic, pastel on paper

123. *Meditation with Buddha,* 1987
from the *Stones of Worship Series*
101.5 x 76 cm (40 x 30 in)
acrylic, graphite, transfer, pastel on paper

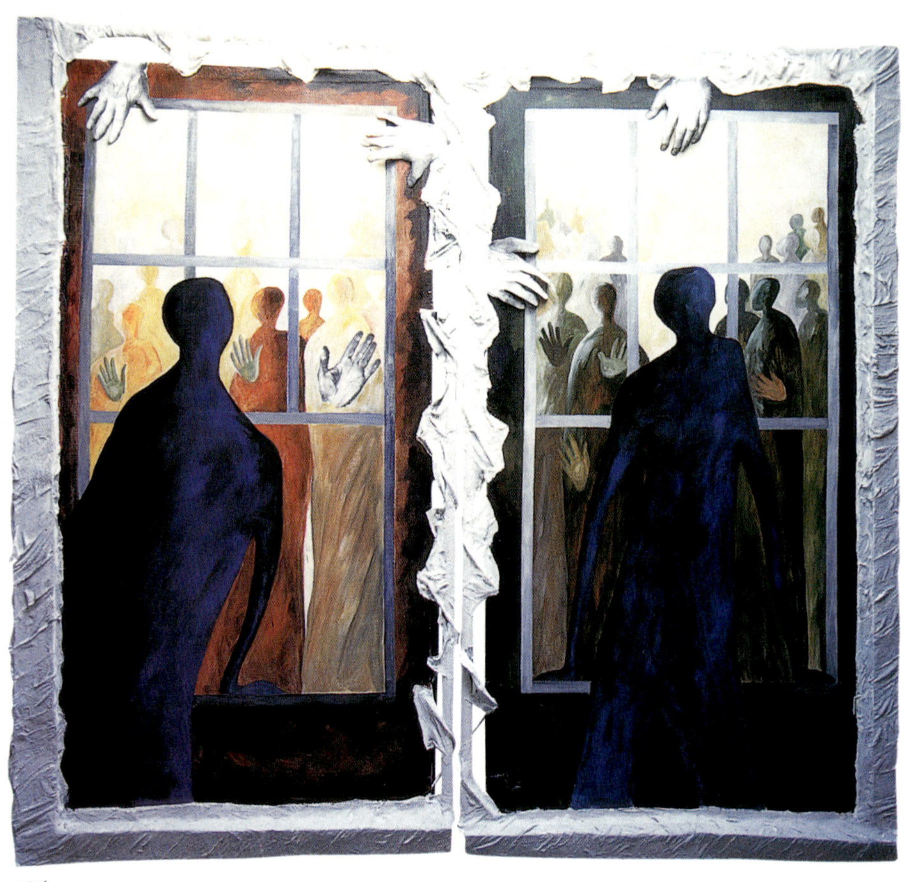

124

The first exhibition of *Fear of Others — Art Against Racism,* was held in Vancouver in 1988. For this Granirer created a diptych entitled *Invisible Barrier,* now in the collection of the United Nations Human Rights Commission in New York City. This was a mixed media piece *par excellence.* Instead of canvas she used plasticized tarpaulin from a garden screen, stretched on aluminum frames. These she covered with plaster, creating a disquieting frame around the work. The lifelike hands reaching out of the window frames are her own, xeroxed and collaged. The window, a transparent, "invisible" barrier, separates the two lonely figures from the group with a disturbing finality.

In 1989 Granirer was part of the organizing committe for the second International juried exhibition of *Fear of Others,* held at the *Roundhouse* in Vancouver. For this occasion she organized a number of panel discusssions dealing with topics such as racism in art and censorship. While searching for participants, she thought of the prominent American artist Leon Golub, whose impressive work on political topics such as

124. *Invisible Barrier,* 1987
diptych, 2(155 x 84 cm) 2(61 x 33 in)
acrylic, collage, plaster on tarp
Collection of the United Nations
Human Rights Commission, New York

125. *From the Flames,* 1988
triptych, 3(111.8 x 76 cm) 3(44 x 30 in)
acrylic, transfer, collage, graphite on paper
Collection of the Yad Vashem Museum, Israel

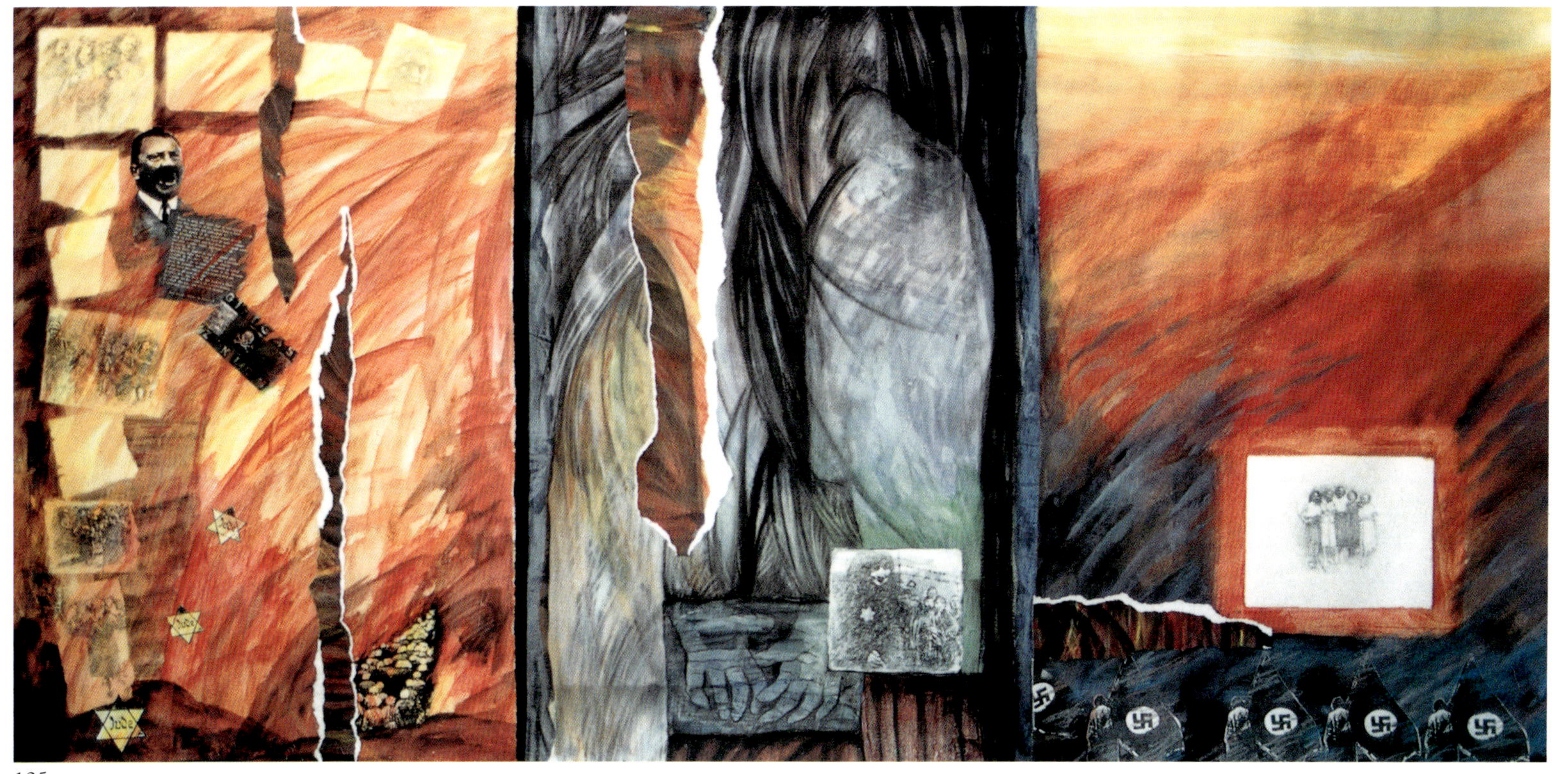

125

the Vietnam war and torture in South America she had seen in museums in Montreal and New York. Granirer called him in New York, inviting him to participate in the exhibition and on one of the panels. His response was immediate and positive. He also offered the participation of his wife, Nancy Spero, the well known feminist artist. The panel, dealing with censorship in the arts, was sponsored by and held at the Vancouver Art Gallery.

For the 1989 exhibition, Granirer produced *From The Flames,* a 1988, 44 x 90-inch triptych (acrylic, collage, photo-transfer, pastel, graphite on paper) now in the collection of Yad Vashem Museum, Jerusalem, which combines the imagery of eternal stone figures surrounded by the flames of the Holocaust and the collaged symbols of Naziism (swastikas), Judaism (stars of David), and the random, candid images of oppressor and victim alike. Granirer graphically underscores the irony of a Nazi culture destroyed in a conflagration of its own making from which emerges, Phoenix-like, a new Israel.

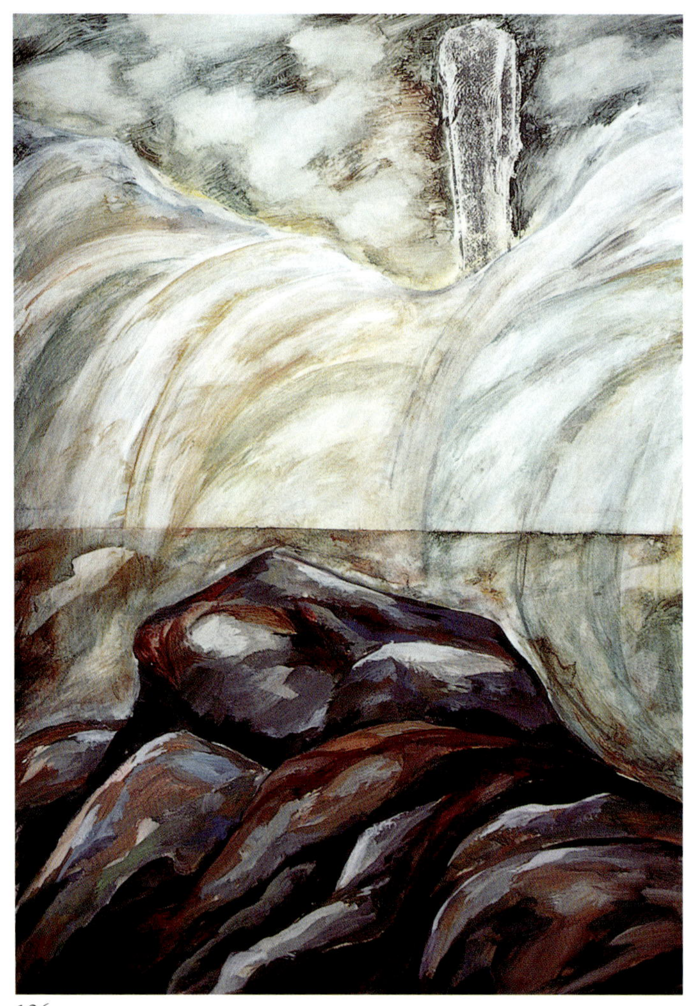
126

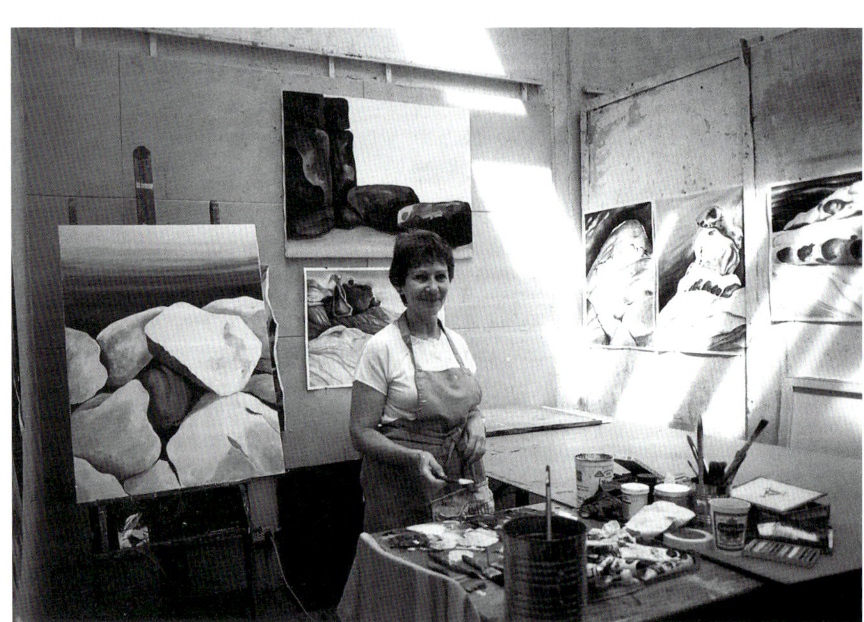
127

126. *Apparition,* 1989
99.5 x 70 cm (39 1/4 x 27 1/2 in)
acrylic, transfer on paper

127. Granirer in her makeshift studio space at Emma Lake, 1989

Emma Lake

In the summer of 1989, Granirer participated in a two-week session of the internationally acclaimed Emma Lake artists' workshop. This event, organized by the University of Saskatchewan since the mid-50's, and inviting guest artists and critics such as Barnett Newman, Jack Shadbolt, Clement Greenberg, Frank Stella, Greg Curnoe, and many others, had become a well-known summer artists' retreat.

The workshop was situated on the shore of Emma Lake, an isolated nature oasis reached after a long drive from Saskatoon through endless fields of yellow canola which stretch far into the horizon. This was the first time Granirer had been given the opportunity to immerse herself totally in making art, removed from all domestic and social responsibilities. The brief but intense experience of Emma Lake had a great impact on her work. She took time to experiment with different techniques, achieving a new freedom in the handling of paint and engaging in more canvas work. Her paint became looser, sometimes permitted to drip freely down the canvas. This technique was to reach a climax with her *Eden Series,* in 1994.

This shift in technique came none too soon. Granirer was now afflicted with arthritis, particularly in her hands, which made it painful and uncomfortable for her to draw or do precise work, as she had formerly done. The freedom of using the brush in great, gestural motions, enabled her to continue painting as an exciting new experience.

While at Emma Lake, Granirer kept a daily journal. Following are some passages, which give insight into her work at the time:

Monday, July 17, 1989

One loses track of time here. I can't believe that in the 3 days (only!) that I've been here so far, I've done one painting and 4 works on paper and started two more . . . It is quite unreal and marvellous to go to the studio at 6:00 a.m. and work as long as one wishes. The only structure is the meals. It is probably something the women here appreciate much more than the men — being free of the cooking chores.

I'd like to simplify more and maybe get more abstraction in the work, perhaps these 2 weeks will help me. I miss talking to someone with positive criticism.

Tuesday, July 18, midnight

The lake was gorgeous this evening. Water like a mirror with lovely pastel pinks and blues. Incredible gold-lined cloud formations.

Wednesday, July 19

Today I did a painting which worked! Yesterday I was feeling so downcast about the canvases — too heavy and literal, really. But the one today — I used very thin paint and let it drip, so that it is quite transparent. Only the

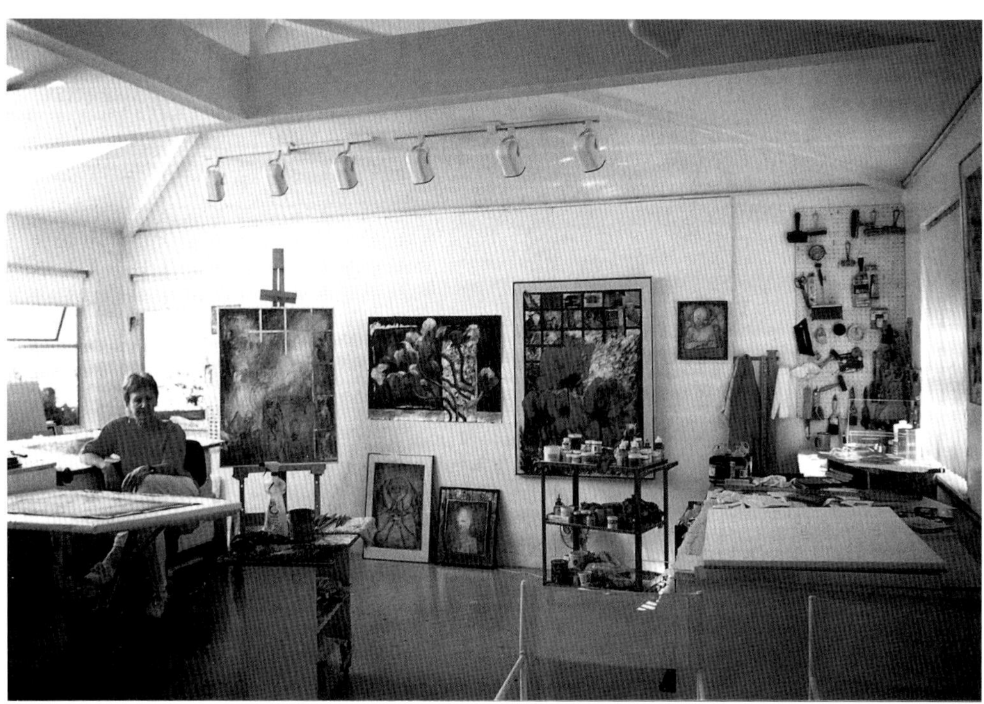

128

128. New studio on the back of the house

129. Exterior view of the new studio. The wall paintings are parts of sets done for *A Midsummer Night's Dream*

rocks are a bit heavier. Then I wiped areas and the white of the canvas showed, it became stylized clouds and I got beautiful textures all over. I was very pleased!

Saturday, July 22, evening

It was a good day. I worked some more on two paper works (big) which I did yesterday. On one I transferred two beautifully stylized goddess figurines of the Cyclades, dating 3500–2800 B.C.

Monday, July 24

I am starting more and more to get a better sense of who I am as an artist, and to care less about the uneven — illogical way art is evaluated. I feel this awareness slowly taking shape here. I look at my work and compare it to others' — and it looks good. Is is very different, indeed, probably does not "fit in", but it is, for this reason, more personal and unique.

Wednesday, July 26

A breakthrough! I did a painting on paper which worked all the way. The sky area which always gives me trouble came out well — painting over light colour with darker paint, then wiping and spraying water and wiping again. I feel really great about it.

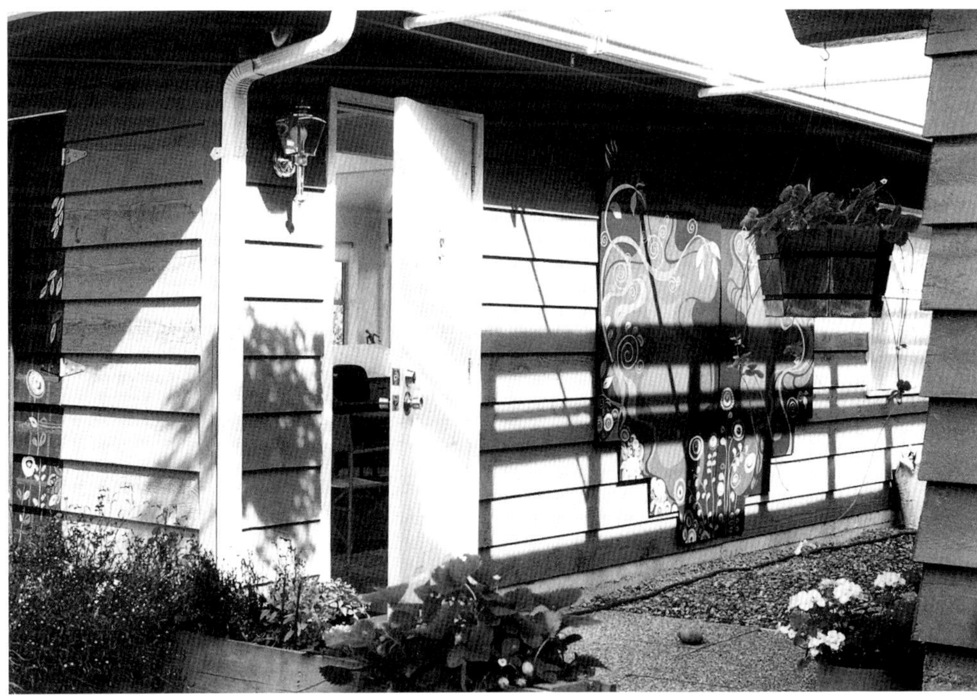

129

Kyoto / Buddha Series

During a trip to Japan in 1990, Granirer was delighted to see how a selected piece of stone placed in waves of raked sand in the formal garden of a monastery was revered by the monks and lay devotees. Seventeen days in Japan not only confirmed her own integration of classical sculptural forms with the forms of nature, but also demonstrated to her the Japanese artistic capacities for simplicity, economy, and restraint, particularly in regard to natural motifs.

Back in her studio, she began graphic evocations of the multifarious Buddha-image and the powerful memories of monastery gardens, in which all aspects of humanity and nature were allegorized in the simple arrangement of natural materials placed in harmony with one another. Most of all, she enjoyed working with images developed from Japanese architecture, which encloses, frames, sets off the visual delight of inexpressibly beautiful and understated, timeless forms.

It would appear that Granirer was not trying to make "Japanese art" — but rather was making an homage, in her own way, to everything that Japanese art represented to her; was integrating her new findings into an overall aesthetic. As with the lessons of Art Nouveau, her general leanings (consciously or unconsciously) toward the Pattern and Decoration movement, her recognition of the subtleties evinced by Northwest Native art, allowed Granirer to incorporate all her experiences into her painting. All of these inquiries have been, incidentally, a skirting of mainstream modern art and abstraction. Nonetheless, she was heading toward these sensibilities.

The classic red gate in a semi-abstract work titled *Torii,* 1990, effectively replaces the window/mullions of Granirer's earlier works,

130. *Buddha with Blue Diamonds,* 1991
76 x 56 cm (30 x 22 in)
acrylic, collage, pastel, silver powder on paper

131. *Stone Garden 3,* 1991
10 x 12.2 cm (4 x 5 in)
acrylic, collage, silver powder on paper

132. *Stone Garden 4,* 1991
10 x 12.2 cm (4 x 5 in)
acrylic, collage, silver powder on paper

133. *Chaleur/Heat,* 1991
76 x 56 cm (30 x 22 in)
acrylic, gold transfer on paper

creating a framing structure for the planes and textures of nature viewed in light and shadow. In a more complex composition, *Phoenix,* 1990, mixed media on paper, the Japanese patterns of regularity and economy represented by post-and-beam construction and classic shoji screens (which are also curiously reminiscent of the bird-cages of Paris) play off against a free painting in gold which depicts a triumphant, utterly free phoenix bird, perhaps signifying the unfettered spirit which rises above all conformity.

In *Buddha With Blue Diamonds,* 1991 (ill. 130), Granirer once again is impelled to create a mixed-media work with stone figures emerging from grey abstracted walls and rocks, accented with square diamonds of sky-colour and one flat red element: variations on the Nature/Culture dichotomy. As it turns out, the Japanese motifs are perfect foils in her ongoing allegories; the raked gravel undulations against the formality of the shoji patterns; the natural stone against the developed carving of myriad Buddhas; the expressiveness of gold against the cooler hues of stone and water. One of the last, and also most inventive, in this general series of Japanese inspiration is *Chaleur/Heat* (ill. 133). It is semi-abstract, featuring a basic fan shape decorated with branches and blossoms (which also brings to mind a section of the planet/globe), standing in front of an aperture with free-standing shoji pattern, with darker "wings" — a swirl of gestural brushmarks in red, white and blue,

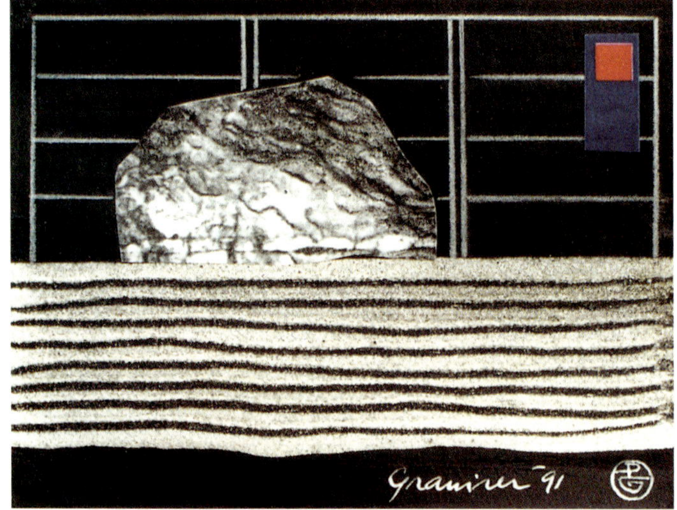

131

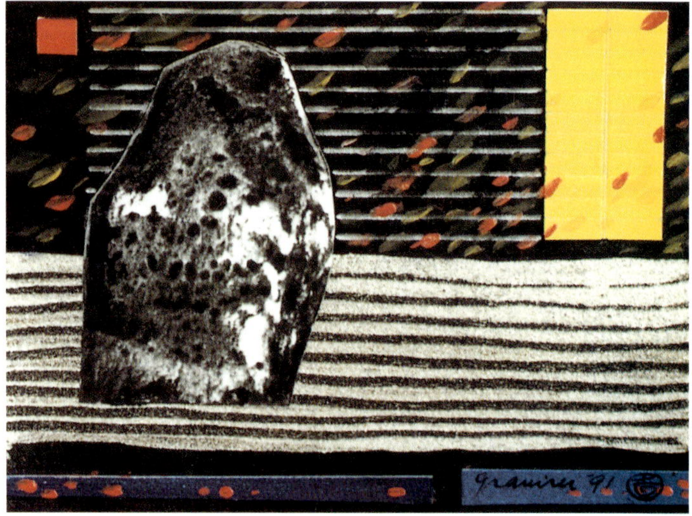

132

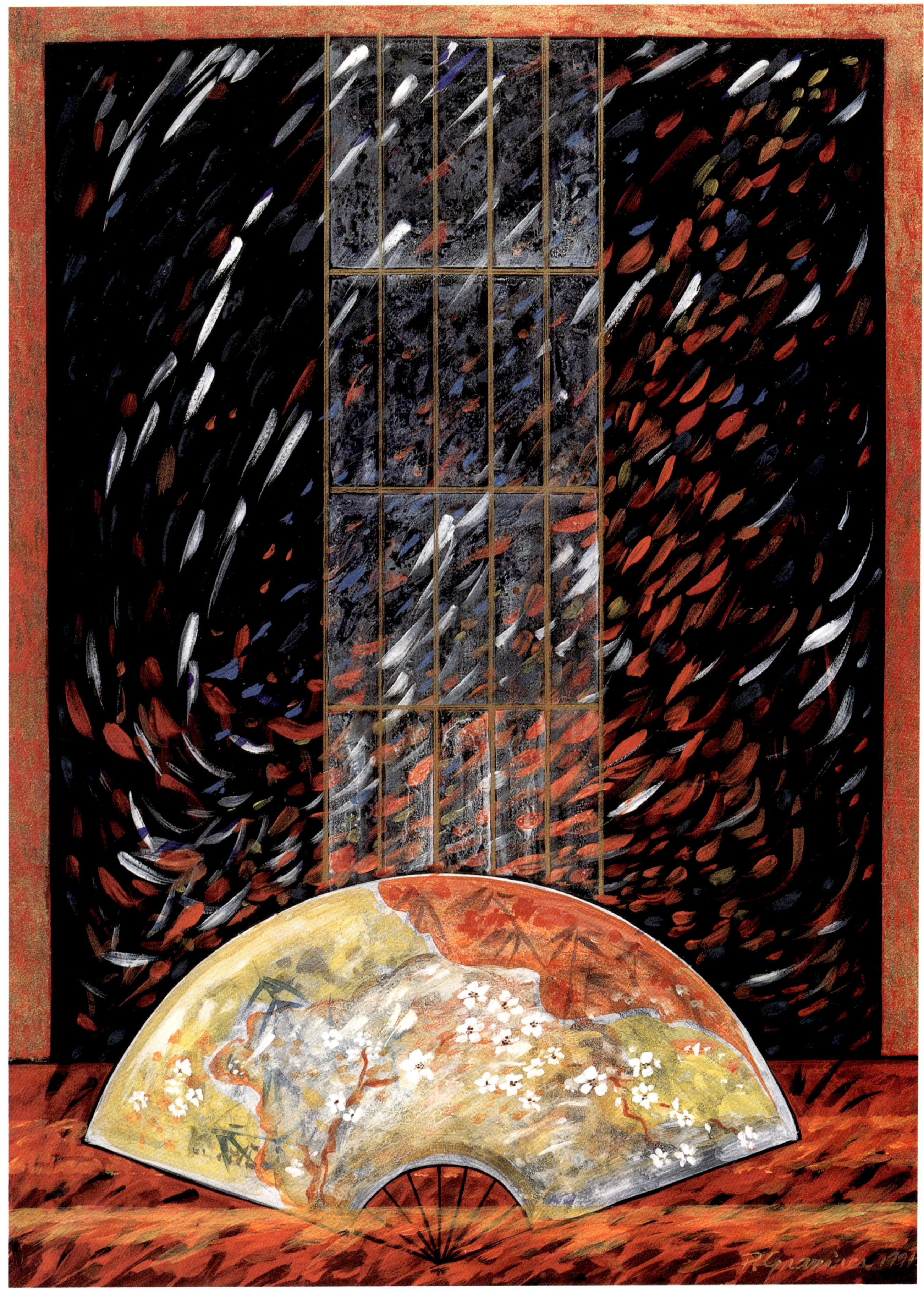

134. *Screens,* 1991
56 x 76 cm (22 x 30 in)
acrylic, collage, transfer, graphite on paper
Collection of Keiko Honda and Dan Granirer

135. View of Procession during the Easter celebrations of the Semana Santa, in Madrid, Spain, taken by the artist.

framed in gold on three top sides and reddish/orange on bottom (a "floor" on which the fan rests).

Kimono, 1991, mixed media on paper, is equally intriguing as a shape which does not need to be read immediately as a kimono (rather, as an abstract configuration) and suggests a tightening grasp on modernist principles.

For twenty-five years Granirer had worked in a small room on the second floor of her house; its only advantage was that it contained a sink. The room's size had actually determined certain methods — the habit of working in panels which combined into diptychs and triptychs — which were easier to handle and store. If she began working on larger canvases, lack of space became prohibitive.

On her return from Japan, she decided that the time had come for her to build a real studio. A spacious new structure was built in the back garden of the house, bathed in north light and facing the huge expanse of Vancouver Harbour and the snow-capped mountains beyond. She finally had a real "room of her own". Although her working habits did not change a great deal, her feeling about her art did. The new studio (ill. 128, 129), with its skylights and spaciousness, its separation from the house proper, led to larger works and new levels of experimentation.

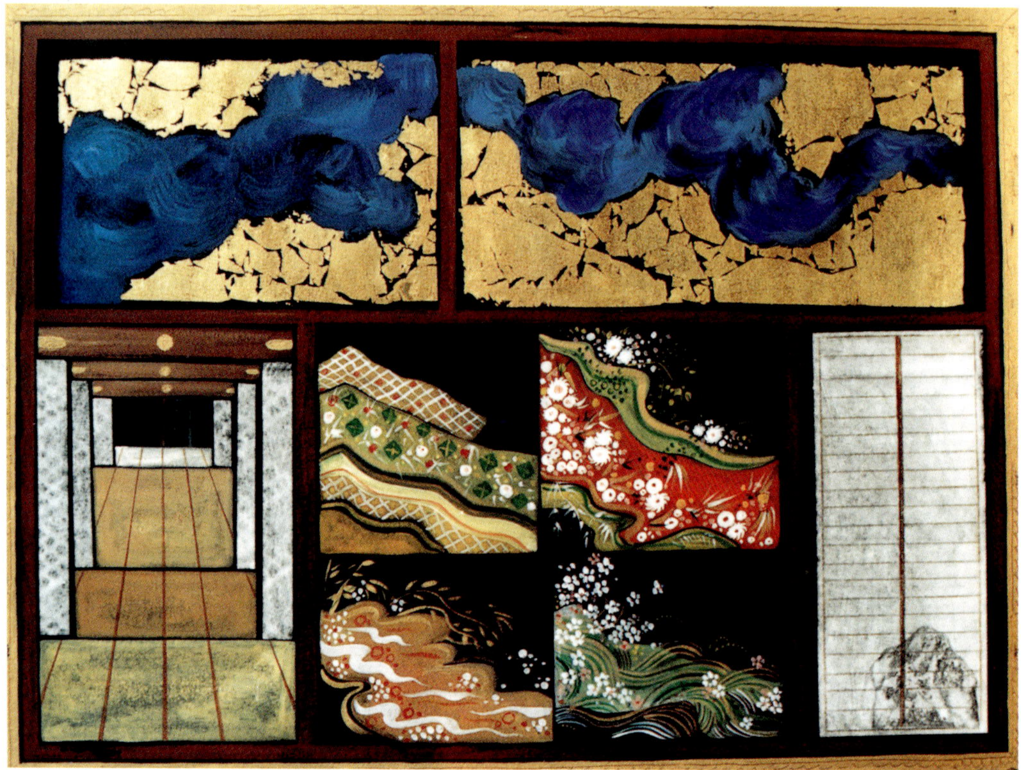

134

Spain — The Alhambra Suite

In much the same way as Japan had inspired the *Kyoto Suite,* Spain in 1992 provided Granirer with a bonanza of visual stimuli, motifs and instinctive associations interwoven with her philosophic outlook. She comments:

In Spain I found the light and the dark again. I saw the Alhambra as the symbol of light, while the Inquisition and war symbolized darkness. In the new series I called "Juxtapositions", I inserted images of this darkness (mainly as small collages of xeroxed images of hooded penitents or warriors from the frescoes from the Salla de las Bataillas at the El Escorial), within the beauty of the garden, a small warning that darkness is always lurking within the light.

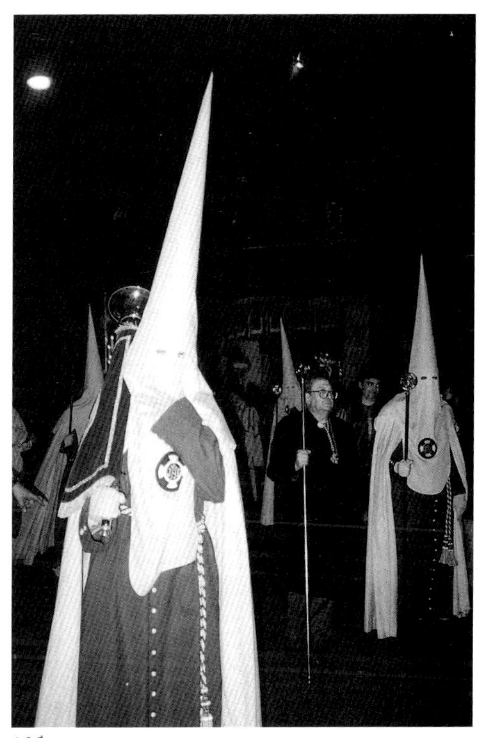

135

The catalyst for the greatest Spanish renaissance was the Moorish invasion from North Africa, which lasted roughly 700 years: Moors, Arabs, Syrians, Egyptians and Berbers created this westernmost province of Islam, beginning in 711, bringing with them artistic forms, science and technology unknown to the Spanish. This was Islam at its most expansive and tolerant: religion was free; women had equal educational chances; libraries, universities, observatories flourished; poets abounded, and musicians were lauded; life was considered glorious in itself, to be ennobled by learning and enlivened by every kind of pleasure.

The Moors were the waterers of Spain, the gardeners: they brought new grace to her culture, they taught her people the techniques of irrigation, and as their own spirit degenerated into excess and sybaritic fancy, so they infused the Spanish stream with additional embryo traces of its romanticism — early inklings of swirl, smoulder, quarter-tone and castanet. To this mix was added the arrival of Gypsies and Jews (not by invasion but by migration) who beneath the tolerant aegis of Islam, enjoyed a golden age for at least three centuries: Spanish Jews became rich, honoured, cultivated and influential.

The remnants of this high culture, the fanciful key-hole doorways, intersecting arches and colonnades, traceries, wrought iron filigrees, gardens, pools, fountains, opulent tilework, carved stone, alcoves and landscaping is what Pnina Granirer saw: the cultivating of nature for the sake of its beauty (a new idea to Europe when the Moors introduced it, as their Koranic theme of Paradise). Moorish Spain is therefore filled with personal implications for her, a parallel to her own predilections and search for humanistic accord in a troubled world.

With *Fountains,* a mixed-media triptych completed in 1992, Granirer recalls the sensuous forms and genial colour combinations achieved by Moorish artisans: the always eccentric and fanciful delineations of pools and streams with backdrops of tiles decorated with star-

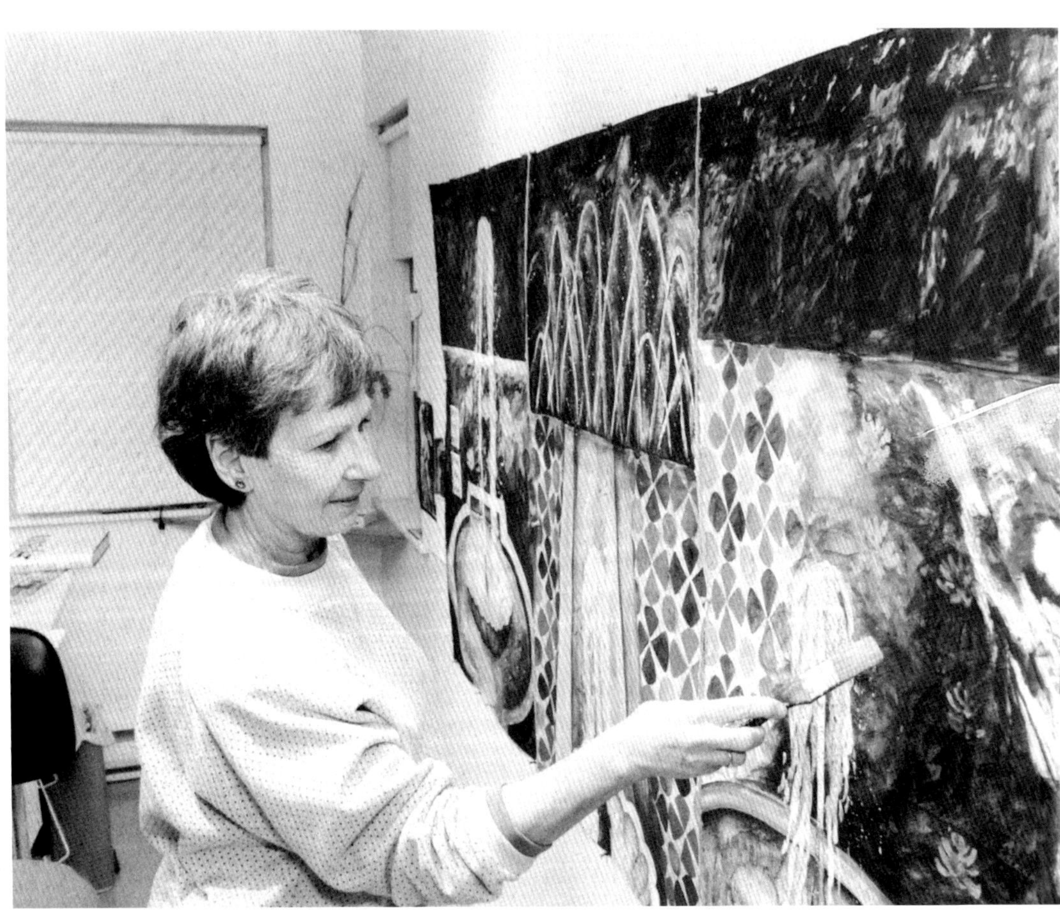

136

136. Granirer painting *Fountains* in her studio

137. *Fountains,* 1992
triptych, 3(101.5 x 76 cm)
3(40 x 30 in)
mixed media on paper

bursts and bold geometries. She is naturally sympathetic to the colour spectrum of that time: copper and manganese produced the greens and purples; cobalt oxide created a spectrum of blues, with rich white copper and golds to bring out the other colours.

In contrast to this Edenic metaphor, Granirer presents the other side of the Spanish coin in *Procession* (ill. 142), also 1992, an arched, candle-lit blaze of yellow and gold surrounding a file of black and white-hooded present-day religious penitents (chillingly reminiscent of Ku Klux Klan attire and ritual) which evokes nothing so much as the Inquisition that followed the Moorish defeat and the cruel expulsion of the Jews from Spain. The light and the dark. *Forever Reaching* (ill. 143), a mixed-media diptych on canvas completed in the following year, underscores even more harshly the provocative Heaven/Hell riddle of humanity. Granirer balances the figure of a swordsman-archangel (the commanding bronze guardian of Franco's immense Falangist graveyard, the Valley of the Fallen) against the nebulous, ephemeral apparition of Paradise. God's hand, such as the hand Adam attempts to touch in the Sistine ceiling, points cryptically toward a cascade of heavenly white foxgloves from Granirer's studio garden.

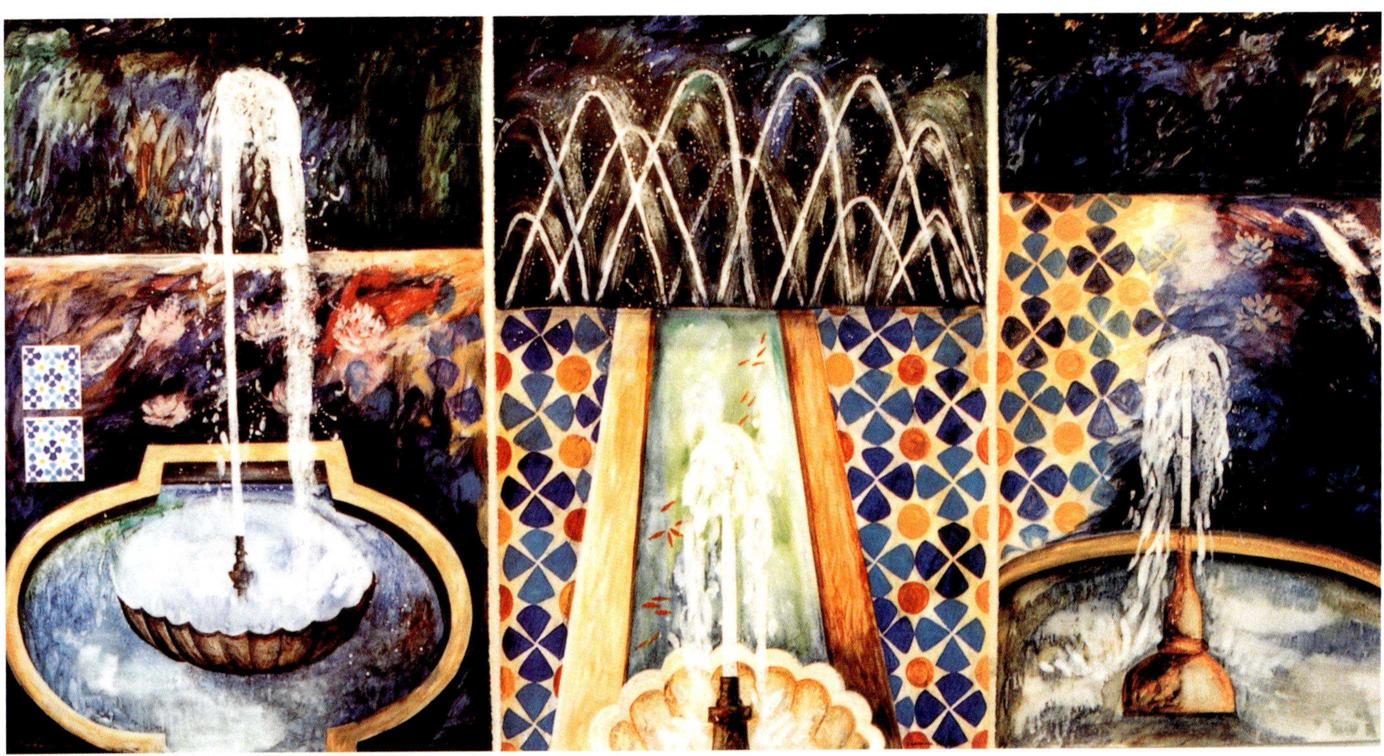

137

The restored gardens of the Alhambra in Granada stand as a monument to a brief time in history when there was a place where there reigned peace, tolerance and a great love of art. Today one walks along paths shaded by oleanders, the air balmy with the heavy perfume of orange trees in bloom. The sound of water trickling from fountains everywhere throughout the garden follows the visitor with its sweet, tinkling music. Water is the main theme of the Alhambra, a symbol of life, of rejuvenation, its coolness healing in the midmorning sun.

I have been working with images from these gardens for the past two years, their beauty and peace a much needed balm for our souls so battered by the constant barrage of headlines screaming with violence, wars, strife and conflict. We need to have a place where we can find respite and healing, where we can find peace even if for a short moment; if not a garden, what better place is there for all of these?

Statement for *Gardens of Spain*, at the Sandstone Studio, on Gabriola Island, June 1994

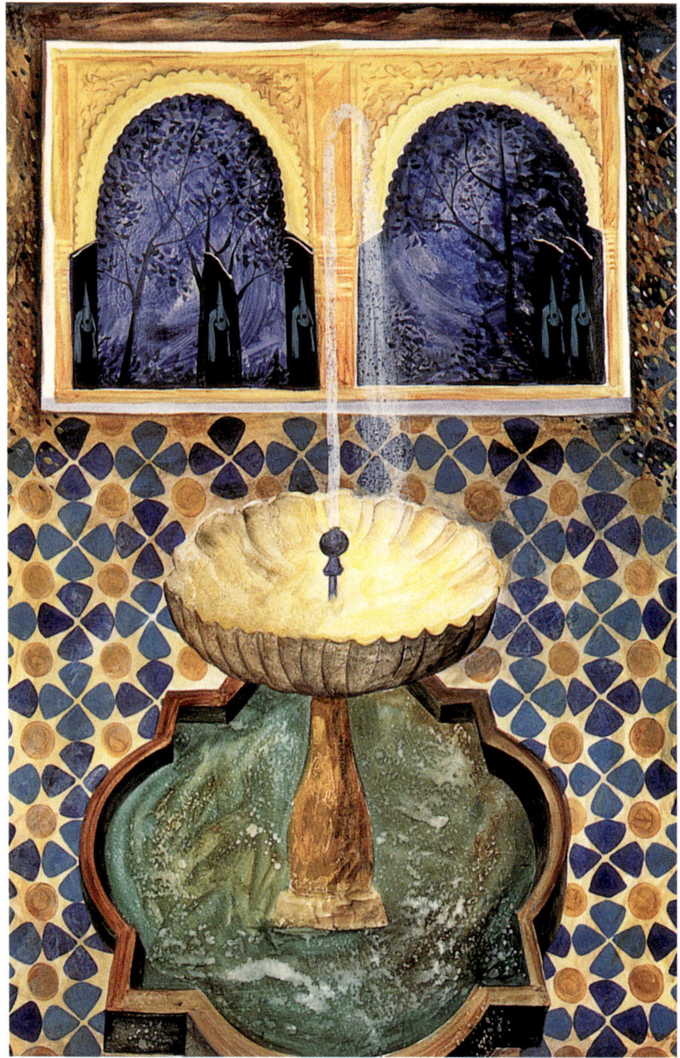

138

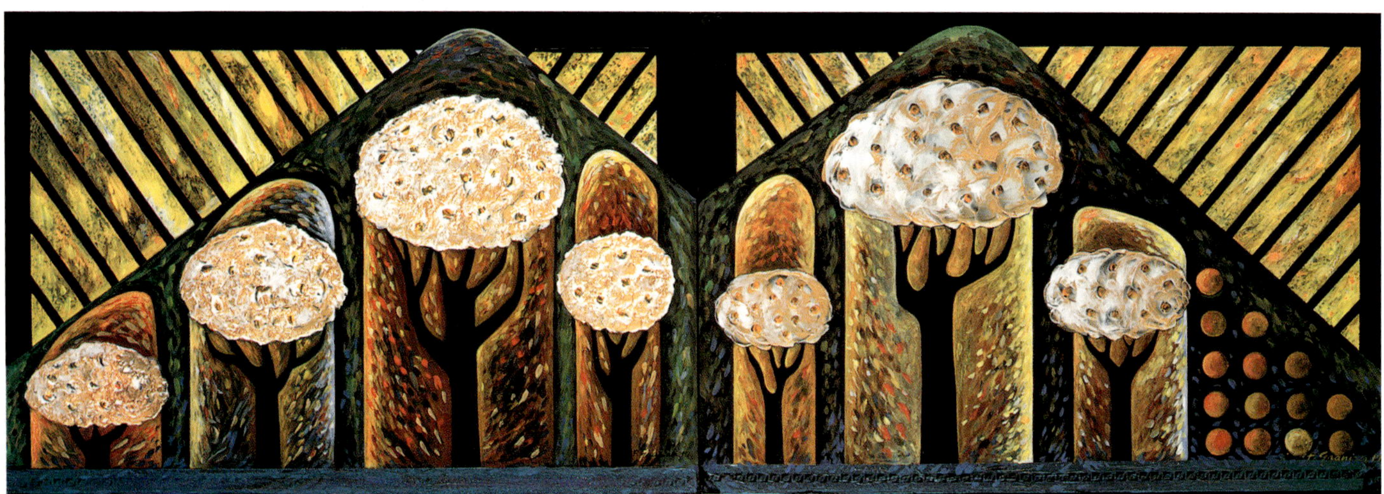

139

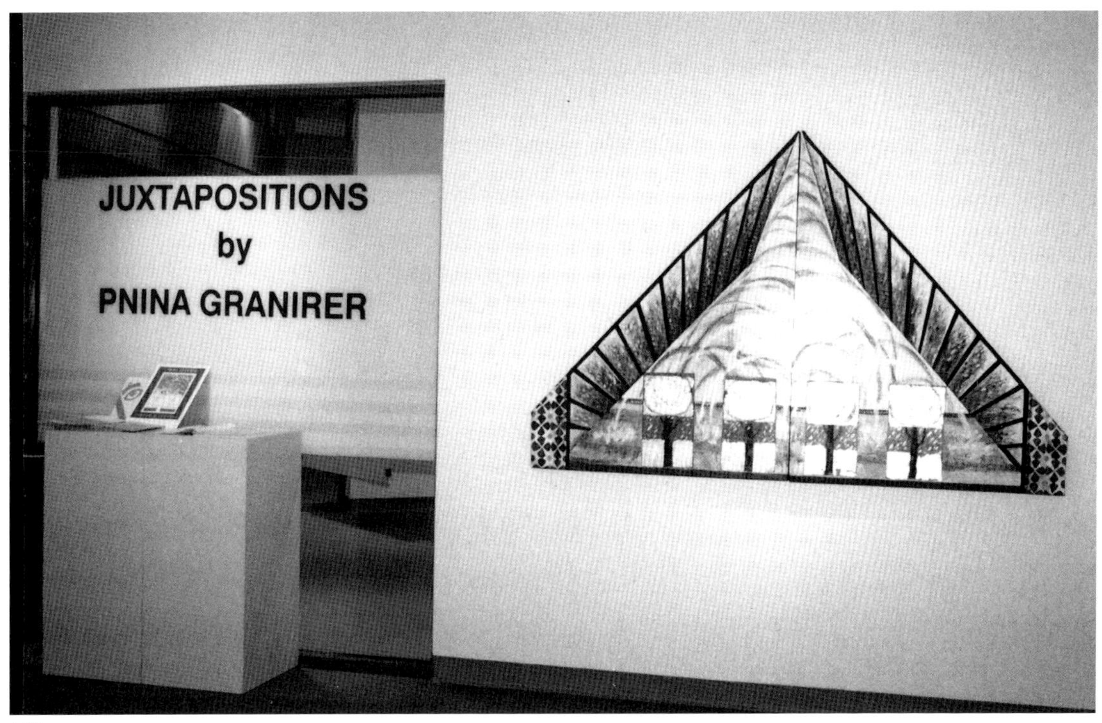

140

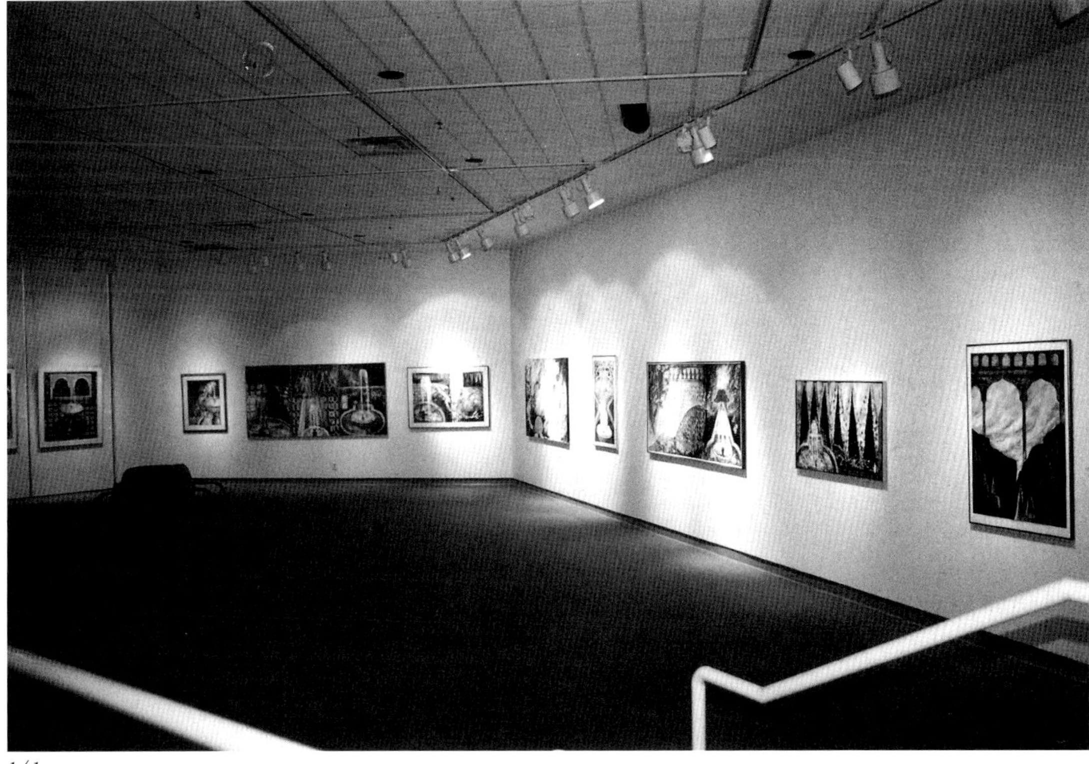

141

138. *Fountain with Shadows,* 1992
101.5 x 76 cm (40 x 30 in)
acrylic, collage, modelling paste on paper

139. *Orange Trees,* 1993
69 x 183 cm (24 x 72 in)
acrylic, modelling paste on canvas

140. *Juxtapositions,* 1993
Exhibition of the Alhambra paintings at the Richmond Art Gallery. Featured here is *Perfect Harmony,* 1993
diptych, 2(120 x 95.2 cm)
2(47 1/2 x 37 1/2 in)
acrylic, collage, modelling paste on canvas

141. Installation view of *Juxtapositions* at the Richmond Art Gallery, 1993

142. *Procession,* 1992
76 x 56 cm (30 x 22 in)
acrylic, collage on paper

143. *Forever Reaching,* 1993
diptych, 2(91.5 x 61 cm) 2(36 x 24 in)
acrylic, collage on canvas

144. *Poppies at Alhambra,* 1994
76 x 111.8 cm (30 x 44 in)
mixed media on paper
Collection of Shelley Nitikman

Through the presence of the poppies, this work represents the transition between the *Alhambra Suite* to the *In Search of Eden Series.*

Perhaps it is here that a number of simple truths begin to present themselves in her work, signalling the shift from the almost Biblical heaviness and profundity to a new, less-burdened, more humanly graspable level of consciousness. With *Orange Trees,* 1993 (ill. 139), for instance, Granirer revels in the multiplicity of rich decoration in a formal design, which could be likened to a stained glass motif, cast against the symbolism of seven trees (cf. the Jewish menorah), which may be read alternately as prosaic Spanish citruses or the ever-elusive trees of Life and Knowledge.

It is the combination, it would seem, of brief sojourns in Japan and Spain that ultimately resolved philosophical problems in Granirer's work: her need to deal seriously with fundamental questions of life's origin, possible meaning and ultimate consequence.

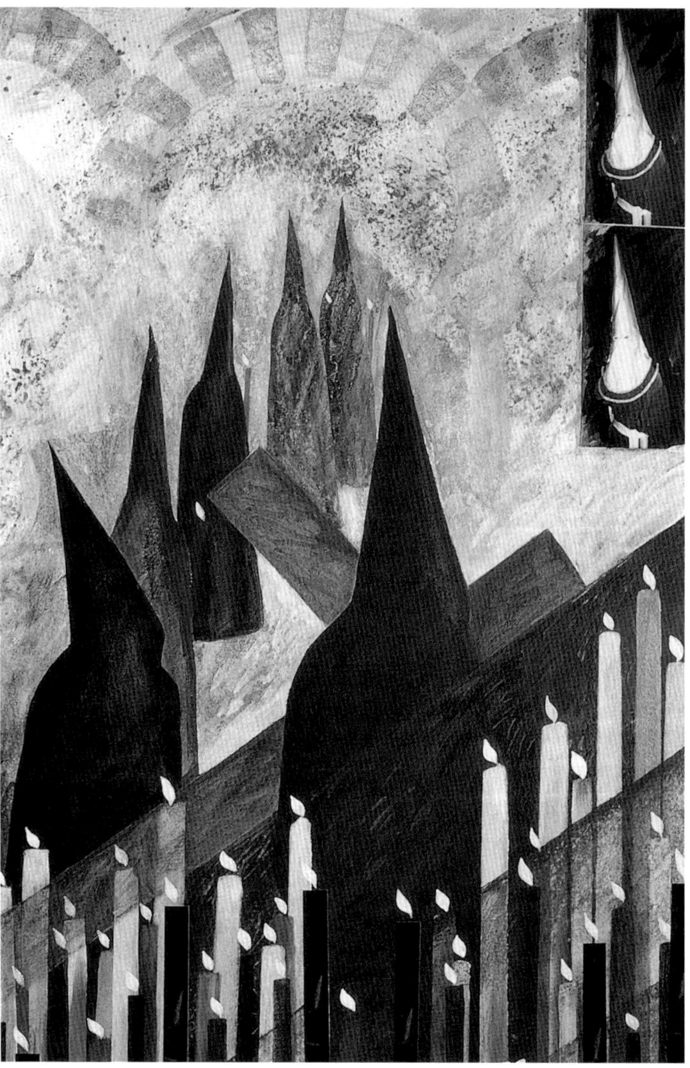

142

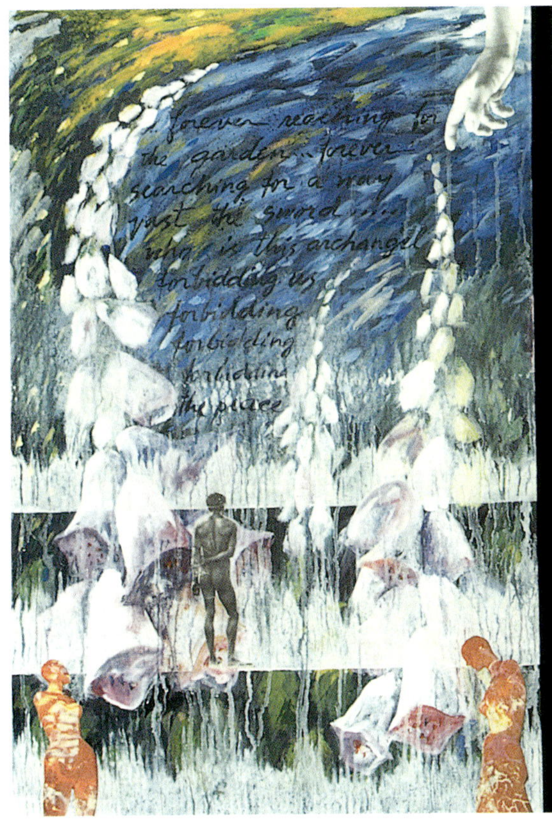
..forever reaching for
the garden..forever
searching for a way
past the sword.....
who is this archangel
forbidding us
forbidding
forbidding
forbidding
the peace

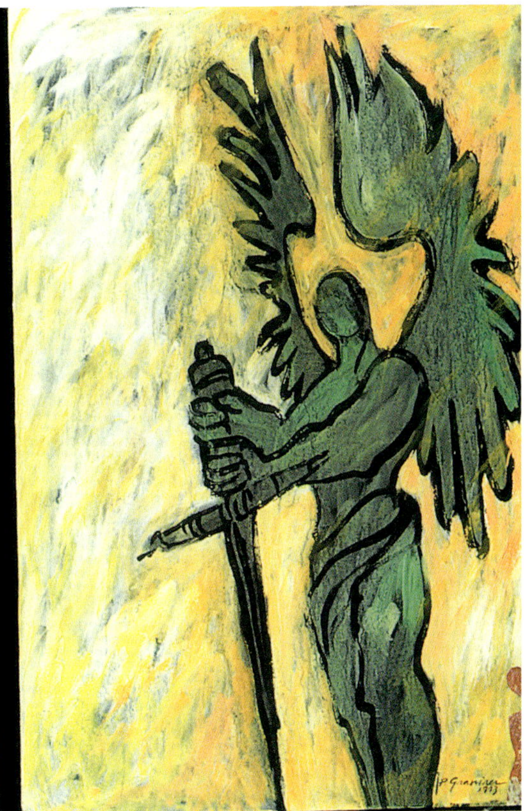

143

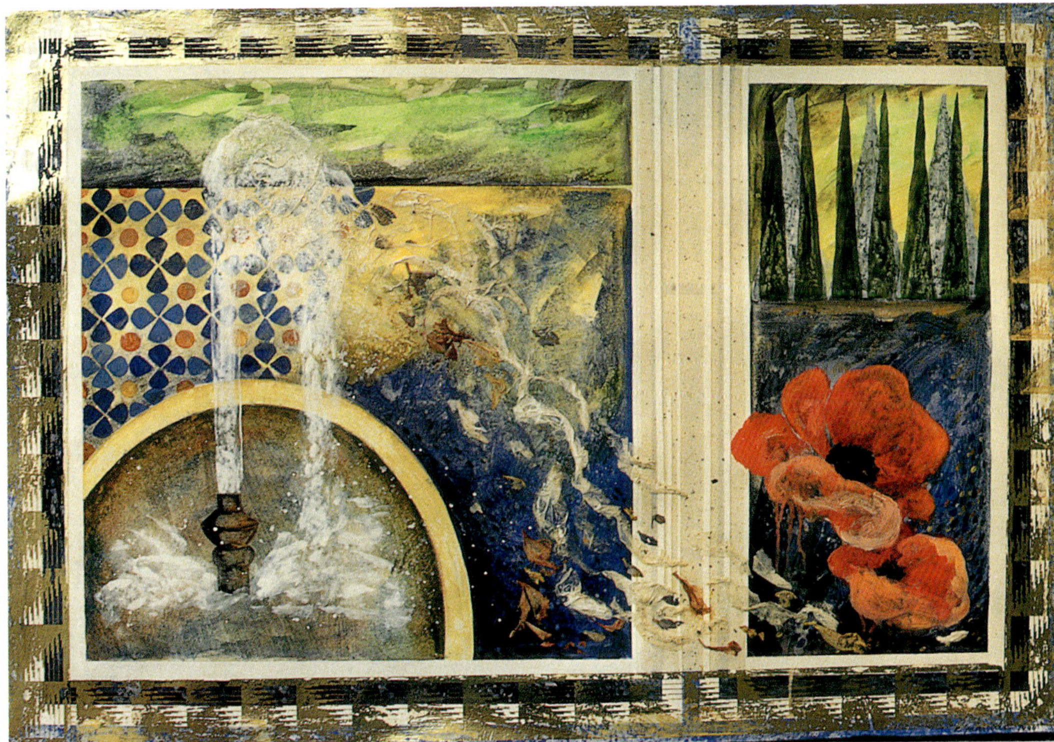

144

VISIT WITH EL GRECO

Today
I shall visit with Domenico Theotocopulos
the Greek.
No need to call for an appointment.
No need to check if he is there,
no need to ring the bell
and wait for footsteps
coming to the door,
or to apologise that I am
four hundred years late.

At the gate,
tourists wait, clutching their tickets
curious and eager, hoping to discover
the secrets of this man,
this anguished painter,
who, by his brush alone found immortality.

I feel embarrassed, like a voyeur
training her fieldglasses
on private territory.

The rooms are small and dark.
The ancient wooden floors creak in protest
aghast at the invasion.
An easel, a few paintings brown with age,
a musty smell of old, neglected objects
once touched by hands which handled brush and paint;
and this is all.

Outside,
the courtyard flooded
by sunshine and the perfume of wisteria.
Behind the house,
The garden looks down
upon the city of Toledo.

Pnina Granirer, May 14, 1992

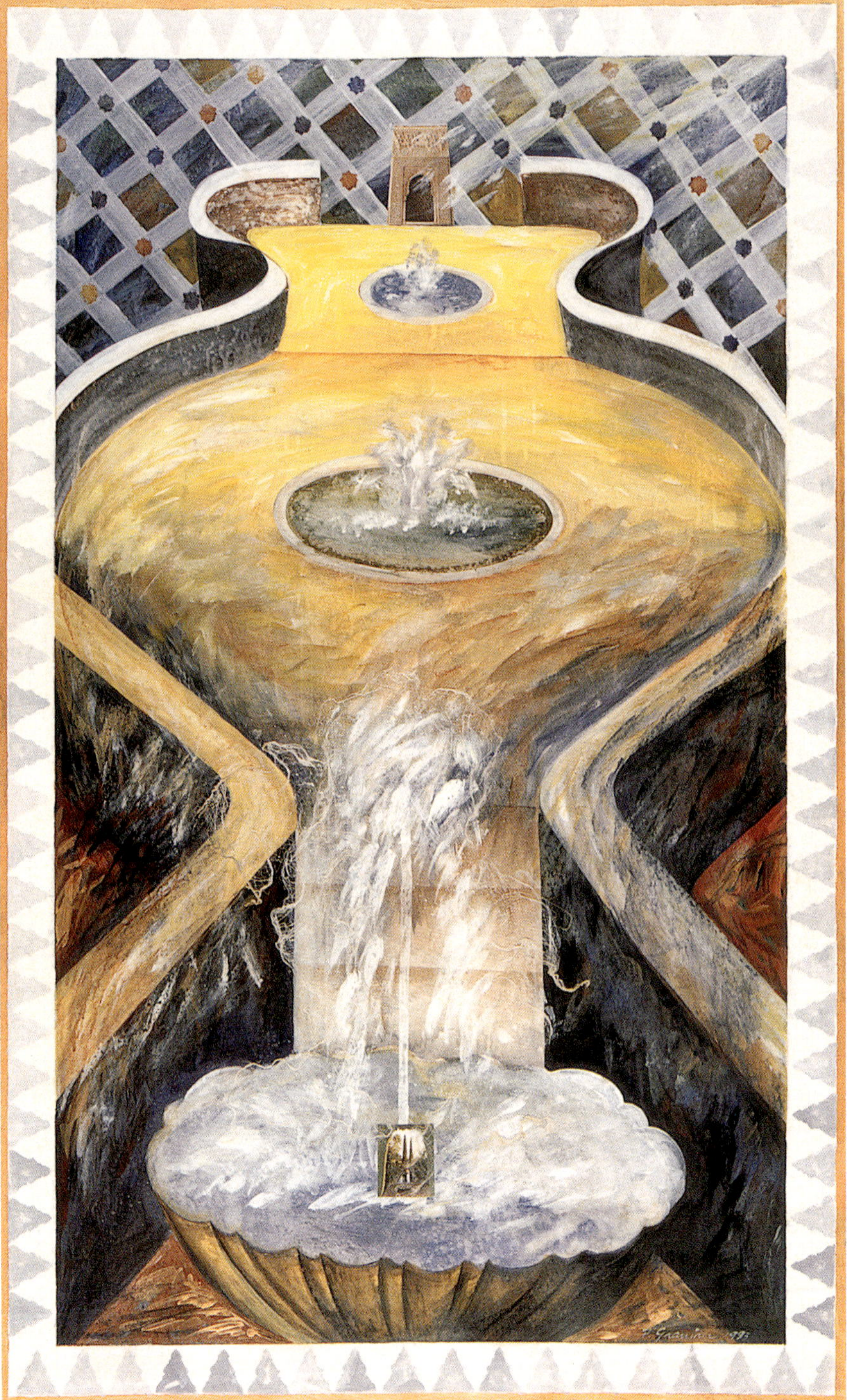

145

145. *Fountainhead,* 1993
108 x 67.3 cm (42 1/2 x 26 1/2 in)
acrylic, collage on paper

Artists in our Midst

In January 1993, triggered by a suggestion made by artist friend Anne Adams to open their studios jointly to the public, Granirer recalled the great Open Studios she saw in Paris' Bastille area. Responding to her pedagogical bent (she taught at Continuing Education classes at the University of British Columbia), she expanded on the idea and, together with Adams, decided to organise a number of artists living in three Vancouver districts, in a communal art event.

The two friends went to work on an annual happening, Artists in our Midst (now in its fifth year and embracing over sixty participating artists), which has proven an unqualified success. Working from her own experience and a reliance on her own devices and resources, Granirer has shared with other artists the imperative for controlling their own destinies and creating their own opportunities, without government grants, strictly through the artists' participation and support from their communities. Artists in our Midst has validated itself again and again as an idea that works.

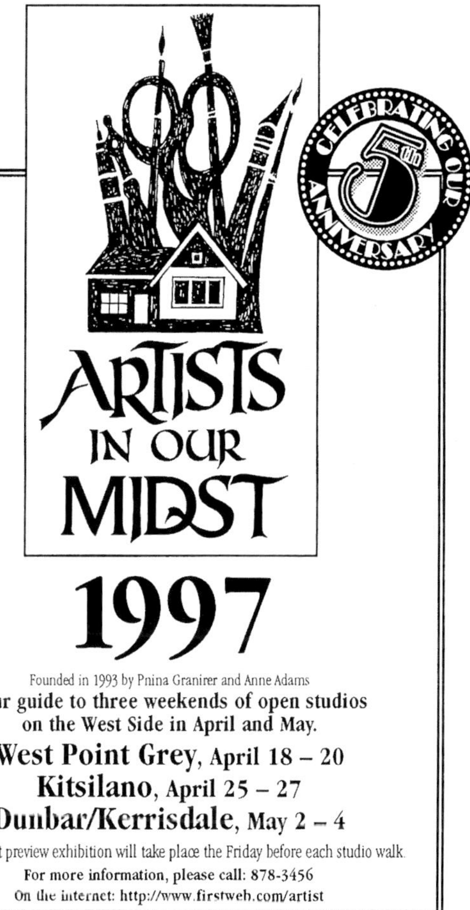

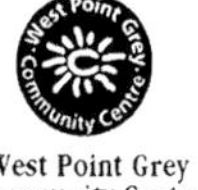

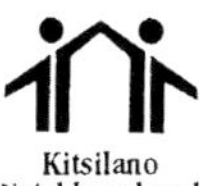

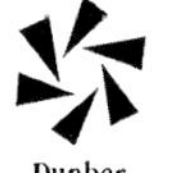

146

146. Cover of information brochure for *Artists in Our Midst*

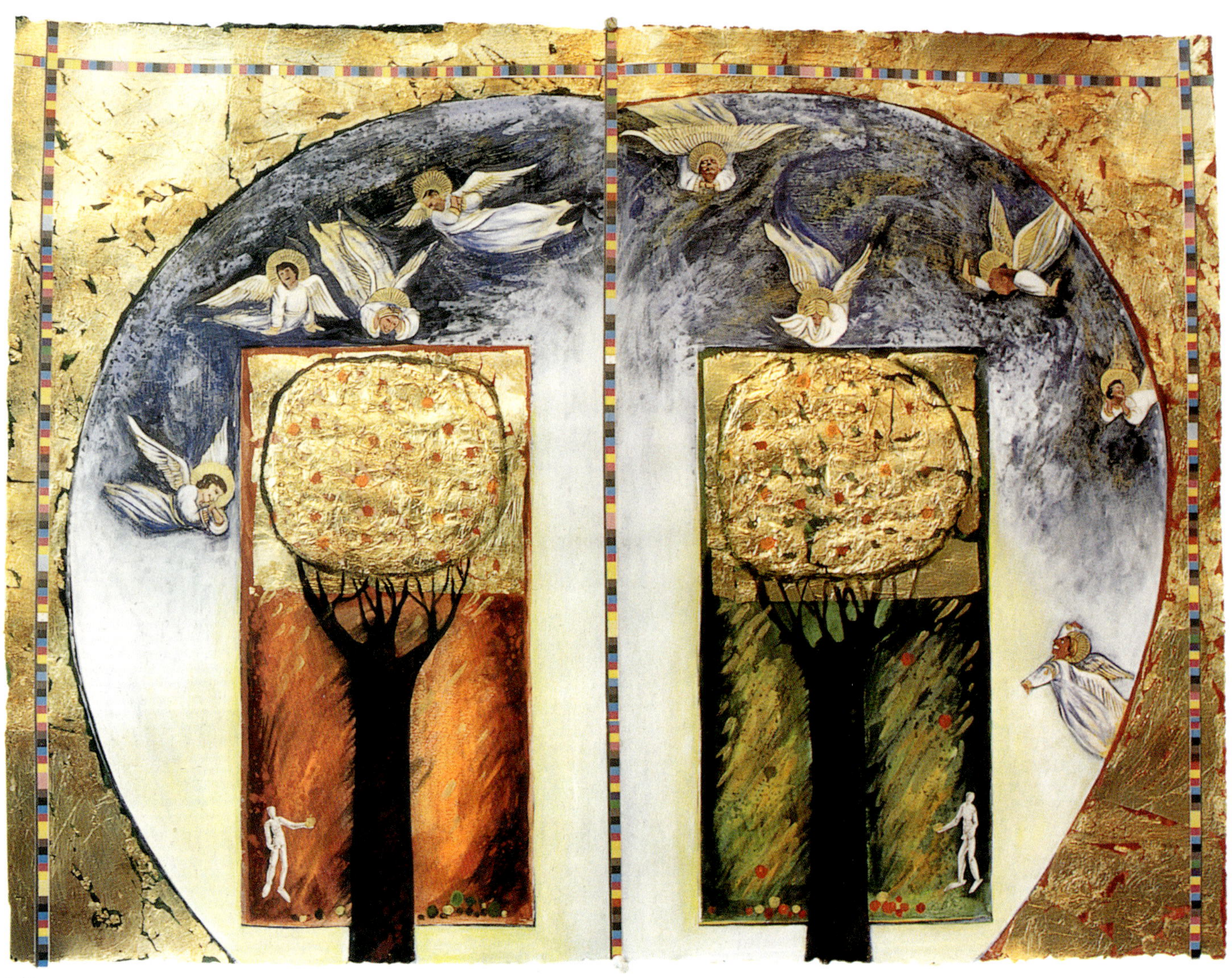

147

147. *Harvest in the Garden,* 1994
56x76 cm (22x30 in)
acrylic, collage, gold leaf on paper
Private collection

148. *Angels' Frolic*, 1995
76x56 cm (30x22 in)
acrylic, collage, oil pastel,
gold leaf on spackled paper
Collection of Dr. Frances Rosenberg

In Search of Eden

In a radically new style of directly brushed images and collage that has come to characterize the *In Search of Eden* series, Granirer momentarily put aside her linear drafting abilities to achieve a more immediate and resonantly expressive statement. The visual elements of her own life become the symbolic angels (spiritual presences) and ecstatic nirvanas (suggesting the extinction of desire of the unattainable) which can be accessed from moment to living, breathing moment. Of her *Eden* series, an artistic denouement which is continuing to this writing, Granirer says:

One of the works is called Harvest in the Garden *(trees of Life and Knowledge abuzz with mischievous cherubs). This theme appeals to me because these were the trees we [humans] were forbidden to touch. On the contrary, I think we should eat as much of their fruit as we can. If we don't taste Knowledge, we don't taste Life.*

In her statement to the exhibition *In Search of Eden,* at the Torres Gallery in April, 1995, she adds to this initial insight:

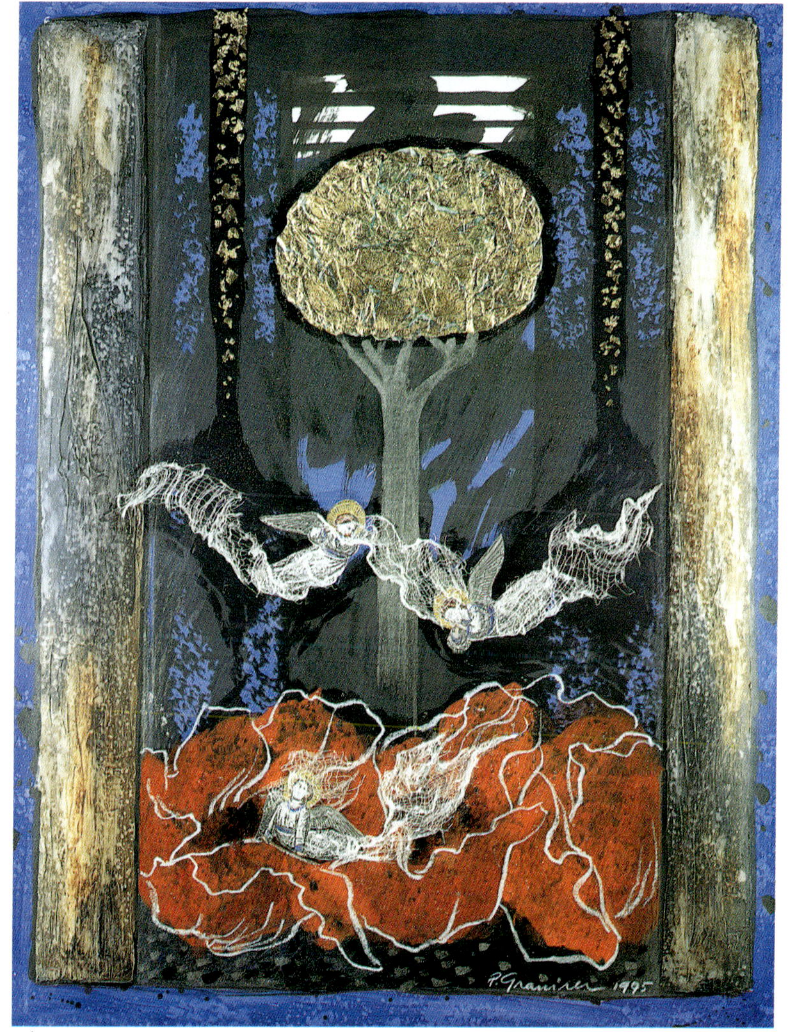

148

Some of the works, This Way to Eden *(1994) and* We the Angels *(1994), for instance, recall altars in places of worship with their formal cross-like arrangements and jewel-like colour. Realizing that we, ourselves, are mythic angels of past belief can be a religious experience. In the poppies series Granirer's use of the grid as a composing and framing device recalls her Alhambra series and the formality of the gardens she painted before. There is a tension created by the contrast of the soft organic flowers and the geometric hardness of the grid, which somehow cannot entirely contain the subject. Throughout this series of works Granirer plays with the formal framing of her images, seeming to comment on the elusive and incategorical nature of her true subject: Eden.*

– Amir Ali Alibhai, *Artfocus,* Fall, 1995

149. *The Joys of Eden,* 1995
triptych, 3(25.9 x 20.3 cm) 3(10 x 8 in)
acrylic, collage, gold leaf, oil pastel on canvas
Collection of David Granirer and Beatrice Scott

This new interpretation of Adam and Eve shows a radical change in world view, which might not have happened had Granirer not first worked her way through *The Trials of Eve.*

150. *This way to Eden,* 1994
4(20.3 x 25.9 cm) plus (91.5 x 61 cm)
4(8 x 10 in) plus (36 x 24 in)
five panels mixed media work on canvas
Collection of Drew Schroeder

We have to make the best of what we have today and every other day of our lives, but unfortunately this wisdom comes late in life. When I walk into my studio, my paintings with their blood-red poppies greet me with a life power which feeds and strengthens me. Their unfolding petals burst into bloom but only for a short moment of total beauty and vibrancy, while their dark seeds hide a constant search for a heavenly place of no return. My angels have human faces. They are whimsical, happy, ironic. They look at the vibrant poppies so full of vitality and seem to say, "You have the gift of this wonderful planet, take good care of it! Are you using your skills as an artist to enhance life, or are you just passing through?"

In effect, working with these images is like therapy for myself — I realize the need to look at the lighter side of life. In spite of the darkness and misery in the world, we have to create our own Edens. In my sixtieth year I have come to accept the fact that Paradise is an elusive goal; I can only keep up the search. If through my paintings I could bring pleasure and joy to the people who care to spend a few minutes in their company, I should be satisfied.

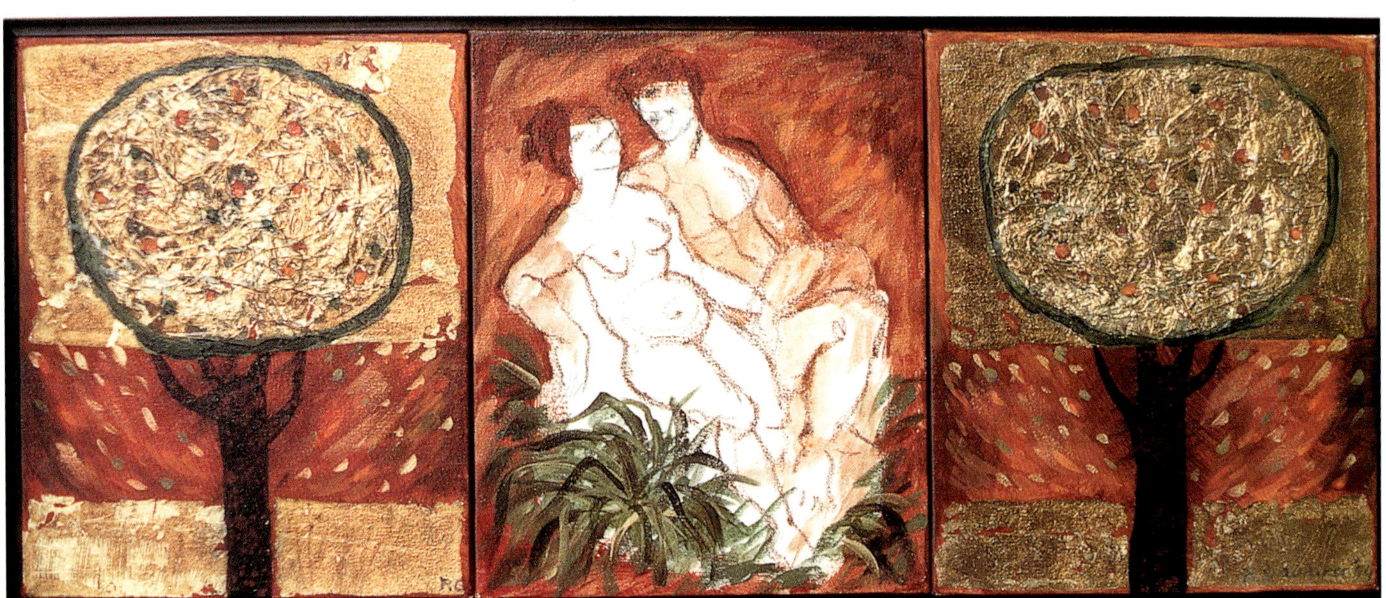

149

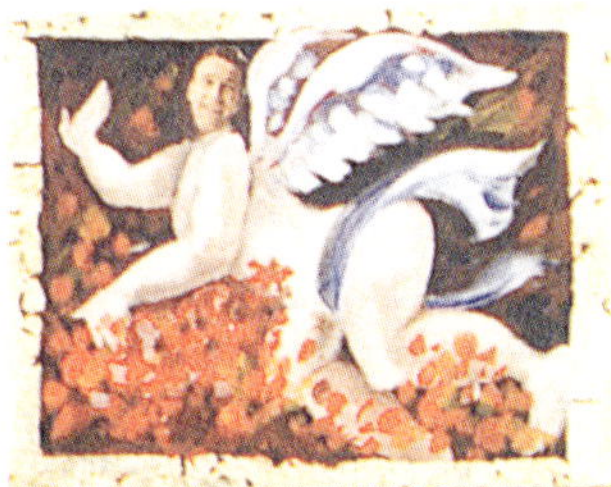

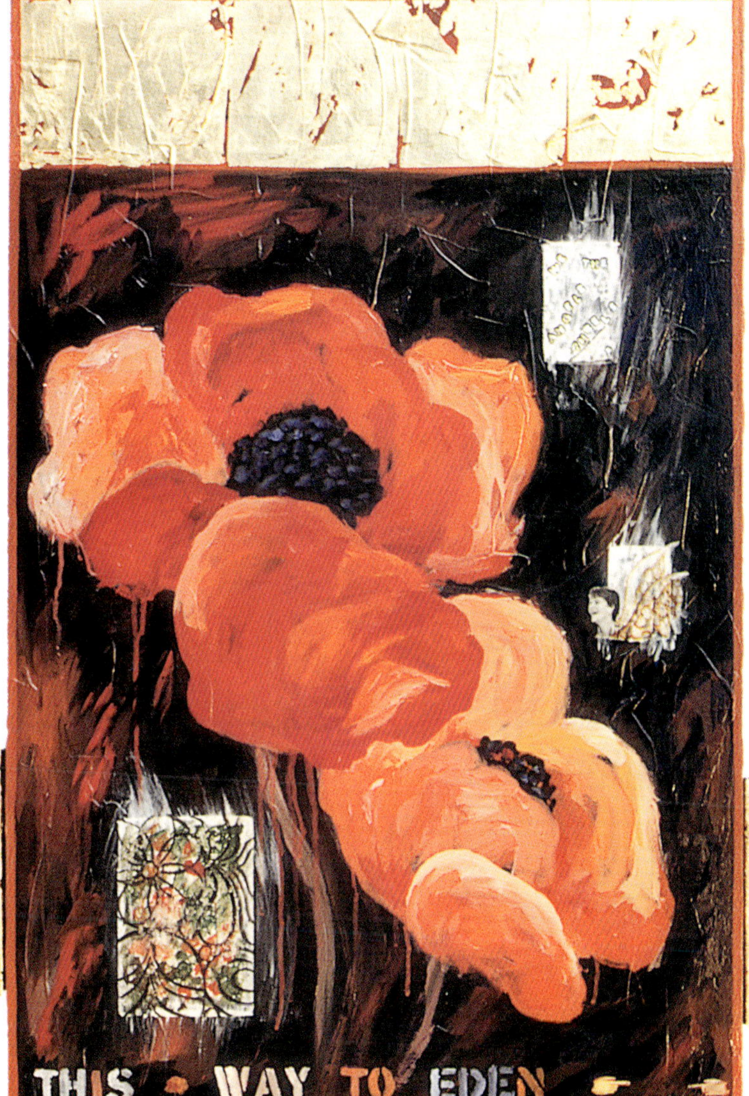

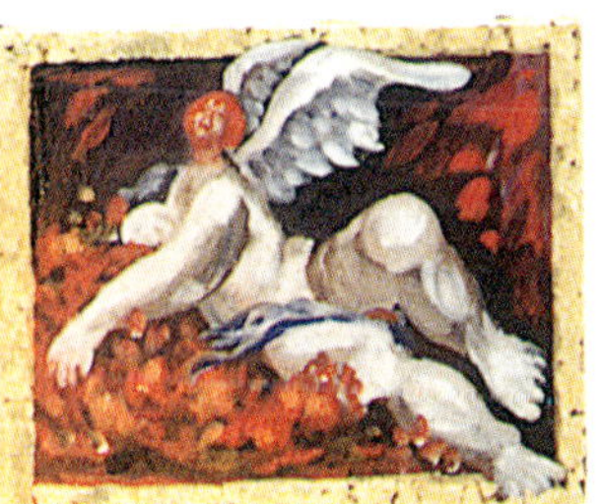

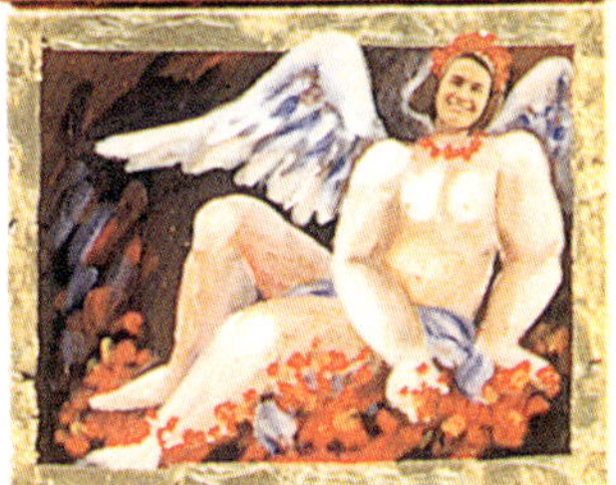

150

151. *Paradiso,* 1985-1994
61 x 91.5 cm (24 x 36 in)
acrylic, resist, collage on canvas

Paradiso, 1985-1994, a re-worked, or "re-opened" painting, is an excellent example of Granirer's new, Eve-like irreverence and animation in style. A mischievous-looking androgynous child with a mop of red hair sprouts wings above a border of lush, juice-weeping poppies. Behind the child there is a night firmament; above, a golden field of blossoms in which rests a cosmic eye. At the base of this composition, Granirer has collaged photos of a massive bolt-studded door, perhaps Spanish. In one photo, a woman is attempting to open it; in another, a man. What is this door, one must ask, which impedes their entry to Paradiso? Why cannot the man and woman simply look up to see the paradise which surrounds them? Granirer suggests an answer with scale: the door appears small and bleak in comparison to what it successfully obstructs.

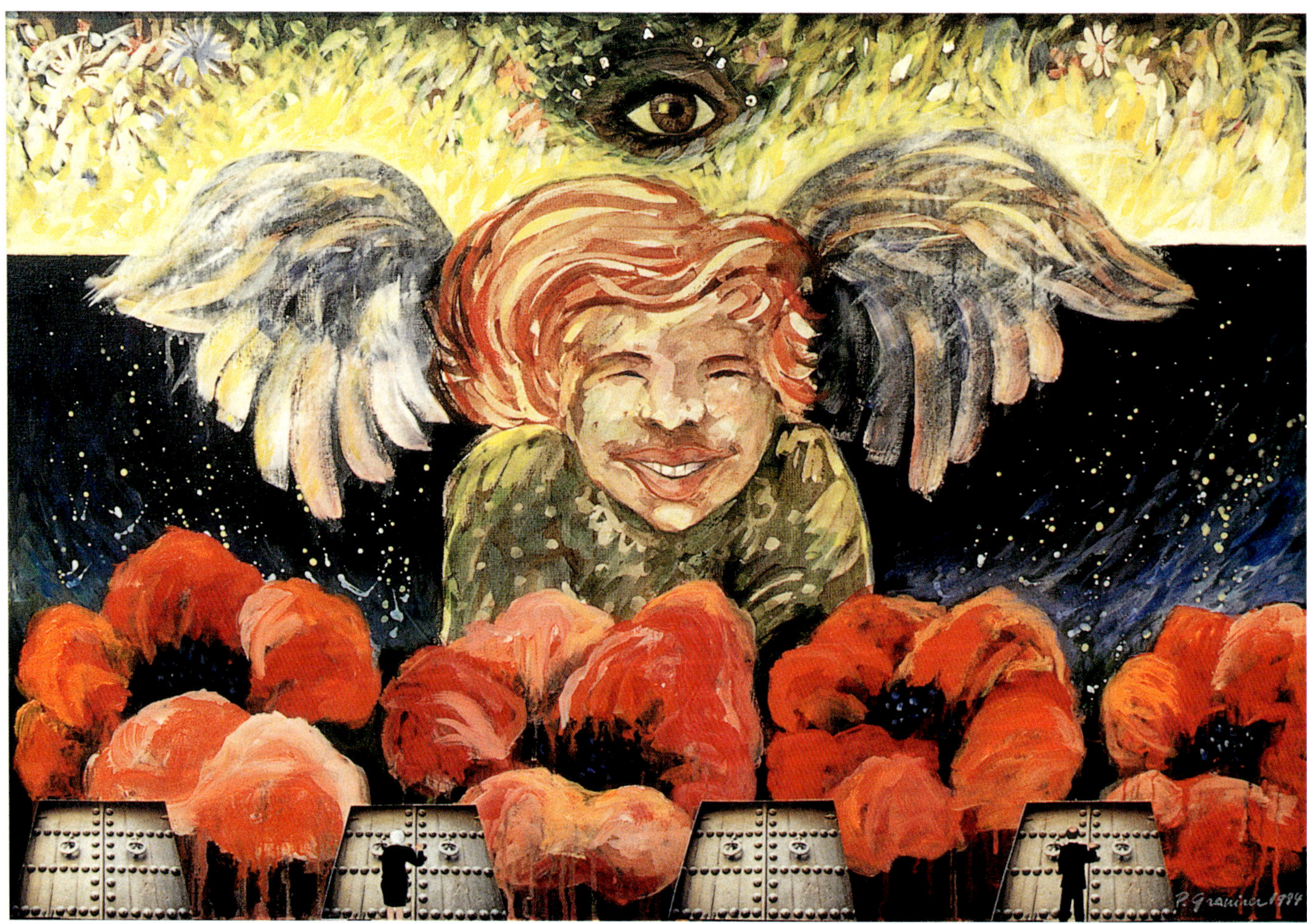

151

Once Granirer has unconditionally engaged the idea of cherubs (or angels) in conjunction with more and more voluptuous poppies in a format of grids, shoji or windows, there is no cessation of variants on this theme. She seems activated, philosophically and stylistically, to emphasize the notion that, however absurdly, we are perhaps our own angels and that, at any moment in time, our present environments may become our de facto paradises, utopias or arcadias.

It is with her *Eden* series that, for the first time, Granirer as an artist becomes almost reckless in her imagery, her lavish use of strong colour and metallic paint, even resorting to burlesque humour to press her vital points. She collages the small-scale heads of contemporary people on the Rubenesque bodies of corpulent cherubs; they lounge and frolic in masses of the symbolically dichotomous poppy.

From 1994 on, there is a general meld, or cross-fertilization, of all Granirer's strongest icons and emblems. Free of the constraints of straight, illustrative narration, she must surprise even herself with certain results or resolutions. Life's riddle, if it is a riddle, has lost the insistent quality of her more self-conscious work. She draws from both the

152. *A Definition of Eden 2,* 1994
diptych, 2(91.5 x 91.5 cm) 2(36 x 36 in)
acrylic, collage, modelling paste on canvas
Collection of Dr. Morton and Irene Dodek

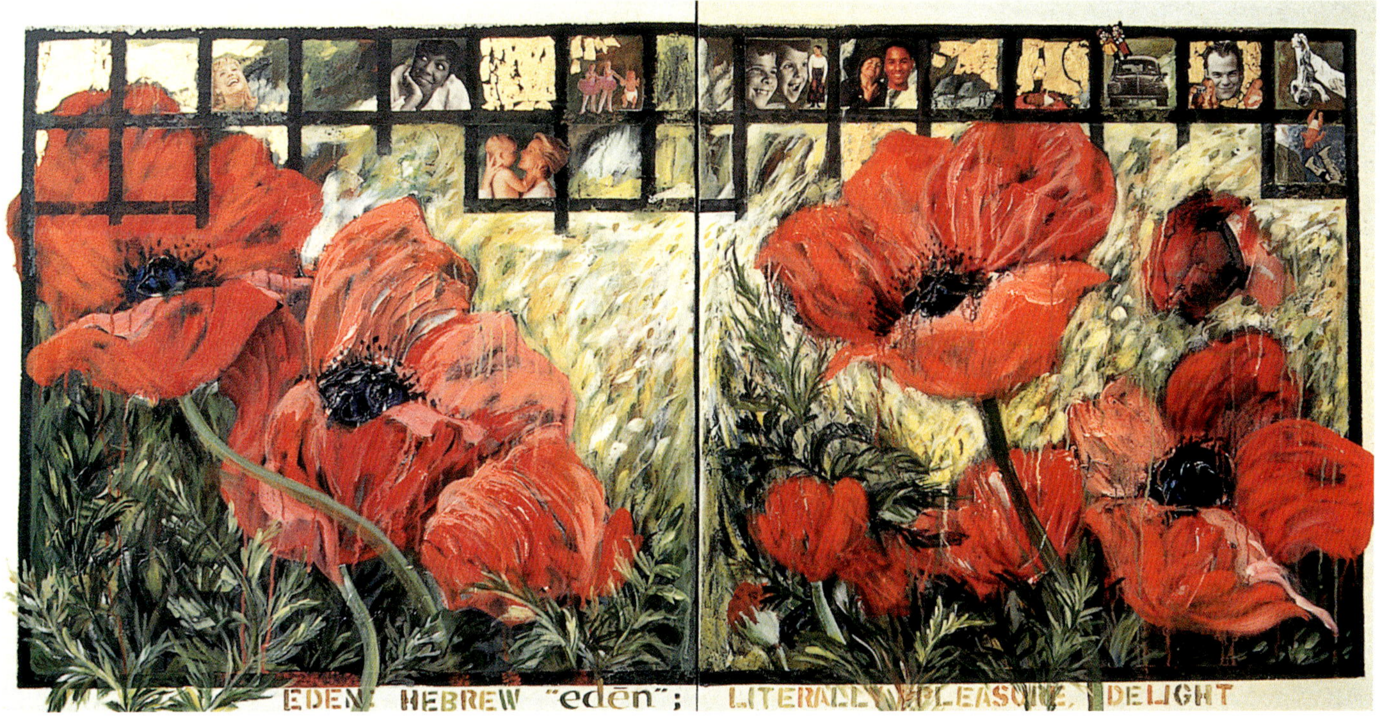

152

153. *Heaven on Earth,* 1995
160 x 110.5 cm (63 x 43 1/2 in)
acrylic, collage, gold leaf on spackled canvas
Collection of Lloyd and Lyn Baron

154. *Definition of Eden,* 1993
150 x 120.5cm (59 x 47 1/2 in)
acrylic, modelling paste, acrylic gel,
collage, gold leaf on canvas

For the group of paintings titled *Definition of Eden,* Granirer simply used the dictionary definition:
Eden, Hebrew: edēn, *literally pleasure, delight.*

The images collaged behind the grid are chosen with great care. They had to represent icons of the earthly Eden, the only one we shall ever know. Some of these images are treated with a measure of humour, such as the soldier marching hand in hand with Mickey Mouse. There are references to other cultural icons, such as Picasso, Van Gogh, or Melina Mercuri, who define our world, i.e. our Eden or our Hell.

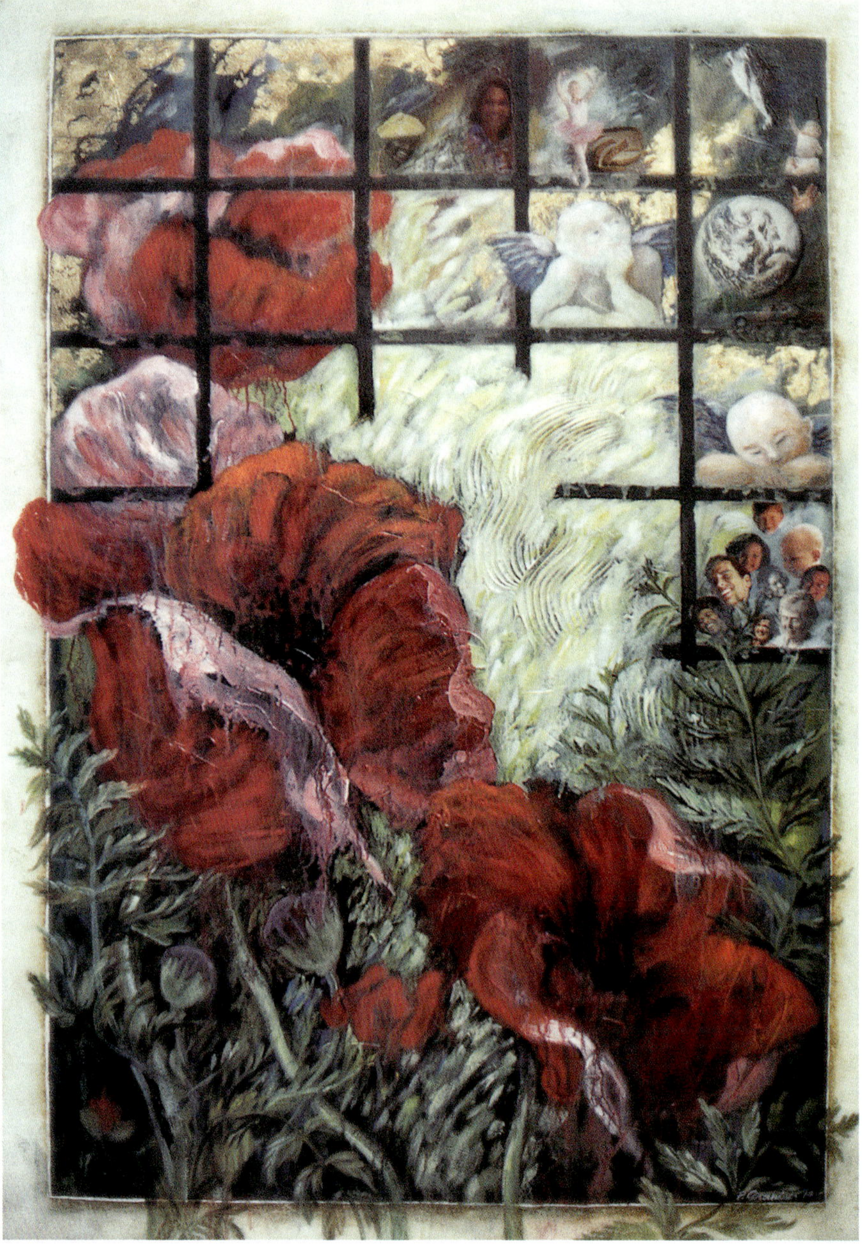

153

sacred and the profane: motifs, insights and memories from experiences as diverse as daily life at home, or major cultural signatures. Increasingly, there is an emphasis on her own inimitable Eden and a deliberate blurring of the angel/devil polarization that insists on a belief in absolutes.

Sorting back through more than a thousand works (most of which are held in private or public collections), which Granirer has recorded on photographic slides, one realizes the progression of her artistic and personal development. There is, in current, postmodernist critical ver-

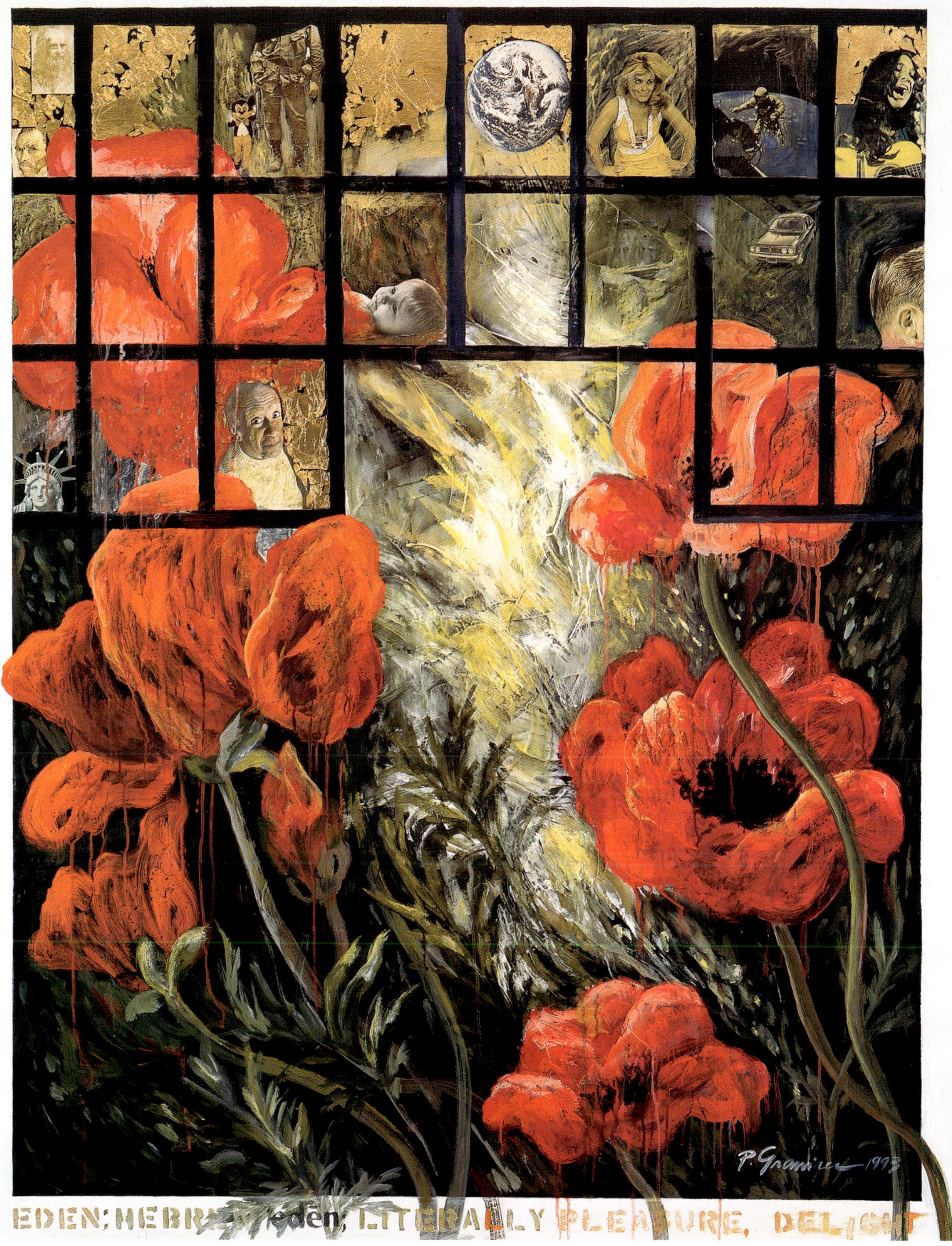
EDEN; HEBREW eden, LITERALLY PLEASURE, DELIGHT

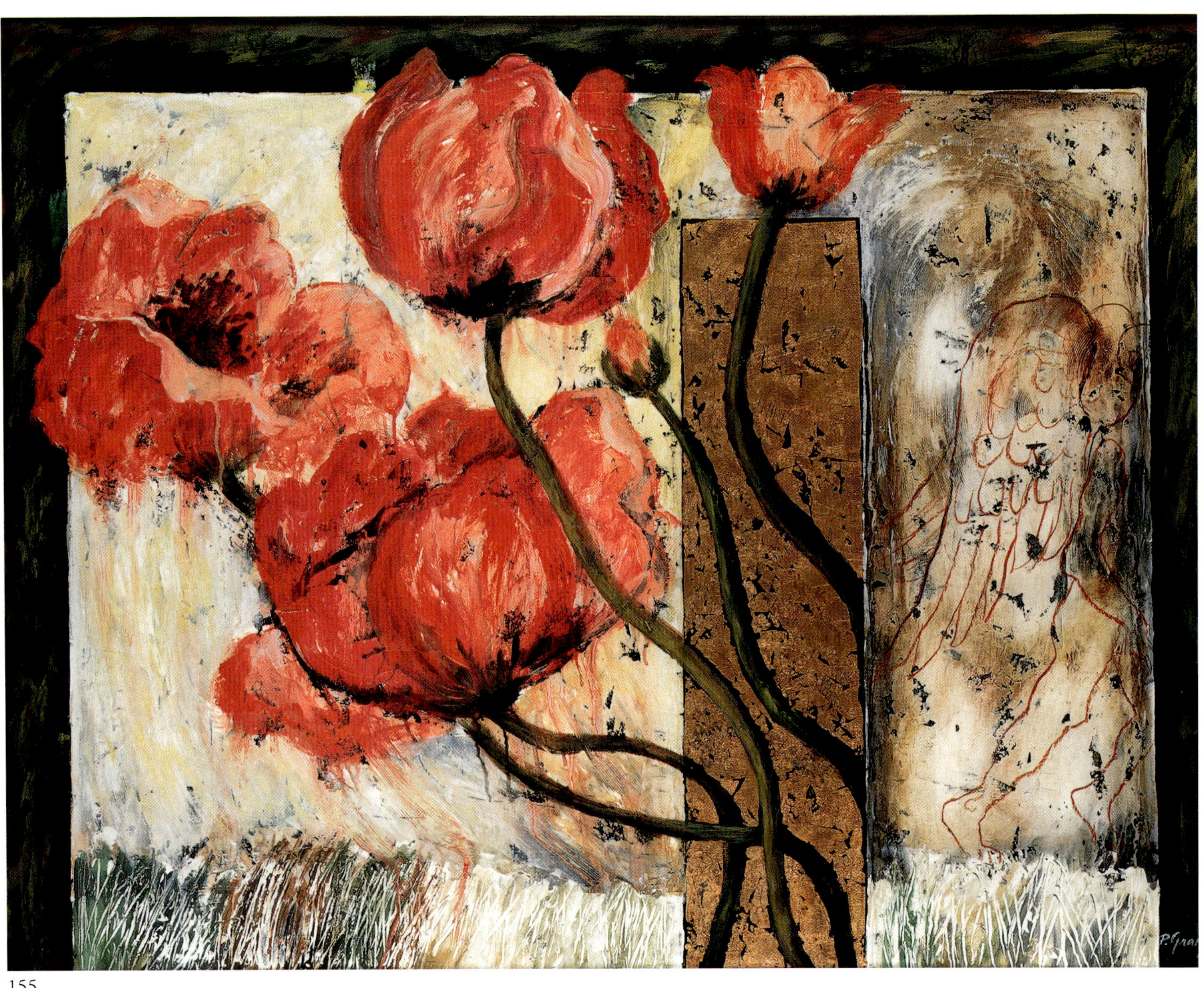

155

nacular, no particular term or phrase which quintessentially describes her artistic growth and production. Surely she is part of a rising tide of individualists who prefer to exist outside "Mainstream Art", if this, by definition, means hyper-intellectualized, text-and-agenda driven Conceptualism. Modern, abstract, increasingly theoretical (and often male-dominant) art was already a fact of life at the time of Pnina Granirer's birth. Because she was stylistically and thematically destined, as it were, to an artistic apartheid — for all the mitigating circumstances of geography, ethnicity, gender and timing — she has had to find her own way to the freedom of expressive abstraction.

155. *Departing Angel,* 1995
91.5 x 122 cm (36 x 48 in)
acrylic, oil pastel, gold leaf on spackled canvas
Collection of Edmond Granirer

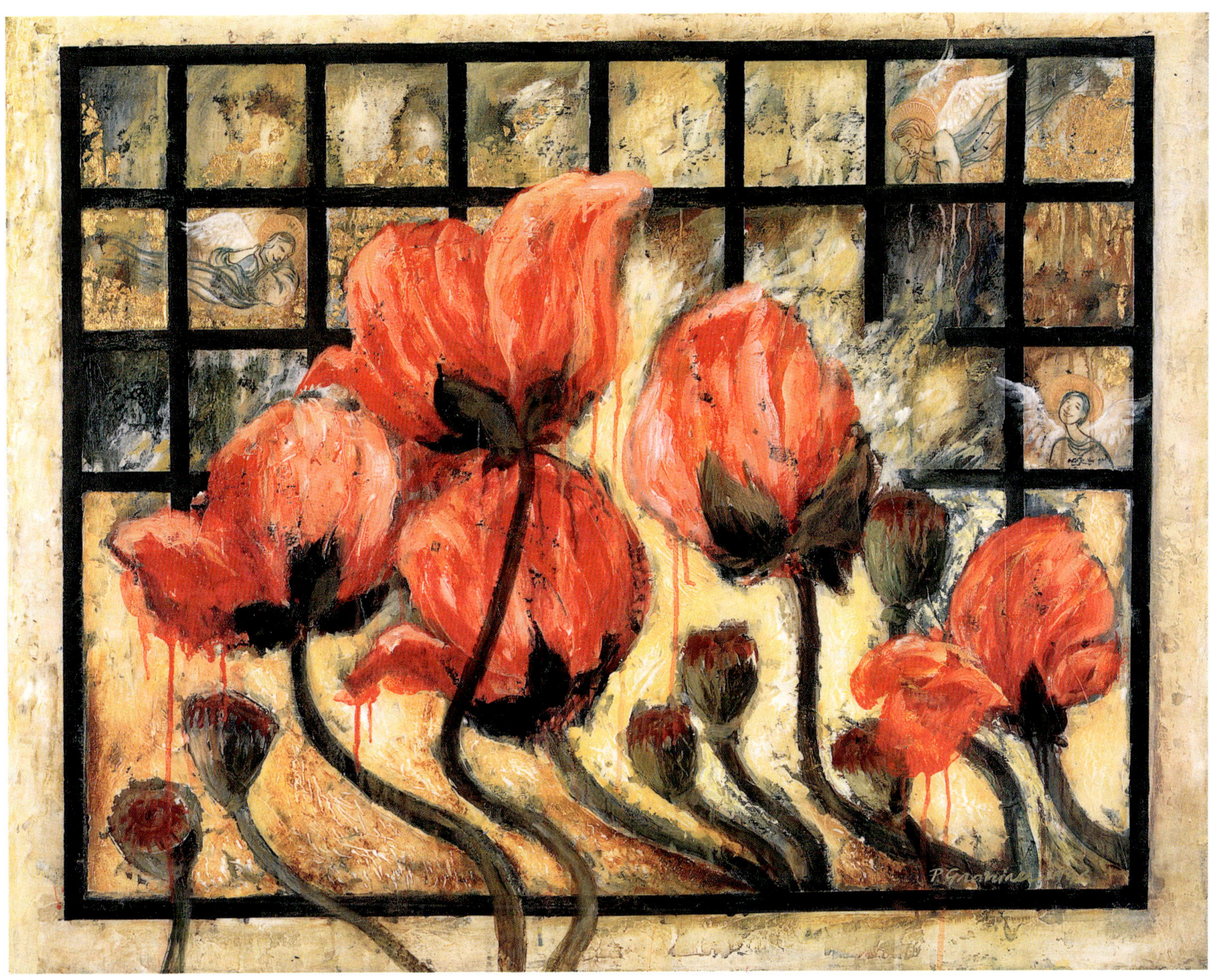

156

Our current art historical/critical overviews, notorious for a kind of reductive, global myopia, merely compound the phenomenon of her determination and success. What we today applaud as refreshing and incomparable, because it departs from the predictability and arrogant sameness of mainstream art, Granirer has achieved by struggling against current fashion, and at the same time adapting her training in graphic design and illustration to innovative collage modes of expression that are rendered in bold, seemingly spontaneous brush strokes. Any independent reading of Granirer's oeuvre demonstrates a major transition from simple illustration and design-oriented compositions to progres-

156. *A Taste of Heaven,* 1995
90 x 118 cm (35 1/2 x 43 1/2 in)
acrylic, gold leaf on spackled canvas

Eden is presented as being here and now, a construct of our own lives. The angels add a sense of humour and lightness that is characteristic of Granirer's recent work. She seems to say that Eden is attainable through living and through our own sensuality; the stuff of Paradise is all around us.
— Amir Ali Alibhai, *Artfocus,* Fall, 1995

157. *Creation 1,* 1995
diptych, 2(30.5 x 22.8 cm) 2(12 x 9 in)
acrylic, collage, oil pastel on
spackled canvas
Collection of Georgina and Peter Bullen

158. *Do Poppies Grow in Heaven?,* 1996
diptych, 2(122 x 61cm) 2(48 x 24 in)
acrylic, collage, oil pastel, plexiglass,
gold leaf on spackled canvas

Granirer produced a number of works with the above title in response to her visit to the huge American cemetery in Normandy. The small poppies sold at Remembrance Day in memory of the lost lives of the two World Wars are sometimes collaged on the canvas.

Part of the oil pastel drawing of the poppies was done on the back of a plexiglass sheet, which was then collaged directly on the canvas. The delicate drawing, in direct contrast with the painted poppies, is captured behind the plexiglass. This is the first time Granirer has experimented with this technique.

sively complex and sophisticated statements of sustaining value. This transition seems less based in hyper-intellectualized theory than in arduous, intuitive eye/hand development, an obdurate, if eventually effective alternative to the intensive, all-embracing art school training of the kind available today.

Granirer has not departed from the determination that art somehow must have pictorial content and "meaning" (that trap of a word), but she would readily admit that she has immensely broadened her notion of "meaning" over the years. One has only to compare her early poster-like works with the protean, painterly works of which she has been capable in the past decade.

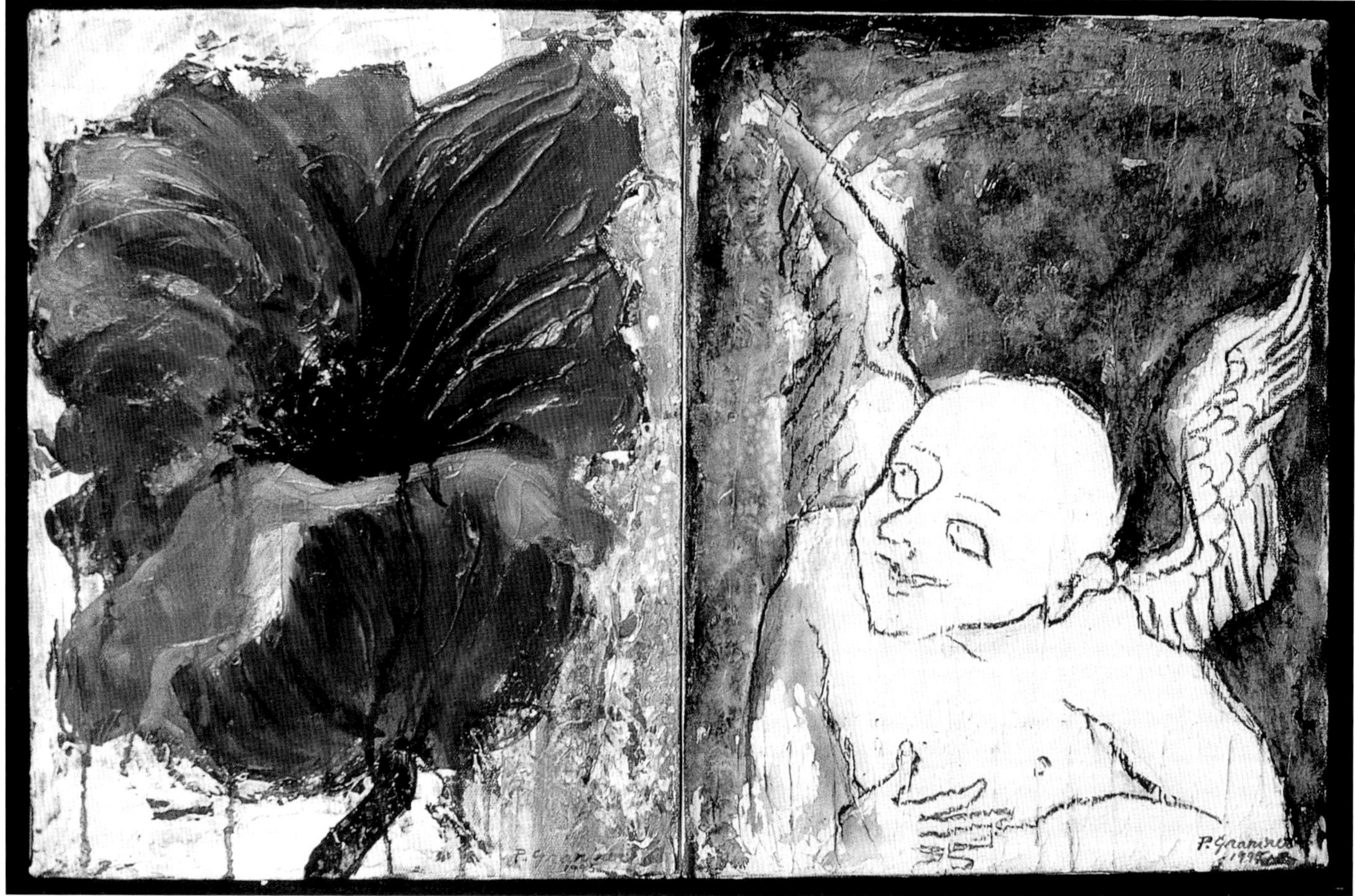

157

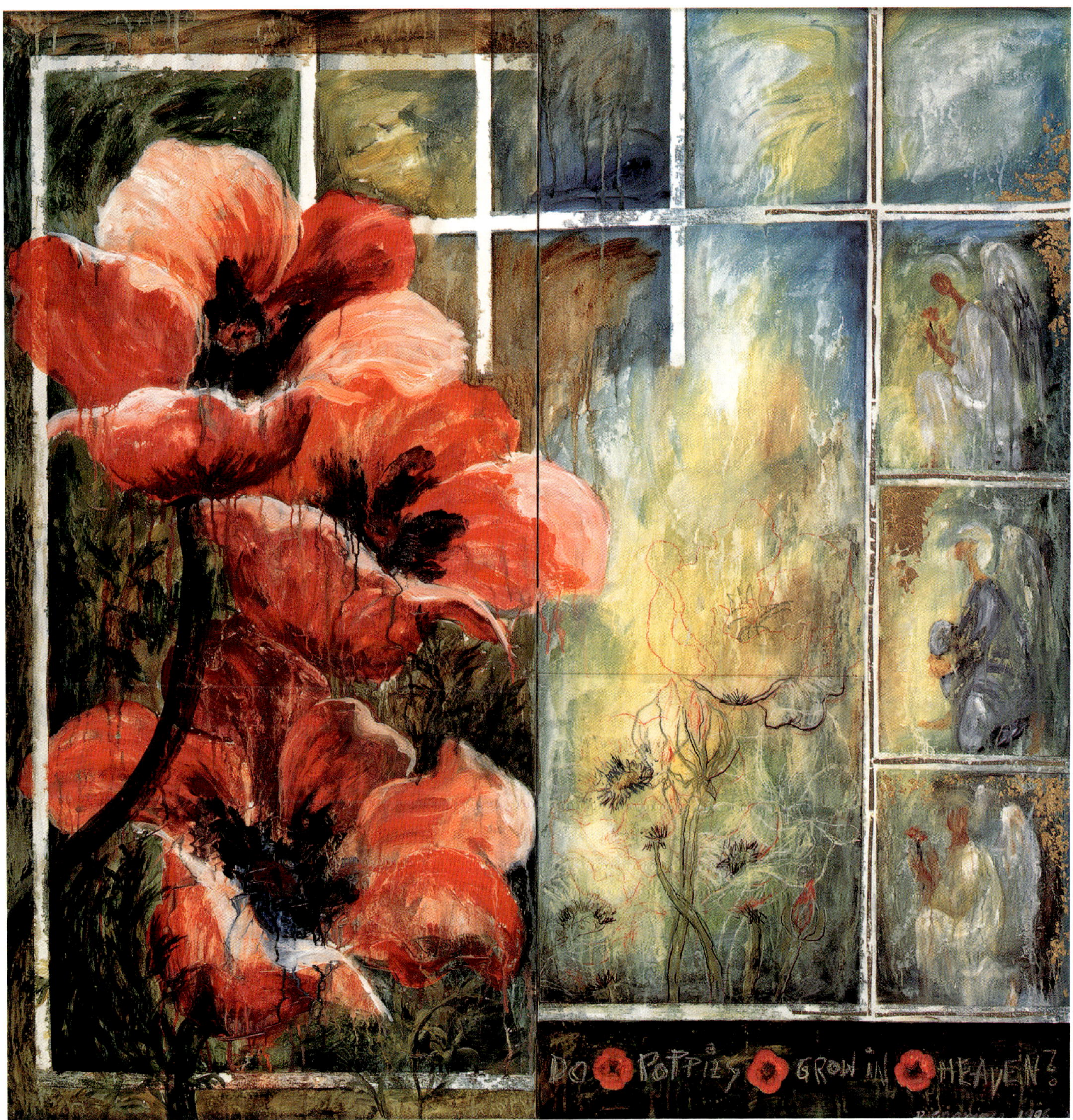

158

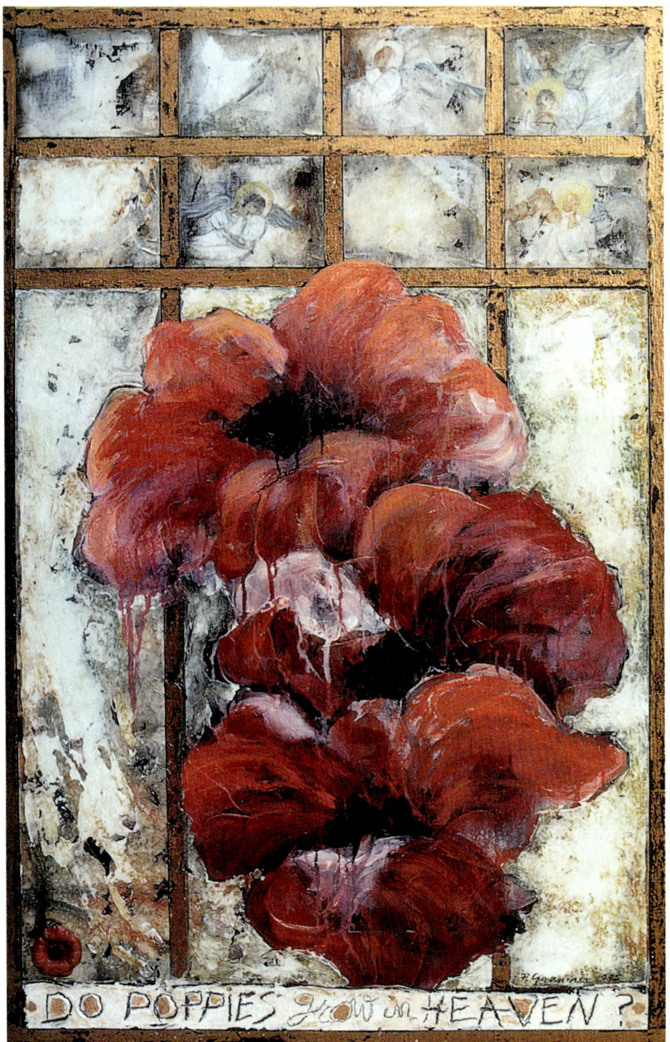

159

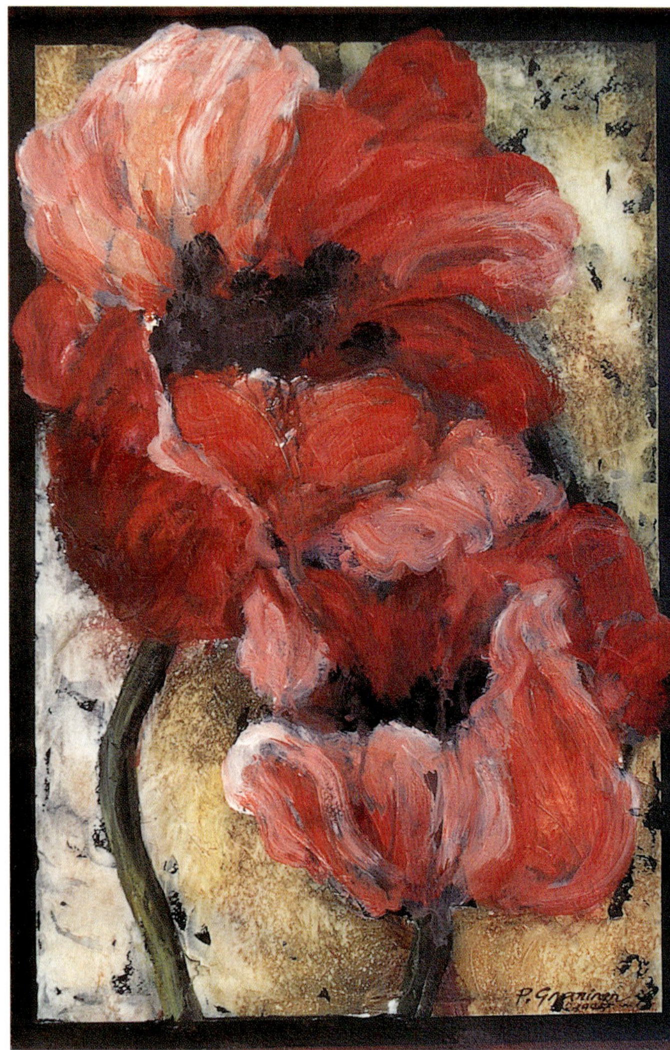

160

159. *Do Poppies Grow in Heaven? – 2,* 1995
91.5 x 61 cm (36 x 24 in)
acrylic, gold transfer on spackled canvas
Collection of Susan Ogul & Lonnie Propas

160. *Two Poppies,* 1996
76 x 55.3 cm (30 x 12 3/4 in)
acrylic, gold transfer on spackled paper

Philosophically, Granirer's preoccupation with cross-cultural creation myths, forces of Light and Dark, the cycles of nature, the vicissitudes of women in a deeply patriarchal society, have ultimately netted her something of the greatest value: a personal creation myth which encompasses all these — an Earth which may be perceived as Heaven or Hell — and for that matter, our Eden or Wasteland.

Pnina Granirer's most recent work appears neither angst-driven nor a vehicle for popular political agendas. Her hard-won artistic feminism (as opposed to "feminist art") is evinced through an emphatic demon-

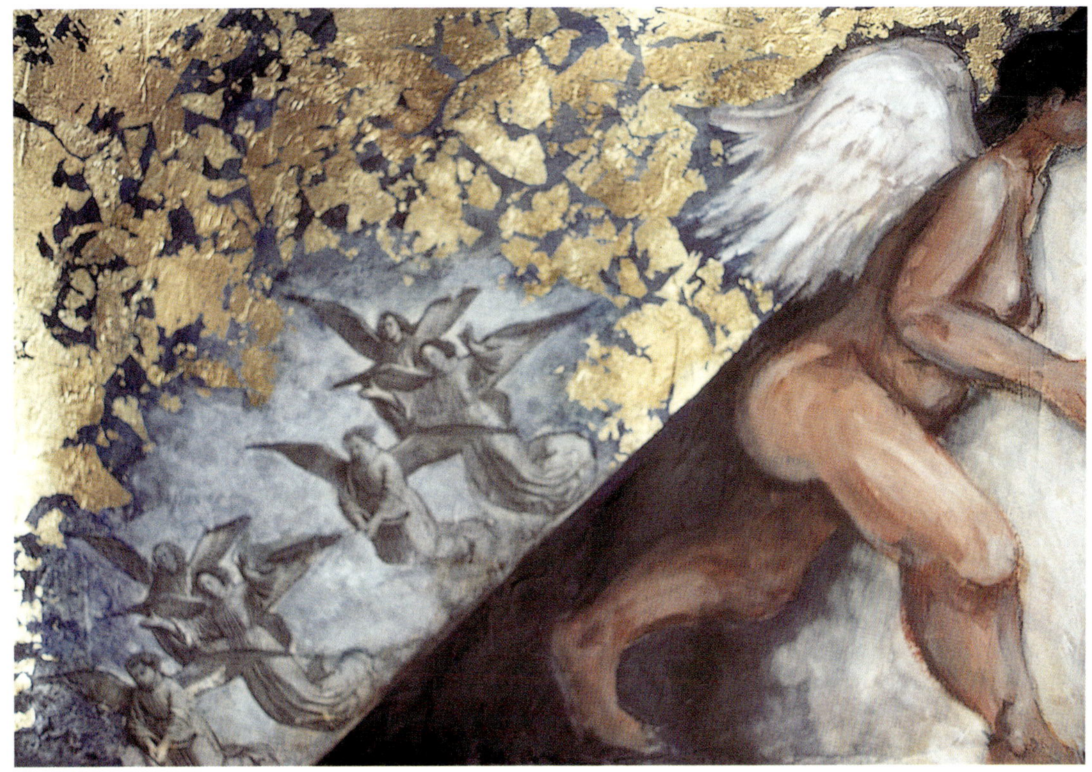

161

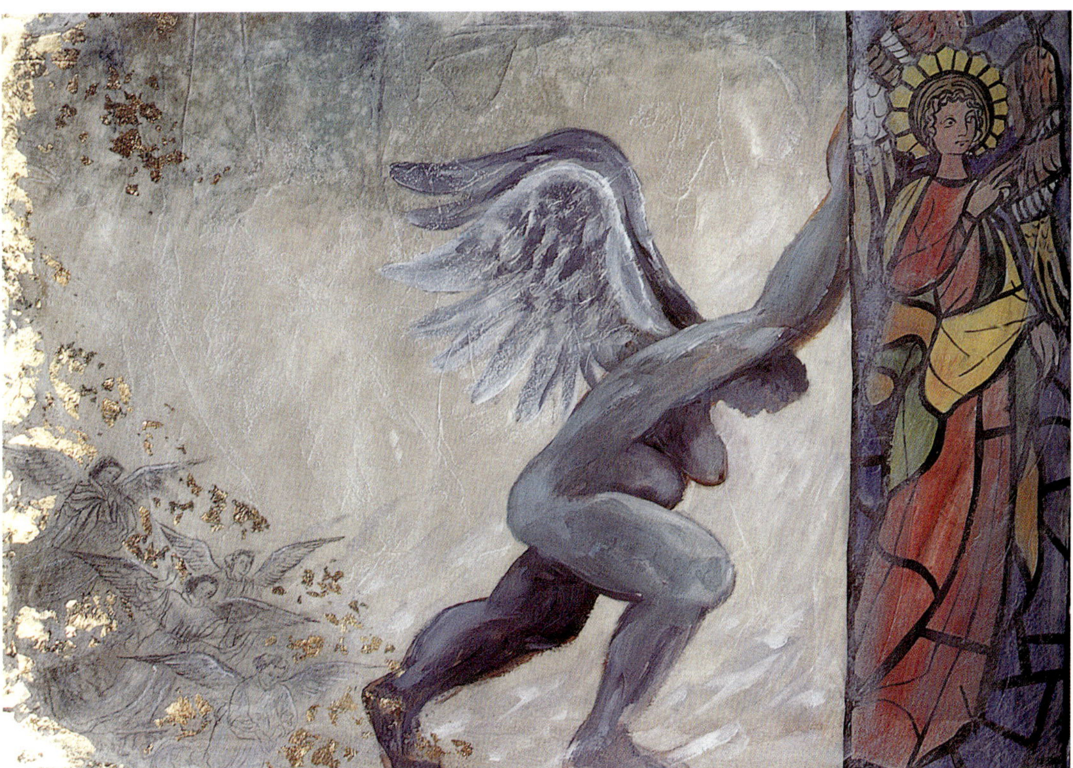

162

161. *Angel Flees Stereotypes,* 1997
40.6 x 56.5 cm (16 x 22 1/4 in)
acrylic, collage, gold leaf on spackled paper

162. *Angel Fights Stereotypes,* 1997
40.6 x 56.5cm (16 x 22 1/4 in)
acrylic, collage, on spackled paper

These two small works summarize my quest for an elusive Eden. The cherub has matured into a woman-angel who does not fit the stereotypes. She flees the slim, pretty, bland image which has defined her until now, or pushes away the idealized vision of the Edenic creatures who are supposed to act as role models as they protect her and direct her life. By doing this, she is at last assuming control over her identity.

WORDS

I am a painter, not a poet.
My words are written
with colour and with line.
I trace my stories
in images
and forms
like ancient hieroglyphs
to be deciphered
by the unitiated eye.

And yet . . .
by speaking, godlike,
one may conjure a universe.
Words
are instruments of power
woven threads of sound and signs
binding the loose pages of our past.

I should so like to plant
a garden of words
in my field of colours.

Pnina Granirer, Vancouver, October 1992

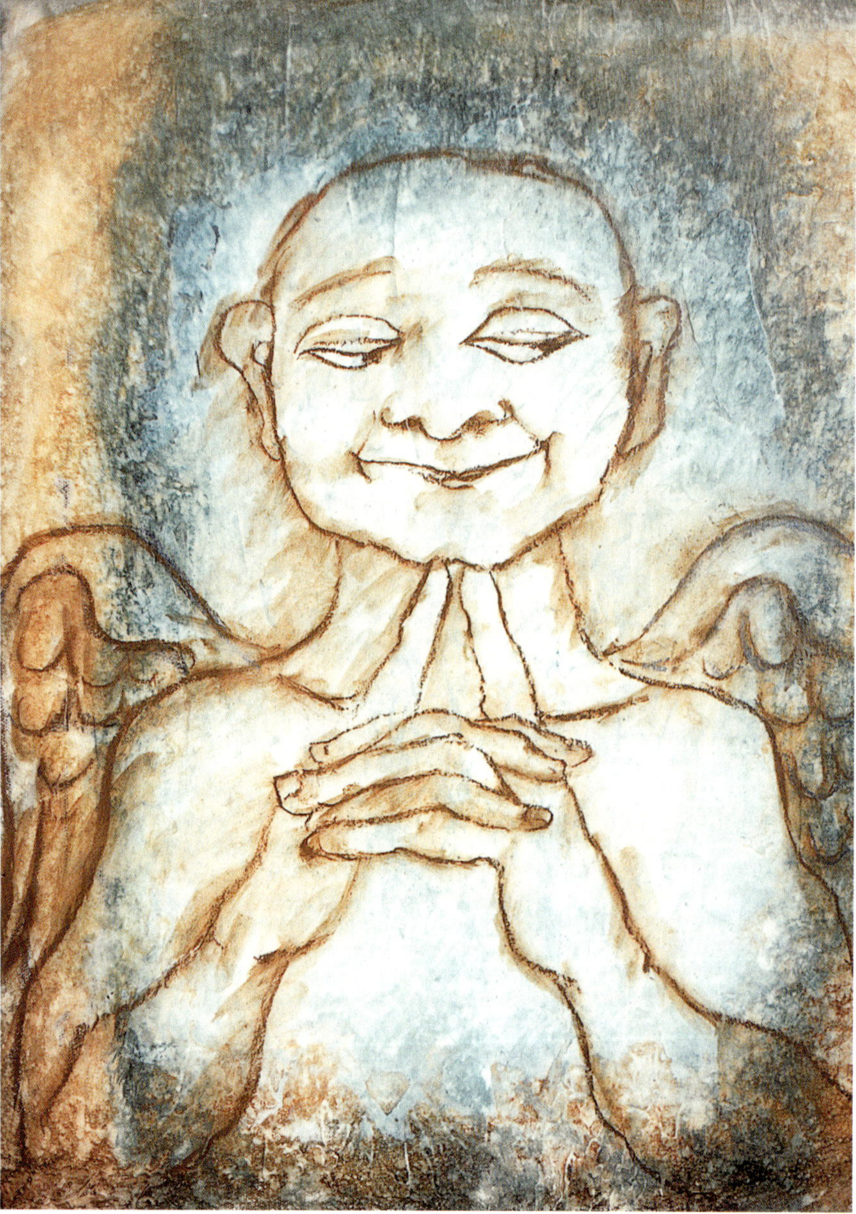

163

stration of a woman's passionate visual experience, sparkling internal fantasy and daring association. On these she builds testimonies and allegories based not on the heroic past or the audacious potential of art, but through an equally persuasive confirmation of principles that have kept her on course to a transmittable and gratifying resolution.

163. *Angelic Thoughts,* 1997
50.8 x 40.7 cm (20 x 16 in)
acrylic, oil pastel on spackled canvas

The Prints

As with many artists who enjoy the diversity and option of new technical vistas, Pnina Granirer, throughout her career, has periodically turned from drawing and painting to various forms of printmaking. Woodblock carving in particular, was a fundamental and practical part of her education at the Bezalel Art Academy in Jerusalem in the late 1950s.

Her mentors were Jacob Steinhart and Jacob Pines, both originally from Germany. Steinhart, born in 1887, had exhibited internationally and had won first prize at the San-Paolo and Venice Biennale in 1955 and 1958 respectively. He worked from a figurative/expressionist tradition which is reflected in Granirer's earliest woodblock prints: scenes and episodes in an ancient locale, often including the oldest examples of architecture and the diverse cultural blend of people on the streets and marketplace of Jerusalem.

Jacob Pines was born in 1917 and had also exhibited internationally. His personal inspiration came from the Japanese woodblock tradition which required a separate block for each colour in a print and was revered in the West for its clean design and spatial illusion, created without Renaissance perspective. As mentioned before, Pines owned an extensive collection of Japanese Ukio-e woodblock prints, which first introduced Pnina to this artform. This "Japanese" influence is echoed again and again in her compositional solutions, both in and out of the printmaking sphere. Granirer comments:

The woodblock printmaking method, which implies drawing the actual image in black and white first, appealed to me enormously. It tied in per-

164. *Mystery,* 1960
5.2 x 6 cm (2 1/8 x 2 3/8 in)
engraving on olive wood
from *Small Verses by* Moshe Hanaami

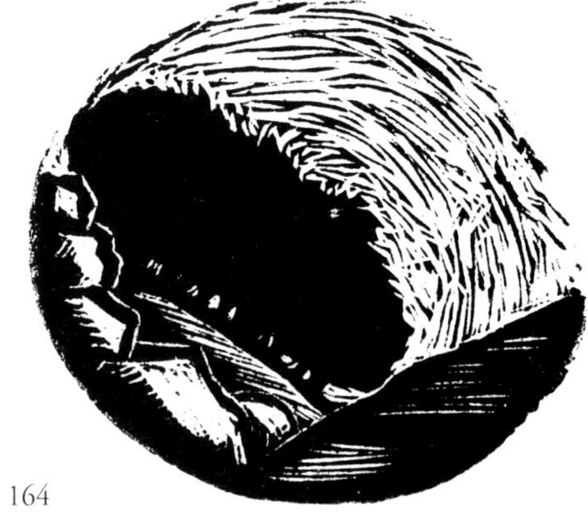

164

fectly with my love of drawing, the use of line and composition. This technique of relief printing means that one draws the image first in black and white, with the awareness that all the white areas will eventually be removed, leaving the uncut, black areas to be inked and printed. The power of this medium lies in its simplicity and its directness.

Doves, 1959, is a very early example of Pnina's wood-relief carving and printing. A simple linear motif of two nesting doves is treated in a balance of opaque black (positive) and white (negative) contrasts against a backdrop of tree trunks from which the ink has apparently been partially wiped, revealing a grey tonality which additionally emphasizes the woodgrain in the block itself.

Two elements in this print presage pictorial themes which will appear in Granirer's work throughout her career: the pattern of massed, vertical tree trunks and the complex decorative potential of birds, birds' wings and intricate feather patterns.

Children, another constant theme in her early work, is invoked in *Togetherness* and *The Blue Apron,* 1958 (ill. 167, 168). Not only are their tiny, compact bodies delightfully stylized, but one can imagine their symbolic importance to a new mother in the freshly invented Israeli society. Against a backdrop of the Holocaust and the struggle for taking root and nurturing, Israeli children were understandably more than objects of sentimental endearment; they represented a crucial future.

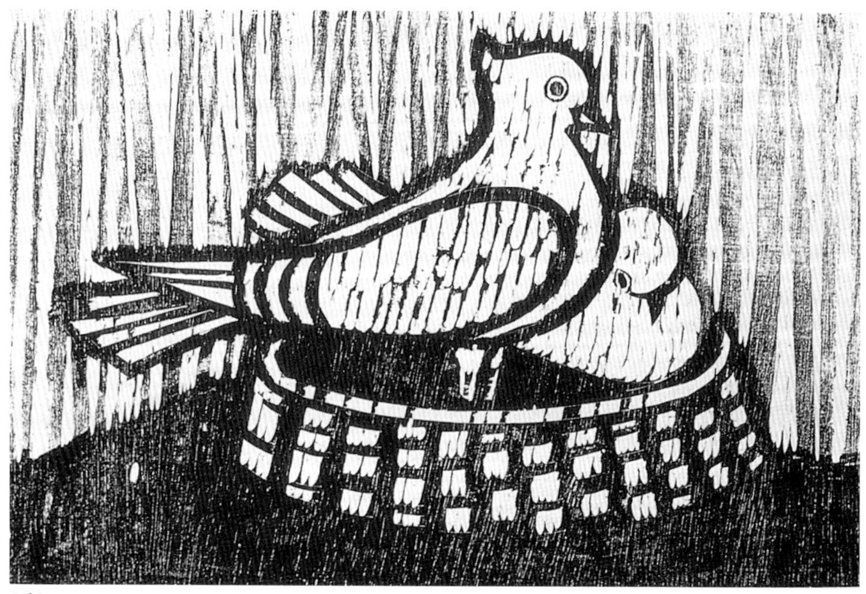

165

165. *Doves,* 1959
21.5 x 33.7 cm (8 1/2 x 13 1/4 in)
woodblock print

In complete contrast, *Gossip/Three Yentes,* 1959, gently mocks the physical and mental attitudes of old fashioned busybodies, scrambling for tidbits like the chickens at their feet. Four colour blocks (including the white and black areas) are employed adeptly to strengthen the contrasts of the composition.

Although Granirer loved the simplicity and directness of both wood and linoleum block printing, she resisted from the start any serious concerns about editioning: producing and numbering a run of identical imprints. Editioning is essentially a marketing device which gives greater value to (particularly) etchings and engravings in their lower numbers, but which tend to be discernably less distinct in higher numbers, as the printing plates wear or become clogged with dried ink.

She much preferred experimentation, varying the colour schemes in a single print, or even over-printing with the same block, as in *Yemenite Dancers,* 1963 (ill. 169), producing six dancers in a tight group

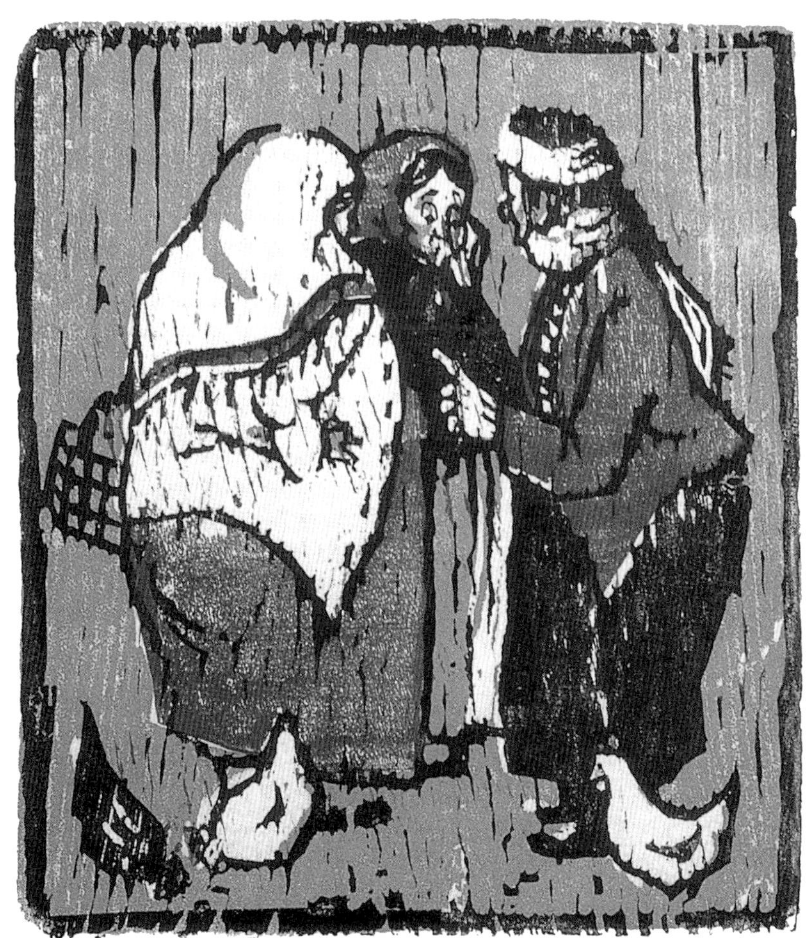

166

166. *Gossip/Three Yentes,* 1951
22.5 x 20.8 cm (8 7/8 x 8 3/8 in)
Four-colour blocks woodcut

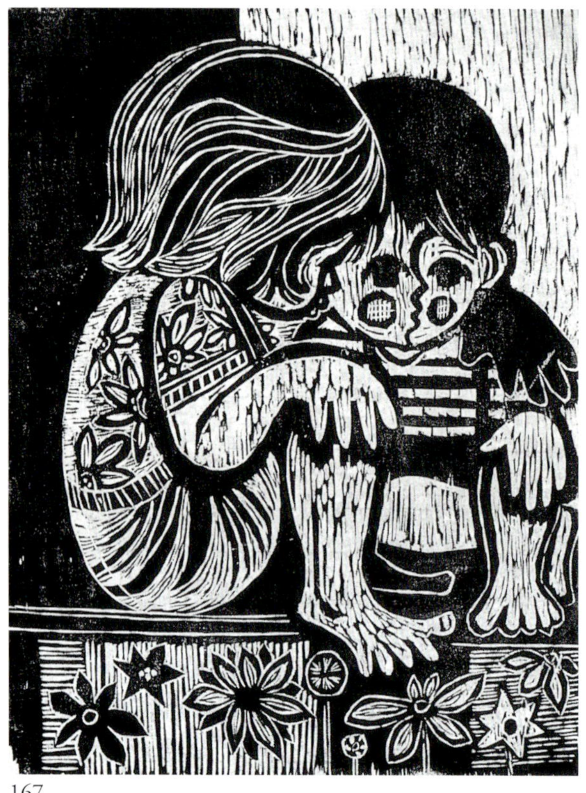

167

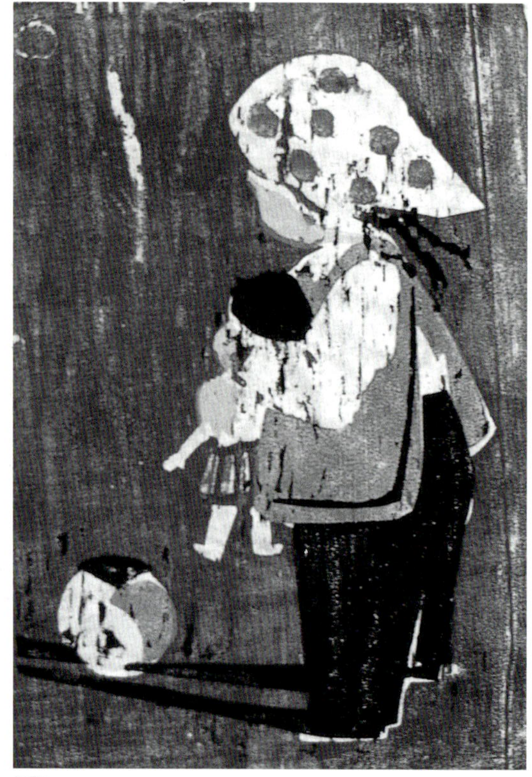

168

167. *Togetherness,* 1971
53.3 x 43.2 cm (21 x 17 in)
woodblock print

The theme of two small children sitting close together was inspired by the friendship which developed between Granirer's son David, age 3, and Mary Jo, age 5. Mary Jo herself was the subject of numerous drawings, such as *Mary Jo with Turtle* (ill.20).

Togetherness was used as a Unicef Poster and the theme was repeated in other drawings (ill.19), monoprints and a linocut.

168. *Blue Apron,* 1958
28 x 19 cm (11 x 7 1/2in)
Four-colour blocks woodcut

169. *Yemenite Dancers,* 1963
56 x 66 cm (22 x 26 in)
woodblock print

This is an example of the use of imagery brought from Israel and developed by Granirer while living in Urbana, Illinois. A block representing two dancers was printed twice and the figures separated and printed individually. The background consists of various pieces of wood, inked and placed separately on the paper. Due to this method, each print in this edition of 20 is different.

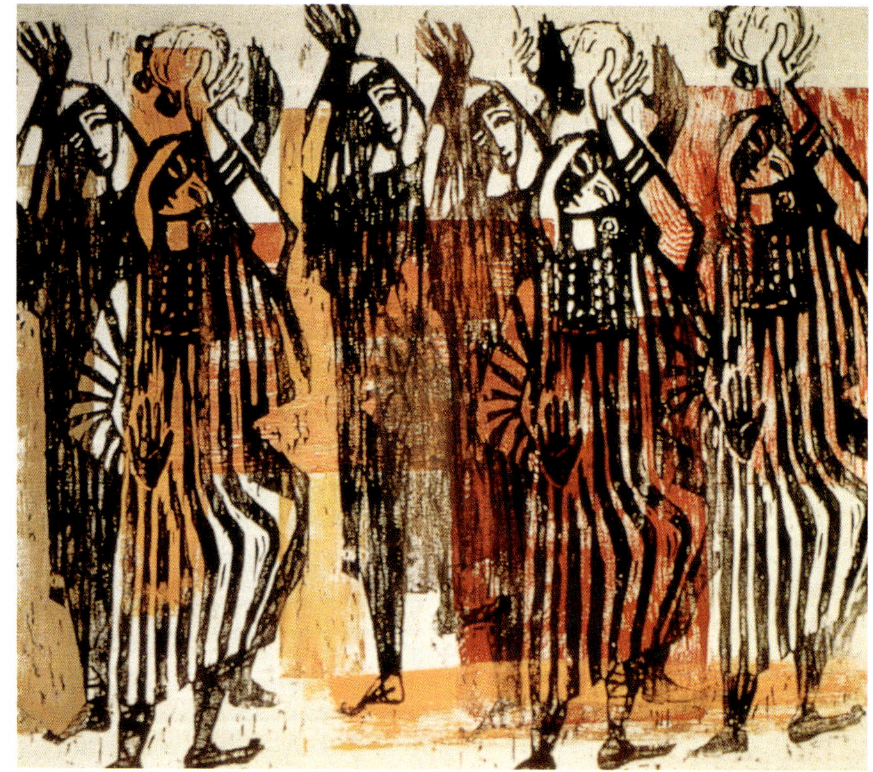

169

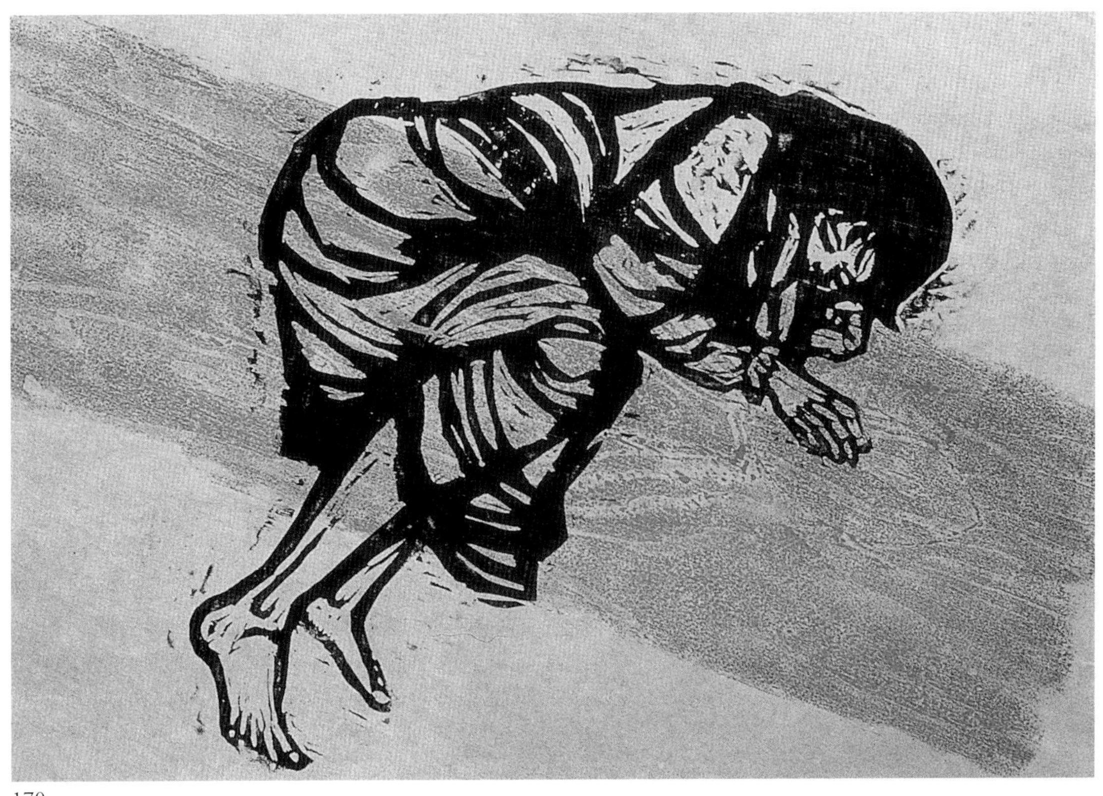
170

170. *Asleep,* 1963
33 x 38.2 cm (13 x 15 in)
Two-colour blocks woodcut

171. *Flower Women,* 1963
50.8 x 83.8 cm (20 x 33 in)
woodblock print on
mulberry paper

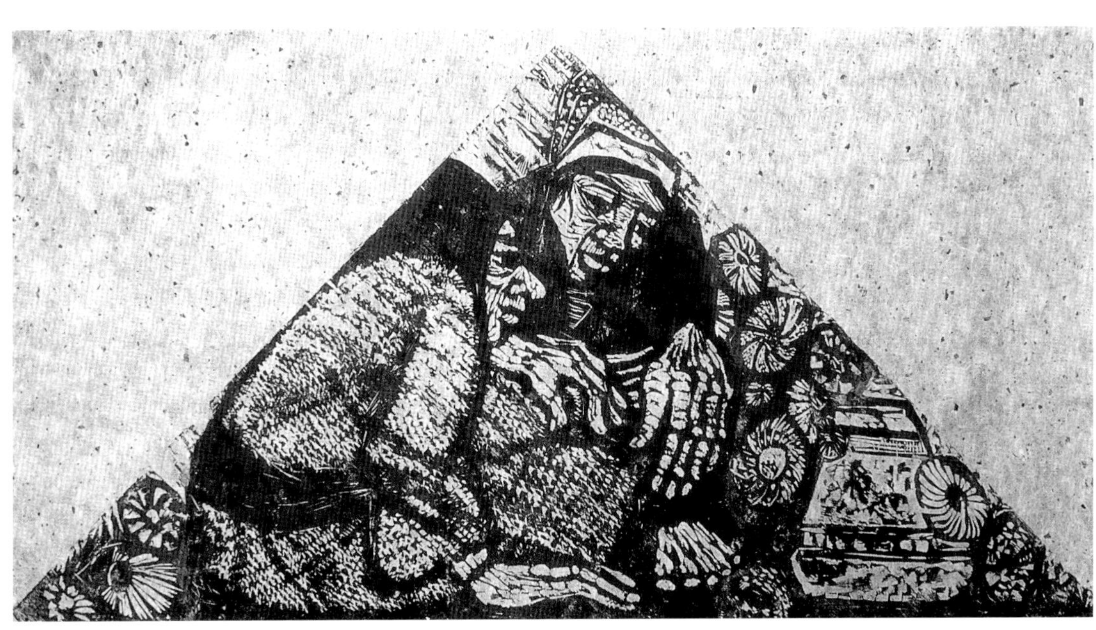
171

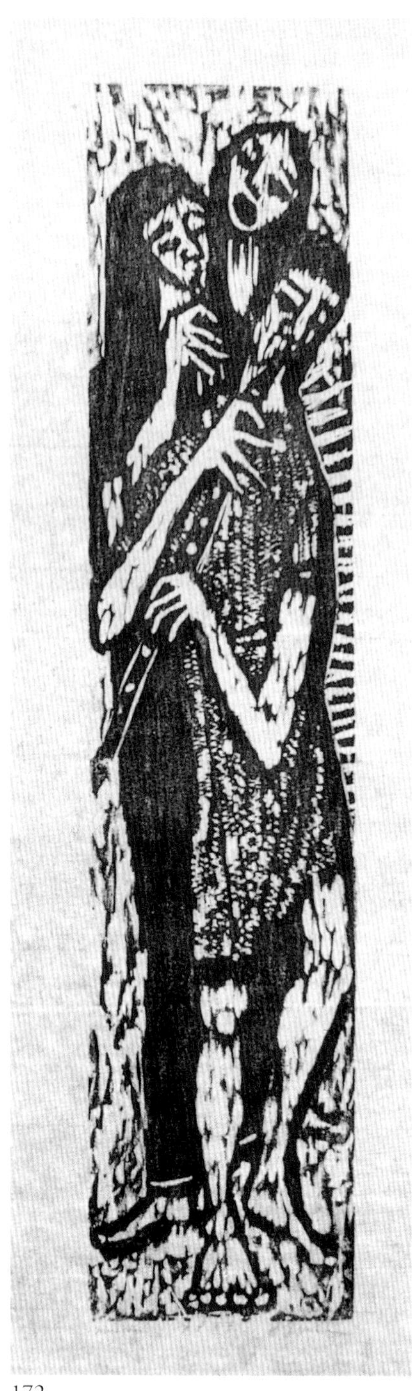

172

172. *Flute Players,* 1963
71.1x15.2 cm (28x6 in)
woodblock print

This print was also printed in colour, using the same experimental method of individual blocks inked in various colours, laid in the background, as in *Yemenite Dancers.* The colour prints are all different from one another.

from the cuts of two figures. This, she was told later, went against the conventions of printmaking, although it was abundantly clear that even then she was intuitively responding to Emerson's observation, "consistency is the hobgoblin of small minds."

In this same period, Pnina also experimented with wood engraving, using small pieces of olive wood. This technique differs from woodcut printing in that it is a method of relief printing from a block sawn across the grain to give a smooth, hard surface suitable to engraving with a burin (a fine steel cutting tool). As in woodcut, the incised areas print white, but the effect is closer to that of intaglio metal engraving and with no wood-grain pattern any longer in evidence. One of these 1960 wood engravings, *Mystery* (ill. 164), which was originally part of a large group of engravings commissioned for a poetry book, was included in *Endgrain — A Survey of North American Wood Engraving,* a comprehensive, limited edition book on the subject, published in 1995 by Barbarian Press, Mission, British Columbia.

Woodblock printing continued to engross Granirer during her residence in Urbana, Illinois, in the early 1960s. Its minimal technical requirements — small pieces of wood, some knives and gouges, a brayer (roller for applying ink) and assorted tubes of ink and papers — were all she needed. She did not even need a press, since perfectly satisfactory prints could be achieved by rubbing a spoon against the backside of the paper after it was applied to the inked block.

Significantly, the content of most of the woodcuts done in Urbana were memories of Granirer's former life in Israel. This is possibly a manifestation of a kind of "artistic culture shock", in which she could not yet visually relate to her new North American surroundings, or see anything innately "artistic" about them. She was not yet in any sense a "nature painter", a tendency for art-making which is peculiarly North American. Her instincts for art were socially or mythologically based and even her more personal, autobiographical insights were explored as creative possibilities.

Titles such as *Iraqi Woman,* 1962, *Old Woman on a Rock,* 1962, *Yemenite Dancers,* 1963 (ill. 169), *The Flight from Sodom,* 1964 and *Flower Women,* 1965 (ill. 171), are all memory snippets of details from sketches brought with her from a former life. The content remains one of memories of the realities of life in Israel, while she wrestles, as it were, to find new content for appropriate "pictures" of her current reality.

Absorbed as she was with her own growing family, images of children, children's fantasies and more universal symbols such as kings and clowns began to emerge in her work. During a one-year stay in Montreal (1966-1967) when she worked in the print studio of Pierre Ayot, she used a traditional printing press for the first and only time to produce a two-colours/two-blocks woodcut entitled *Masquerade.* More importantly, Ayot taught her the essentials of intaglio printing, where the design is cut or etched into the surface of a metal plate and the ink is held in the incisions or pits, as in metal engraving, drypoint, etching and mezzotint which variously stress line, texture or tonality.

Her first etchings, such as *Clown* (ill. 175), printed in a variety of colour combinations, and *Incantation* (ill. 27), both in 1967, awakened a new talent for exploiting and controlling a vastly more delicate line than was possible even in wood engraving. Etching, with its further possibilities, seems to have contributed to freeing Granirer from the heavy traditionalist implications of woodcut and its seemingly restricted subject matter, although there was a continued lag-time in content when she returned to Vancouver. *CHIMOVATONE* (a made-up acronym from CHIcago, MOntreal, VAncouver, TOronto, NEw York) and *Exit–Terre des Hommes* (woodblock and linocut) both reflect her experience in former locations.

Montreal had been her first residence in a large city, and *Exit–Terre des Hommes* (ill. 29) was among her first truly "contemporary" prints. Like nothing before, it evokes a sense of alienation and loneliness along with the textures, lines and veneers of this richly heterogeneous society.

Forest with Green Moon, 1973, is a collaged, experimental print comprising the imprints of reliefs as various as a roof shingle, a piece of tea crate and a wood engraving, with which the printmaker has created a repeated border along the lower edge. Nominally a landscape, diverse textures and exaggerated, brilliant colour turn it into a semi-abstract design which refers to no specific place or event but exists only for itself.

Although by the 1970s Granirer's drawing and painting career was now well established, her interest in printmaking continued. She took a summer course in 1978 with California printmaker Garo Antresian at the Vancouver School of Art (now Emily Carr College of Art and Design). The workshop was in lithography, a method of surface printing in which the design is drawn or painted (with a greasy crayon or ink) directly onto a polished limestone block. Through a process dependent on the natural antipathy of grease and water, prints can be produced without cutting into the block (as in relief or intaglio printing) and the effects may range from tonalities of soft granularity to contrasted clear and stippled colour areas. In its most simple, monochromatic form, lithography

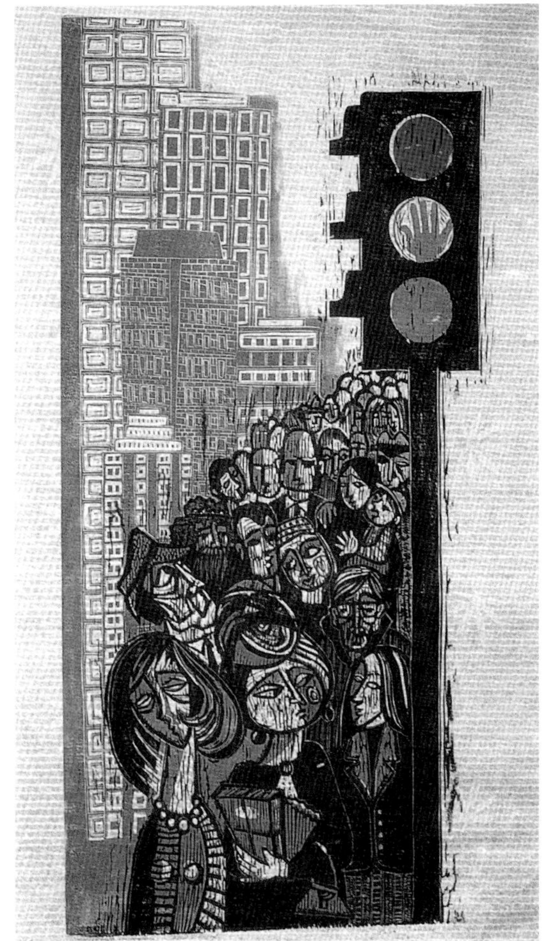

173

173. *CHIMOVATONE,* 1972
101.5 x 58.5 cm (40 x 23 in)
linoleum and yellow cedar print

174. *Trio,* 1967
22.8 x 20.7 cm (9 x 8 2/8 in)
four-colour linoleum blocks

175. *Clown,* 1967
18.8 x 15.3 cm (7 3/4 x 6 in)
colour etching

176. *Heron,* 1966
29.8 x 22.8 cm (11 3/4 x 9 in)
colour etching

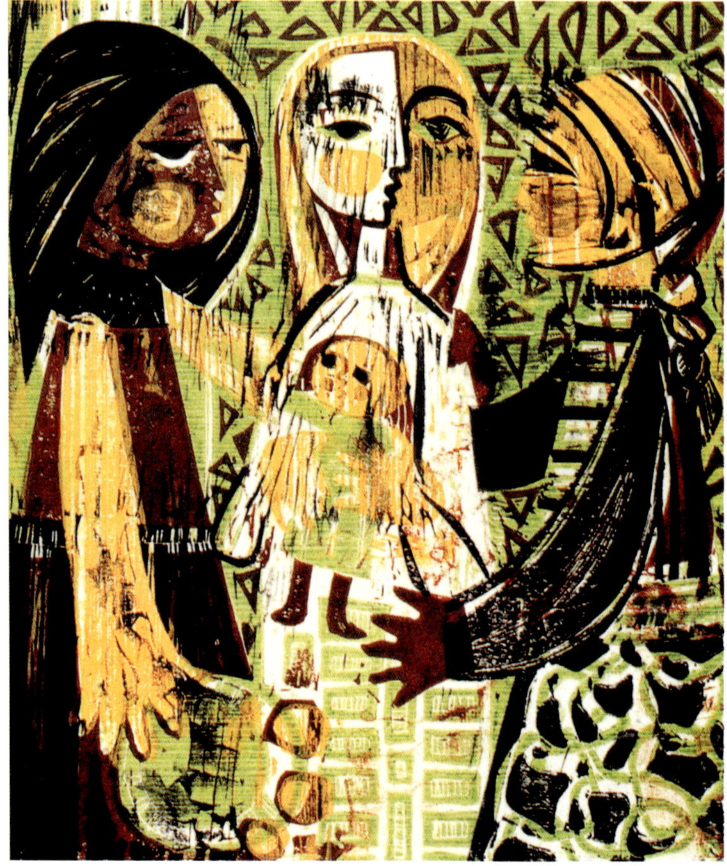

174

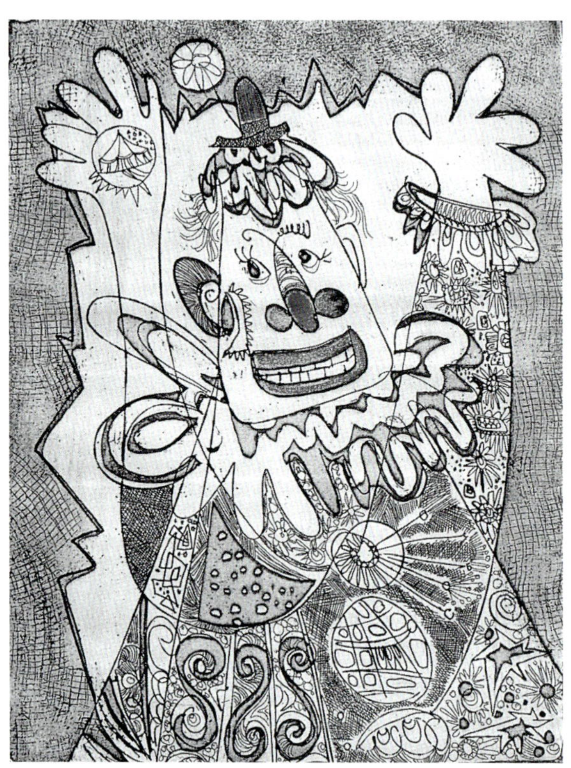

175

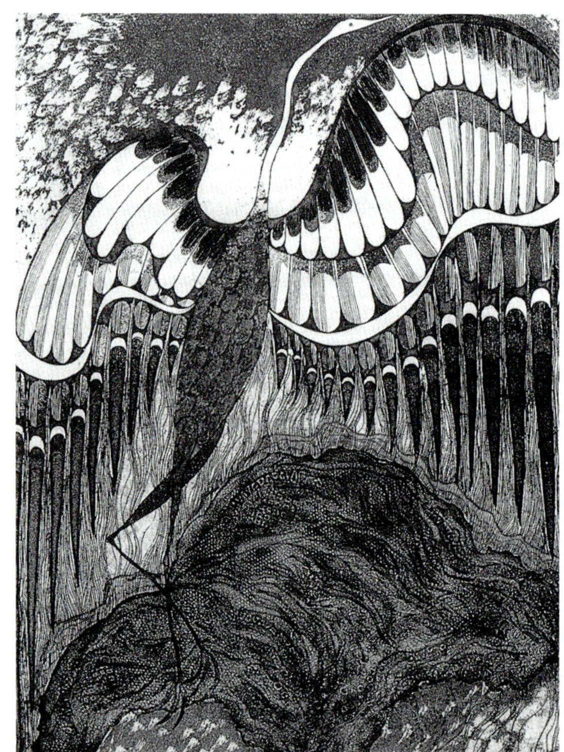

176

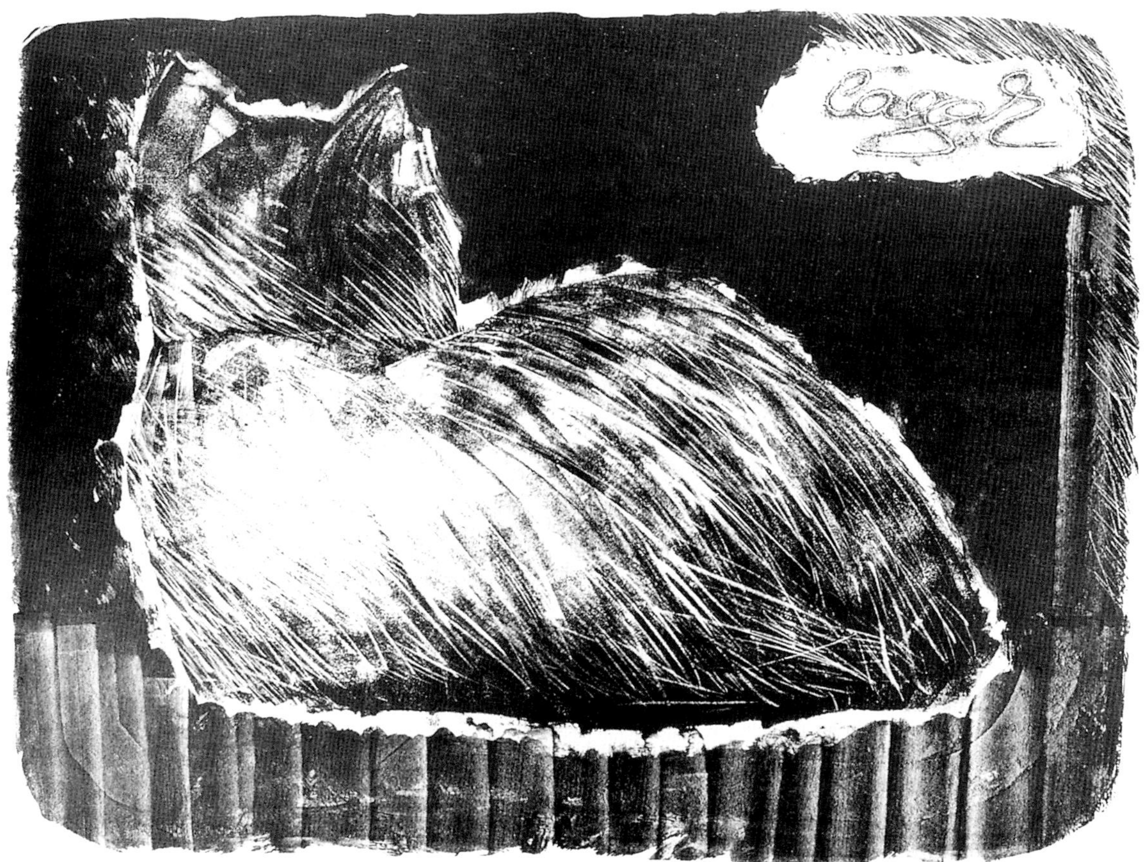

177

can emulate the subtle tonalities achieved in charcoal or graphite drawing — even the most photographic — which is why the process found favour in commercial illustration (à la Daumier) prior to the invention of photogravure.

Granirer's lithograph *Caesar,* 1978, is an excellent example of a soft image which stresses texture over line. Although aquatint and mezzotint etching could produce similar effects, nothing can be as direct or verifiable as direct drawing or painting on a stone surface which precisely reiterates every nuance in the ensuing print.

The same year Granirer went on to work with professional printer Rob Wilson of Crown Printers in Vancouver. With his assistance, she was able to produce far more complex compositions in colour, closer to her original drawings of fantastical birds and lush, Art Nouveau landscapes. *Loon* and *Wild Man of the Woods,* 1978 (ill. 178), mark a breakthrough of sorts in that the artist could now confidently produce multiples of compositions which were similar to her current style of drawings.

177. *Caesar,* 1978
36.8 x 48.3 cm (14 1/2 x 19 in)
black and white lithograph

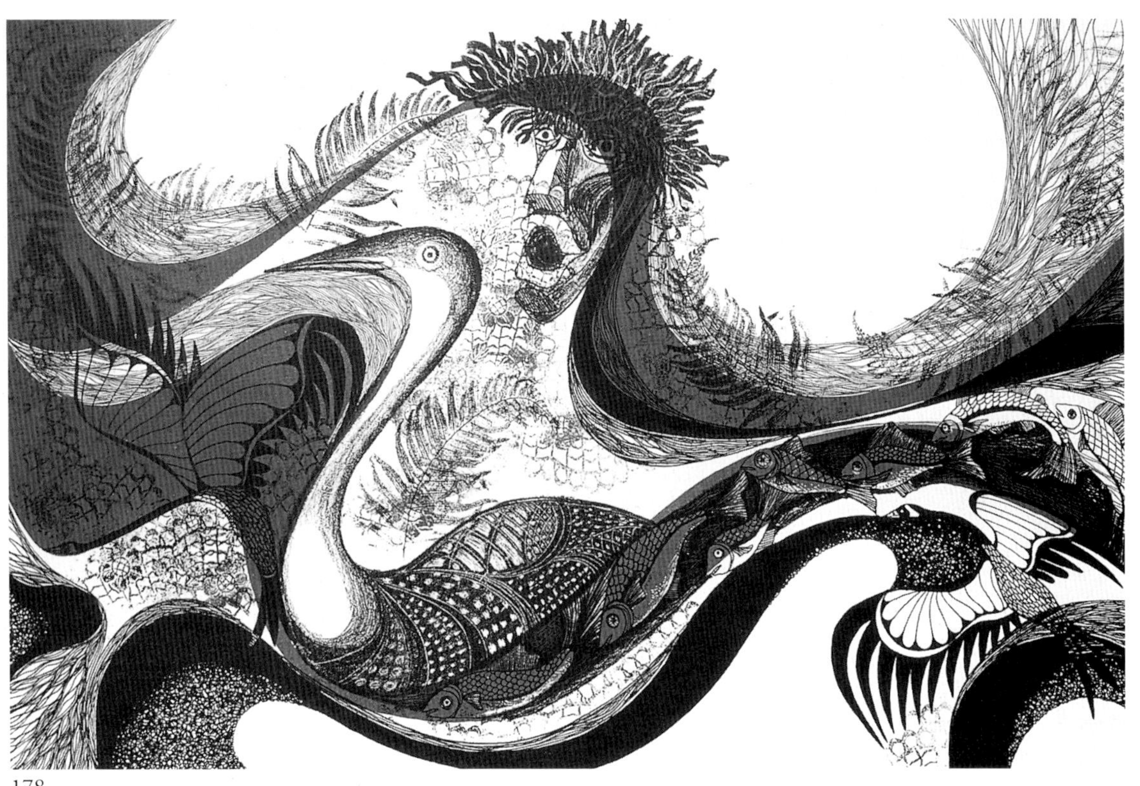

178

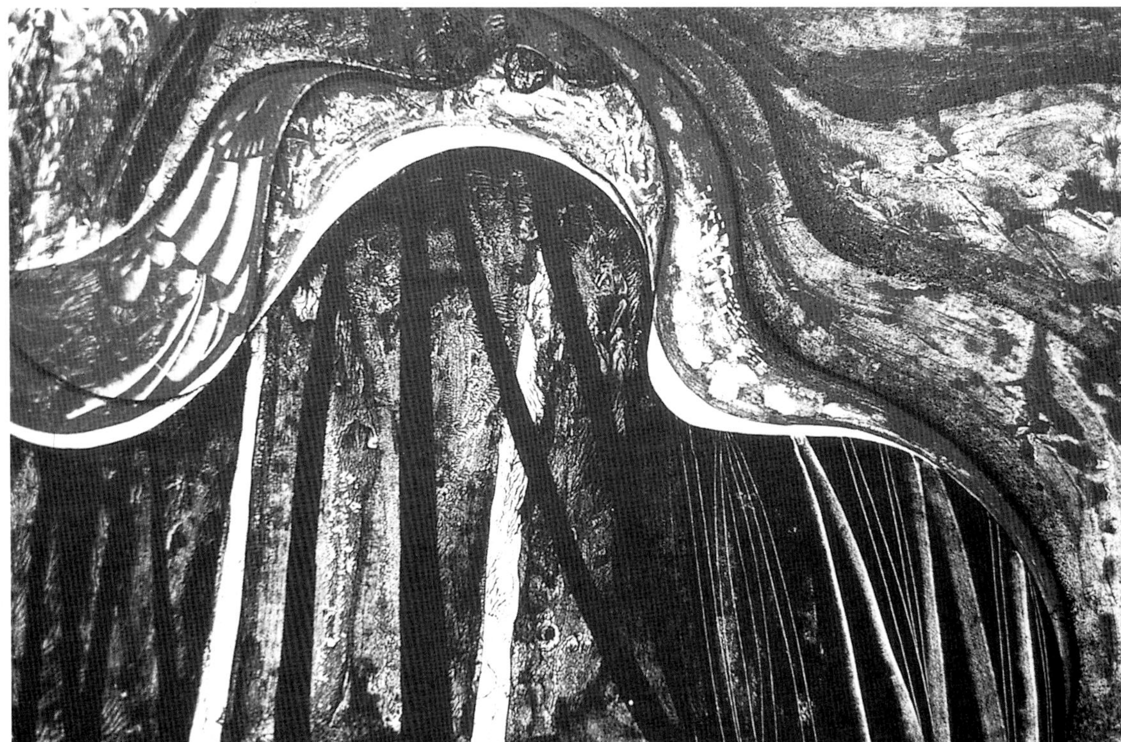

179

178. *Wild Man of the Woods,* 1978
36.2 x 56.5 cm
(14 1/4 x 22 1/4)
two-colour lithograph

179. *Deep Forest,* 1980
31 x 48.3 cm
(12 1/4 x 19 in)
two-colour lithograph

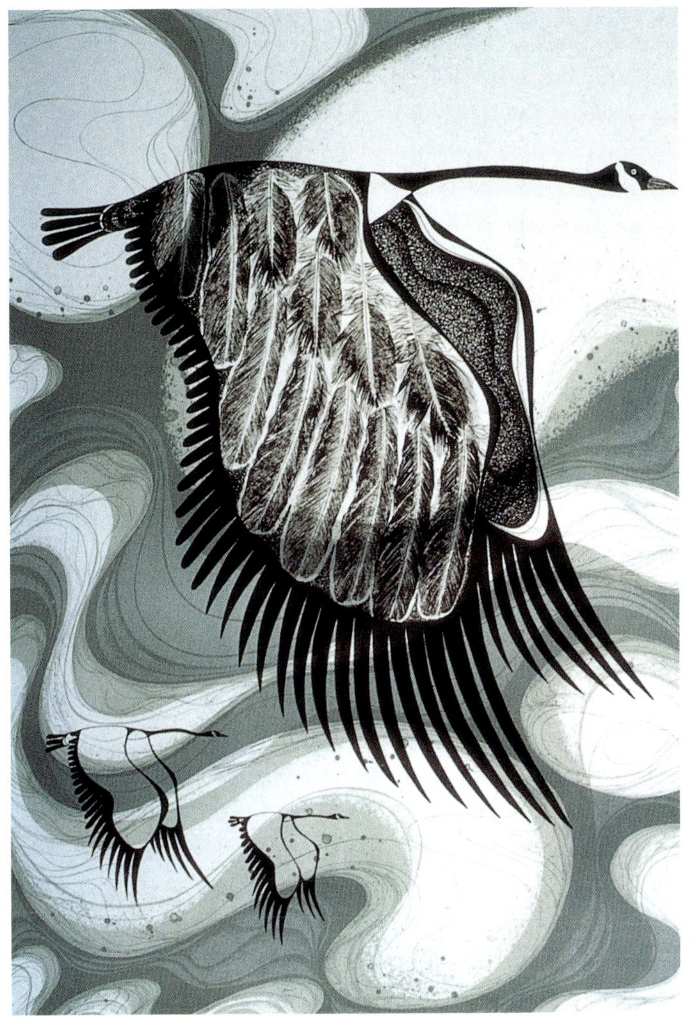

180

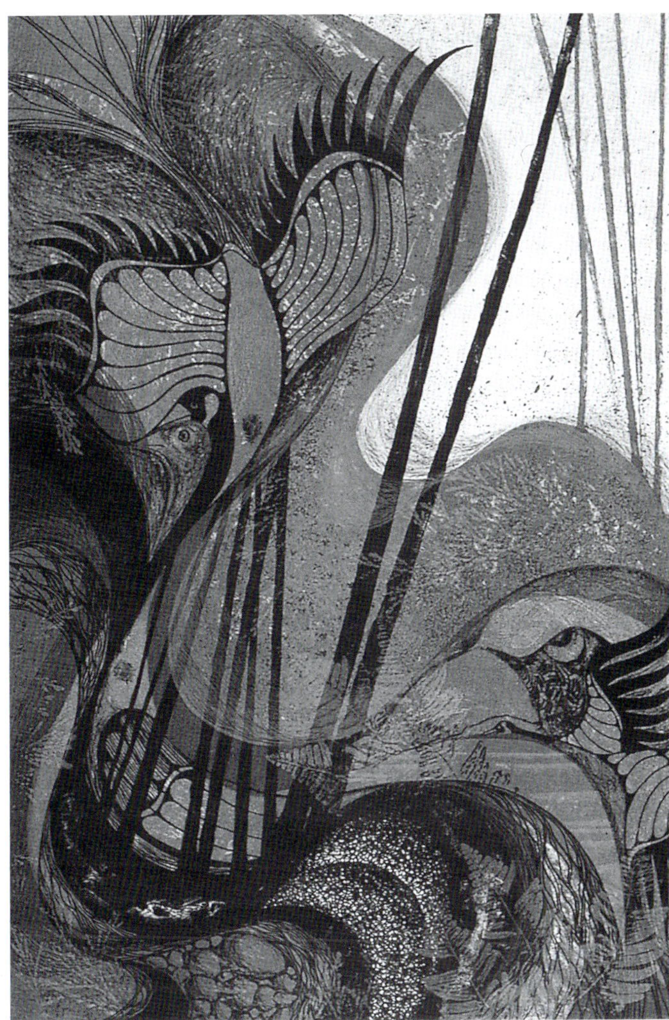

181

Two years later, in Paris, she worked with another master printer, Yann Samson, at the Atelier Clot, Bramsen & Georges. Samson had worked for a few years in California with Garo Antresian, but disliked the precise, scientific American approach. He both amused and liberated Granirer as far as stone etching technique was concerned: he was shockingly imprecise and slap-dash as far as mixing acid, wiping plates and timing were concerned, but he seemed to sense intuitively the conditions for a perfect print — more artistic and less scientific. This approach, which allowed for originality and discovery, appealed to Granirer's innate sense of herself as an artist rather than a printmaker.

Granirer worked with Yan Samson on several lithographs, incorporating imagery she had brought with her from British Columbia. *Pas-de-Deux,* 1980 (ill. 80), celebrates the balletic ascent of a pair of highly styl-

180. *In Flight,* 1980
70.5 x 49 cm (27 3/4 x 19 1/2 in)
colour lithograph

181. *Morning Mist,* 1980
69.3 x 53.4 cm (27 1/4 x 21 in)
colour lithograph

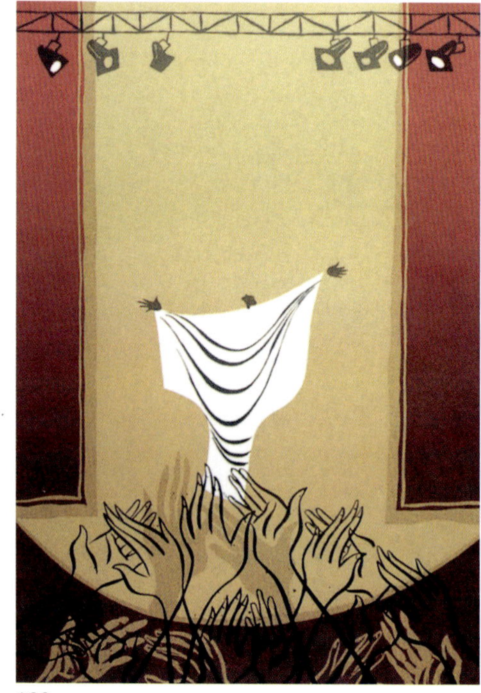

182

ized Canada geese amidst a vortex-like rainforest backdrop. The artist used this print as a poster for an exhibition during the same year, in Strasbourg. For prints such as *Morning Mist,* 1980 (ill. 181), an illusory meld of flora and fauna locked in an undulating, caressing embrace of a transparent grey wraith, she had brought feathers from home, which were incorporated into the image.

Actual feather imprints are even more apparent in *In Flight,* 1980 (ill. 180), done at the same time. *Deep Forest* (ill. 179), finished in the Paris studio, expresses her maturing reverence for and understanding of the canopying rainforests of British Columbia. Aware of her formidable rivals among B.C. nature-artists — Emily Carr, for one — Granirer had carved out a set of graphic stylizations which were uniquely her own.

The millstone quarry on Gabriola Island remains one of Granirer's most enduring visual inspirations. Although the circular cuts in a ribbon of limestone were man-made, their abandonment to nature and eventual rediscovery places them in the realm of alien, geometric phenomena in the midst of organic asymmetry. Her 1987 hand-coloured lithograph, *Quarry at Gabriola,* may be seen as a kind of "literalist abstraction", which plays on the psychological tension between realism and universal symbolism. There is an additional irony reflected in this print, if one remembers that the block on which the image was drawn is also *limestone,* or considers Pnina's general fascination, in this phase of her work, with the venerable qualities of stone itself.

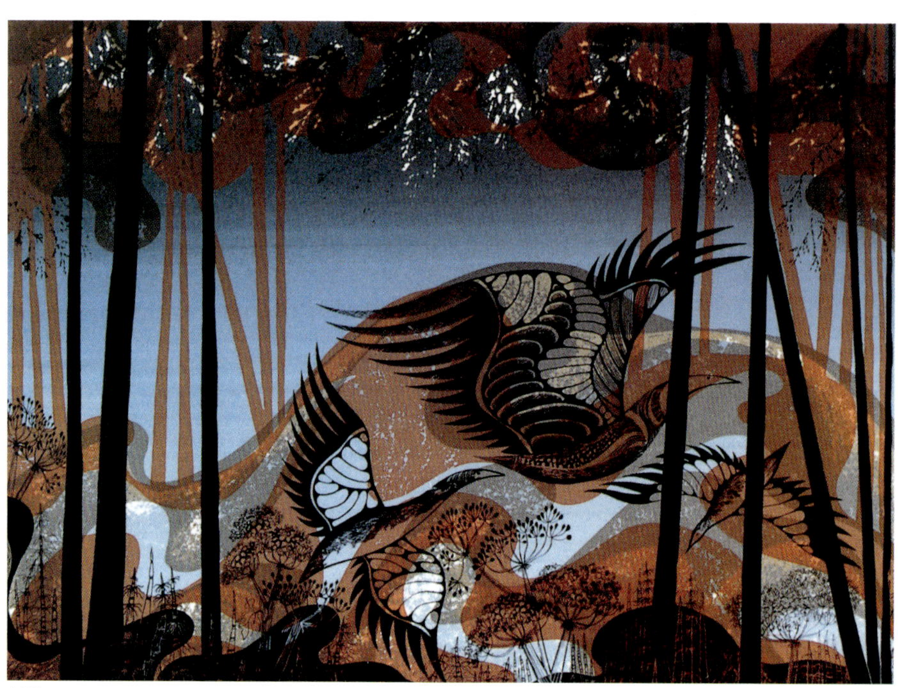

183

182. *Standing Ovation,* 1983
59 x 43.2 cm (23 1/4 x 17 in)
colour silkscreen

183. *Evening Flight,* 1985
45.5 x 63 cm (17 7/8 x 24 3/4 in)
colour silkscreen

Another planographic method, serigraphy or silkscreen printing (which is related to lithography only because it, too, utilizes a flat rather than engraved plate), is actually employed as a kind of stencil glued to a stretched, finely woven permeable mesh, through which inks or dyes can be pushed. Beginning in 1976, working with serigrapher David Schapira, Granirer found this printing technique particularly strong in line and flat colour values. Silkscreen produces no distinctive tonality or texture of its own, but it can be unerringly responsive to the finest detail. Prints such as *Wild Goose,* 1976, or *O Canada,* 1978, attest to what is perhaps a highpoint of Granirer's ever-popular, stylized birds in their most meticulous detail.

In 1981 she began working with print-technician and artist Michael de Courcy, producing first *Dreamskeeper,* a surreal portrait of a domestic (but provocatively inscrutable) cat, clutching a printed fabric emblazoned with images of nature and a sleeping child — and then *Spring Winds Through my Window.* Here white window mullions were employed as a compositional device, separating multiple variations of stylized birds, trees and undulating currents of atmosphere. This print was used as a poster for the artist's exhibition at the Gold Design Gallery in Calgary. *Evening Flight,* another print done in Michael de Courcy's

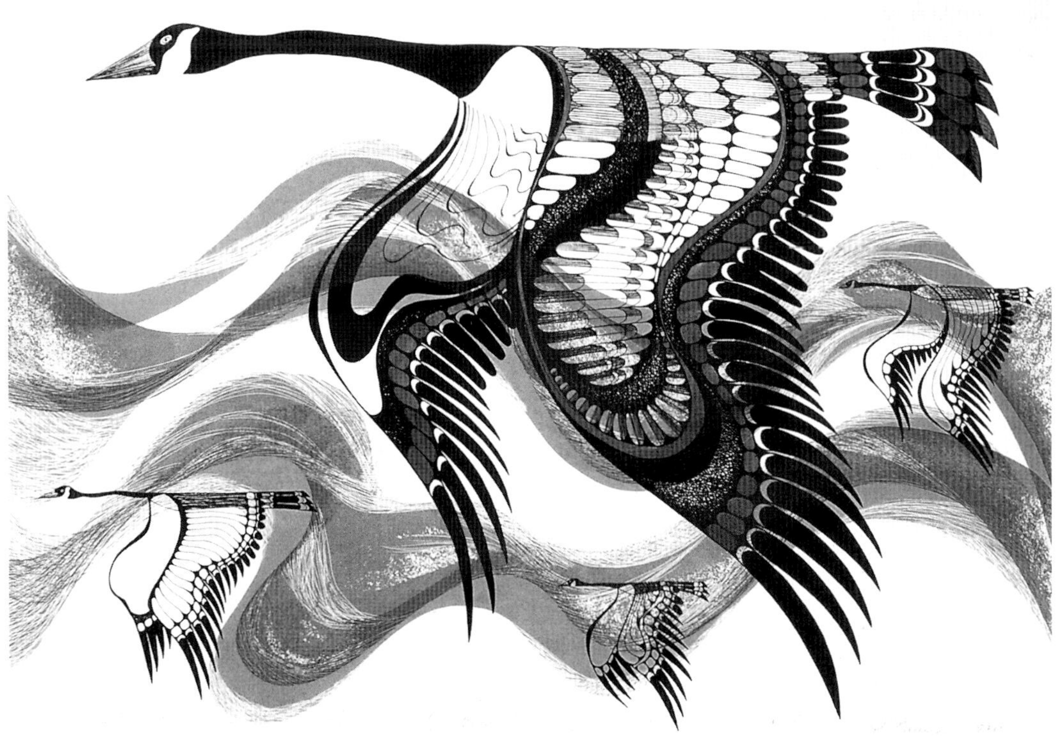

184

184. *O Canada,* 1977
44.5 x 71.2 cm (17 1/2 x 28 in)
colour silkscreen

185. *Games,* 1973
63.5 x 84 cm (25 x 33 in)
experimental woodblock print, never editioned.

studio, captures the flutter of birds' wings on their flight through the translucent evening sky.

When, in 1983, Granirer became peripherally involved with the Shakespeare Festival in Vancouver's Vanier Park, designing sets for *A Midsummer Night's Dream* and *As You Like It,* she also created the serigraphs *Othello* and *Standing Ovation* (ill. 182) for the Festival's fundraising auction. The print *Danzig,* 1989, with its Torah-like opened scroll in blue and gold, depicting the Nazi-destroyed synagogue of the city of Danzig, in Poland, was donated by the artist as a fundraiser print during the Danzig Exhibition at the Vancouver Museum.

When Granirer's hands were affected by arthritis at the beginning of the 90's, she lost some of her ability for delicate detail work and the physically demanding control of carving tools. As has been seen, she moved in response into an optimistic phase of broader and freer brush painting which has produced some of the strongest and most vivid paintings of her life as an artist.

185

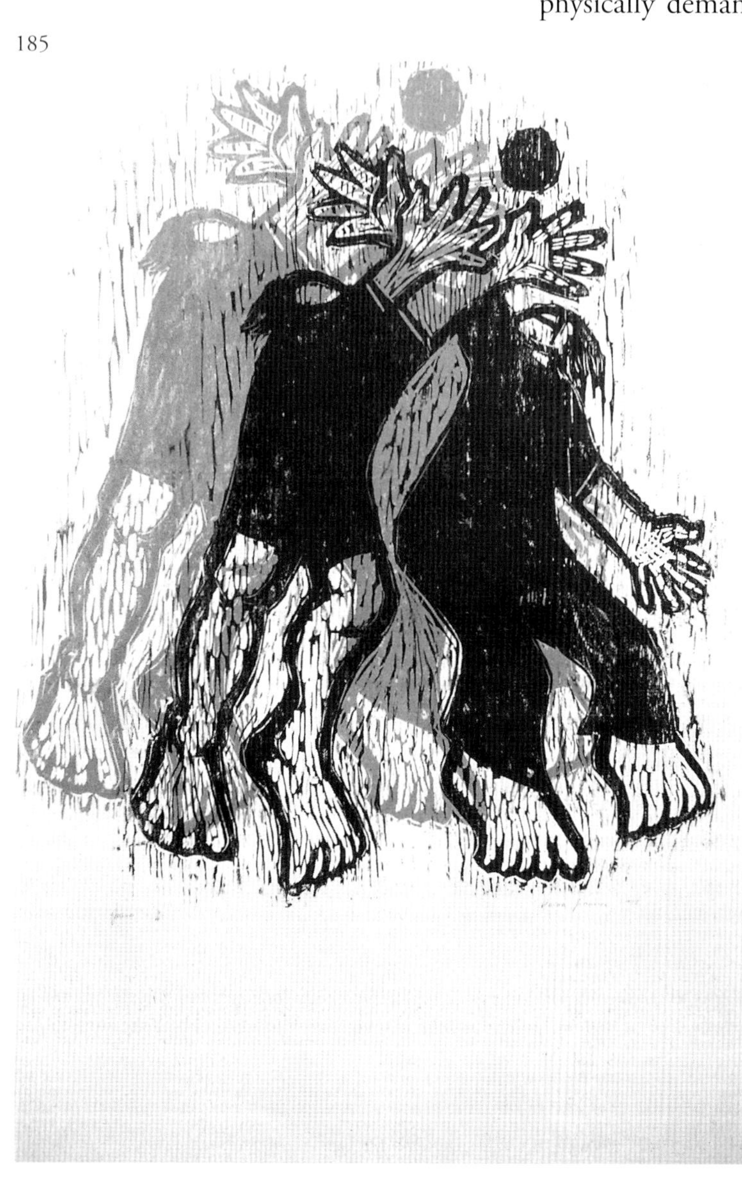

Because her forays into printmaking were always more experimental than mass-production-for-market driven, Granirer has benefited in a way which is well-understood by many artists: each distinctive technique mastered by the artist informs the next technique taken up. As drawing, in a sense, informs painting, painting prepares the way for etching and lithography in a way unavailable to those who are uninitiated with the brush. Silkscreen printing's incisive lines and edges can induce a certain "snap" in hard-edge painting (which often relies on structures of masking tape).

If one compares Granirer's drawing/painting/collaging career chronologically and comprehensively with her printmaking career (the two are inextricably entwined), one realizes the literal meaning of progressing from strength to strength. Neither of these careers can be regarded as separate or finite: she is neither "Pnina Granirer the printmaker", nor "Pnina Granirer the painter", which is why we have the useful, all inclusive word, appropriated from the worlds of theatre and performance: the word "artist".

Exhibitions

GROUP EXHIBITIONS

1997 **Artropolis–Browser 1997**, Roundhouse, Vancouver, British Columbia
Ars Mundi, 4th International Conference of the Visual Arts, Vancouver, British Columbia
Artists in Our Midst, Vancouver, British Columbia

1996 **Quay Gallery**, Gibsons, British Columbia, invitational
A Child's View, Richmond Art Gallery, Richmond, British Columbia, invitational

1995 **Artists in Our Midst**, Vancouver, British Columbia
A Jewish Beaux Arts, Zack Gallery, Vancouver, British Columbia, juried

1994 **Artists in Our Midst**, Vancouver, British Columbia
Unravelling the Patterns–Reweaving the Future: Women & a Sustainable Development Conference, University of British Columbia, Vancouver

1993 **Artists in Our Midst**, Vancouver, British Columbia
Mona in Brno, Gallerie Mladych, Brno, Czech Republic
11th Annual Vancouver Exhibition, Community Arts Council, Vancouver, British Columbia, juried
La Couleur de Mon Art, Studio 16, Vancouver, British Columbia
Canadian Art in Prague, Prague, Czech Republic, juried
The Canadada Elvis Stamp Series, Smash Gallery, Vancouver, British Columbia
Art Can't Hurt, NEWZONES Gallery, Calgary, Alberta

1992 **Canadian Women Artists**, Canadian Embassy, Paris, France
The Stendhal Effect, Emily Carr Art College, Vancouver, British Columbia
Christmas Show, Patrick Doheny Gallery, Vancouver, British Columbia
Rainforest of the Mind, Gallery Alpha, West Vancouver, British Columbia, invitational
Genesis, Victoria Jewish Centre, Victoria, British Columbia, invitational

1990 **A Celebration of the Female Spirit**, Coe Gallery, Portland, Oregon, invitational
Bumbershoot, Seattle, Washington, USA, juried

1989 **Emma Lake Artists' Workshop**, Emma Lake, Saskatchewan
Fear of Others: Art Against Racism, The Roundhouse, Vancouver, British Columbia, international, juried
The New Landscape, Pitt Gallery, Vancouver, British Columbia, invitational
BC Festival of the Arts, Vancouver, British Columbia, juried
Gallerie Annual 1989, Community Arts Council, Vancouver, British Columbia

Pnina Granirer & Peter Davenport, The British Columbia Club, Vancouver

1988 **Fear of Others**, Firehall Gallery, Vancouver, British Columbia, invitational

Mona Lisa, Surrey Art Gallery, Surrey, British Columbia, invitational

1987 **Réverbérations**, Canadian Cultural Centre, Paris, France, juried

Biennale de la Societé des Beaux-Arts, Grand Palais, Paris, France

1986 **B.C. Artists at the Square '86**, Robson Media Centre, Vancouver, British Columbia, juried

Jewish Visions '86, Vancouver, British Columbia, juried

Festival Francophone '86, Robson Media Centre, Vancouver, British Columbia, juried

101 Vancouver Artists, Pitt International Gallery, Vancouver, British Columbia, invitational

Sacred Arts, St. Andrew's Wesley Church, Vancouver, British Columbia, invitational

1985 **B.C. Women Artists 1885-1985**, Art Gallery of Greater Victoria, Victoria, British Columbia, invitational

Theatre Arts, Queen Elizabeth Theatre, Vancouver, British Columbia

1984 **B.C. Artists at the Square '84**, Robson Media Centre, Vancouver, British Columbia, juried

A Canadian Collection '84, Peretz School, Calgary, Alberta, invitational

Jewish Visions, Vancouver, British Columbia

1983 **A Canadian Collection '83**, Peretz School, Calgary, Alberta, invitational

Print Fair, Bern, Switzerland

Three Artists, Alliance Française, Vancouver, British Columbia

Viewpoints, A Reality Show: Working Women, Working Artists, Calgary Board of Education, Calgary, Alberta

1982 **A Canadian Collection '82**, Peretz School, Calgary, Alberta

Two Artists (with Alistair Bell), Bau-Xi Gallery, Vancouver, British Columbia

1981 **A Canadian Collection '81**, Peretz School, Calgary, Alberta, invitational

Emerging Canadian Artists, Muttart Gallery, Esso Collection, Calgary, Alberta, invitational

1980 **A Canadian Collection '80**, Peretz School, Calgary, Alberta

13 Women Artists, Gallery Move, Vancouver, British Columbia

1979 **Focus One Gallery**, Vernon, British Columbia

Kamloops Public Gallery, Kamloops, British Columbia

Hogar Gallery, Lima, Peru

1978 **The Archives Collection of the Society of Canada**, Society of Painters-Etchers & Engravers, Art Gallery of Hamilton, Hamilton, Ontario, juried

The Artist's Work as a Reflection of his Environment, Ottawa, Ontario, juried

Lincoln Centre, New York, NY, USA

WomanArt Gallery, New York, NY, USA

1977 **Accent on Art Gallery**, Winnipeg, Manitoba

WomanArt Gallery, New York, NY, USA

Third Annual Malaspina Print Show, Helen Pitt Gallery, Vancouver, British Columbia, juried

For the Birds, Fine Arts Gallery, University of British Columbia, Vancouver, invitational

14th Annual Calgary Graphics Exhibition International, juried

Civic Center, North Vancouver, British Columbia

King County Arts Commission Center, Seattle, Washington, USA
Four Canadian Artists, Zagreb, Yugoslavia
USA National Print Exhibiton, Hunterdon Art Centre, Clinton, NY, USA, juried

1976 **Civic Centre**, Community Arts Council, North Vancouver, British Columbia
Four Canadian Artists, Maribor, Yugoslavia
Four Canadian Artists, Moderna Galeria, Ljubljana, Yugoslavia
Nordau Annual, Vancouver, British Columbia

1975 **International Woman's Year**, Simon Fraser University, Burnaby, British Columbia, invitational
Dawn, Women Artists of BC, Student Union Building Gallery, University of British Columbia
Malaspina Printmaker's Society, Helen Pitt Gallery, Vancouver, British Columbia
Perth Drawing International, Perth, Australia, juried
Creative Women, Fantastic Gallery, Vancouver, British Columbia

1974 **Mido Gallery**, Vancouver, British Columbia
50 B.C. Women Artists, Student Union Gallery, University of British Columbia, Vancouver
11th Annual Graphics International, Alberta College of Art, Calgary, Alberta, juried
ISIS, travelling exhibition, Vancouver & British Columbia, juried
Canadian Painters-Etchers & Engravers, travelling exhibition, Toronto & Alberta, juried
Canadian Artists Exhibit, Student Union Gallery, International Math Conference, University of British Columbia
Dimension Gallery, Vancouver, British Columbia

1973 **Deer Lake Printmakers' Society**, Burnaby Art Gallery, Burnaby, British Columbia, juried
Three Artists, H & S Canvas Art Gallery, Vancouver, British Columbia

1972 **SCAN**, BC Artists, Vancouver Art Gallery, Vancouver, British Columbia
Canadian Painters-Etchers & Engravers, 56th Annual Show, Toronto, Ontario, juried
Private Patrons Collects, Simon Fraser University, Burnaby, British Columbia, invitational

1971 **Canadian Painters-Etchers & Engravers Annual National Graphics**, Toronto, Ontario, juried
Picture Loan Juried Show, Burnaby Art Gallery, Burnaby, British Columbia
H & S Canvas Art Gallery, Vancouver, British Columbia

1970 **United Nations Permanent Collection**, New York, Boston, Montreal
Four Artists, H & S Canvas Art Gallery, Vancouver, British Columbia

1968 **Canadian Painters-Etchers & Engravers Graphics National Show**, Toronto, Ontario, juried

1967 **Picture Loan Gallery Show**, Pointe Claire, Quebec

1965 **Annual Art Show**, Ithaca, NY, USA

1963 **Central Illinois Artists' League**, National Juried Show, Champaign, Illinois, USA

1960 **Union of Israeli Artists**, Jerusalem, Israel, juried

ONE PERSON SHOWS

1998 **Pnina Granirer: Celebrating a Life's Work, a 40 Years Survey**, Richmond Art Gallery, Richmond, British Columbia

1997 **Synchronicity**, Oktavia Gallery, Vancouver, British Columbia

1995 **Lecture and exhibition of *The Trials of Eve*** original drawings and book, Gabriel Books, Vancouver
In Search of Eden, Torres Gallery, Vancouver, British Columbia
Pacific Exchanges, Dr. Sun Yat Sen Garden, Vancouver, British Columbia
Pnina Granirer: 1985–1995, Zack Gallery, Vancouver, British Columbia

1993 **Lecture and exhibition of *The Trials of Eve*** originals and book, Alliance Française, Vancouver, British Columbia
Screening of Film *Trials of Eve,* opening remarks by Hon. Mary Collins, Minister for the Status of Women, and Wendy Carter, Regional Director for the Secretary of State, Canada, Pacific Cinémathèque, Vancouver, British Columbia
Juxtapositions, Richmond Art Gallery, Richmond, British Columbia
Heart of the Stone, Art Centre of New Westminster, British Columbia
Launch of paperback edition of *The Trials of Eve,* Fotobase Gallery, Vancouver, British Columbia

1991 **Lecture and exhibition of *The Trials of Eve*** originals and book, Richmond Public Library, Richmond, British Columbia

1990 **Carved Stones Suite**, Smash Gallery of Modern Art, Vancouver, British Columbia
Book Launching of *The Trials of Eve,* Women in Focus, Vancouver, British Columbia
Exhibition of *The Trials of Eve* originals and book, panel discussion "The Story of Eve, Myth and Reality," University Women's Club, Hycroft, Vancouver, British Columbia
Launch of *The Trials of Eve* book and exhibition of originals, Bowie & Weatherford Booksellers, Seattle, Washington, USA
Launch of *The Trials of Eve* book and exhibition of originals, The Great Northwest Bookstore, Portland, Oregon, USA
Back to the Source, The Sandstone Studio, Gabriola, British Columbia

1989 **Carved Stones**, Alliance Française, Vancouver, British Columbia
Carved Stones Series, Art Gallery of the South Okanagan, Penticton, British Columbia
Carved Stones Series, Galerie Rochon, Toronto, Ontario

1988 **New Works**, Gateway Gallery, Richmond, British Columbia
Carved Stones, Threshold Gallery, Vancouver, British Columbia

1987 **Les Rochers Bleus**, Galerie Aktuaryus, Strasbourg, France

1986 **The Blue Rocks Series**, Atelier Gallery, Vancouver, British Columbia

1985 **Family Portraits**, The Koffler Gallery, Toronto, Ontario

1984 **Cannibal Bird Suite & Trials of Eve**, The Sunshine Coast Arts Centre, Sechelt, British Columbia
Family Portraits, Bau-Xi Gallery, Vancouver, British Columbia
Family Portraits, Chrysalis Gallery, University of Western Washington, Bellingham, Washington, USA
New Works, Civic Centre, North Vancouver, British Columbia

Family Portraits, Calgary Jewish Centre, Calgary, Alberta

1983 **Du Canada**, Galerie Artal, Strasbourg, France

New Works, Gold Design Fine Arts, Calgary, Alberta

1982 **Cannibal Bird Suite & Trials of Eve**, Burnaby Art Gallery, Burnaby, British Columbia

New Works, Shalom Gallery, Vancouver, British Columbia

The Captive Birds Suite, Gold Design Fine Arts, Calgary, Alberta

1980 **West Coast Series**, Queen Elizabeth Theatre, Vancouver, British Columbia

New Works, Bau-Xi Gallery, Vancouver, British Columbia

West Coast Series, Gold Design Fine Arts, Calgary, Alberta

Les Oiseaux Cannibales, Galerie Artal, Strasbourg, France

1979 **Pnina Granirer: New Works**, Fleet Gallery, Winnipeg, Manitoba

Pnina Granirer: New Works, Topham Brown Gallery, Vernon, British Columbia

Pnina Granirer: New Works, Kelowna Art Association, Kelowna, British Columbia

Pnina Granirer: New Works, Kamloops Public Art Gallery, Kamloops, British Columbia

New Drawings, Bau-Xi Gallery (Jan. '79), Vancouver, British Columbia

Coast Forest Images, Bau-Xi Gallery (Dec. '79), Vancouver, British Columbia

1978 **New Works**, Maples Gallery, Saanich, British Columbia

New Works, Minotaur Gallery, Mission, British Columbia

Pnina Granirer, WomanArt Gallery, New York, NY, USA

Childhood Magic, Bau-Xi Gallery, Vancouver, British Columbia

1977 **New Drawings**, Presentation House, North Vancouver, British Columbia

New Works, Bau-Xi Gallery, Vancouver, British Columbia

1976 **Queen Elizabeth Theatre**, Vancouver, British Columbia

1975 **West Coast Images**, University Women's Club, Hycroft, Vancouver, British Columbia

West Coast Images, Bau-Xi Gallery, Vancouver, British Columbia

1972 **The Kite Series**, Burnaby Art Gallery, Burnaby, British Columbia

1970 **Pnina Granirer: Batiks**, Unitarian Church, Vancouver, British Columbia

1966 **Pnina Granirer**, Danish Art Gallery, Vancouver, British Columbia

Pnina Granirer, Pandora's Box Gallery, Victoria, British Columbia

Pnina Granirer, Art Den Gallery, Montreal, Quebec

1962 **Hillel House**, Urbana, Illinois, USA

Student Union Gallery, University of Illinois, Urbana, Illinois, USA

Awards & Commissions

1997	Two paintings for the Vancouver International Airport
1996	Painting for Temple Shalom, Vancouver, BC
	Christmas card for the Cancer Society
	Cover for the Greater Vancouver Jewish Telephone Directory
1995	Works featured on TV show *Strange Luck*
1994	Works featured on TV show *Sliders*
1992	Print Portfolio of 18 B.C. Artists for Wildlife Rescue, Vancouver, BC
1989	The Alcuin Citation Award for *The Trials of Eve*
1985	Christmas Card for Amnesty International
1984	Mural for Jewish Centre, Calgary, Alberta
	Sets for *The Comedy of Errors*
1983	Sets for *A Midsummer Night's Dream*
1978	Cover for University Singers record, University of British Columbia
1978	Cover for *Playboard Magazine,* Vancouver, BC, March
1977	Cover for *Prism International,* University of British Columbia, Fall issue
	Cover for *Two Plays* by George Woodcock, Talon Books
1976	Cover and 8 woodblock prints for *Canadian Fiction Magazine,* Feb/March, no. 20
	MAKARA Magazine, full page drawing, vol.1, no. 2
	First Prize Graphics, *Nordau Annual,* Vancouver, BC
1975	*The Upper-Left-Hand Corner, a Writer's Guide for the Northwest,* Burnaby, BC, pp. 1, 49, 81, 115
	Poster for *Canadian Fiction Magazine*
	Poster for Vancouver UNICEF
1974	Cover and 8 drawings for *Canadian Fiction Magazine,* summer issue
1965	Mural for TREE ISLAND factory
1964	Illustrations for slide lecture "Striving for Independence," Cornell University, Ithaca, NY, USA
1960	Wood engraving illustrations for *Small Verses,* by Moshe Hanaami, Jerusalem, Israel
	Illustrations for *Chamber Music* by James Joyce, translation Moshe Hanaami, Jerusalem, Israel
1960–62	Illustrations for children's books, Jerusalem, Israel
	Illustrations for children's stories for filmstrips, Department of Culture, Jerusalem, Israel

Collections

Archives of the Society of Canadian Painters-Etchers and Engravers, Ontario
Agnes Etherington Gallery Rental, Ontario
B.C. Ferry Corporation, BC
Bettison Management, BC
Burnaby Art Gallery, BC
Canada Northwest Land Ltd., Calgary, Alberta
Canada Northwest Energy Ltd., Calgary, Alberta
City of North Vancouver, BC
City of Strasbourg, France
Dal Cor Corporation, BC
Daon Development Corp., BC
Dominion Securities Pitfield, Toronto, Ontario
Environmental Management Assoc., Calgary, Alberta
Esso Canada Resources, Calgary, Alberta
Glenbow Museum, Calgary, Alberta
Gulf Oil of Canada, Calgary, Alberta
Human Rights Commission, UN, New York, NY
J.E.D. Management, BC
Jewish Centre, Calgary, Alberta
Jewish Community Centre, Vancouver, BC
Lions' Gate Hospital, North Vancouver, BC
London Regional Art Rental, London, Ontario
Merlin Resources Ltd., Calgary, Alberta
The Peter Savage Collection, Calgary, Alberta
Pan Canadian Petroleum, Calgary, Alberta
Richmond Art Gallery, BC
Rogers Group, BC
Shell Oil of Canada, Calgary, Alberta
Simon Fraser University, BC
Sun Tower, Toronto, Ontario
Supreme Petroleum, Toronto, Ontario
Toby, Russell, Buchnell & Partners, Vancouver, BC
UNICEF Collection, New York, NY
Vancouver Art Gallery Art Rental, Vancouver, BC
Vancouver International Airport, Vancouver, BC
Yad Vashem Museum, Jerusalem, Israel

Professional Activities & Studies

PROFESSIONAL ACTIVITIES

until 1996 Instructor, Art Department, Centre for Continuing Studies, University of British Columbia
1995 "Eve and her Image in Literature," lecture at Langara College, Vancouver, BC
1994 "Eve and her Image in Literature," lecture at Langara College, Vancouver, BC
"On The Trials of Eve," Centre for Research and Women's Studies and Gender Relations, the University of British Columbia
"On The Trials of Eve," Vancouver Public Library, City Poets Series
1993 Co-Founder of "Artists in Our Midst," a new concept for community participation in the Arts, Vancouver, BC
Public presentation at the Pacific Cinémathèque, Vancouver, BC
Organizer, panel discussion on the image of Eve in literature, history and art, Alliance Française
Production of multi-media Flamenco performance for JUXTAPOSITION exhibition, Richmond Art Gallery, Richmond, BC
1989 An organizer of the international exhibition "Fear of Others: Art Against Racism," held in Vancouver in 1989. Facilitator, panel discussion involving Leon Golub and Nancy Spero among others.
Founder of the Art Gallery at Temple Shalom, Vancouver, BC
Founding member of the Jewish Festival of the Arts, Vancouver, BC
Lecture on *The Trials of Eve,* the Richmond Public Library, BC
"Eve: Myth or Reality?" — panel discussion at the University Women's Club, Vancouver, BC
1970's Presentations and workshops at Vancouver area schools
Invitational lectures on own work at various clubs and organizations

STUDIES

1989 Emma Lake, Saskatchewan
1984 Stage painting with Ted Roberts, University of British Columbia
1980 Lithography at Atelier Clot, Bramsen & Georges, Paris, France
1978 Lithography with Garo Antresian, Vancouver School of Art
1969-72 Printmaking at the Print Studio, Vancouver
1967 Printmaking at La Guilde Graphique, with Pierre Ayot, Montreal
1956-60 The Bezalel Art Academy, Jerusalem, Israel

Bibliography

1998 *Pnina Granirer: Portrait of an Artist* by Ted Lindberg, Vancouver: Ronsdale Press

1997 "In Search of Eden" in *Patterns in the Lives of Jewish Women,* edited by Rachel Josefowitz Siegel and Ellen Cole, New York: Haworth Press

Canadian Woman Studies, Women and Spirituality, vol.17 no.1, Toronto, pp. 81, 91

Ars Mundi — 4th International Conference for the Visual Arts (catalogue), Vancouver

1996 *Singing Waters, Celebration* — Commemorative Book of the Jewish Community Centre of Greater Vancouver, p. 31

1995 "Mystery" in *Endgrain: Contemporary Wood Engraving in North America,* Mission, BC: Barbarian Press

"In Search of Eden," Profile by Amir Ali Alibhai, *Artfocus* Magazine (Fall), Toronto, pp.18–19.

"The Framing of Eve," in *Matriart,* Toronto, vol. 5 no. 3, p. 27

"Mystery on Gabriola," in *Continuing Studies Calendar* (Spring/Summer), University of British Columbia, cover, pp. 2, 8

1994 "The Trials of Eve," Cathy Berson, *Outlook* (March), Vancouver, pp. 19, 20

Unravelling the Past–Reweaving the Future, Women & A Sustainable Development, catalogue for University of British Columbia International Conference

The Feminine Viewpoint (catalogue), Jacob

1993 *Discerning Woman* (May), Vancouver, p. 9

Canadian Artists for the Olga Havel Foundation (catalogue), Galerie Palles, Prague, Czech Republic

1990 *The Trials of Eve,* film by Gretchen Jordan-Bastow, based on book by Granirer of the same name

Western News, profile (July 12), Vancouver

1989 "Pnina Granirer: artist's statement," *Gallerie,* Vancouver, pp. 60–61

Pnina Granirer: Profile of an Artist, 28 min. video, Knowledge Network, BC, shown nationally on Educational Networks and Vision Network

Lilith Magazine, New York (Fall), pp.18–20

Fear of Others: In Search of Tolerance (catalogue), Vancouver, p. 44

1988 *Mona Lisa and Others,* Mail Art Presents (catalogue), curated by Ed Varney & Ann Rosenberg, Surrey Art Gallery

Fear of Others: Art Against Racism, International Exhibition (catalogue), Vancouver, p. 27

1987 *Poésie et Modernité* (catalogue), Centre Culturel Canadien, Paris, France

1986 *VIII Festival Francophone* (catalogue), Vancouver, p. 7

Book and Program Cover for *The Jewish Family Service Golden Jubilee,* Vancouver

1985 *1885–1998 BC Women Artists* (catalogue), Art Gallery of Greater Victoria, BC

1983 "Gallery," *Western Living* (January), Vancouver, p. 78

"Dawn," "Forest Ghosts," Program for the Conference of the Canadian Association of Orthodontists, Vancouver

1982 *Pnina Granirer, Recent Works* (catalogue), Burnaby Art Gallery, Burnaby, BC

"Pnina Granirer, Une Artiste de l'Ouest Canadien," Jeanne Maranda, *Canadian Woman Studies,* vol. 3 no. 3, Toronto, pp. 4–6

1981 *Emerging Canadian Artists* (catalogue), The Esso Collection, Muttart Gallery, Calgary, Alberta

1978 "Freedom, Harmony, Endurance and Motion," Melanie Gold, *ARTS WEST,* (May-June), vol. 3, no. 3, Winnipeg, pp. 8–13

Works and Words, Womanart at the Lincoln Center (catalogue), New York

The Archives Collection of the Society of Canadian Painters-Etchers & Engravers (catalogue), Toronto

The Artist's Work as a Reflection of his Environment (catalogue), Canada-Israel Cultural Foundation, Ottawa

Four Canadian Artists, catalogue for exhibition in 3 museums of the former Yugoslavia

1977 *14th Annual Calgary Graphics Exhibition (International)* (catalogue), Calgary, Alberta

Atlantis: A Women's Studies Journal, vol. 4, no. 2, Acadia University, Nova Scotia, pp. 13, 180

1975 *Dawn,* Women Artists of BC (catalogue), Student Union Gallery at the University of British Columbia, Vancouver, BC

Perth Prize for Drawing International (catalogue), Western Australian Art Gallery, Perth, Australia

1973 *Three Hours Later,* Vancouver, p. 93

1969 "Cover," *UNICEF Calendar,* New York

RADIO & TELEVISION

1996 Interview with Hélène Deggan on CBC Radio Canada, Pacific Exchanges

1995 *The Trials of Eve,* Women's Television Network (17 min), December

In Search of Eden, interview with Hélène Deggan on CBC Radio Canada, April

Artists in Our Midst, interview with Christian Bernard on French CBC Radio, April

In Search of Eden, reportage by Thérèse Champagne, French CBC TV, April

1994 *The Trials of Eve,* Women's TV Network — The Creators, December

Artists on Our Midst, interview with Joyce Janvier, CBC French TV, April

Artists in our Midst, interview with Hélène Deggan, CBC Radio Canada, April

Artists in Our Midst, CBC Newshour, April

Artists in Our Midst, Rogers Cable — News Item, May

Almanac, interview with Cecilia Walters, CBC Radio, March

1993 *Juxtapositions,* Producer Nina Ferretti, interview with Ara Parker, Knowledge Network TV — Arts Edge, November

Juxtapositions, 30 min. interview with Denise Christie, Rogers Cable TV, November

News spot with Joyce Janvier, CBC French TV, April

The Trials of Eve, panel discussion with Sylvie Beauregard for International Woman's Week, CBC French TV, March

The Trials of Eve, interview with Hélène Deggan, CBC Radio Canada, March

1991 *The Kyoto Suite*, interview with Hélène Deggan, CBC Radio Canada, October

The Trials of Eve, interview with Leslie Allison, Co-Op Radio, March

1990 "Back to the Source," interview with Hélène Deggan, CBC Radio Canada, July

"Profile" on Roger's Cable, Gabriola, BC, July

Interview with Elizabeth Roux, CBC French TV

Launching of *The Trials of Eve* at *Women in Focus Gallery,* Vancouver, BC, CBC French TV — reportage by Thérèse Champagne, January

The Trials of Eve, interview with Michael Eizenstadt, QMFM, February

The Trials of Eve, Roger's Cable, North Vancouver, BC, January

1989 *The Carved Stones*, TV interview on exhibition at the Art Gallery of the South Okanagan, Penticton, BC

1988 Interview with Porte Ouverte, CBC Radio Canada, Vancouver, BC, November

Interview, CBC Radio, Art Beat, April

Interview with Hélène Deggan on L'Orient Express, CBC Radio Canada, April

Interview with Christian Bernard on Horizons, CBC Radio Canada, April

1987 Interview with Michel Serplet, CBC International, Galerie Aktuaryus, Strasbourg, France, February

1984 Interview with Hélène Deggan, CBC Radio Canada, April

1980 TV Documentary for TF1, Strasbourg, France, December

REVIEWS

Les Affiches-Moniteur, Strasbourg, France (Jean Christian) — April 4, 1980, Feb. 10, 1987

Artmagazine (Deanna Levis) — Oct./Nov., 1977, May/June, 1980

Arts West — May/June, 1984

The Bellingham Herald, Bellingham, WA (Jerry Szymanski) — Oct. 5, 1984

BC Bookworld — winter, 1993

Borba, Yugoslavia (Prvoslav Mitie) — Sept. 4, 1976

Burnaby Today — April 18, 1985

The Burnaby & New Westminster News (Michael Ajzenstadt) — Feb. 18, 1990

The Calgary Sun (Kerry McArthur) — Feb. 19, 1982

Canadian Jewish News, Toronto, ON (Ron Csillag) — April 18, 1985

Coast News, Sechelt, BC — Jan. 9, 1984, Jan. 17, 1984

Coast News, Sechelt, BC (Belinda McLeod) — Jan. 23, 1984

The Columbian — March 14, 1969, March 8, 1974

The Courier (Maureen Korman) — June 17, 1990, Aug. 12, 1990

The Courier (Ann McLaughlin) — Nov. 25, 1992

The Courier (Fiona Hughes) — Jan. 1993, April 28, 1993

The Daily Sentinel, Kamloops, BC — April 8, 10, 1979

Dernieres Nouvelles d'Alsace, Strasbourg France — April 18, 1980, Feb. 11, 1987
The Gabriola Sounder (Phyllis Reeve) — June 1990, June 10, 1994
Georgia Straight, Vancouver (Joyce Woods) — April 6, 1984
Illustrierte Neue Welt, Vienna (Ursula Ucicky) — June-July, 1987
The Jewish Star, Calgary (Gila Wertheimer) — Oct. 9, 1981, April 2, 1982, March 25, 1983
The Kamloops Daily Sentinel — Aug. 4, 1979, April 10, 1979
The Kitsilano News — May 12, 1993
The Montreal Gazette — Dec. 24, 1966
News Gazette, Urbana, Illinois, USA (Nancy Levner) — Oct. 9, 1963
North Shore News, (Archie Graham) — Oct. 20, 1991
Le Nouvel Alsacien, Strasbourg, France — April 19, 1980, March 30, 1983
Penticton Herald (P.M. Ritchie) — July 11, 1989
Richmond Review — Sept. 22, 1993
The Sechelt Press — Jan. 17, 1984, Jan. 10, 1984
Le Soleil de Colombie (Louise Lassagne) — April 14, 1989
Le Soleil de Colombie (Jeanne Baillault) — April 28, 1955
The Times Colonist, Victoria, BC (Robert Amos) — July 27, 1991
The Vancouver Province (Art Perry) — Oct. 3, 1975, June 1977
The Vancouver Sun (David Watmough) — March 3, 1966
The Vancouver Sun (Christopher Dafoe) — June 11, 1970, March 18, 1971
The Vancouver Sun (Joan Lowndes) — Dec. 9, 1971, April 14, 1972
The Vancouver Sun (Jamie Craig) — March 30, 1973
The Vancouver Sun (Mary Fox) — Sept. 15, 1976
The Vancouver Sun (Wayne Edmonstone) — June, 1977, Feb. 19, 1977, Sept. 2, 1977, Dec. 19, 1980
The Vancouver Sun (Anne Tempelman-Kluit) — Nov. 27, 1982, Aug. 6, 1983, Oct. 27, 1982, Feb. 15, 1990
The Vancouver Sun (Anne Rosenberg) — March 16, 1991, Nov. 2, 1991
The Vancouver Sun (Peter Wilson) — May 14, 1993, April 21, 1994
Vanguard (Jill Pollack) — Summer, 1984
Victoria Daily Colonist (Robert Amos) — July 16, 1966
Western Front, Bellingham, WA (Liisa Hannus) — Oct. 12, 1984
Western Jewish Bulletin, Vancouver — April 29, 1976, April 16, 1982, April 22, 1982, May 13,1982, Feb. 9, 1984, March 1, 1984, Aug. 2, 1984, Nov. 2, 1984, Aug. 2, 1984, Nov. 23, 1986, April 9, 1987, April 7, 1988, Feb. 15, 1990, June 28, 1990, Dec. 3, 1992 June 23, 1994, Dec. 1, 1995
The West Ender (Liz Gilbert) — August 11, 1983, (Mia Johnson) — July 29, 1989
The Winnipeg Tribune (Anne-Marie Holden) — Oct. 10, 1980

Selected Reviews

Artfocus (Toronto) Fall 1995: 18–19

PNINA GRANIRER: In Search of Eden

By Amir Ali Alibhai

In Search of Eden, a series of new works by Vancouver-based artist **Pnina Granirer** was held from April 13 to May 6 at the *Torres Gallery* on the west side of the city. The show marked the 60th birthday of the artist and 30 years of her art-making in Canada. The title of the show underscores her process and intentions and speaks not only of her current interests, but of her life-long search as an artist.

In this expressive and painterly series, Granirer explores images of flowers, specifically poppies, and utilizes strategies which make use of collage and mixed media techniques. As a result of her many years of prolific output, the artist demonstrates easy control of her tools and skills. Images and symbols reoccur and manifest themselves – another clue to process. There is a definite sense of freedom and joy expressed in these works which convey moments of understanding and enlightenment, mixed with passages of questioning and confusion.

Born in Romania, educated in Israel, Montreal, Paris and Vancouver, and having travelled extensively, Granirer brings a great deal of experience and knowledge to her work. The sources are diverse, ranging from Northwest Coast First Nations oral culture and imagery, to Muslim gardens at the Alhambra in Spain, to the Bible and the Torah. She uses these sources to create her own vocabulary of images by adding, removing and transforming elements from them with each new series that she makes.

One must reconsider past work when viewing current work by this artist. For instance, there are strong connections between the *Alhambra Series* (1992/93), where Granirer was re-interpreting the formal and conceptual meaning of these gardens in Granada, and the current poppy motif. It is as if the new work grew directly out of the search being carried out in the preceding series. The gardens that so enamoured the artist in Spain, were built by Muslim "invaders" who created their own Eden within an impenetrable fortress in the hills.

Granirer's continuing fascination with the story of Eden and its effect on Western history and society, found a place to focus in the gardens of the Alhambra. Perhaps this is where the search for Eden began for the artist, or maybe it was during the *Trials of Eve Series* and bookworks (1981/82, 1989) when Granirer reexamined and satirized the biblical account of Eve? Or maybe it was during the *Cannibal Bird Series* (1982) when she explored the stories and beliefs of a non-Judeo-Christian-Islamic culture? All these series contained their dark sides, the unanswerable questions, the fears. In *In Search of Eden* there is a sense of closure and resolution of many of these issues.

Back home and in her own backyard, as it were, Granirer discovered Eden anew. The bright and robust poppies growing in her own garden (not a garden 1000 miles away), became the vehicle for her exploration and understanding. She relinquished the tightness and draughtmanship that is characteristic of many of her past works and squarely faced her subject. I suppose that there were moments of self-doubt when she felt that these poppies were not political or socially relevant enough to be taken seriously and would be better left to the hobby painter. But her commitment to her work led her to a deeper search, one begun years before.

The poppy has many connotations and associations. It is often viewed as exotic and foreign; it is a symbol for those who lost their lives in war; and it is associated with the making of opium, heroin and morphine. It is a breathtaking flower, an example of great natural beauty and design – an apt metaphor for Paradise. Granirer explores many of these themes in the current series.

Personally, I could not help but associate the poppy with opium production. Nor was I able to forget the phrase "Chasing the Dragon", which refers to the narcotic and hallucinogenic properties of the plant's resin. The poppy's duality, that is its beauty and potential, countered by the dangers of addiction and escape, sets up an interesting metaphor for the human journey to enlightenment. Whether or not that was the intention of the artist, or part of her subject, I do not know. But the connections between the idea of "Chasing the Dragon" and "In Search of Eden" seem real to me.

Do Poppies Grow in Heaven? (1994) is the title and text of a painting that poignantly addresses the futility of war. *A Glimpse of Heaven* (1994) and *Heaven on Earth* (1995) are both paintings in which the artist presents us with luscious images of bright red poppies, framed by a grid-like trellis that contains images of angels. Eden is presented as being here and now, a construct of our own lives. The angels add a sense of humour and lightness that is characteristic of Granirer's recent work. She seems to say that Eden is attainable through living and through our own sensuality; the stuff of Paradise is all around us.

Throughout this series, Granirer's use of bright colour (lots of red against contrasting dark grounds and golds), varied textures (gold leaf and collage), appeal to the viewer's senses and emotions directly. Some of the works, *This Way to Eden* (1994) and *We the Angels* (1994), for instance, recall altars in places of worship with their formal cross-like arrangements and jewel-like colour. Realizing that we ourselves are mythic angels of past belief can be a religious experience. In the poppies series Granirer's use of of the grid as a composing and framing device recalls her *Alhambra Series* and the formality of the gardens she painted before. There is a tension created by the contrast of the soft organic flowers and the geometric hardness of the grid, which somehow cannot entirely contain the subject. Throughout this series of works, Granirer plays with the formal framing of her images, seeming to comment on the elusive and incategorical nature of her true subject: Eden. Poppies break through formal borders, growing into the picture plane, from the outside; the paint drips, taking the path of least resistance and animates the images of petals.

Granirer also revisits her *Trials of Eve* series by using images of the Tree of Life. *Temptation 1 and 2* (1995), are small mixed media works on canvas that depict hands plucking fruit from these mythical and symbolic trees. This is a contradiction to the directions given to Adam and Eve, and thus all humanity, by the God described in the Bible. But being mortal, Granirer tells us that it is only through the fruits of knowledge and life that we may touch and know Paradise. This message is more obvious in works such as *The Joys of Eden 1 and 2* (1994, 1995), where depictions of intimate couples are flanked by images of the Trees of Knowledge and Life. There is a culmination of meaning and realization in work like *Harvest Time in Eden* (1994) where marionettes from *The Trials of Eve* reappear to feast with the angels on the fruits of these trees.

Over 30 years ago, when Granirer began her career as an artist, she began a process where questioning and self-reflection were important in her work. That attitude of search has led her to look at many different sources for inspiration and skills. It has also made her an artist that works in series, each series leading to and informing the new ones. Each variation on a theme answers and solves old questions and problems, but also poses new ones. Granirer's search for Eden is ageless and endless, and will, I am sure, ensure many more years of output from this dedicated artist.

Amir Ali Alibhai is an artist, curator, educator and writer based in Vancouver.

North Shore News (North and West Vancouver) Wednesday, November 20, 1991: 32

Sombre contemplations: Artist Pnina Granirer crosses the border between culture and nature

By Archie Graham

Pnina Granirer: The Carved Stones Suite at Smash Gallery of Modern Art, 160 Cordova St. October 25-November 21

If the Bau-Xi is the smart-set's Holt Renfrew of art venues in Vancouver, Smash Gallery is a neon-lit, nose-thumbing version of the Army/Navy Surplus Store. While the one deals in classy, exlusive, designer-labelled high priced art, the other traffics in deliberately impertinent, proletarian workmanship at affordable prices.

Both have something to offer, but each serves up an entirely different menu and caters to its own loyal patrons.

One hardly ever finds an artist crossing the abyss between these polarities, but Pnina Granirer is attempting it. The change in venues is a reflection of the alteration in her work. Purely pleasant, airy, graphic explorations into the mythological interior of nature give way to moody, sombre contemplations of stone.

"Stone," she says, "is the common denominator between culture and nature."

Granirer means this in both a material and a figurative sense. Stone is not only the substance of a great deal of human architecture and the base stratum of the natural environment, but a concrete emblem of stability and eternity. This show of mixed media works on paper ranges from the literal to the experimental.

Stones of Worship — the Buddha, for example, is one of a number of relatively conventional narratives that comment on the womb-like character of stones and their sacrilegious significance in other cultures.

The series that involves a headless Venus de Milo, however, or the Winged Victory emerging from a rocky landscape beneath swirling skies, is a more adventurous attempt to develop the theme of feminist liberation, one with apocalyptic overtones.

But is is the most recent pieces in this exhibition which, though somewhat less conceptually resolved, are the most daring and ambitious. Here the artist effectively uses the methods of deconstruction, torn fragments, stencilled texts and juxtaposition of incongruous imagery to focus attention on the process of image-making itself. The resulting effect is intended to undermine our confidence in the orthodox and essentially male formulations of both women and nature's traditionally conceived femininity.

Though Granirer's methods may be associated with the newest trends in the contemporary art scene, her aim is the wistfully old-fashioned one of reconstruction and wholeness.

In this exhibition we sense the groping of a keen mind in its search for suitable icons in a world from which the sacred has already been excised. Even if we do not share the artist's optimism we cannot help admiring the spirited effort. Perhaps this is one of the reasons why the owner-curator of Smash Gallery, the self-named 12 Midnite, is showing Granirer's art. At any rate, it is mounted along with the gutsy and provocative multimedia work of Fiona Bowie and Gabriele Gottsclag.

It may be fitting that the one is exhibited upstairs, the others downstairs. While Granirer is carrying on a hopeful discourse, Bowie and Gottsclag are engaged in a troubling debate about the bars of a prison cell.

The Western Jewish Bulletin (Vancouver) Thursday, June 28, 1990

Artist Granirer wins national prize

by Michael Ajzenstadt

Local artist Pnina Granirer has won the second prize for book design in the 1990 Alcuin Society Citation Awards. These are the only national awards for excellence in book design in Canada. First prize was not awarded this year.

Granirer won the prize for the limited edition of her book *The Trials of Eve* which she published privately on Gaea Press. The book has already been purchased by libraries, universities and individual art collectors. The original series of 12 mixed media drawings has been exhibited all over town and reviewed on these pages a few months ago. The current prize warrants an in depth look at *The Trials of Eve* as a book and the issues it deals with.

In her introduction to the book, Granirer states that "these works are a feminist interpretation of the story of woman. It is structured as a play in three acts." The use of a theatrical term to describe a work which is anchored in visual arts and comprises poetry, is rather unique. Usually visual artists seem to be alienated by the world of the performing arts. But Granirer embraces here a very clear theatrical structure.

There is no doubt that the 12 drawings and poems which comprise this book are a clear drama. And although visual art does not really speak, at least not in the way an actor speaks on stage, here the additional poems provide a clear voice. It is the voice of the artist, of the omnipotent narrator who guides us through her work.

Act 1 of this play begins with *The Set-Up.* "The curtain rises," we read. "On centre stage, the tree, with its fruit of forbidden knowledge." This is the basic premise of our tale. Immediately some questions follow, questions that have mystified human beings for many centuries. Why is the fruit forbidden? Why is knowledge forbidden? Or "who is this God who sets the trap for His own creation?" The drawing is as strong as the words. A baffled puppet-like Eve looks with puzzlement at the tree.

Next come *Adam and Eve Tempted by Cannibal Birds.* This is where we encounter for the first time Granirer's use of Native Indian birds instead of the original serpent. It lends local colour to the work and it never disturbs. After all, the snake was only a symbol. Here the meaning — "a devouring will to know" — is still pertained. The Adam and Eve puppets are now closer to the tree. They have made the first step to the act which will eventually change their life. In *The Framing of Eve,* Granirer is harsh and to the point. Eve, the first woman, has been trapped for posterity. And the result is obvious. After all, "it is so safe-and-easy to adore a trapped adventuress!"

Once the first act sets the stage for our tale, the second one takes us a step further into this feminist interpretation of mythology. *The Fall* depicts hungry and malicious birds side by side with modern skyscrapers. The everlasting craving for knowledge and power is presented as Adam and Eve leave paradise. We all try to return to that blissful beginning, but will we ever get there?

The text for *The Trial* is most perplexing. In the drawing, Eve is in a small, caged prison for her trial. The verdict, Granirer suggests, is that "the softness of life-giving womb is cursed now, a painful duty and not the joy of life created." Many women will no doubt argue with this statement.

In the next drawing-poem, *The Verdict,* we see four huge mythical birds with open beaks pecking at Eve. She is doomed and so are the people who tried her, so is the society which enabled such a thing to happen. Once the guilty verdict was decreed, we move in *The Sentence* from an a-religious myth to a very Christian one. In a stained glass window we see Eve lying at the feet of her Adam. The sentence, Granirer tells us, is "forever to love and to obey."

The *Pay-Off* brings us to a world in which gender discrimination has always existed. Eve is now outside of the canonized world of men. She is in front of a fence, lonely, bewildered. Knowledge, we read, was meant for men only, not for women. And if until this moment one was searching for the clear feminist approach of Granirer, here the artist spells it out.

The *Trials of Eve* is not about God trying the first woman. It is about a society in which men discriminate against women, about a society in which women exist only as pretty objects in a menagerie — to look at, to adore and to play with.

By the end of the second act the artist ironically suggests that harmony does still exist in the world, at least when women are concerned. The *Labelling of Eve by Unanimous Consent,* decrees very clearly that "As long as she is good and plays the parts," woman will be adored. But the parts — the mother and the whore — are those that men have proclaimed. Woman is not allowed to have a say.

The long second act of *The Trials of Eve* moves us through a multitude of ideas and symbolism which present the artist's main thesis – men are to blame for what they made of women. But it is the rather short Act 3 which leaves behind the harsh criticism and calls for a future in which changes can take place.

The final act begins with *Eve Tries Again* — in this context a rather sudden realization that men have brought the world to naught. They are willing to give Eve another chance and send her out on parole. The corresponding drawing is one of Granirer's best. The contrast between Eve in her electronic kitchen and Adam conversing with one of these huge Indian birds, is startling.

And then the conclusion — *Adam and Eve Puzzle; To Be Assembled With Love.* This is a most soothing ending to a rather pointed criticism: "Two halves of one whole, one needing the other."

One might question Granirer's optimism here. Her work leaves almost no illusion regarding the role of men in society *vis à vis* their women. Why does she believe that Eve will be given another chance? Maybe the work would have made more sense if Granirer's Eve would have tried to go against her Adam and imprint her own feminine stamp on society.

But this might have caused confrontation and the artist here finishes with a call for a truce: "Let's start again, it's worth a try." Yes, it is but only if one can start from the very beginning without any misconceptions. Otherwise the case is doomed yet again.

As the last drawing tells us, however, the puzzle is here to be assembled. And all of us, men and women, need to do it with care. As Pnina Granirer tells us in her invigorating *Trials of Eve,* "It's worth a try." Even more so, it is our last resort.

The original art and the book will be on display in October at the University Women's Club, Hycroft Manor and will then travel to Seattle and Portland. The book itself can be purchased from Gaea Press, (604)224-6795, or from William Hoffer Booksellers Ltd.

Les Affiches-Moniteur d'Alsace et de Lorraine (Strasbourg, France), No. 12, 10 février 1987

OEUVRES RECENTES DE PNINA GRANIRER

Jean Christian

Il s'agit d'aquarelles et de dessins, mais sans doute aussi d'oeuvres plus complexes dans lesquelles Pnina Granirer introduit d'autres éléments encore pour leur donner un pouvoir magique. Toute la première salle de la Galerie Aktuaryus, 23 rue de la Nuée-Bleue à Strasbourg, en est comme illuminée, transfigurée. Car l'ensemble de l'exposition dégage une sorte de clarté presque magique, tout à fait inhabituelle, en tout cas de nos jours.

Cette magie l'artiste d'origine roumaine, mais installée au Canada depuis plus de vingt ans, est allée la chercher sur les bords du Pacifique, du côté de Vancouver, où le hasard a voulu qu'elle fût quasiment initiée à un autre monde.

Certes chacun pourrait y découvrir les îles rocheuses et les étranges figures que les vents et les marées ont sculptées tout au long des millénaires. Mais Pnina Granirer a pénétré plus profondément dans le paysage, découvrant notamment une carrière abandonnée de meules découpées à même le rocher et qui constitue aujourd'hui un site étrange qu'on pourrait attribuer depuis longtemps à une lointaine civilisation depuis longtemps révolue. Car, dans ces cavités géométriques l'herbe a poussé, l'eau s'est accumulée et le ciel s'y reflète comme dans de profonds miroirs.

Pnina Granirer a tiré de ces lieux secrets une merveilleuse série qu'elle a intitulée "Découverte à Gabriola" et qui apporte à l'ensemble de l'exposition son sceau spécifique qu'elle seule a pu se réserver.

Aussi bien, si l'artiste qui par deux fois déjà avait exposé à Strasbourg ne nous est pas inconnue, nous a-t-elle plus que surpris par cette nouvelle ascension qui justifie plus qu'amplement la réputation internationale qu'elle a acquise depuis bon nombre d'années déjà. D'autant plus que, loin d'en rajouter, elle traite les thèmes les plus originaux avec une belle maîtrise et une sobriété qui pourrait évoquer le silence des lieux, traversé tout au plus par la rumeur de l'Océan et les cris lancinants des mouettes. Et par une bouleversante poésie.

NEW WORKS BY PNINA GRANIRER — TRANSLATION

The show consists of watercolours and drawings but also more complex works into which Pnina Granirer introduces new elements, giving them magical powers. All of the first room at the Aktuaryus Gallery, 23, rue de la Nuée-Bleue in Strasbourg, is as if illuminated and transfigured by them. This exhibition as a whole emanates an almost magical clarity, quite unusual these days.

The artist, of Romanian origin, but settled in Canada for over 20 years, went searching for this magic on the shores of the Pacific near Vancouver, where, by a quirk of fate, she was initiated into a new world.

Of course, anyone could discover rocky islands and strange figures carved by the winds and the tides over thousands of years. But Pnina Granirer has penetrated much deeper into the landscape, discovering an abandoned quarry of millstones cut out of the living rock, today a strange site one might attribute to a long lost civilisation.

Wild grasses have grown in the geometrical cavities, water has filled them and the sky is reflected in them like in some deep mirrors.

Pnina Granirer has put her very own personal stamp on the exhibition, by creating a marvelous series out of these secret places, entitled "Discovery at Gabriola".

Even though the artist has already exhibited twice before in Strasbourg and thus is not a stranger to us, she still surprised us by this new height which more than justifies the international reputation she has developed for quite a few years now. All the more so, since far from repeating herself, she treats the most original themes with great control and sobriety, suggesting the silence of the space disturbed by the rumbling of the ocean and the piercing cries of the seagulls. And also by an overwhelming poetry.

The Bellingham Herald (Bellingham, WA), Friday, October 5, 1984

WOMEN, Black Roses: Subtle loss of innocence

by Jerry Szymanski

The fall gallery season has started on the Western Washington University campus with an intriguiging and expressive exhibit in the Chrysalis Gallery.

The show "Of Women and Black Roses", features drawings and paintings by Vancouver, BC, artist Pnina Granirer, a Romanian-born emigré to Canada whose international outlook is quite obvious in her work.

Granirer completed her art studies at the Bezalel Art Academy in Jerusalem before moving to Canada in 1965, and has been a prolific artist who looked not only at the world as a source of material for her work, but also as a place to exhibit. To date she has exhibited in the United States, Canada, England, Peru, France and Yugoslavia and her work has been featured on the cover of the UNICEF calendar. She has also been exhibited in the United Nations permanent collection, and will exhibit shortly in eastern Canada.

The reason for such interest in Granirer's work is that it is just plain good. It's also nostalgic — in a wistful sort of way — and her drawings hark back to the kind of sketchy exuberance found in Paris in pre-Cubist days. Such a visual reference is rather difficult to pull off. All too often what comes across is the kind of schlock seen in the home accessories department of major stores. Fortunately, Granirer's work is much too subtle for such an association, and the drawings literally draw the viewer into responsive gaiety.

Yet the subject matter of the works in the Chrysalis exhibit is definitely on the black side. Full of foreboding and the loss of youthful innocence in young women, the works function as a reminder of the process of aging and the loss of enthusiastic promise. The subject is of specific reference to women, yet can capture the attention of anyone; it deals not so much in "women's issues" as it reflects on the loss of so much by all who have made it to middle age.

Various techniques are used by Granirer to highlight the conceptual nature of each piece. The drawings concerning young women are usually light and expressive. With some wash and crayon line, Granirer portrays the exuberance and seemingly secure futures of the young. She captures the spirit of young girls for whom aging and broken promises have yet to become a reality. But sometimes, very quietly, she includes a visual reference that portends the coming years.

This is apparent in "In the Garden," which centers on five young women in a happy, playful pose in a formal garden. The girls are presented in a combination of washes and delicate linework, the lightness emphasizing their youth. Surrounding the five is a trellis, the kind used for roses, and on the trellis are black roses. Roses are used by Granirer in much of her work to signify middle age, a time when the decay of expectations and hope is as much a certainty as bodily degeneration.

The black roses fulfill their function well, and most effectively in "In the Garden." They seem to place the viewer in the uncomfortable position of joining the artist in knowing the future before the young subjects of the drawing will. The effect is to temper the gaiety of the young women and the drawing with a touch of melancholy; one wishes he could keep these girls locked into their current time, yet knows he cannot.

The process of aging — in both body and soul — continues in those works dealing with middle-aged women. These works, such as "They Never Promised her a Rose Garden," take a more heavy-handed approach. The light sketchiness of youth gives way to a solid look, and visual information is presented in more solid colors and a two-dimensional treatment that fills in the negative spaces.

Granirer's older women are overshadowed by the visual "props" surrounding them. Curtains are used extensively, often overpowering the images and reflections of these women. These works I found harder to deal with, as they contained not so much the romanticism of Parisian youth as elements suggestive of the realities of communist-block Europe.

The human figures in these works are pale imitations of themselves; perhaps a reality intended by the artist. The treatment certainly is not complimentary, although the viewer is left to decipher the meaning of these women figures and their situation.

Therein lies Granirer's appeal. She does not include too much visual information, nor hammer the viewer with anti-male propaganda. Whether the unfulfilled expectations and broken promises are due to male indifference and insensitivity is left strictly to the viewer, although some wedding references in a few works point the way for the more socio-politically oriented.

Factors other than male/female relationships are allowed to rise to the surface, and are there for those willing to work for their visual rewards. Because of her sensitivity in dealing not only with the subject matter but with the viewer, Granirer's exhibition achieves a success that belies the seeming simplicity of her works. Most effective in the exhibition is the transition one sees in moving around the gallery: the child gives way to the youth, who eventually becomes the middle-aged recluse. The works carry the concept mercifully and with subtleties one does not apprehend until much later.

While the works are uneven in style and treatment, they do carry the message most effectively. The exhibition will be on view through Oct.20.

Jerry Szymanski reviews visual arts for The Bellingham Herald.

Le Nouvel Alsacien, Der Elsässer (Strasbourg France), samedi, 19 avril, 1980

Dessins et gravures de Pnina Granirer
Quand les Canadiens se distinguent par le sérieux et l'originalité

– G –

STRASBOURG — La Galerie Artal (rue du Bain-aux-Plantes) présente actuellement et jusqu'au 24 avril une exposition consacrée à l'artiste canadienne Pnina Granirer. Il s'agit içi de la première apparition de cette graphiste à Strasbourg. Les artistes canadiens qui ont exposé à Strasbourg (ils ne sont pas nombreux) se sont toujours distingués par le serieux et l'originalité de leur travail. C'est le cas de Pnina Granirer dont la technique mixte — combinaisons d'encre, d'empreintes et d'aquarelle — lui permet de réaliser des oeuvres d'une indéniable qualité. Originaire de Vancouver, Pnina Granirer a fait ses études à Jérusalem et a beaucoup voyagé. On pouvait craindre que son art ne subit des influences disparates et, partant, néfastes. Il n'en a rien été et, bien au contraire, cette artiste s'est forgé un style très personnel et non moins expressif. Le dessin y est d'une finesse et d'une délicatesse qui n'excluent en rien des prises de positions catégoriques. Le Canada, avec sa faune certes, mais surtout avec son côté mystérieux, ce fonds de magie qui vient de la nuit des temps est célébré içi dans un délire presque mythique. L'oiseau y prend une place fort importante, mais l'homme également, avec ses empreintes, par une présence invisible presque, mais tellement sensible. Le rythme de ces dessins et gravures est, un peu comme la large pulsation d'un grand coeur généreux. Il y a beaucoup de musique dans cette oeuvre et Pnina Granirer ne s'en défend nullement, elle qui nomme "Sonate à quatre mains" l'une de ses oeuvres, dans laquelle les quatre mains s'envolent sur le battement de deux ailes silencieuses. Le genèse du monde est évoquée, l'intrusion de l'homme dans la nature, dans le paysage; le paysage y figure également dans une conception presque abstraite.

Voilà les composantes d'un oeuvre dont on est heureux de saluer la force, la puissance même. Ce qui n'empêche que l'oeuvre de Pnina Granirer est typiquement féminine avec cette souplesse, cette séduction, cette expresivité imagée. Une exposition qui mérite beaucoup plus que le détour, qui mérite qu'on se laisse conduire vers les mystères de la création artistique, reflet de la création originelle. Elle sera visible jusqu'au 24 avril.

WHEN THE CANADIANS
DISTINGUISH THEMSELVES
BY SERIOUSNESS AND ORIGINALITY
— TRANSLATION

STRASBOURG — The Artal Gallery (rue du Bain-aux-Plantes) is currently showing until April 24, an exhibition dedicated to the Canadian artist Pnina Granirer. This is the first appearance of this graphic artist in Strasbourg. The Canadian artists who have shown in Strasbourg in the past (not many of them), have always distinguished themselves by the seriousness and originality of their work. This is the case with Pnina Granirer, whose mixed media technique — combinations of inks, imprints and watercolours — allows her to create works of unquestionable quality. Coming from Vancouver, Pnina Granirer has studied in Jerusalem and has travelled extensively. One might worry that her art could have gone in a negative direction due to too many disparate influences. But this is not the case, quite the contrary; this artist has created a very personal and expressive style for herself. The fine and delicate drawings do not exclude the taking of categorical stands. Canada, certainly with its fauna, but especially with its mysterious aspects, its background of magic which emerges from the darkness of time, is celebrated here with almost mythical rapture. The bird occupies a central place, but man does too, with his footprints, his almost invisible but sensitive presence. The rhythm of these drawings and prints is like the pulsations of a great, generous heart. There is much music in these works and Pnina Granirer does not apologise. In one of her works which she calls "Sonata for Four Hands", four hands take flight on two silent wings. There are works which refer to the creation of the world, the intrusion of man into nature, into the landscape; the landscape itself appears in an almost abstract way.

Here are works whose strength, power even, we are happy to salute. At the same time, Pnina Granirer's work is typically feminine, with its flexibility, its seductiveness and its imaginative expressivity. This exhibition deserves more than just a casual visit; it deserves to be allowed to lead the viewer towards the mystery of the artistic creation, the reflection of the original creation itself.

It will be on view until April 24.

Artmagazine (Toronto), May/June 1980

Pnina Granirer at Bau-Xi Gallery (December 10–22)

By Ed Varney

Pnina Granirer uses impressions or feelings remembered from childhood, transmuted by a sense of participation in her physical environment to create a densely layered, technically brilliant and evocative series of paintings. In this show at the Bau-Xi, her central concerns seem to have moved away from bird forms which have dominated recent work and into a series of forest scenes in which leaf and tree forms are the predominant image. These forms, however, upon close inspection, are made up of layers of other images, i.e. the recurrent birds, wave-like swirling patterns and, in some cases, the ghost-like remains of the original inhabitants of our west coast forests.

As well as layering imagery, she uses a wide variety of techniques in these paintings which are overlaid on top of each other such as watercolour, pastel, pencil, ink, embossed line, electrostatic photo transfer and monoprint impressions of various natural objects, including leaves and feathers. She uses the oval shape as a recurring organizational form; sometimes it is cut off by the frame of the painting and sometimes it is wholly contained within it and echoes or reverberates much like the visual echoes which turn up so often in network logos on TV.

Some of Granirer's paintings are reminiscent of Emily Carr and reveal the forest backlit and infused with light. Others are darker and more brooding, but they have in common a printmaker's sense of design and simplicity of image combined with a painter's sense of density and detail. They are evocative of the west coast landscape but they also contain a sense of a private and eclectic mythology which combines elements of west coast and prairie Indian art, Eastern European folk art and a sense of decorative image which functions as a symbol for a state of mind or emotion.

Several of the paintings in this exhibition are three, four and five panel works and, as such, are the largest works Granirer has done. Although many of them share common concerns, there is a progression of thought and, therefore, image, which explores different aspects or visions drawn from the same source. This exhibition represents a major artistic statement by Granirer which is developed and amplified by a high level of craftsmanship and commitment. With this work, she has shown herself capable of using her excellent graphic sensitivity and her skilled manipulation of colour as the means to a coherent and satisfying whole.

Arts West (Winnipeg), volume 3, number 3, May/June, 1978

FREEDOM, HARMONY, ENDURANCE AND MOTION

by Melanie Gold

The impetus for Pnina Granirer's Romantic expression is dreams — remnants from her childhood and somnambulist visions of the present. Her art verifies these dreams.

Often decried as escapist, Granirer's Romantic attitude may more justly be described as sympathetic to reality — an emotional response to external stimuli.

Externals, for Granirer, have been influenced by her Romanian upbringing and her art education in Israel. This Eastern European background, which from economic necessity deals with life on a subsistence level, has provided the empathy and social consciousness that prevail throughout her work. Now, after a brief stay in the United States, a Canadian citizen residing in Vancouver, Granirer shows that her creative foundation has undergone a number of radical changes and, finally, a cultural synthesis with Western influences.

Granirer's ink drawings show her resolution of the fundamental differences between the more traditional Eastern European and Western avant-garde attitudes. These distinctions are based on approach and application. Representational and figurative subjects are most common in Eastern composition, relating an individual experience to the universal. The human factor is of major importance. Western affluence has all but removed such overt human consciousness from art. Its artists are more concerned with abstract cognitive effects. In the interest of enlightenment and education, the Western artist speaks to, rather than with and about people who are then forced to "view" rather than experience the art.

The common ground on which these disparate ideologies walk is the desire to create a universally significant statement. The polemics of the Western avant-garde are intended to arouse a new understanding of time, space, colour and their interaction. Eastern European artists, on the other hand, are compelled by the nature of their environment to recount the human profile of subsistence. Humanity is both the subject and the object.

Correspondingly, Pnina Granirer deals with the enigmas of existence: evolution, birth, the yearning for freedom. She responds to these perpetual dilemmas with an attitude of introspective spirituality. At the same time, she assumes the "once-removed" Western position, acknowledging the emotions, yet always observing and recording for the purpose of general enlightenment. She seeks the ultimate synthesis.

Narrative content, then, is both the motivation and the function of Granirer's artform. Through a vocabulary of ideistic symbols, she interprets and lends credence to the reality of our imaginings: birds and wings as they relate to the concepts of freedom, harmony, endurance and motion; the goose and eagle epitomizing the beauty and strength of these concepts. The oval and circle are elements of totality and continuity which Granirer relates to the evolutionary process of the womb, birth and the life cycle. Ancient Hebraic letters represent a key to the artist's own roots as well as artifacts of civilization and in particular, the word, "Breshit" (braysheet), the first word of the Old Testament, meaning "In the beginning." Angels and devils are part of Granirer's childhood memorabilia. The cat, present throughout her work, acts as narrator and ultimate spectator, quietly surveying the illustrations. The notions of constancy and anticipation of that constancy are maintained as the impulse of existence.

It is important at this point to note the similarity of function in both Granirer's and primitive art. Each relates strongly to the psychological climate. Both use symbols suggestive of innate powers. They have in common a simple design structure and limited element format, providing not only a pure aesthetic, but a narrative of familiar life experiences created for and about people. Granirer is not a primitive artist, yet the basis for her inspiration and expression is similar.

The simplicity of Granirer's imagery is deceptive. Its symbolism is conveyed, in part, by placement on the design field and the rhythms or tensions of supporting lines. These lines provide spacial definition as well as an elegant structure and flow for her highly decorative, almost lyrical compositions. They form the connecting link between the format and the idea. The success of the drawings is partly a result of another deception — the singularity of a daydream. Made visible, our subconscious imaginings are remarkably similar, in substance if not in detail. The realizations of common thought patterns and experiences are interwoven, binding the creator and spectator.

Much as they would in the landscape of our subconscious, Granirer's symbols float across the design field. The drawings are almost devoid of conventional background, yet they are skilfully controlled by the decorative sensitivity of the artist.

The decorative nature of Granirer's ink drawings is derived from the finely etched, textural quality of her lines. They are tracings of "found" objects: a dried cactus weed, a piece of old lace, wire mesh, printed hands and feet. They lend depth and atmosphere, and are important as interpretive as well as compositive elements. They are physical ties with reality.

The printed hands and feet, for example, suggest uniqueness, individuality, and proof of our earth-bound existence. Granirer inks her drawings in black or sepia with the occasional introduction of gold, ochre and aqua. Her limited palette is well suited to the high contrasts of her subjects. It re-enforces the narrative flow.

Through line, colour and form, each drawing is an exploration in decorative harmony. Granirer's success has been achieved by making her works visually resonant through sensation and recollection.

The Tribune (Winnipeg), October 10, 1979

Original Approach – Granirer's art truly unique

by Laura Anne Holden

The compelling drawings and prints of Pnina Granirer at the Fleet Gallery, 173 McDermot Ave., are the product of a very original approach to two-dimensional art.

The results of her combinations of ink, pencil, crayon, monoprints and watercolours truly suits the term unique. Pnina's work is the kind that you could live with for years and still discover something new.

Birds are the common denominator of the collection. They are everywhere, hidden and exposed, revered and exploited. In *Sonata for Seagulls in Wings Sharp,* some of the gulls are sneaked into the composition and some are obvious, but all are in a pattern of spiralling flight, the way seagulls usually perform. *O Canada,* a serigraph of four Canadian geese, has a Prairie Indian quality of simplicity. The back of the largest goose has been flattened to form the top frame of the composition. Ms. Granirer uses this technique in several of her pieces to define space. *O Canada* is also the best example of the artist's abilitiy to give a sense of air, a reminder that the space around her birds is not really a void.

There are two pictures in this show that are converses to one another. *Magic Circle 2* is composed of a spiral of birds flowing into a circle containing two footprints; *Magic Circle 4* is a series of footprints leading to a circle of birds. This type of gimmick does not always work well, but the artist is subtle enough to carry it off.

It is not that we are being fooled, we are just being presented with visual affects we never thought possible. A canoe full of people tucked into the hill, supported by a half-legendary, half-real bird whose wing is also a part of the hill, in the second frame of *Forbidden Plateau,* is such a visual trick.

All of the artist's other unlikely combinations of media are to be found there as well — the ethereal white chalk overlays, lines drawn in and "taken out," the empty space that beautifully offsets the intensity of the multi-layered coloured areas, the monoprints that could be drawings beside the drawings that could be prints, the washed in offtones that form the backdrop of most of her pieces.

The historic pictures in the show are just as well executed. The dull antique gold that exists only in *Images of Past Glories* and nowhere else in the collection is a very dramatic touch.

Despite all of the intelligent documentation, it is the birds we will remember. It is the artist's understanding of these, the way she stops them in time and flight, the way she closes the distance between them and us, that is the major attraction of this collection.

After the birds, it is Pnina Granirer's ability to interpret in her own terms the traditional art of the West Coast Indians, and use it without plagiarization, that stands out as remarkable in her work.

The show closes October 18. Try to see it.

Artmagazine (Toronto), Oct/Nov 1977

Pnina Granirer at the Bau-Xi Gallery

by Deanna Levis

The new works of Pnina Granirer recently on display at the Bau-Xi Gallery, are painstakingly rendered (but by no means static) dual compositions. From a distance, the viewer perceives striking combinations of colour and fluid line which carry the eye around as if the work were in motion. Viewed closely, a diverse selection of details ornament and inform. At any distance, they are visual delights.

Granirer studied and graduated from the Bezalel Academy of Art, in Jerusalem. In 1967, she moved to Canada, and worked for a year in Montreal with Pierre Ayot, during the beginnings of *La Guilde Graphique.*

Her training in graphics is reflected in the exhibition, which comprises three series of drawings: *The Musical Suite, In the Beginning,* and *Human Landscapes.*

As a medium, the artist uses India ink, which she mixes herself, then paints with a brush onto 100% rag paper. The coloured inks, when mixed, produce earthy tones of terra-cotta to brown, and soft greens; incredibly rich hues against the white backgrounds or "negative spaces," themselves an integral part of each work. When the ink is dry, she creates texture and softens the flat ink surface with details worked in graphite pencil (she uses pencil a great deal), leaf or cork patterns, handprints, or by scratching into the paper surface. Usually, a work will contain a combination of these elements. Also, two personal symbols appear frequently in the drawings. One is the *Imp of Lincoln Cathedral,* given in the form of a charm by her parents when she was very young. In her private mythology, it becomes a serpent, or harbinger of doom. The other is a lace cherub; her angel image, which derives from a design on a sheet she used as a child.

She is not a landscape painter. She feels that "an artist has a lot to say and should say it." The statement she is making through the drawings is that we should keep what we have that is beautiful in the world, not destroy it; less a pretentious stance, in her case, than a sincere desire to keep life intact.

The core of her present work is the womb, symbolized by round or oval shapes. "The oval shape has been constant in my work, and now has become focal; of overwhelming importance."

In the Beginning evolved from an earlier idea of a "magic circle," which she developed from a conversation with her son, then four, who wondered why "children can do magic, but when they grow up they can't anymore." The circle became the yolk of an egg: the "life-giving starting point for everything." Though sometimes foreboding, there is in this series a strong sense of the universality of man in cohabitation with animals. Also a base, along with the womb image, are the ancient Hebraic letters for *In the beginning.* The letters are hidden within one of the drawings, titled *When the Earth was Young and Fertility was a Goddess.*

Human Landscapes grew naturally out of the "beginning" series. The womb becomes a landscape in which the embryo resides. At times, Granirer plays Creator, as in *Insert Cut-outs into Landscape,* where empty spaces are left in the landscape (in this case, a mountain) with the matching life forms drawn elsewhere, like puzzles. A whimsical idea taken from cartoon cut-outs, it has led the artist into a fascinating and possibly new series with puzzles.

A departure from the more metaphysical concepts of the rest of the exhibition, and my personal favourite, is *The Musical Suite.* A dazzling equation of form and content, these works fairly sing with rhythm and movement. Here, the abstract form displays to the full Granirer's ability as a graphic designer. Even the titles are rich in lyrical cadence, like *Sonata for Feathers in Gold Flat,* or *Symphony #1 in Wings Major.* She says: "*The Musical Suite* is a direct result of my habit of working while listening to music. The idea is simple: take a few constant elements, just as music is using a few constant notes, and see what different works and variations can be achieved. In this case, the elements were: birds, the eagle, printed skeleton leaves, fine lines and sweeping colour areas. The birds take the part of violins or flutes; the eagle, the cello or the piano. By using these elements in different ways, I compose quartets, sonatas, or symphonies." Listening to her poetic manner of speaking, one wonders if she might also have made a mark as a writer.

Of the nearly 30 drawings, many show the influence of Primitive and Oriental art, both of which she admires. Also strongly evident throughout is the Canadian Indian culture, which, she says "was not a conscious thing, although I remember I was fascinated by a book on Canadian Indian art which I saw in art school."

Together, the three series form an open-ended cohesive unit: a growing out from earlier works, and a transition into a possible new series with puzzles. "My drawings are living things," she says, "I stand by and watch them grow, change and grow again."

The Trials of Eve, softcover edition, 1993

Foreword & Introduction

These complex images undermine the myth of Eve, the original sinner, by their very puppet forms. The introduction of indigenous flora and fauna raises the specter of different origin myths, combining those of several cultures.

Granirer is another Eve, recreating herself in the image of a more inclusive humanity. *The Trials of Eve,* unlike those of Job, are to be conquered in the name of compassion and understanding. Responsibility replaces guilt; grace is internal.

— Lucy Lippard, art critic and writer

These are a dozen images and as many poems that are full of reference and ideas. Granirer has drawn upon sources as diverse as Boticelli, Michelangelo, William Blake and Judy Chicago. She has combined these borrowings with visual devices that are her own. The result is a suite that is eclectic and contentious, as provocative as the subject it tackles. After seeing and reading Granirer's *The Trials of Eve,* we will not think of Eve, the fall from grace or the expulsion from the garden in the traditional way again.

— Ann Rosenberg, artist, writer and curator

Index

(Page numbers in ***italic bold*** refer to illustrations.)

PHOTO CREDITS — All photos by Pnina Granirer, except: ANNE ADAMS illustration nos. 24, 55, 62, 64, 66, 77, 99, 103, 105, 106; BENWELL ATKINS illustration nos. 87, 89, 90, 91, 92; MARY BLADE portrait of the artist, no. 100; STURDY PHOTOGRAPHY portrait of the artist, ill. no. 136, portrait of the artist, front flap; WEEKES PHOTO GRAPHICS illustration nos. 45, 46, 61, 63, 116, 118, 130, 133, 138, 139, 145, 154, 155, 156, 158, frontispiece.

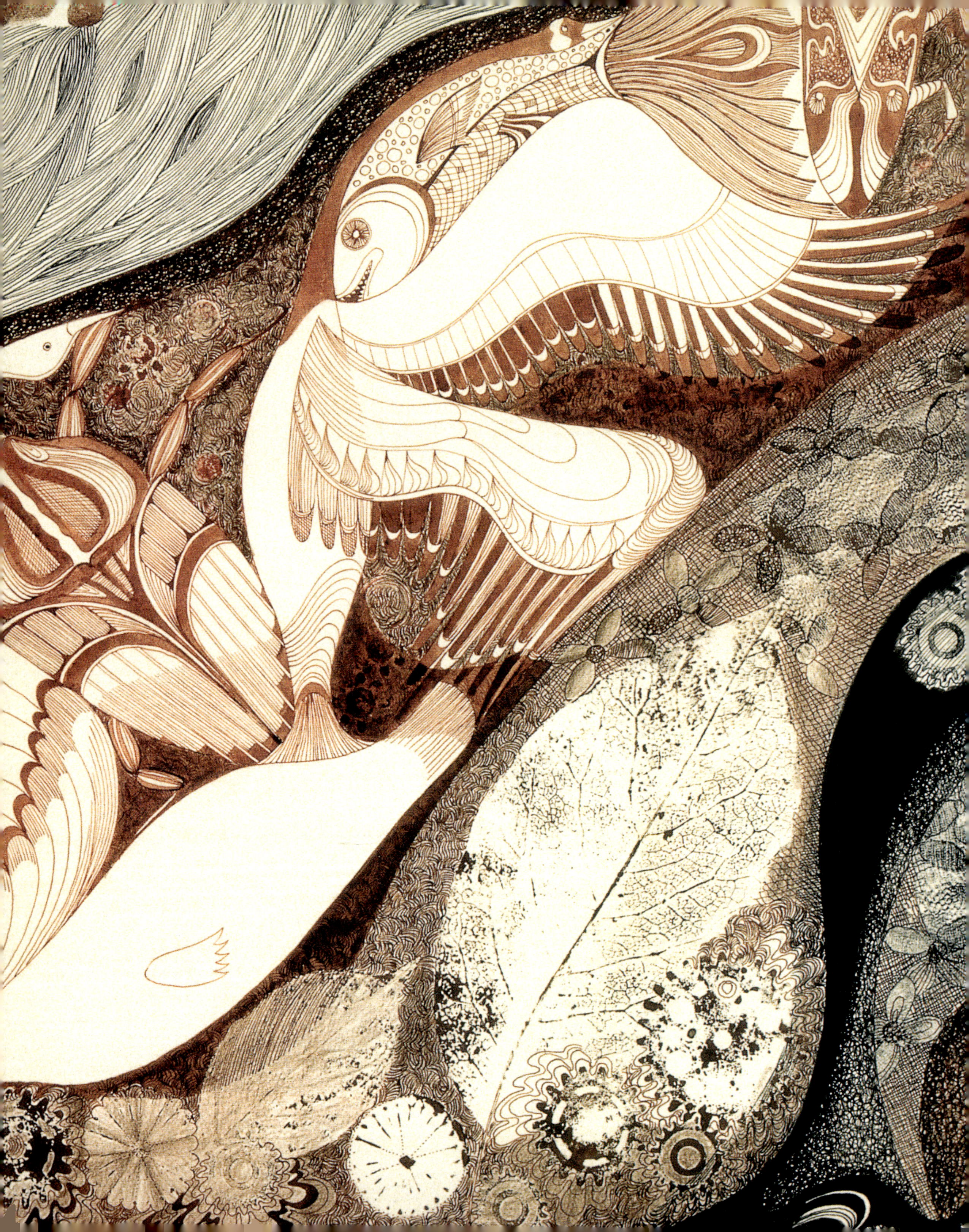